The Historic Turn in the Human Sciences

The Historic Turn
in the
Human Sciences

Terrence J. McDonald, Editor

Ann Arbor

THE UNIVERSITY OF MICHIGAN PRESS

1999   4   3   2

A CIP catalog record for this book is available from the British Library.

Library of Congress Cataloging-in-Publication Data

McDonald, Terrence J.
    The historic turn in the human sciences / Terrence J. McDonald,
editor.
        p.   cm.
    Includes bibliographical references and index.
    ISBN 0-472-09632-X (hardcover : alk. paper).—ISBN 0-472-06632-3
(pbk. : alk. paper)
    1. Social history.   2. Social sciences.   3. Sociology.   I. Title.
HN28.M4   1996
306'.09—dc20   96-18773
                                                        CIP

Contents

Acknowledgments

These essays were born at a conference on "The Historic Turn in the Human Sciences" organized by the Program for the Comparative Study of Social Transformations (CSST) at the University of Michigan and financed by grants from the University's Presidential Initiatives Fund and the Office of the Vice President for Research. A large number of University of Michigan faculty made comments then and since that assisted all the authors in the clarification of the themes in this volume. They include Kathleen Canning, Fernando Coronil, Linda Gregerson, F. Muge Gocek, Janet Hart, Sally Humphreys, Howard Kimeldorf, Silvia Pedraza, William Rosenberg, David Scobey, Ann Stoler, Ron Suny (now of the University of Chicago), Hitomi Tonamura, Ernest Young, and Mayer Zald. Michael Kennedy performed the immeasurable service of reading and providing written comments on early versions of all the essays in the volume. Conversations with, and the work of, Andrew Abbott of the University of Chicago and Eric Monkkonen of UCLA helped me with the introduction to the volume. Excellent help was provided by Rusty Bush with the conference itself, and Mary McGuire with the many tasks necessary to see the volume through to the press. Susan Whitlock and Kevin Rennells, of the University of Michigan Press, made the volume's progress through the press as easy as possible.

Three of the essays in this volume appear by permission of other presses. Early versions of the essays by Sherry Ortner and Joan Scott were given at the conference but each was also published elsewhere. Scott's essay, "The Evidence of Experience," was first published in *Critical Inquiry* 17 (1991): 773–97, and it appears here courtesy of that journal and the University of Chicago Press. Ortner's essay, "Resistance and the Problem of Ethnographic Refusal," was published in *Comparative Studies in Society and History* 37 (1995), and is reprinted here by permission of that journal and its publisher, Cambridge University Press. A somewhat revised version of Steve Mullaney's essay, "Discursive Forums, Cultural Practices," will appear at almost the same time as this volume in *Alternative Shakespeares Two,* edited by Terence Hawkes and published by Routledge (1996), and is used here by permission of the publisher.

Introduction

Terrence J. McDonald

One of the most distinctive aspects of the current intellectual epoch is a turn toward "history" that is in progress across the humanities and social sciences in America today. The signs of a significant transformation of the intellectual agendas of the human sciences are apparent in the appearance of, among other things, the "new historicism" in literary and legal theory, a revived interest in "history in philosophy," a historically oriented "new institutionalism" and other historical approaches in political science and economics, "ethnohistory" in anthropology, "historical sociology" in sociology, and even a more self-consciously reflexive and historicist methodological discussion in history itself.[1]

This transformation is "historic" in at least three senses. First, it represents an epochal turn *against* the science of society constituted at least in part in opposition to "history" in the immediate post–World War Two years. Second, it involves a contentious and by no means well-defined turn *toward* history— as past, process, context, and so on, but not necessarily as discipline—as a component of intellectual investigations across a wide variety of fields. Finally, it is producing renewed inquiry into the construction *in* history of disciplinary discourses and investigators.

This historic turn has seemed to originate primarily within different fields and, therefore, to proceed under different names, toward different destinations, and against different oppositions. For this reason, most programmatic statements on or collections of this new work remain single-discipline endeavors or catalogs of how an apparently stable element called "history" has been added to or deployed by a variety of other changing disciplines (e.g., Skocpol 1984; Rorty et al. 1984; Veeser 1989; Cox and Reynolds 1993; Monkkonen 1994; Kohen and Roth 1995). While useful, these approaches that isolate the disciplines from one another—or leave the profession of history itself out altogether—minimize the challenge that the historic turn presents to the way the human sciences go about their business. There are, in fact, important similarities in the way the disciplines have reached out to history and the dilemmas encountered because they have done so.

The purpose of this volume is to permit a closer look at these similarities by presenting in one place a series of reports from the field, as it were, from several disciplines within which this historic turn is ongoing: namely, sociology, political science, law, literary studies, and history itself. The authors have been selected both because of the way their work has stood at the junctions of disciplines or approaches within disciplines and also because of their willingness to write about the implications of these developments. This latter criterion turned out to be an important one; while many are apparently willing to write history today, far fewer are interested in considering the implications of that work. One well-known historical social scientist invited to contribute to this volume spoke for many when he declared that he would "leave to others the question of how to write history," while continuing himself simply to do it.

As the reader will see, if the essays in this collection demonstrate anything it is that the historic turn has rendered this position completely untenable. Outside of the skillfully produced world of the commercial, "just doing it" is neither easy for historical actors nor wise for historical analysts, and for pretty much the same reason. For just as historical actors make history but not always under the conditions of their own choice, historical analysts work at a particular moment in the history of their own theory and practice. Today, the leakage of history out of its professional disciplinary container has allowed the development of new models for its practice at the same time as its old and new practitioners have subjected it to theoretical challenges from critical social theory, literary criticism, and newer interdisciplinary projects like feminist studies and cultural studies. This does not mean that history is impossible, but it does mean that the term now has multiple meanings and that it has been appropriated for many different reasons by the different disciplines.

If ever there were a kind of agreed upon "manual" of historical practice (and one of the points of these essays is that historians, on the whole, have been extremely reluctant to provide one) there is none today. With this point in mind, then, this volume makes no attempt to provide a new one but instead charts the terrain of recent ventures into the historicizing enterprise. This introduction begins, appropriately enough, with a brief historical account of the growth of this new concern with history out of an American intellectual environment that was ahistorical in important ways. It then proceeds to summarize the common themes among the essays in the volume.

When sociologist C. Wright Mills published *The Sociological Imagination* in 1959 he rightly felt iconoclastic in declaring that "every social science—or better, every well-considered social study—requires an historical scope of conception and a full use of historical materials" (Mills 1959, 145). The contrary attitudes of the mainstream were well represented three years later, when, as Rogers Smith notes in his essay, political scientist William Riker dismissed "traditional methods—i.e., history writing, the description of institutions, and legal analysis as able to produce only wisdom and neither science nor knowledge. And while wisdom is certainly useful in the affairs of men, such a result is a failure to live up to the promise in the name political science" (Riker 1962, viii). It was in part because of attitudes like this that philosopher Quentin Skinner noted with some surprise in his 1985 introduction to *The Return of Grand Theory in the Human Sciences* that times had "certainly changed," when "the study of history has increasingly proved to be a fertile source of inspiration and evidence" (Skinner 1985, 5, 11). What had happened in the meantime was a dynamic and dialectical interaction between historical events, historical practice, and social theory.

Although historical work had by no means stopped in the 1950s and 1960s, voices like Mills's stood out because of a variety of seemingly disparate developments in the United States that seemed to add up to a declaration of the "end" of history. Political intellectuals declared an "end to ideology"—and with it the historical combat over ends—and celebrated a new historical epoch where technical means would take the center of politics. Political scientists and historians focused on what they took to be the historically unprecedented issues of abundance and consensus. The consolidation of structural-functional social theories and pluralist political theories lent credibility to a vision of the historical process as one that was equilibrium-seeking, efficient, and politically teleological. At the same time, theories of modernization and convergence proposed an end stage of development that looked remarkably like a view of contemporary America (Pells 1985; Ricci 1984; Gouldner 1970).

The problem with these views from the standpoint of this volume is not—as is so often and sometimes misleadingly claimed—that they were naive artifacts of the "consensus" politics of America in the 1950s but rather that they created ahistorical effects—unintentionally in most cases. For if the central challenges of the period were historically unprecedented (e.g., Americans had "always" enjoyed a level of consensus remarkably like that of the 1950s or "never" experienced such abundance), if the present had arrived as a result of a historical process that was both efficient and teleological, if the interest group politics praised in pluralist theory somehow represented a "mature" political society, and if the other nations of the world were modernizing toward a "convergence" with American society, then the past had, to a great extent, become irrelevant to the present.

These ahistorical effects were reinforced by another development in this period that was—indeed almost had to be—more self-consciously antihistorical and that was the consolidation of the long campaign to remake the social sciences in the image of the natural sciences. The attempt to move the social sciences further from their historical-institutional origins in the early twentieth century and toward more concern with theory and method had picked up momentum with the organization of the Social Science Research Council in the 1920s. These activities grew in influence during the 1930s and World War Two itself when social scientists used their new theories and methods to analyze foreign propaganda and domestic attitudes. The shift toward quantitative methods and testing of hypotheses derived from "middle-range theory" took on new momentum in the postwar years, and the publication of works like Mills's revealed the widespread impression that this effort had been successful. Because the social sciences had been "born" in history it was almost inevitable that their new scientized versions of themselves would be portrayed as "not historical" (i.e., not merely institutional or historical), while at the same time the status of science would legitimate claims that this new social science was "transhistorical" (i.e., applicable at all times and places).

While these scientized human sciences in America increasingly converged on the belief that the proper route to the development of cumulative social science theory was through the rigorous testing of middle-range theory by means of observations of behavior in the present, most of the historians interested in interaction with the social sciences in this period gave more thought to the problem of history as a social science than to the social sciences as history. A series of conferences and volumes sponsored by the Social Science Research Council between 1954 and 1963 framed the debate among historians over "the social sciences in historical study" rather than the reverse, and the program for these historians was the borrowing of the middle-range theories and methods of the social sciencs (Novick 1988).

These developments were all influenced, in turn, by the conjunction between American power and economic might, the rise of the national security and social welfare state with its needs for research and information and willingness to support research offering "scientific" analysis, and the rapid growth of the research university into the conglomerate of activities that would come to be known as the "multiversity" by the 1960s. It would be wrong, however, to reduce these developments only to their political and institutional contexts. It was, in the end, the way that these contexts interacted with theory and method that made the difference.

Whether or not this generation of scholars cared about history, however, it was surely not exempt from it, as the decades of the 1960s and 1970s were so brutally to demonstrate. With the benefit of more than thirty years of history, in fact, one reads some of the more overconfident promises of the scientized human sciences with an almost archaeological interest, as if they were clay shards left behind by a civilization destroyed by an earthquake. The rise of the civil rights movement, the "rediscovery" of poverty, and the prosecution of the war in Vietnam revealed, in their turn, the inability of theories of consensus and status attainment, abundance, and modernization to explain current events. The domestic social movements arising in response to these events—for example, civil rights, antiwar, welfare rights, and parallel movements for the rights of women and others—placed both agency and history back on the agenda. The sheer existence of these movements reawakened and stimulated the theories of social movements and collective action while their political agendas stimulated new inquiries into the histories of social movements, race-making and state-building in America (Schwartz and Lemert 1988). By the late 1960s, the ground was well plowed for E. P. Thompson's classic work on the English working class, which would make clear that working-class history—and by analogy that of all oppressed groups—was not just lived but made and that both liberal and Marxist social theory would have to change to accommodate that fact (Thompson 1968).

The essays in this collection leave little doubt that the contemporary historic turn is in part a response to these demonstrations of the power of history as reflected in these movements and events. All of the authors are members of the age cohort that experienced these historic developments and, as some of the essays point out, some of the subdisciplines under discussion—for example, historical sociology and social history—enjoyed a recruitment of people active in politics. But once again, it would be wrong to reduce this complicated set of developments to any simple list of political and institutional determinants that minimize the way that historical events interacted with historiography and theory. A broad stream of new historiographies—of African-Americans, workers, women, immigrants, and others—flowed out from these events and across disciplinary boundaries. And they interacted dialectically with antifunctional social theories. At first, the idiom for this interaction was primarily structural: histories focusing on the structural locations and possibilities of various groups in society interacted with primarily structural theories of race, class, and gender along with theories of the structural prerequisites for social and political protest and change. As new histories interacted with new theories, the balance between structure and function became almost totally replaced by structure and agency (Dirks, Eley, and Ortner 1994).

At the same time that these developments placed more importance on action and the agent, however, critical theories of subjectivity assaulted the notion of the unitary bourgeois subject as the main actor in history. Poststructural theory affected not only the theory of structure, of course, but also of agency. Agency and the agent have, therefore, taken on critical importance at precisely the same time that the concept of the agent has been evacuated of much of its content. Rather than a colossus bestriding the pages of history, the agent must now emerge from those pages. Similarly, the meaning of agency must emerge from the historical reconstruction of its possibilities, not from deductions based on a putative map of social structures and accompanying subject positions. The importance of theorists of the local and contingent operations of power and ideology as otherwise different as Geertz and Foucault; the prominence of such theoretical terms (constantly redefined and contested) as hegemony, discourse, and identity, the multiple shifts from the global to the local, from the macro to the micro, and from structure to conjuncture and event in the distinctive intellectual practices of the era—for example, feminist theory and history, cultural studies, subaltern studies, and the new institutionalism—are all both symptomatic and constitutive of these developments (Geertz 1973, 1983; Foucault 1978–88).

Originating from a different point but intersecting completely with these changes has been the rise of a new history and sociology of science and social science that has transformed the social analyst, too, from the anonymous, omniscient voice of science to the identified and contextualized actor in history. Thomas Kuhn's pathbreaking 1962 book in the history of physics, *The Structure of Scientific Revolutions*, disrupted the image of science as following a cumulative path toward greater and greater truth and replaced it with the notion of the paradigm and the struggle for its centrality as the guide for "normal" science. By rehistoricizing the natural science that had served as the model for the scientized human sciences, Kuhn's work helped to unleash a flood of works on the history of social science published in the 1980s and 1990s that have raised the level of historical self-consciousness in all the disciplines (Kuhn [1962] 1970).

Just as a lack of historical self-consciousness was a factor in the reduced concern with history forty years ago, this increasing historical self-consciousness generates a number of notable points of consensus among the authors in this volume concerning both the problems affecting historical practice today and the prospects for a more historicized human science in the future. The former cluster around the point that Margaret Somers makes here that history must not be just subject matter but rather an epistemology, a "historical epistemology" concerned with exploring how both the formative issues in theory construction and analytical practice became what they are. A lack of self-conscious commentary on the meaning of history and the maintenance of constructed boundaries among the disciplines that belies their increasing convergence are among the issues that such an exploration reveals.

As Nicholas Dirks points out in his essay, the rush to history has not, on the whole, been accompanied by much "serious theoretical reflection about history itself." The problem here begins, admittedly, with the bad example of historians who have for the most part refused to put their own practices at risk by much methodological or theoretical writing, preferring instead to know history when they see it and therefore being more proficient at boundary maintenance—identifying what is "not history"—than at theorized reflection on their own practice. But at the same time, the appropriation of history by other disciplines has been ironically similar to the much decried "borrowing" of theory from other disciplines by historians. As Somers notes, for example, sociologists have been less interested than they should be in the histories of their own knowledge cultures, the way that certain questions have come to be investigated and others not and, therefore, the intellectual and political history embedded in central theoretical concepts. An interesting example of this problem is given in William Sewell's essay, which contends that, for all the writing on historical sociology, very little attention has been paid to a concept absolutely central to history—namely, the event itself. This has occurred in part, he argues, because of theoretical frameworks defining time in more acceptably—if "uneventful"—scientific ways. Similarly, Craig Calhoun makes the important point that much of the history of interest to sociologists (and members of other social science disciplines) has come from the typologies contained in the canon of classic works of social theory—including those of Marx, Weber, and Durkheim—rather than from a direct encounter with the past itself. This last problem has led to one of the most interesting and little noted ironies of contemporary social science: namely, that these conceptions of history have influenced the middle-range theory "borrowed" by historians to structure the accounts that have, in turn, been borrowed as facts by other social sciences.

The metaphor of the borrower, of course, is part and parcel of a whole series of distinctions between history and other practices that have been key to constructing and maintaining boundaries between the disciplines that the authors of these essays are eager to deconstruct. The dichotomies that Sewell, Calhoun, Smith, and Geoff Eley criticize include those of historians as "useful drones" doing the tedious work of collecting archival data and writing narratives that historical sociologists would use to produce "grander and more theoretically sophisticated analyses"; historical facts as "inferences from relics" and the facts of social science as the result of inferences from new, more perspicacious data and methods; "sensitive interpretation" versus the "logic of scientific methods"; and even "history" and "theory." These distinctions have become so familiar in the discourse of the social sciences that it is easy to forget that they, too, have a history.

As I contend in my essay, it should come as no surprise that, having been "born" in history, the social sciences would increasingly attempt to distinguish themselves from it by emphasizing theory and method in the years after the 1930s. But this separation was a two-way street. Historians in the 1950s turned to the social sciences in part at least for protection against relativism, constructing their theoretically subordinate role vis-à-vis social science so as not to have their enterprise destabilized in its turn by the responsibility of producing "theory." At the same time, by maintaining an image of history as merely a source of "facts" or historical "data points," social scientists protected themselves from the potentially corrosive effects of historical self-consciousness.

The paths that leading historians and sociologists have taken since then have been significantly different. Many senior members of the current generation of historical sociologists have worked hard in their own ways to repair rather than to break down these boundaries. Concerned about attacks on their own work as being too "interpretive" or "idiographic," some historical sociologists have outdone the sociological mainstream in their incessant concern about method and in continuing attempts to distinguish themselves from history and historians in the name of "science." On the other hand, for many historians as Eley suggests, this originally subordinate theoretical position nonetheless planted a seed of theoretical competence and interest that has grown into the current situation wherein historians are more and more comfortable acting as their own theorists both by tracing the effects of theory on historical practice and by propounding it themselves.

Boundary crossing like this underscores the disciplinary-ideological function of boundary maintenance and highlights instead a remarkable convergence of theoretical frameworks and analytical agendas across the disciplines involved in the historic turn. Consider the following quotations from the essays in this collection:

The literary is thus conceived neither as a separate and separable aesthetic realm nor as a mere product of culture—a reflection of ideas and ideologies produced elsewhere—but as one realm among many for the negotiation and production of social meaning, of historical subjects, and of the systems of power that at once enable and constrain those subjects.

In order to realize its potential both within sociology and in relation to an interdisciplinary historical and theoretical discourse . . . historical sociology needs to address problems of the changing constitution of social actors, the shifting meanings of cultural categories, and the struggle over identities and ideologies. These need to be conceived as part and parcel of social relations, not separate topics of inquiry, and still less as the turf of other disciplines.

[Political science needs to investigate] not only how various structural contexts constitute political agents with certain capabilities and constraints, but also how far those agents reconstitute their contexts.

The first quotation is from new historicist literary analyst Steven Mullaney, the second from Calhoun, and the third from Smith. This convergence of analytical agendas is a response not just to the historic turn but one kind of response to the more generalized development in this period, which Eley here calls the "antireductionist turn." This multidimensional challenge to "normal" social science refers both to theory and practice: the authors in this volume are simultaneously moving away from both the totalizing social theories (whether liberal functionalist, Marxist, or otherwise) and the parsimonious practice of previous social analysis. The search for a theoretical point of "determination in the last instance" whether in economic base, social function, or systemic equilibrium has been abandoned along with various maps of "the social" or unexplained "fixed and exogenous" preferences and with them the urge for the explanatory "elegance" of parsimonious and reductive models.

This theoretical move is, however, remarkably eclectic. Although the historic turn is occurring simultaneously with other "turns"—perhaps most significantly, the so-called linguistic turn—it is by no means identical with them. Within literature, as Mullaney notes, the historic turn is conducted primarily within poststructural theory, but in political science, as Smith reveals, it encompasses hermeneutic and poststructural theory as well as an eclectic mix of theories of institutional and state formation. In anthropology, meanwhile,

Sherry Ortner charts the effects of practice theory, feminist theory, and theories of subalternity, while among historians a broad range of all these theories has been deployed.

It is this commitment to theory that eliminates any desire by the authors here to return to history as an atheoretical narrative of "one damn thing after another" or to abandon the search for explanation. As Sewell and Smith agree, the product of the historic turn will indeed be similar to narrative history in its commitment to change over time and to the effectivity of events, culture, and individuals. But at the same time, attention will be paid to explanation of causal regularities and patterned behaviors as well as the effects of the past, which are the sediments and precipitates of culture and history.

The notion of history shared by these authors is less a "place"—the "past"—than a historicizing process. Deceptively simple, this process requires the recognition that the past is constructed—made and made sense of—as Dirks writes and therefore requires "nothing more nor less than the constant asking of questions about how something came to be and about what effects things have had over time." The list of "things" to be included in the "past" is of course extremely broad: social categories and identities, events and responses to events, structures and their transformations, and so on. As Joan Scott argues, however, it must also include "all explanatory categories usually taken for granted," so that its own interpreting movement is, as Dirks puts it, "part of the historicizing field."

For most of the authors in the collection the technique for producing such a history will resemble what Ortner here calls the "ethnographic stance," which refers not just to the practice of ethnographers but as she puts it to "first and foremost a commitment to what Geertz has called 'thickness,' to producing understanding via richness, texture, and detail, rather than parsimony, refinement, and (in the sense used by mathematicians) elegance." The goal of such a stance is a fully contextualized actor, understood as socially and culturally constructed, embedded in the matrix of local relations of power and conflict but also fully capable of action within that context. Such an actor will live in what Sewell calls an "eventful" past, one where social relations are affected by (and affect) path dependency, temporally heterogeneous causalities, and global contingency.

The notion then of historically self-conscious analysts reconstructing fully contextualized historical actors and representing them in a theoretically sophisticated narrative that takes account of multiple causes and effects is at the heart of the vision of the historic turn. It should come as no surprise, however, that even among those disciplines making this turn there is ambivalance about how far and how fast to go on this road. As Dirks notes, anthropologists now take for granted that there are "immense differences in the way in which the past, narrative, event, historicity itself can take form in different cultural contexts," and because, as Somers puts it, each of the disciplines possesses its own "knowledge culture," the place for history will vary within each.

As Robert Gordon's essay regarding legal history makes clear, law is an extreme case of historical practice that is almost predicated upon the removal of history from its context. In order to give the past its present effect, lawyers—whether they have argued for legal stasis or change—have conventionally "ripped" historical texts from their contexts to render them serviceable for a legal project that requires the past to be part "of a homogenous—or at least continuous—piece with the present." In a well-known comment, Charles Tilly has said much the same thing about sociology, that a "hidden piece of history"—the piece the analyst is living—roots most sociology in the present (Tilly 1981). The historically contextualized actor or text, therefore, has not always fit comfortably into these enterprises. Sewell's call for an "eventful" conception of temporality, Calhoun's demand for an end to sociology based on theories with "massive (unexamined) historical induction," and Somers's plea for a sociology aware of the histories embedded in its presuppositional categories call for a major change in the way even mainstream historical sociology views itself. It is for this reason that they all call for the spread of "historical" approaches to the discipline as a whole and reject their containment in a subfield of historical sociology.

Smith's analysis of political science similarly calls for a historical and institutional renewal to help solve the problem of the disparity between the discipline's knowledge that politics—and individual agency in politics—"matters" and "scientific" theory and methods, which have subordinated the importance of political action to exogenous, impersonal "forces." Smith's history of the search for "science" in political science since World War Two tells a story that is true for almost all the scientizing disciplines, and his hope for historical renewal is balanced against a disciplinary history where that path has been rarely taken.

Among those familiar with the presentation of "timeless" rituals and texts in anthropology and literature the historic turn raises the question of how and how much culture can be (or has been) historicized. On the one hand, as Mullaney points out, the new historicism has used cultural theory to decisively shift literature from the realm of the aesthetic to the realm of power, the terrain where it becomes not a collection of timeless canonical texts but an inquiry into the power of literary forms to shape ideas, subjects, and practices. But, on the other hand, Dirks asks whether the same anthropologists who have been eager to "explode" history with culture have been as eager to see their own practices historicized, to realize that their own histories, texts, and traditions have been constructed in history. At the same time, Ortner wonders whether a more fully historicized ethnohistorical actor is the answer to what she calls the "ethnographic refusal."

Among historians, meanwhile, the assumptions about what Eley calls the "determinative coherence of the social" that launched the "new" social history have themselves become the objects of historical analysis in the wake of the theoretical recognition that "there is no overarching structural coherence" or other principle of order from the economic or social systems. On the contrary, as he and Scott contend, the "social" is not the framework for history but a moment in history itself, and therefore the emergence of new concepts and identities—like the social—are themselves historical events in need of explanation. Furthermore, as Scott points out, even "experience," once thought of as the historian's touchstone, is now not the origin of explanation but—always both an interpretation and in need of it.

As the response to Scott's previously published essay suggests, historians themselves have bridled at the historicization of their own ground. Like the lawyers in Gordon's account, they have learned—sometimes to their regret— that "whenever [they] embraced historical methods and evidence they could never get rid of them, even when the company became uncomfortable." History becomes most uncomfortable when, like Marx's old mole it burrows and burrows until it seems to dig out the ground beneath the analyst, whether that analyst is a historian or other practitioner of history.

Although Eley may be correct that at the level of theory "all bets are off," in some ways, in spite of these controversies, a huge wager has been placed on history. It will take some time to see whether that bet will pay off. It is not clear that the historical branches of some disciplines can renew the rest, that calls for history will outweigh calls for science, or that historians will continue to participate in this effort by putting their own culture at risk. Whatever the long-term outcome of the historic turn, however, we can say for now, with Dirks, that it is surely a turn for the better.

NOTE

1. Because all of these tendencies are more thoroughly discussed and cited in the essays in this collection, citations in the introduction are illustrative only and make no attempt to be comprehensive.

REFERENCES

Abbott, Andrew. 1988. "Transcending General Linear Reality." *Sociological Theory* 6:169–86.

Abbott, Andrew. 1994. "History and Sociology: The Lost Synthesis." In *Engaging the Past: The Uses of History across the Social Sciences,* edited by Eric H. Monkkonen, 77–112. Durham, NC: Duke University Press.

Cohen, Ralph, and Michael S. Roth. 1995. *History And—: Histories Within the Human Sciences.* Charlottesville: University Press of Virginia.

Cox, Jeffrey N., and Larry J. Reynolds, eds. 1993. *New Historical Literary Study: Essays on Reproducing Texts, Representing History.* Princeton: Princeton University Press.

Dirks, Nicholas B., Geoff Eley, and Sherry B. Ortner, eds. 1994. *Culture/Power/History: A Reader in Contemporary Social Theory.* Princeton: Princeton University Press.

Dryzek, John S., and Stephen T. Leonard. 1988. "History and Discipline in Political Science." *American Political Science Review* 82:1245–60.

Foucault, Michel. 1978–88. *The History of Sexuality.* 4 vols. New York: Pantheon.

Geertz, Clifford. 1973. *The Interpretation of Cultures.* New York: Basic Books.

Geertz, Clifford. 1983. *Local Knowledge.* New York: Basic Books.

Gouldner, Alvin. 1970. *The Coming Crisis in Western Sociology.* New York: Basic Books.

Halliday, Terrence C., and Morris Janowitz, eds. 1992. *Sociology and Its Publics: The Forms and Fates of Disciplinary Organization.* Chicago: University of Chicago Press.

Higham, John. 1983. *History: Professional Scholarship in America.* Baltimore: Johns Hopkins University Press.

Hunt, Lynn, ed. 1989. *The New Cultural History.* Berkeley and Los Angeles: University of California Press.

Kavanaugh, Dennis. 1991. "Why Political Science Needs History." *Political Studies* 39:479–95.

Kuhn, Thomas. [1962] 1970. *The Structure of Scientific Revolutions.* 2d ed. Chicago: University of Chicago Press.

Mack, Arien, ed. 1992. Frontiers in Social Inquiry. *Social Research* (special issue, winter) 59:4.

March, James G., and Johan P. Olsen. 1989. *Rediscovering Institutions: The Organizational Basis of Politics.* New York: Free Press.

Mills, C. W. 1959. *The Sociological Imagination.* London and New York: Oxford University Press.

Monkkonen, Eric H. 1994. *Engaging the Past: The Uses of History across the Social Sciences.* Durham, NC: Duke University Press.

Novick, Peter. 1988. *That Noble Dream: The "Objectivity Question" and the American Historical Profession.* New York: Cambridge University Press.

Pells, Richard H. 1985. *The Liberal Mind in a Conservative Age: American Intellectuals in the 1940s and 1950s.* New York: Harper and Row.

Ree, Jonathan. 1991. "The Vanity of Historicism." *New Literary History* 22:961–83.

Ricci, David M. 1984. *The Tragedy of Political Science: Politics, Scholarship, and Democracy.* New Haven: Yale University Press.

Riker, William H. 1962. *The Theory of Political Coalitions.* New Haven: Yale University Press.

Rorty, Richard, J. B. Schneewind, and Quentin Skinner, eds. 1984. *Philosophy in History.* Cambridge: Cambridge University Press.

Schwartz, David, and Charles Lemert, eds. 1988. "Breaking Boundaries: Social Theory and the Sixties." *Theory and Society* (special issue) 17:5.

Seidelman, Raymond, and Edward J. Harpham. 1985. *Disenchanted Realists: Political Science and the American Crisis, 1884–1984.* Albany: State University of New York Press.

Seidman, Stephen, Robert A. Jones, R. Stephen Warner, and Stephens Turner. 1985. "The Historicist Controversy: Understanding the Sociological Past." *Sociological Theory* 3:13–28.

Skinner, Quentin, ed. 1985. *The Return of Grand Theory in the Human Sciences.* Cambridge: Cambridge University Press.

Skocpol, Theda, ed. 1984. *Vision and Method in Historical Sociology.* New York: Cambridge University Press.

Smith, Dennis. 1991. *The Rise of Historical Sociology.* Philadelphia: Temple University Press.

Social Science Research Council, Committee on Historiography. 1954. *The Social Sciences in Historical Study.* New York: Social Science Research Council.

Social Science Research Council, Committee on Historical Analysis. 1963. *Generalization in the Writing of History.* Chicago: University of Chicago Press.

Thompson, E. P. 1968. *The Making of the English Working Class.* New York: Vintage.

Tilly, Charles. 1981. *As Sociology Meets History.* New York: Academic Press.

Veeser, Aram H., ed. 1989. *The New Historicism.* New York and London: Routledge.

White, Hayden. 1987. *The Content of the Form: Narrative Discourse and Historical Representation.* Baltimore: Johns Hopkins University Press.

Part 1. Historic Encounters

Is Vice Versa? Historical Anthropologies and Anthropological Histories

Nicholas B. Dirks

The problem now is to explode the concept of history by the anthropological experience of culture.

—Marshall Sahlins

To articulate the past historically does not mean to recognize it "the way it really was." It means to seize hold of a memory as it flashes up at a moment of danger. Only that historian will have the gift of fanning the spark of hope in the past who is firmly convinced that *even the dead* will not be safe from the enemy if he wins.

—Walter Benjamin

The Concept of Culture

The concept of culture has been anthropology's signal—and perhaps single most important—contribution to recent social theory. In American cultural anthropology, the name most recently and most clearly associated with the development of culture as a concept is Clifford Geertz, who has provided elegant definitions of culture and inspired much of the most interesting work in cultural analysis. Geertz's definition of culture has always been a semiotic one, predicated on the notion that culture has to do with meaning, with the way experience is construed rather than with some unmediated notion of experience itself, and with the centrality of symbols for conducting and expressing meanings that are systematic as well as shared.

Although Geertz gave culture a new set of glosses and spins, he developed his sense of the concept out of certain fundamental traditions in anthropology, as also out of his ethnographic encounters in Indonesia and Morocco, not to mention Chicago and Princeton. His culture, like anthropology's culture more generally, was not Arnoldian, not the high (and capitalized) culture that had in the nineteenth century been identified with Western civilization and a Kantian aesthetic of the sublime, the very view that in the 1980s was accorded the official sanction of the National Endowment for the Humanities (NEH) and the National Endowment for the Arts (NEA). Anthropology has been guilty of reifying and, in Said's sense, orientalizing other cultures, but in identifying non-Western cultures as coherent, meaningful, and integral structures it has also been instrumental in shifting culture from its high Enlightenment position to the terra firma of lived social experience.

It is no accident that when social historians sought to register their concern about the exclusion of politically marginal groups from the master narratives of history they turned to anthropology and its notions and examples of cultural life to enrich their own sense of what it meant to study historical "experience." Historians had first turned to quantitative methods and formal social science, which made possible the recuperation of the myriad numbers and reports that had been compiled to document and control nonelite social groups. But quantitative methods could not answer some of the most basic questions about the meaning and shape of lived experience among ordinary people. Nevertheless, when historians turned to anthropology for inspiration about such questions as tradition, community, family organization, and agrarian social structure, they tended to borrow concepts and attitudes out of the contexts of disciplinary debate within anthropology, often ending in a parody of their own political justifications for social history in the first place. As Bernard Cohn has elsewhere warned, historians should beware of buying used concepts from other disciplines. When historians entered anthropologyland, they left their political scruples at home (Cohn 1987).

If anthropology might be said to have invented culture, it no longer owns it. As in other areas where the incitement to consume is endemic, Cohn's warnings have stopped nobody. *Culture* is a term that is cropping up all over. The "sociology of culture" is a new growth industry in sociology departments. Cultural studies programs are being set up in many American universities, reflecting not only the currency of anthropological notions of culture but more generally the current rapprochement between the traditional humanities— English, comparative literature, history of art, critical theory—and those areas in the social sciences that have until recently been more keen to cultivate their affinity to the sciences than the softer humanities. All of these groups, and perhaps last of all anthropologists too, have become increasingly aware of a parallel interdisciplinary phenomenon, or movement, in Britain called "cultural studies." This movement has been of tremendous importance in calling for increased attention to the political character of culture.

The Politics of Culture

British cultural studies has often been located in departments or programs of sociology but grew out of the literary criticism of Raymond Williams and Richard Hoggart and the social history of E. P. Thompson and Eric Hobsbawm. It is now principally associated with the activities of the Centre for Contemporary Cultural Studies at the University of Birmingham and the writings of Stuart Hall and Raymond Williams. According to Richard Johnson, "Cultural processes do not correspond to the contours of academic knowledges, as they are. No one academic discipline grasps the full complexity (or seriousness) of the study. Cultural studies must be interdisciplinary (and sometimes anti-disciplinary) in its tendency" (1986-87, 42). He goes on to say that, for him, "cultural studies is about the historical forms of consciousness or subjectivity, or the subjective forms we live by, or [. . .] the subjective side of social relations" (43). As interesting as these statements are, culture appears in these formulations as little more than class-specific subjectivity. We are left to wonder why cultural studies has not adequately theorized its concept of culture (and the lack of a vigorous interest in culture among British social anthropologists is perhaps one of the problems). However, Stuart Hall is clearer and more interesting when he notes that cultural studies grew out of a sustained and even dialectical reading of structuralism and culturalism in the light of a concern about the residual determinisms in any mode of production, be it social or cultural. Hall, following Williams and others, takes a Gramscian reading of hegemony as central to any study of cultural phenomena, and the constant concern with the political and class-based dynamics of culture finds its justification here (see, for example, Hall 1980, 57–72). In any case, cultural studies is as cultural studies does. People associated with the label have worked on the cultural forms and activities of marginal and nonelite groups, as for example the worlds of factory workers, Rastafarian slum dwellers, Pakistani immigrants, or dispossessed women. Cultural studies has continued as well to focus on cultural production, in particular on film and mass media, popular literature, and the functions and festivities of ordinary folk. In all its guises, the cultural studies movement has debated and adopted different approaches to the "politics of culture."

The strengths of British cultural studies have in part to do with the level of political commitment and engagement that have been fundamental to the movement. At last, culture has been genuinely politicized in academic writing. However, this very engagement has led to certain weaknesses as well. In particular, the definition of culture is somewhat narrowly tied to the neo-Gramscian interest in hegemony and counterhegemony, leading to an emphasis on consensus within class boundaries and resistance across them. This concern does not allow a lot of room for critical discussion about the assumptions implicit in most notions of consensus and resistance, for example, the conventional categories of agency, subjectivity, and experience. In addition (and not unrelatedly), the cultures chosen for analysis are principally contemporary and located within Britain itself. Class and ethnicity are taken to be the foundational categories of analysis in ways that seem to those of us looking at other parts of the world as peculiarly rooted in contemporary postcolonial British society. While anthropology has still not successfully engaged its own historical implication in European colonialism, it has at least insisted that if culture be celebrated as a popular rather than an elite phenomenon, the populace—and our theories of cultural production—must be genuinely international. Nevertheless, British cultural studies has demonstrated some of the weaknesses of anthropology's culture concept, and anthropologists are increasingly recognizing that their notion of culture can no longer be silent about the continual political valence and mobility of all cultural forms. Williams is turning up as a reference for considerations of the culture concept almost as frequently as Geertz in recent anthropological writing.

Culture and History

In American cultural anthropology, the first major reconsideration of a semiotic theory of culture came more from an insistence on the recognition of the historicity of cultural forms than it did from the academy's engagement with the politics of class. One of the most dramatic interventions of this kind has been that of Marshall Sahlins, who through his own appropriations of French structuralism had locked himself into a far more formal cultural semiotics (see Sahlins 1976) than the fluid Weberianism of Clifford Geertz. In his recent writing (1981, 1985), Sahlins has regaled us with stories of what happened when Captain Cook went to Hawaii. As he did so, he also announced with great fanfare that he had discovered history or, rather, the event. He argues persuasively that a Saussurean theory of structure cannot withstand the pressures of the conjuncture, and in several brilliant theoretical essays he undermines the structuralist foundations of his own earlier claims about meaning and cultural form.

However, Sahlins neither provides examples of what historical process might look like apart from dramatic moments of culture contact and colonial conquest nor does he sufficiently incorporate his notion of event into the contingent complexities of cultural formation. As always, Sahlins is elegant, and his gesture toward history has clearly had a salutory impact on anthropological practices in America. As his last word in *Islands of History,* he writes that "The truer issue lies in the dialogue of sense and reference, inasmuch as reference puts the system of sense at the risk of other systems: the intelligent subject and the intransigent world. And the truth of this larger dialogue consists of the indissoluble synthesis of such as past and present, system and event, structure and history" (1985, 156). What this seems to mean is that systems of meaning have constantly to be practiced, and that, as he says elsewhere, "Every implementation of cultural concepts in an actual world submits the concepts to some determination by the situation" (149). But systems of meaning, or culture, are formulated prior to and autonomously from the moment of risk or determination, and the situation, or the intransigent world, is, like the British and American military forces that came back to wreak revenge for Cook's murder, nothing more (or less) than a periodic, if occasional, check on the steady reproduction of cultural systems. Culture may have become situated in history, but culture has still not been genuinely historicized. Sahlins may be correct to assert that we should attempt "to explode the concept of history by the anthropological experience of culture" (72), but by leaving his concept of culture unexploded by history he has instead reproduced the tendency for interdisciplinary formulations to swing mostly in one direction. If history should be exploded by culture, then culture should likewise be exploded by history.

The structuralist modes of reasoning deployed by Sahlins engage history at a level that makes little sense to most historians, who tend to feel much more comfortable turning to Geertz, Turner, or Evans-Pritchard. In a recent essay on historical anthropology, Aletta Biersack recommends Sahlins to historians, saying that Sahlins resolves many of the fundamental debates in the historical study of culture (Hunt 1989, 72–96). But while Biersack is correct to point out that Sahlins engages these debates with extraordinary skill and clarity, he does so in ways that are specifically situated in anthropological discourses and problematics. Sahlins's work reveals some of the fundamental commitments of anthropology as a discipline and why it is that historical anthropology still looks so different from history when practiced by historians. Most historians find it difficult to relate to Sahlins's principal concern, namely, his argument that no synchronic theory of structure can account for the way in which structures must always reproduce themselves and that in every moment of reproduction the structure is at risk. Although Sahlins insists that "cultural schemes are historically ordered" (vii), his elaboration of the concept of culture is little different from his concept of structure (as Roseberry recently commented [1989, 8], if you look up the word *culture* in the index to *Islands of History* one reads, "see structure"). Historians are perplexed by the fact that for Sahlins meaning itself is as much about the structuring principles of social determinations as it is about ideas, signs, or beliefs. Whereas for Sahlins the event enters as a disruptive force, challenging structuralist assumptions about reproduction, for historians events are everywhere, challenging structuralist notions of structure itself.

The Subjects of Culture

Sahlins views culture as "the codification of man's actual purposeful and pragmatic action" (1976, 55). This concern with collective codes as sediments of human action underplays for most historians the importance of the historical actor or agent; indeed, historians find it difficult to recognize any theoretical space at all for agency, for individual actions or voices. Historians believe in the need to identify and privilege historical subjects. So although for Sahlins culture may be subject to history, it is culture itself that is for him the universal subject of history. Historians recognize this kind of concern from other structuralisms, particularly from Althusser's insistence that subjects are produced by history rather than the other way around, but they are rarely persuaded. Instead, historians tend to prefer vague notions of experience to formal conceptions of either structure or culture, and, as Joan Scott (1991) has noted, the notion of "experience" is used to establish the prior existence of subjects. Even so, there is much in anthropological views of culture that is similar, say, to E. P. Thompson's notion of experience, in which class is both the determination and distillation of subjective meaning, and the conceit of experience becomes specifically tied to the material life and social position of a class. Sahlins and Thompson represent tendencies in cultural anthropology and social history to focus on ideas, cultural practices, shared beliefs, and attitudes, at the same time that their theoretical commitments, to culture and class respectively, tend to elude the historicizing emphasis of their polemics. But despite all this and their culturalist readings of Marx, Sahlins and Thompson write, and are read, in ways that reflect their own disciplinary cultures, with all their differences and alterities.

Sahlins's insistence that culture is the subject of history, for example, flies directly in the face of the concerns of historians about agency and subjects.

Historians are usually reluctant to engage the totalizing propensities of structuralism, even in Sahlins's version of a historical anthropology. But Sahlins raises one issue to which historians, I believe, must attend, and that interestingly aligns poststructuralist critiques of the unitary/originary subject with anthropological commitments to the specificity of cultural regimes. Sahlins makes with particular force the anthropological point that different cultures entail different historicities. Indeed, not only does anthropology insist that experience is never immediate, never the kind of unmediated reality—whether affective or cognitive—that Scott so effectively critiques in her essay, anthropology suggests that there are immense differences in the way in which the past, narrative, event, and historicity itself can take form in different cultural contexts. If historians at some level would invariably align themselves with Collingwood's "commonsensical" notion of experience, anthropologists are aware of how culture-bound this desire is. But to insist that experience itself is culture-bound is not to solve the problem of how to bound culture. Experiences differ radically within single cultural domains, according to such factors as class, race, and gender. The notion of the uniform character of cultural experience (within variably defined cultural domains) seems unlikely to survive either the scrutiny of historians or the poststructuralist commitment to multiplicity. If anthropology correctly insists that at one level culture is the subject of history, we must remember that different groups have different histories, as also that the subject (or, rather, the unitary bourgeois subject lurking behind most historical understandings of the subject) has been fractured and dissolved in recent critical theory.

It has been many years since anthropology as a discipline was defined by a particular preoccupation with primitives, and because of the decolonization both of the world and of anthropology's geographical (and theoretical) provenance there is no longer any defensible reason that the notions of a people and of a culture should be seen as in any sense coterminous. One of the most important implications of Geertz's insistence that culture be defined semiotically has been that culture could be detached as an analytic domain from any particular social referent. But anthropologists nevertheless too often continue to think of culture as writ large, as most meaningful when descriptively attached to such labels as "Nuer," "American," or "Indian"; as the largest possible domain of agreement, belief, and shared understanding; and as bounded by such modern social units as nation, tribe, or island. While culture as a category clearly does operate at these levels, social historians among others have now established that cultural forms are developed, transformed, manipulated, and appropriated in different ways within what have traditionally been deemed as anthropological units of analysis. In this respect, E. P. Thompson has only been one of many historians who has claimed that when history is practiced "from below" it changes, that a commitment to study the life worlds of various subaltern groups genuinely subverts master histories.

The theoretical locus of much recent rethinking of the tensions and disjunctions in cultural configurations across social/class groups has been the work of Antonio Gramsci, in particular his suggestions about the nature of hegemony. Gramsci uses the concept of hegemony in at least two ways: to mean domination itself and to refer to the means by which the consensus that allows rule to take place is formed and transformed. For Gramsci, hegemony is never total; it is always multiple, contradictory, and contested. As Raymond Williams has made clear in his cogent reading of Gramsci, hegemony always implies counterhegemony: "[Hegemony] does not just passively exist as a form of dominance. It has continually to be renewed, recreated, defended, and modified. It is also continually resisted, limited, altered, challenged by pressures not at all its own. We have then to add to the concept of hegemony the concepts of counterhegemony and alternative hegemony, which are real and persistent elements of practice" (1977, 112, 113). For Williams, as indeed for all those who have been influenced by Gramsci, hegemony dramatically supplements any previous definition of culture because it insists that culture is a human activity that always exists in relationship to dominance and subordination. Culture is thus linked to the continuing and pervasive processes of rule, politics, and struggle. The units of anthropological and historical analysis must now contain multiple cultures and histories.

Gramsci does not address the question of the subject itself, though he is concerned about the way in which hegemonic processes limit the extent to which culture is a purposeful human practice. But when historians learn from Gramsci's insights, they tend to celebrate those very subjects whose subjectivity is shown to have been most in question throughout history. Gayatri Chakravorty Spivak has recently discussed this problem in her provocative essay "Can the Subaltern Speak?" (Nelson and Grossberg 1988, 271–313). But she begins her essay, and today it seems difficult to imagine doing otherwise, with a consideration of the powerful critiques of the subject that have emerged from poststructuralist theory. Without doubt, the most penetrating critique of the subject, and the most powerful linkage of subjects with subjection, comes in the writing of Michel Foucault.

Foucault developed and refined Althusser's sense of subject production, writing that "It is a form of power which makes individuals subjects . . . power applies itself to immediate everyday life which categorizes the individual, marks him by his own individuality, attaches him to his identity, imposes a law of truth on him" (1982, 212). In works such as *Discipline and Punish* and the *History of Sexuality,* as well as in essays and interviews of the late 1970s and early 1980s, Foucault insisted that subjects recognize themselves as individual, purposeful, autonomous, and originary in relation to the operations of power. The subject itself is one of the effects of power. Even in his early writings, Foucault proposed the fundamental historicity of the subject, with man himself not arriving on the scene fully formed until the seventeenth century. The unitary subject has been further demolished by Derrida's deconstruction of the metaphysics of presence and by Lacan's psychoanalytic insistence that the supposedly immediate certainty of self-identity is imaginary. If poststructuralism has a single dogma, one that also expresses its genealogical connection to structuralism itself, it is that the imagined sovereign bourgeois ego is a product of ideology.

The poststructuralist assault on the subject does not, however, provide the basis for any simple recuperation of older anthropological notions of culture. As noted above, Sahlins's insistence on multiple cultural forms and historicities is always made in the context of his sense that cultures are total systems with internal uniformity of structure and signification. And Sahlins's turn to history seems similarly limited by his location of events outside of culture. The problem is not so much that Sahlins has not worried about the question of agency as much as historians would like but that his conception of culture has remained largely impervious to the historic turn. Sahlins has added history but failed to historicize either culture or his own historical intervention.

The History of Culture

Sahlins is by no means the only anthropologist to have made the historic turn. In fact, other anthropologists have gone much further in historicizing culture, seeing it as contingent, conjunctural, invented, transacted, and manipulated. A recent book of essays by William Roseberry (1989) takes on both Geertz's and Sahlins's sense of culture by referring to some of the same social theorists whose names already grace the endnotes of this paper. There is much in Roseberry's book that parallels my own critique. He writes, for example, that Sahlins emphasizes practice as a theoretical category "rather than the practices of differently situated and positioned actors within contradictory social relations" (1989, 10). He also notes that Sahlins finally fails in an effort to incorporate events "within preexisting conceptual schemes" (9). And Roseberry criticizes Geertz for removing culture from the process of cultural creation and historical production, thereby making possible "the constant reproduction of an antinomy between the material and the ideal" (29).

But there is something in the critique that falls flat, and it is worth examining the rhetoric of this particular anthropological polemic in order to isolate some of the strengths and weaknesses of anthropology's turn to critical theory and historical analysis. For, having begun to make an important intervention in the anthropological debate about culture, Roseberry then reinvokes—without reflection—the same antinomy between the material and ideal that he began by criticizing. He writes that "The resolution of the antinomy, and the concept of culture that emerges from that resolution, must be materialist" (26). Roseberry reverses the terms of the debate; he accuses Sahlins of subordinating history (by which both Sahlins and Roseberry mean material process) to culture and counters by subordinating culture to history.

Roseberry's hero is Eric Wolf, for whom history is a "material social process, one characterized by economic and political inequality and domination, and by transformation not only of the relations among cultural terms but of entire social orders" (11). And Roseberry asserts that Wolf's approach is completely incompatible with that of Sahlins or Geertz. Whereas for Sahlins and Geertz "the Other . . . [is] different and separate, a product of its own history and carrying its own historicity," for Wolf "the Other . . . [is] different but connected, a product of a particular history that is itself intertwined with a larger set of economic, political, social, and cultural processes to such an extent that analytical separation of 'our' history and 'their' history is impossible" (13). While there is much in this critique that rings true, Roseberry's characterization leaves all terms other than culture unexamined. Roseberry seems content to be the flip side of Sahlins's coin and by invoking Wolf as his primary exemplar leaves his claims about the importance of such theorists as Gramsci and Williams entirely without explanation. Roseberry also lays claim to a universal history that necessarily consigns other histories (and other historicities) to a position of relative insignificance.

Roseberry's general formulation becomes clearer if we examine some of his concrete examples. In his critique of Geertz, he refers to a recent article by Taylor and Rebel about the meaning of Grimm's folk tales. According to Roseberry, Taylor and Rebel situate the tales in the real historical context of the late eighteenth and early nineteenth centuries and suggest that the tales were, in the final analysis, "attempts by peasant women to respond to the disruption of families and the drafting of their disinherited sons" (28). Thus, the tales recommend that "inheriting daughters should renounce their inheritance, move from the region, marry elsewhere, and offer a refuge for the fleeing brothers." The ultimate historical evidence is demographic, despite the acknowledgment that "it cannot yet be demonstrated whether the process they suggest actually occurred" (28). While Roseberry is undoubtedly correct in suggesting by analogy that Geertz could have situated his analysis of the cockfight more saliently in the political and economic contexts of mid-1960s Indonesia than in his own narrative account of ethnographic empathy, the above example does not shed nearly as much light on what is missing in Geertz's (or in other brands of) anthropological analysis as Roseberry asserts. Roseberry seems unconcerned that he is reducing cultural meaning to historical process, that he is reifying a concept of the purposive subject (the collective rational subjects identified as peasant women) in ways that are completely compatible with bourgeois social theory; that history itself might as a procedure and a context be more than demographic trends, family maintenance, and dilemmas concerning inheritance; and indeed that history as his ultimate referent might be more (or less) than what "actually occurred," whether we know it "yet" or not.

Roseberry seems equally limited in claiming elsewhere in his book that the work of Arnold Strickon demonstrates his own putatively postantinomial sense of historical anthropology. Roseberry argues that Robert Redfield's sense of cultural and historical transformation in the Yucatan was limited by his lack of attention to the "transformation of ecology and economy in the area as a result of the development of estate agriculture and ranching." Strickon's work, we are told, "shows that all of the communities can only be understood in terms of that history" (214). As with Sahlins, history continues to exist outside of culture. But whereas Sahlins introduces history after culture (and shows how it is often determined by it), Roseberry puts culture after history (and demonstrates the same logic of determination).[1]

Roseberry's lineage within anthropology, revealed both by his choice of ancestor and his world of reference and association, is clearly identifiable as a distinctly anthropological brand of political economy. He prefaces his book by announcing that he wishes to explore the nature of a "political economic understanding of culture," something, he notes, that is dismissed equally by critics of political economy and most practitioners of political economy itself. But in attempting "to place culture and history in relation to each other" (ix), Roseberry has simply widened the net of subjects that political economy can address and explain, proceeding then in much the same way as it has done when on more familiar ground. My purpose in rehearsing this attempt is not to vindicate Sahlins (or Geertz) from critique but to suggest that Roseberry takes culture as a fixed and unproblematic category. Roseberry proceeds to argue that culture should be explained not in reference to itself (as he argues Sahlins and

Geertz do) but as it is determined by what "political economy" highlights as historical and material process. Not only does Roseberry fail to attend to recent developments in critical theory that call into question some of the theoretical terms and assumptions of his own political economy (and precisely his own assumptions about historical and material process), he fails to suggest any ways in which anthropological analysis might be of interest to the growing group of people committed to cultural studies, most of whom begin their studies of culture with apparently compatible premises, such as the need to politicize and historicize the study of culture. As it turns out, not only does Roseberry disavow the complex dynamics of cultural production, he seems genuinely uninterested in cultural analysis itself.

The Culture of History

If Sahlins failed to explode his own sense of culture through his turn to history, Roseberry has failed to explode his own sense of history. Even when critiquing the parallel antinomies between the ideal and the material and between culture and history he resolutely keeps history exempt from culture. In this failure he is not alone. The recent turn to history on the part of many disciplines in the human sciences has generally been in response to specific disciplinary debates and concerns but has rarely been accompanied by any serious theoretical reflection about history itself or how historical process and method might be examined in light of different disciplinary dilemmas. At least Sahlins and Geertz have used their sense of anthropological method to call history into question. I have already suggested some of the difficulties in these formulations, but it is worth remembering some of the ways in which cultural anthropology has anticipated poststructuralist critiques of the objectivist and unitary master history of Enlightenment thought before engaging in yet another critique of anthropological practice.

Sahlins, for example, has quite explicitly argued that "different cultural orders have their own modes of historical action, consciousness, and determination—their own historical practice" (34). In the case of Polynesian cultures, Sahlins lays out a notion of heroic history, which has to do with the social fact that in "heroic polities the king is the condition of the possibility of community" (36). Thus, he quotes Feeley-Harnik to underscore one of his points, that "History is not evenly distributed because to have it is a sign of politico-religious power and authority" (49). This uneven distribution is valorized through chiefly logics of hierarchy, which seem unjust to modern Western ideologies of social formation. All very well, except that cries of injustice seem mostly to valorize a capitalist logic of putative equality. As Sahlins notes, "The native 'Boo-jwas' theory is that social outcomes are the cumulative expressions of individual actions, hence behind that of the prevailing state of people's wants and opinions, as generated especially out of their material sufferings. The society is constructed as the institutional sum of its individual practices" (52). Sahlins forcefully parodies the market-driven conceits of bourgeois rationality: "The prevailing quantitative, populist, and materialist presuppositions of our social science can then be no accident—or there is no anthropology" (53). By implication, Western assumptions about universal historicities are deeply problematic and profoundly tied to the ideological formation of capitalism.

One problem with Sahlins's critique is that he reserves his hermeneutic of suspicion for contemporary Western ideologies. Sahlins's version of "chiefly politics" replaces one conceit with another, and never includes a politics of hegemony or resistance, of domination or dissent. As "Western" as these terms may be, their anthropological opposites are no less foreign to the fundamental categories of Western social thought.[2] When Sahlins suggests that the main relationships of Fijian society work through persons of authority, he invokes the standard antinomy of "consensus" (or influence) and "coercion." And, perhaps even more worrying, Sahlins is strangely uncritical of European descriptions and sources that provide the evidence for and ground of much of his ethnographic characterization. He fails to deploy his hermeneutic of suspicion against anthropological knowledge itself, permeated as it is so clearly by ideologies and histories of capitalism and colonialism (see Dirks 1996). Sahlins's commitment to extreme anthropological relativism may be linked to his own critique of capitalist ideology but is equally subject to it, as well as to forms of nostalgia that themselves depend upon capitalist alienation. Surely a version of a cultural order that is depicted as a seamless whole and as exempt from critical theory's attack on the conventional categories of political theory requires serious interrogation.

Recent critical attention to anthropology, and its implication in the discourses of colonial rule, has identified the tropes of reification and denigration that lurk just below the textual surfaces of much cultural anthropology (see Clifford and Said). For a variety of reasons, though perhaps primarily because of increasing attention paid to the way our forms of knowledge are shaped by the relations of power and interest (from the influence of Foucault), we must now question the integrity, possibility, and authenticity of any properly anthropological object. We are now correctly suspicious of the categories of "otherness" and "difference" that have historically been caught in logics of domination, whether "orientalist," "primitivist," or "colonialist." And we must maintain this suspicion despite the fact that Sahlins uses his anthropological characterizations to critique Western thought and assumption, in particular the values of capitalist accumulation, predicated as he sees them on the Augustinian tragedy of unending desire and material obsession (Sahlins 1987). One of the central critiques of Sahlins from within anthropology has been that he denies non-Western or precapitalist peoples economic rationality, a charge he would happily acknowledge. Indeed, Sahlins provides a salient example of how anthropology has always promised the possibility of encountering other worlds and other modes of being that can work to defamiliarize and denaturalize the world we take for granted. But even the most salutary aims in anthropology may carry dangerous cargo. The operations of difference seem always to produce hierarchical relations between "us" and "them" (however these categories are constructed) and never exist outside of representation itself.

The realization that anthropology has its own history and politics of representation does not, however, solve the methodological or theoretical problems raised in my consideration of the relations of history and culture. And if otherness is a category that must always be suspected, that continually reinscribes colonialism into the postcolonial procedures of anthropology, it nevertheless may facilitate our attempt to listen to the voices of anthropological informants and colonized subalterns. Reflexive anthropology seems often to suggest that we have a choice to make as to whether we read the anthropological text as a product of either the subject or the object, the author or the informant (or, even more simply, that the incorporation of objects as subjects and informants as authors removes the politics from representation). But this is not a choice that should have to be made, any more than the recognition that meaning is contingent and conditional need necessitate a suspension of our effort to engage the effects of the world "out there" (or the acceptance that god is dead lead necessarily to suicide).

Similarly, we should not have to choose between forgetting anthropology's colonial legacies and forfeiting anthropology's insistence on the importance of studying cultural difference. The critique of anthropology's role in reflecting and enabling colonialism as a historical practice and mode of thought simply raises the stakes of the historicizing enterprise. The question remains, however, as to what exactly it might mean to historicize both anthropology and its concept of culture.

The Concept of History

Historians have typically made less impact on social theory than anthropologists, literary critics, or other disciplinary practitioners in part because of their resolute refusal to theorize, to put their own culture of history at risk by the reference of metahistorical thinking. If there is, as Terrence McDonald suggests, a historic turn—a general turn to history by anthropologists, sociologists, political scientists, and literary critics—it is also the case that these nonhistorians are often sorely disappointed when historians fail to appreciate what they do and sometimes even to recognize it as history. Nonhistorians are often deeply puzzled why those very professional academics who would seem from the outside to hold the keys to the kingdom of enlightenment refuse to think helpfully about E. H. Carr's age-old question, what is history? Historians are quick to say what history is not but find it much more difficult to say what it is.

Most historians would agree that history is fundamentally about change. It is certainly the case that anthropology has generally been held up by historians as unhistorical because it has not been primarily concerned to delineate change. But aside from the fact that change can be as fetishized a concept for the past as continuity is for the present, it is clear that many historians seek to identify change only to control it. Change is seized to be normalized, to be explained by reference to structural conditions or personal actions. Positivist historians are explicit in their attempts to identify not just causes but the universal laws that determine historical properties. Narrative historians are far less concerned with laws but are committed to the task of isolating and narratively encoding the finite segments of the past that render the particularities of the historical record comprehensible in retrospect (White 1978, 54, 55). Revisionist historians, regardless of method, find themselves most deeply implicated in changing forms of historical knowledge at precisely the moments when they most accept the terms, categories, and problematics of history that have come before.

If historical interpretation is about control, about mastering narratives of the past and establishing authoritative ways to order events into logics of causation and explanation, interpretation is always characterized by ambivalence. The more the historian reflects about the selection and evaluation of evidence, and the more credit a scholar gives to the imaginative acts of analysis and interpretation, the more the past is acknowledged to be constructed. But historians have for the most part responded skeptically at best to the assertions of theorists such as Hayden White that history is basically about interpretation. As White has noted, "Once it is admitted that all histories are in some sense interpretations, it becomes necessary to determine the extent to which historians' explanations of past events can qualify as objective, if not rigorously scientific, accounts of reality" (51). Concerns about objectivity lead to claims about the character of reality, the irreducibility of facts, the ultimate referent of truth. And these concerns tend to controvert the historicizing impulse, which should lead instead to the subversion of essential categories and the celebration of doubt.

Historicizing is nothing more nor less than the constant asking of questions about how something came to be and about what effects things have had over time. To historicize is to accept that the past is constructed, that things are not given but made and made sense of. The historicizing operation probes the way categories and identities become formed and fixed, and in so doing it must of necessity be reflexive, framing its own interpreting movement as part of the historicizing field. And the historicizing operation is concerned not only with causes (always multiple) but with effects, with the residues and consequences of the past itself, as also with the present significance of these residues and effects. As LaCapra has suggested, "historians are involved in the effort to understand both what something meant in its own time and what it may mean for us today. The most engaging, if at times perplexing, dimensions of interpretation exist on the margin, where these two meanings are not simply disjoined from one another, for it is at this liminal point that the dialogue with the past becomes internal to the historian" (1983, 18). But LaCapra writes without the urgency and the political commitment of Benjamin, who puts the point about history better than anyone else. As genealogists of the past, historians are responsible for the safety of the dead. History is really about the dangers that haunt both the living and the dead.

Despite the urgency and clarity of Benjamin's call to history, most historians do not accept it. When historians are most political and critical they tend to be uninterested in epistemological questions that might lead to the suspension of the reality effect. And when historians are most concerned about the crafted conceits of narrative representation, they tend to be least interested in making explicit the specific ways in which the past has been made a compelling story by them, for certain purposes, and with particular effects. And in spite of the politicization of history in recent years through social and feminist history, historians have only begun to examine critically the ideological effects of their story making in terms of the kinds of concerns about historicizing mentioned previously. As just one example, there has so far been remarkably little critical concern about the way in which history is organized in terms of the imagined communities of nations.[3] We think far too little about how historians legitimize and naturalize the boundaries and political imperatives of the nation-state as a form (as well as of some nation-states vis-à-vis others)—not to mention the political organization and balance of power in the world today—through their curricula, their professional training and reproduction, and their teaching. If anthropologists have traditionally neglected the political dimensions of social and cultural life, historians have typically been dominated by them.

Debates about the extent to which history is interpretive, about the relationship between interpretation and objectivity, and about the status of historical reality have in recent years been conducted around the metaphor of textuality. Although most observers would attribute this turn to the cancerous influence of literary criticism, the initial textual turn was taken by historians largely through the influence of anthropology, and especially the work of Clifford Geertz. Although Geertz himself acknowledged the literary influences of scholars such as Paul Ricoeur, Kenneth Burke, and Northrup Frye, he grounded his statements about texts in anthropological terms and with reference to the large world of cultural meaning. In his well-known essay on the Balinese cockfight, he wrote that "The culture of a people is an ensemble of texts, themselves ensembles, which the anthropologist strains to read over the shoulders of those to whom they properly belong" (1973, 452). Geertz's sense of textuality had principally to do with interpretive strategy; his injunction was that the anthropologist should read culture as if it were a text. Because of his emphasis on reading, Geertz could extend the metaphor of the text beyond the usual range of cultural products. As he wrote in *Negara,* "Arguments, melodies, formulas, maps, and pictures are not idealities to be stared at but texts to be read; so are rituals, palaces, technologies, and social formations" (1980, 135). All of culture is a text, not so much because it looks like one but because it can be read as one.

Historians could invoke Geertz's influence because it seemed tremendously liberating to be able to engage in interpretive readings of the stuff of history, of symbolic actions, social movements, material remains. And Geertz seemed far less threatening than White, who suggested that historical writing itself was textual, prefigured by its rhetorical tropes and ideological commitments. Geertz only pointed the way. Historians now debate their methods, politics, and epistemes in reference to an increasingly wide range of literary theories.[4] But the debate continues for the most part to be the same, and textuality is seen less as a metaphor inviting a new range of critical interpretive practices than an invitation to nihilism and relativism. If historical reality is a text, then it can neither be important nor real.

If the metaphor of textuality seems to invite the same old antinomies and debates, as even the deconstructionist historian LaCapra acknowledges (19, 20), Foucault's use of the term *discourse* has radically shifted the terms of debate. Not only is discourse not the same as text, discourse is defined in ways that sharply distinguish it from language. Discourse is about the conditions under which the world presents itself as real, about the way institutions and historical practices become regimes of truth and of possibility itself. While most historians have continued to view Foucault as if he is only concerned with language (and not material reality), Foucault has provided new ways to think about the past: for example, how the effects of history are more salient for historical investigation than the causes, how knowledge and power are inexorably linked, how historical categories themselves are produced by and in relationship to the objects of historical scrutiny. Foucault has trained his skeptical eye on practices as various as philology and sex and on institutions such as the clinic and the prison, and he has shown in these stunning historical exercises that the institutional history of modernity is riddled with terror and contradiction. If there are numerous problems with Foucault's theoretical proposals and practical investigations, historians should at least recognize that for Foucault theory is nothing more nor less than history itself.

Suspicion and the Supplement

Within anthropology, attempts to theorize a new relationship between "culture" and "history" have so far failed. And historians have been of little help. Typically, one of the two terms is subordinated to the other, and despite attempts to set some kind of dialectic in motion we are left with a sterile debate. This failure accounts at least in part for why anthropology is seen as far less relevant than it should be, and by all historical accounts ought to be, to recent developments in cultural studies in the American academy. This failure also accounts in part for why it is that historians have begun to turn from anthropology to other disciplines in their most recent attempts to understand cultural history.

Although the theoretical failure I have identified is itself only part of a larger set of problems in the human sciences, I would suggest that Derrida's notion of the supplement might provide a way to rethink the categories of history and culture both within and outside the disciplinary borders of anthropology. Supplementarity reveals, as LaCapra has put it, "why analytic distinctions necessarily overlap in 'reality' and why it is misleading to take them as dichotomous categories" (152). Reflecting on Rousseau's notions about the relations of writing and speech, Derrida proposed that when writing supplements speech it does far more than add a new, and for Rousseau unnatural, dimension to language. Derrida writes that "The supplement adds itself, it is a surplus, a plenitude enriching another plenitude, the fullest measure of presence" (1974, 144). Derrida challenges Rousseau's conviction that nature after culture can be imagined ever to have existed, that nature could any more be seen as self-sufficient. He goes on to say that the supplement "adds only to replace. It intervenes or insinuates itself in-the-place-of; if it fills, it is as if one fills a void" (145). A supplement is something that is added as if external to the thing itself, but its necessity paradoxically proclaims the essential inadequacy of the original. Supplementarity suggests why every dialectical structure must remain open, why no synthesis can be anything more than provisional. The supplement coexists with that which it supplements in a fundamentally destabilizing way.

If we can now consider the relationship between culture and history as supplemental rather than additive, as subversive rather than complementary, it becomes clear that neither Sahlins nor Roseberry have adequately reconsidered their fundamental categories. "Cultural orders" and "historical processes" have survived relatively intact. The suspicion that should be generated from recognizing the logic of the supplement has not been deployed against the foundational assumptions of analytic practice.[5]

The utility of supplemental reasoning for a historical reading of culture can be seen by contrasting the sense of historicizing that I have outlined with Fredric Jameson's call to "Always historicize," with which he begins his most influential book of Marxist literary criticism, *The Political Unconscious.* Jameson predicates his injunction on the contention that there are two distinct paths for the historicizing operation: namely, the path of the object and the path of the subject. The first path is that of the historical origins of the things themselves. The second path is that more intangible historicity of the concepts and categories by which we attempt to understand these things. I argue instead that these paths are necessarily indistinct, that the things themselves are never separable from the categories and concepts that make it possible to recognize and taxonomize those things. History too must be seen as having historicity.

Sahlins is correct to suggest that history should be exploded by culture, but as I earlier observed, the explosion must work both ways. Supplementary reasoning promises the theoretical means to develop some sense of how the terms *culture* or *history* can continue to have utility while at the same time never representing isolable or essential referents, whether empirical or analytic. Richard Johnson may perhaps be correct that what is needed more than interdisciplinary research is an antidisciplinary attitude. Anthropologists and historians should both feel uncomfortable with their forms of interdisciplinary appropriation. The commitment to multiple historicities—whether anthropological or poststructuralist—should disfigure, to use a phrase of Peter de Bolla's (1986), the certainties of historical analysis. And the commitment to refiguring a concept of culture that can be simultaneously historical and subject to its own historicizing moment might well dissolve for good the anthropological commitment to seeing culture in terms of words like *system* or *order.*

Proposing Derrida's concept of the supplement still hardly clarifies what kind of historical anthropology I would recommend over that of Sahlins or Roseberry. In the second part of this essay I will attempt to provide some examples to illustrate what I have in mind and how I see culture and history as useful categories insofar as they destabilize each other.

Culture in History

Benjamin rescues history by insisting that the safety of the dead depends upon it. Analysis is not just a game; it has real stakes and real effects, even when its epistemological claims would seem to compromise the possibility of knowing the real in any absolute way. Benjamin has anticipated this worry by arguing that history is not about ascertaining how things really were but seizing hold of memories and fanning the sparks of hope.

Similarly, anthropology need not be about establishing in some absolute or abstract sense what things really mean but rather about contesting meanings that appear to be natural and exploring the means by which cultural forms are inscribed into the world of nature. Culture thus appears not as something that is simply arbitrary rather than natural in the usual terms of semiotics but as a particular conglomerate of constructions set in motion by agents, produced within and through social practices (especially practices involving power and inequality) operationalized in the modern age through the agencies of the state and the activities of capital. Culture in the end must be contested through institutional means that themselves have been naturalized through the very denial of history that is encoded in most cultural experience. Culture can no longer be assumed to be about consensus or shared meanings, and culture can no longer be happily abstracted from the conditions of its production or the effects of its use. At one level, culture can be seen as a material force, as it must be analyzed in relationship to the interests and identities of ruling classes and institutions. But insofar as culture is genuinely political, implicated as it is in state projects that naturalize the social and claim to liberate the cultural, we must challenge those claims about determination and reflexivity that depend upon economistic epistemologies (see Taussig 1987). Culture (like power) is and can be contested; but at another and perhaps more fundamental level culture (or power) is the abstraction of discursive and institutional sites that contain contest, define its antipodes, seal its interpretations, and configure its possible resolutions. Thus, the political components of culture are made invisible. Like the state itself, the "political" deploys cultural hegemony through paradoxical forms of preemption and deferral.

To illustrate these claims, I will summarize some of my recent work on the history of the caste system in India. For anthropology, and for social theory more generally, culture in India has always been principally defined by caste. Caste has been seen as always there in Indian history and as one of the major reasons why India has no history and certainly no sense of history. Caste defines the core of Indian tradition, and caste is today the major threat to Indian modernity. However, by subjecting caste to historical analysis, I have been able to demonstrate that much of what has been taken to be timeless tradition is in fact the paradoxical effect of colonial rule, where culture was carefully depoliticized and reified into a specifically colonial version of civil society.[6] In my fieldwork, in my reading of texts traditionally dismissed as so much myth and fabulous legend, in looking for the historicity of caste or kingship, in reading colonial texts, and in charting the contradictory effects of colonial hegemony, I found that the categories of culture and history constantly engaged and subverted each other. Historical methods revealed that modern notions of caste were produced both indirectly (e.g., through the introduction of new revenue systems) and by the cumulative impact of colonial discourse and legislation specifically about caste.

This is not to suggest that caste was invented anew by the British but rather that caste was refigured as a "religious" form of organizing society in a context where politics and religion had never been distinct domains of social action. The religious definition of caste made colonial procedures of rule possible through the characterization of India as a culture essentially about spiritual harmony and liberation. When the state had existed in India, it was despotic and epiphenomenal, extractive but fundamentally irrelevant. British rule could thus be characterized as enlightened even when it denied Indian subjects the minimal rights extended to propertied males in nineteenth-century Britain. This is not to suggest that one culture simply gave way to another nor that the politics and historicity of caste in the seventeenth century were the same as the politics and historicity of caste today. Rather, I am suggesting the complex ways in which certain cultural forms became represented as nonhistorical at the same time that these representations were profoundly situated in the historical conditions of colonialism. Under colonialism, the colonizers and the colonized were increasingly implicated in new discourses on social identity that led to subtle shifts in social relations and political control. The success of colonial discourse was that through the census, landholding, and the law, inter alia, some Indians were given powerful stakes in new formulations and assumptions about caste. This was a version of caste that increasingly resembled the theoretical statements of anthropologists such as Louis Dumont, which are putatively based on an Indological reading of Indian civilization. Caste became the essence of Indian civilization through historical process and through the history of colonialism.

The turn to history does not, however, make culture go away. To find a politics in culture does not necessarily make culture readily comprehensible or subject to economistic or reductive materialist appropriation.[7] Social relations in precolonial India had a distinct and complex politics, having to do with notions and procedures of kingship, order, control, domination, and rule that were specific to a particular historical moment. This formation, however much historical study and analysis is directed at it, remains resistant to final interpretation and understanding. Attention to cultural difference can enable a better and more historically grounded appreciation of the epistemic conditions and limits of interpretation than most historians and other disciplinary advocates of the historic turn would be willing to concede. An anthropological commitment to alterity can also raise serious questions for both historical practice and critical theory. And if anthropology can help demonstrate that there are multiple histories and multiple historicities, historians and critical theorists alike may have to reconsider what they mean when they attempt to "Always historicize."

History and Truth

If anthropology is still compromised by its colonial past, it may also be remembered that it has other histories as well. Indeed, anthropology has often played an unsettling role in social theory, providing grounds and opportunities for social criticism of a variety of kinds. Whether in Rousseau's suspicion of social contracts, Engel's dislike of private property and modern family formation, Leiris's modernist disdain for certain conventions of realism and civility, or finally Sahlins's debunking of bourgeois culture, anthropology can render other worlds and ways of living not only plausible but the ground of radical critique. Given this background, we might ask whether it is possible that anthropology's traditional concerns with such subjects as kinship, ritual, myth, witchcraft, shamanism, and possession, to leave aside the usual utopian appropriations of stateless societies and egalitarian communities, might not raise serious questions about the categories and conventions of even the most critical contemporary social theory. This latter concern is amplified, as we have seen, by recent calls to remember that the so-called universals of Western thought—the unitary subject, the character and consciousness of history, modern rhetoric and narrative, reason itself—are highly particularistic, profoundly Western, and essentially modernist. In critical theory's historicizing turn, the Enlightment project is being dismantled by a concept of history that was produced by the Enlightenment itself.

The concept of history of greatest attraction in the last few years for historical anthropology has come to be placed under the banner of the "invention of tradition" (Hobsbawm and Ranger 1983). Recent work, including my own on the history of caste, has delighted in demonstrating that those very traditions that had been thought to be timeless have histories of their own, that state rituals celebrating nations or monarchs (see Cannadine, Cohn, and Hobsbawm), symbolic markers of identity such as kilts or turbans (see Trevor-Roper, Cohn), and institutions such as the village community and the tribe (Bremen, Ranger) were all invented at specific times, often in ways that served the purpose of some class interest or ruling power. One of the most promising revisionary movements in anthropology has been the recognition that many of the old chestnuts of anthropological assumption were produced through encounters with colonial powers and modern influences rather than representing the residual hold of the past in "traditional" (as opposed to "historical") societies. But in our enthusiasm for this kind of historicizing there are certain dangers, perhaps not least of which is the loss of the possibility of otherness.

For Hobsbawm and Ranger, historicizing tradition means finding the historical means by which a tradition was first invented and then naturalized as tradition. Tradition is sharply distinguished from custom, "which dominates so-called 'traditional' societies." Custom is not invariant because life in traditional societies is not invariant, but neither is custom subject to historical scrutiny. Custom simply refers to a set of practices that combines flexibility in substance with formal adherence to precedent, and Hobsbawm stresses the practical character of custom as well as its embeddedness in institutional forms such as peasant society. Tradition, on the other hand, is a set of rituals and symbolic practices that are fundamentally ideological rather than practical. Tradition, as Hobsbawm uses it, is bad because it is usually a kind of modern ideological mystification that is installed as a constant by the elites and governments whose real interests are thereby served. To show that traditions are invented is in effect to show that traditions are neither true nor real nor legitimate.

While I share Hobsbawm's concern that traditions are frequently appropriated, invented, and manipulated by elites and states, it is also true that elites and states can assert cultural hegemony by defining certain things as tradition and certain things as bogus, that the same technique of separating tradition from custom—or the legitimate from the illegitimate—can and has been used in far more sinister ways than Hobsbawm concedes possible. Indeed, in colonial situations states and colonial elites invented tradition precisely by engaging in the kind of history Hobsbawm seems to advocate, at the same time that colonialism deauthenticated certain colonized history as tradition by deploying a universal sensibility of what historical consciousness should entail. All tradition (and all "custom" too) is historical, but it also engages different forms of historicity. Attention to these alternate historicities might compromise our confidence in debunking fraud and mystification, perhaps even exposing the forms of mystification that are part of our own historicity.

The clearest example of how the "invention of tradition" ploy can go wrong can be seen in Hugh Trevor-Roper's article "The Invention of Tradition: The Highland Tradition of Scotland" (Hobsbawm and Ranger 1983, 15–41). Trevor-Roper begins by arguing that the kilt, the tartan, the clan, and even the bagpipe, rather than being signs of great antiquity and cultural distinction, are "in fact largely modern." If these things existed before the union with England at all, Trevor-Roper asserts, they did so only in "vestigial form" and as signs of "barbarism." Trevor-Roper goes on: "Indeed, the whole concept of a distinct Highland culture and tradition is a retrospective invention. Before the later years of the seventeenth century, the Highlanders of Scotland did not form a distinct people" (15). And so Trevor-Roper proceeds to demonstrate, with convincing historical flair and wit, the recent vintage of Scottish national culture.

The only problem with Trevor-Roper's argument is that while Hobsbawm debunks mystification in general as well as in the particular forms of its manipulation by states, ruling classes, or colonial powers, Trevor-Roper also debunks the necessary claims of Scottish nationalists—necessary because of the hegemonic terms that became set in the eighteenth century for nationalist or populist political aspirations—that Scotland had its own authentic traditions, epics, and histories. Indeed, Trevor-Roper's argument has a genuine colonial ring to it, for, in recounting the invention of clans and kilts and the forgery of the great epic *Ossian,* it uses smug notions of authenticity and historical privilege to contest what appear to be absurd claims about Scottish customs and traditions. At the same time, and with similar colonial resonance, Trevor-Roper uses his historical mastery to conceal his own moral position, one that appears to justify, or at least to support, the unification claims of the British state. The effort to historicize tradition and custom can thus both expose the mystifications of cultural hegemony and be appropriated by them. When historical methods are used as if the methods themselves are exempted from historical scrutiny and critique, history becomes a way of deauthenticating everything but its own authority, denigrating difference, and displacing the categories and logics of historical discourse. It can become far too easy to end up privileging certain kinds of histories, texts, or traditions over others rather than realizing that all such "things"—including our own histories, texts, and traditions—are constructed in historical and ideological contexts.

Trevor-Roper's argument about historical authenticity both recounts and recapitulates arguments over the authenticity of a text that was said by one James Macpherson in 1760 to be the national epic of highland Scotland. Macpherson apparently put together fragments of written poems and tales, oral traditions of Highland Scot families, Irish ballads, and material of his own (including passages evocative of Milton and Shakespeare) to create—he said discover—the epic poem *Ossian.* The epic provided Scotland with a heroic and distinctive past, a claim to epic glory, and a legitimate folk tradition. In particular, the epic marked off Scottish history from Ireland's and established the basis for the rise of a new cultural nationalism in the wake of England's suppression of the Highland clans after the Jacobite Rebellion of 1745. Or, as Trevor-Roper puts it, through *Ossian* "the Scottish Highlands had acquired—however fraudulently—an independent ancient culture" (18). And Trevor-Roper is fully aware of the political implications of culture; the tone of his history dismisses outright any distinct Scottish political or cultural aspirations.

The debate over *Ossian* took the form of a scholarly inquiry into the question of textual authenticity and forgery.[8] Samuel Johnson, perhaps the most influential arbiter of letters in his day, declared the text to be an imposture and the author a sham. Indeed, it was through the Ossianic controversy that Johnson set himself up as champion of the truth, committed not to sentiment but rather to precise empirical standards for textual scholarship and historical investigation. David Hume was equally scornful of the authenticity of the text. However, as embarrassed as he was by Macpherson's forgery and by Macpherson's attempt to restore interest in the clan system, Hume was deeply offended by Johnson's attack. Johnson betrayed his prejudice by writing in his account of his journey to Scotland and the Western Islands that he considered Gaelic "the rude speech of a barbarous people, who had few thoughts to express," announcing wrongly that the language never had a written form.

Ossian had its critical defenders. Dr. Hugh Blair, a literary critic, theologian, and friend of Macpherson's, published a "Critical Dissertation on the Poems of Ossian, the Son of Fingal" in 1763 and argued that Ossian, Homer, and Aristotle enjoyed a natural affinity, the first two having been inspired by nature, the latter having studied it in Homer. Although Blair admitted that there were legitimate queries and felt embarrassed by Macpherson's inability ever to produce the originals of his text, he held fast to his defense and was by no means alone in making it. In Germany, Herder and Lessing gave further credence to the poems and their heroic traditions by celebrating Macpherson's accomplishment. And in Scotland scholars attempted to find ways to defend Gaelic traditions without allowing the critiques of Macpherson to serve as some kind of final judgment. The controversy raged on, and in 1797, a year after Macpherson's death, the Highland Society of London established a committee to investigate the authenticity of *Ossian*. The committee circulated questionnaires through the Highlands and commenced an extraordinary scholarly effort to discover the folk and textual bases for the Ossianic tradition. The final report, completed after seven years, consisted of a 155-page essay and 200 pages of documents. The committee reported that although it found impressive examples of a revival of interest in Scottish literature and culture, including myriad examples of Gaelic oral and literary tradition, there were few direct parallels to Macpherson's text in what they collected. The report makes for fascinating reading, as it documents the extraordinary changes in Gaelic oral tradition during the second half of the eighteenth century as well as the deliberate attempt on the part of many respondents to withhold or refashion information so as not to tarnish the reputation of a man they considered their cultural hero. Although the committee admitted that Macpherson had tampered with tradition, changing what was "too simple or too rude for a modern ear," they stopped short of charging him with forgery. Some critical reviews of the report in London found sufficient evidence to declare Johnson vindicated. Sir Walter Scott, who wrote a review of the report in the *Edinburgh Review* in 1805, was more ambivalent. Although Trevor-Roper reads his review to suggest that Scott "decisively rejected the authenticity of the epic which the Scottish literary establishment in general, and the Highlanders in particular, continued to defend" (18), Scott in fact took a nuanced view of the question of authenticity and at the same time questioned the empirical premises of both Johnson and Trevor-Roper. Scott wrote that Macpherson had been "capable not only of making an enthusiastic impression on every mind susceptible of poetical beauty, but of giving a new tone to poetry throughout all Europe." And Scott went on to reproduce the poetic effort of Macpherson by publishing his own "Border Poems."⁹

The Ossianic controversy illustrates how the development of empirical procedures in textual criticism collaborated with England's confidence in its own cultural heritage—confidently extended by all educated Britons in the eighteenth and nineteenth century to the Hellenic past—and its general assumptions about the barbarism of marginal places and peoples. Oral traditions had to be sanctified by the kind of canonization and appropriation directed at Homer in order to be appreciated; closer to home in time and place these same heroic traditions were ridiculed and dismissed. Educated Scots found themselves in a difficult predicament, forced by the logic of the debate to choose between truth and culture. It was ironically only Walter Scott, who came to have a critical role in the development of the English novel as well as in the development of the standards of historical narrative that have since become basic to our empiricist historical sensibility, who was able to see the issue more clearly. Scott was certainly aware that Macpherson had contributed to the general history of English poetry and directed welcome public attention to the myriad and extraordinary folk traditions of the Highlands, even if he had exaggerated the Homeric character of these traditions and misrepresented his own role in the production of the Ossian text.

In part because of the limited professional opportunities available in Scotland, in part also because of the growing importance of India for Britain's political, military, and economic fortunes, an extraordinary number of gifted Scots played key roles in the operations of the East India Company in the late eighteenth and early nineteenth centuries. Scots seemed particularly ubiquitous among those East India Company servants who became known during this period for their specialized knowledge about India, often as antiquarians and orientalists. The names of Alexander Dow, Montstuart Elphinstone, Thomas Munro, Francis Buchanan-Hamilton, Colin Mackenzie, Walter Elliott, and John Malcolm represent just a few of the growing cadre of British officers who studied Indian languages, history, and society. I can cite no direct evidence to suggest that Scots were more inclined to participate in the study and recuperation of Indian textual and historical traditions than their English colleagues in the East India Company. However, the antiquarian obsessions of men such as Colin Mackenzie could not have been formed without some kind of critical awareness of the Ossianic controversy.

In Mackenzie's case a logic of displacement seems particularly plausible.

Mackenzie, born in the Outer Hebrides in 1754, went to India in the army as an engineer in the 1780s and rose to become the first surveyor-general of Madras in 1807 and of India in 1815.[10] Through his long career in southern India as cartographer and surveyor, Mackenzie was obsessed with collecting texts and facts to supplement the maps he and his associates made of Hyderabad, Mysore, and other regions of the southern peninsula. On his own initiative and with his own resources he hired and trained a group of Brahman assistants who helped him collect local histories of kingly dynasties, chiefly families, castes, villages, temples and monasteries as well as other local traditions and religious and philosophical texts in a wide variety of Indian languages. When Mackenzie died in 1821 he had amassed a collection of 3,000 stone and copperplate inscriptions, 1,568 literary manuscripts, 2,070 local tracts, and large portfolios and collections of drawings, plans, images, and antiquities (see Taylor 1858, Wilson 1828, and Mahalingam 1972 and 1976). This collection contains by far the largest set of sources for the study of southern Indian history and literature.

Two things distinguished Mackenzie and his general project from most of his colonial contemporaries. First, Mackenzie was unusual in his respect for and reliance on local Indians for information and scholarly assistance. Second, Mackenzie was unusually open to and interested in the wide variety of texts and sources that were collected through his local assistants and contacts. Whereas his contemporaries tended to disparage the scholarly judgment of any Indians or dismiss out of hand genealogical or "mythical" sources as completely lacking in historical sensibility and value, Mackenzie realized that historical genres and sensibilities differed in India. It is not that Mackenzie had the kind of anthropological sensitivity to multiple historicities that Sahlins might advocate but rather that Mackenzie believed that history and literature were alive and well in India, both in India's traditions and in India's literati. And while the East India Company professed its admiration for Mackenzie's zeal, it rarely shared his enthusiasm for his actual researches, often complaining that his collections of materials other than inscriptions seemed worthless. Empire and India softened and sometimes obscured the kind of debate that took place between Hugh Blair and Samuel Johnson, but in fact this debate took place over and over again in the colonial theater. The Enlightenment project was not only always organized in the service of empire, but it gave shape to and then progressively intensified the taxonomical fault line between history and culture. History and culture could only be united when both were hegemonic, that is, when both were mutually enabling conditions of power and domination.

Historical methods and textual empiricism were about far more than establishing truth and detecting forgery. They concerned questions about what tradition and history could consist of, about regimes of epistemic possibility. Because all history and tradition is fabricated, we must realize the potentially pernicious effect that historicizing culture or tradition can have. The experiences of Macpherson and Mackenzie suggest not only that there are many histories but that there are also many truths, truths that take many cultural forms. In our general turn to history and in our enthusiasm that the historicizing move will settle the debate or solve the problem, we must never assume that history itself should not be called into question or that our capacity to outrun the historicizing imperative is ever more than partial and provisional. And in the present academic climate, it seems clear that some kind of attention to the concept of culture, however flawed and unhistorical the concept might be, can help.

Postscript: History, Anthropology, and Cultural Studies

In recent years, the emergent field of cultural studies has been attracting a great deal of excitement in the human sciences in the United States. As I noted earlier, culture has become a buzzword, fueling new subfields and professional enthusiasms in a wide range of disciplines (e.g., the new cultural history, the new sociology of culture, and the new importance attached to film and media studies in general). And the term *cultural studies* itself, which used to refer specifically to the activities of the Birmingham Centre, now signifies factional affiliations in English departments, cross-disciplinary institutes, centers, and conferences, and an increasingly distinct constellation of theoretical and practical interests that may yet produce a new academic discipline. What is particularly noteworthy about cultural studies today is its general commitment to considering the politics of culture—in part an inheritance from the pioneering work of Hoggart, Williams, and Hall—and also its capacity to bridge the usual chasms between the humanities and social sciences in the American academy.

Nevertheless, it is clear that much of the enthusiasm for cultural studies in the American academy today comes from members of the traditional humanities. It is also clear that anthropology no longer has any proprietary claim to culture. In a recent and extensive survey of cultural studies in Britain and America by Patrick Brantlinger (1990), anthropology is conspicuous by its absence. For anthropologists this is particularly alarming because of the way Brantlinger problematizes cultural studies. As he writes, "'difference'—the threat or promise of 'the Other'—will continue to be the central organizing category for postmodernist cultural and literary theory" (163). But instead of calling on anthropologists here, the case for "otherness" and "difference" is made for him by literary-cultural critics such as Houston Baker, H. L. Gates, and Gayatri Chakravorty Spivak. As the subaltern is finding her voice in the American academy, anthropology has grown hoarse.[11]

In my opening critique of British cultural studies I noted that one of the problems with the Birmingham Centre as a model for a new culture concept is that the activities of the Centre have been based and oriented solely within the borders of Britain. A similar ethnocentrism affects the growth of cultural studies in America.[12] It is time for anthropologists and comparative historians to argue and demonstrate that the theoretical excitement and power of cultural studies need not be limited to, and is seriously compromised by, its domestic provenance. If history and culture—as conceived by professional historians and anthropologists—need to supplement each other, cultural studies needs them both.

Brantlinger makes the point that cultural studies should provide the space for a dialectical encounter between the two fundamental problematics engaged in studying the "other": relativism and universalism. In the first, the other seems totally different, incommensurable, and incomprehensible. In the second, the other reveals a deeply shared common humanity. Both seem flawed, the first by sacrificing critical engagement for fear of misplaced judgment, the second by sacrificing difference itself.[13] But given the limited scope of his academic canvas, Brantlinger's worries seem exemplified only in the debates over the canon that preoccupy American professors today. As important as these debates are, they do not seem to provide Brantlinger with a sense either of the costs of epistemic violence—as for example does the history of colonialism—or the contingency of his own epistemological concerns—as more attention to anthropology might afford.

I have only begun to suggest some of the ways history and anthropology might better engage each other, as well as some of the uses of this engagement for developments in cultural studies in America today. In addition to exploring the limits of the concepts of culture and history that animate current interdisciplinary discussions and debates, I could have attempted to conduct more thorough ethnographies of other historical-narrative sensibilities (e.g., providing an analysis of either Macpherson's or Mackenzie's texts) or other forms of subjectivity and agency (e.g., an analysis of possession) in order to question further the constructional certainties of our current metadisciplinary discourse. If culture and history are riddled with difficulties, so too are the meanings implied by terms like *voice, subject, agency, event, experience,* not to mention the *other.* But I hope at least that I have illustrated some of the problems with the historic turn in anthropology, at the same time that I have indicated that, when all is said and done, it has been a turn for the better.

NOTES

This essay is being published substantially as it was written for the conference on "The Historic Turn" in October 1990. Many things have changed since then, but major revision would risk losing the conjunctural urgency of a moment in interdisciplinary experimentation that continues to underlie a great many theoretical discussions around the ideas and disciplinary deployments of "culture" and "history." I am grateful to all of the participants in the Comparative Study of Social Transformations (CSST) conference for their reactions and critiques. I owe special thanks to Michael Kennedy and Ann Stoler, the discussants of my panel; to Terry McDonald, who made the conference so enormously stimulating; and to Bill and Ellen Sewell, who provided an extraordinarily acute and helpful commentary on the essay after the conference. In addition to acknowledging many other debts generated in the writing of this essay, I would like in particular to thank Bernard Cohn, Linda Gregerson, Marilyn Ivy, John Pemberton, Adela Pinch, Gyan Prakash, and Joan Scott.

1. I am in general agreement with much of Roseberry's analysis and concur with him that Redfield's modernization schema misses the way in which the antipodal poles of his analysis do not correlate with traditional and modern but rather with the complementary products of modern historical change. However, Roseberry's sense of this transformation is similarly limited by his analytic insistence that the modern world system necessarily and inevitably produces only certain kinds of products and meanings.

2. See my critique of Louis Dumont in *The Hollow Crown: Ethnohistory of an Indian Kingdom* (1987).

3. I take the phrase imagined communities, of course, from Benedict Anderson.

4. Curiously, with the exception of only a few historians, these literary theories tend to be the ones that are least concerned with history.

5. A similar call for postfoundational scholarship has been made by Gyan Prakash, in a recent review of Indian history (1990). Prakash traced the ways in which Indian historiography in its different stages and modalities has always relied upon certain foundational categories and procedures: for example, the nation, civilization, or class. Prakash has proposed that a postorientalist historiography "visualizes modern India, for example, in relationships and processes that have constructed contingent and unstable identities," thereby displacing "the categories framed in and by that history." But Prakash is no epistemological nihilist and recommends concrete strategies for historicizing the analytic object (Indian history) without taking one's own analytic categories as foundational or, to use Derrida's language, as essences that can be conceived apart from the supplement of some subsequent analytic operation.

6. This is an extremely compressed summary of one of the major arguments in my book. Also see my essay "The Original Caste" (1990).

7. As has recently (well after this essay was written) been forcefully argued by Aijaz Ahmad in his *In Theory* (London, 1992).

8. See Blair (1763); Samuel Johnson, *Journey to the Western Islands of Scotland;* James Boswell, *The Journal of a Tour to the Hebrides;* Mackenzie (1805); Saunders (1968); deGategno (1989); Stafford (1988); and Macpherson (1847).

9. Collected with the assistance of John Leydon, who went on to become a noted orientalist in India and Indonesia.

10. See my essay "The Invention of Caste" (1989). Also see Wilson (1828).

11. This observation implies a critique of both cultural studies and anthropology, the former for its ethnocentrism and conventional academicism, the latter for its inability to address the concerns and issues that have been importantly raised in cultural studies. Indeed, my critique of Sahlins and particularly of Roseberry is meant to suggest some of the reasons why the insularity of anthropology is both unwise and unnecessary.

12. An important exception here has been the publishing work of Carol A. Breckenridge and Arjun Appadurai. See their new and pathbreaking journal *Public Culture.*

13. For an interesting analysis of the anthropological use of the ideology of relativism, see Mohanty (1989).

REFERENCES

Ahmad, Aijaz. 1992. *In Theory: Classes, Nations, Literature.* New York: Verso.

Anderson, Benedict. 1983. *Imagined Communities: Reflections on the Origin and Spread of Nationalism.* London: Verso Publications.

Benjamin, Walter. 1968. "Theses on the Philosophy of History." In *Illuminations.* New York: Fontana/Collins.

Biersack, Aletta. 1989. "Local Knowledge, Local History: Geertz and Beyond." In *The New Cultural History,* 72–96. Edited by Lynn Hunt. Berkeley and Los Angeles: The University of California Press.

Blair, Hugh. 1763. "A Critical Dissertation on the Poems of Ossian, the Son of Fingal." Reprinted in Leipzig edition, MacPherson (1847).

Boswell, James. [1786] 1984. *The Journal of a Tour of the Hebrides.* Edited by R. W. Chapman. New York: Oxford University Press.

Brantlinger, Patrick. 1990. *Crusoe's Footprints: Cultural Studies in Britain and America.* London: Routledge.

Cannadine, David. 1983. "The Context, Performance, and Meaning of Ritual: The British Monarchy and the Invention of Tradition, c. 1820–1977." In *The Invention of Tradition*, 101–14. Edited by Eric Hobsbawm and Terence Ranger. Cambridge: Cambridge University Press.

Clifford, James. 1983. "On Ethnographic Authority." *Representations* 1 (2):118–46.

Cohn, Bernard S. 1983. "Representing Authority in Victorian India." In *The Invention of Tradition*, 165–210. Edited by Eric Hobsbawm and Terence Ranger. Cambridge: Cambridge University Press.

Cohn, Bernard S. 1987. *An Anthropologist among the Historians and Other Essays.* Delhi: Oxford University Press.

de Bolla, Peter. 1986. "Disfiguring History." *Diacritics* 16:49–58.

deGategno, Paul J. 1989. *James Macpherson.* Boston: Twayne.

Derrida, Jacques. 1974. *Of Grammatology.* Baltimore: Johns Hopkins University Press.

Dirks, Nicholas B. 1987. *The Hollow Crown: Ethnohistory of an Indian Kingdom.* Cambridge: Cambridge University Press.

Dirks, Nicholas B. 1989a. "The Invention of Caste: Civil Society in Colonial India." *Social Analysis* 25 (autumn): 42–53.

Dirks, Nicholas B. 1989b. "The Policing of Tradition." Unpublished manuscript.

Dirks, Nicholas B. 1990. "The Original Caste: Power, History and Hierarchy in South Asia." In *India Through Hindu Categories*, 59–77. Edited by McKim Marriott. Newbury Park, CA: Sage Publications 59–77.

Dirks, Nicholas B. 1996. "Reading Culture: Anthropology and the Textualization of India." In *Culture/Contexture.* Edited by E. Valentine Daniel and Jeffrey Peck. Berkeley and Los Angeles: University of California Press.

Foucault, Michel. 1982. "The Subject and Power." In *Michel Foucault: Beyond Structuralism and Hermeneutics*, 208–26. Edited by H. Dreyfus and P. Rabinow. Chicago: University of Chicago Press.

Geertz, Clifford. 1973. *The Interpretation of Culture.* New York: Basic Books.

Geertz, Clifford. 1980. *Negara: The Theatre State in Nineteenth-Century Bali.* Princeton: Princeton University Press.

Hall, Stuart. 1980. "Cultural Studies: Two Paradigms." In *Media, Culture, and Society*, 57–82. Vol. 2. Newbury Park, CA: Sage Publications.

Hobsbawm, Eric, and Terence Ranger, eds. 1983. *The Invention of Tradition.* Cambridge: Cambridge University Press.

Hunt, Lynn, ed. 1989. *The New Cultural History.* Berkeley and Los Angeles: University of California Press.

Jameson, Fredric. 1981. *The Political Unconscious: Narrative as a Socially Symbolic Act.* Ithaca: Cornell University Press.

Johnson, Richard. 1986–87. "What Is Cultural Studies Anyway?" *Social Text* 16 (winter): 38–80.

Johnson, Samuel. [1775] 1984. *A Journey to the Western Islands of Scotland.* Edited by R. W. Chapman. New York: Oxford University Press.

LaCapra, Dominick. 1983. *Rethinking Intellectual History: Texts, Contexts, Language.* Ithaca: Cornell University Press.

Mackenzie, Henry, ed. 1805. *Report of the Committee of the Highland Society of Scotland.* Edinburgh: Edinburgh University Press.

Mackenzie, W. C. N.d. *Colonel Colin Mackenzie: First Surveyor-General of India.* Edinburgh: W. & R. Chambers, Ltd.

Macpherson, James, trans. 1847. *The Poems of Ossian.* Leipzig: Bernhard Tauchnitz.

Mahalingam, T. V. 1972-76. *Mackenzie Manuscripts.* 2 vols. Madras: University of Madras.

McGann, Jerome J. 1987. *Social Values and Poetic Acts.* Cambridge: Harvard University Press.

Mohanty, S. P. 1989. "Us and Them: On the Philosophical Bases of Political Criticism." *Yale Journal of Criticism* 2(2): 1–31.

Nelson, Cary, and Lawrence Grossberg, eds. 1988. *Marxism and the Interpretation of Culture.* Urbana: University of Illinois Press.

Prakash, Gyan. 1990. "Writing Post-Orientalist Histories of the Third World: Perspectives from Indian Historiography." *Comparative Studies in Society and History* 32 (April): 383–408.

Ranger, Terence. 1983. "The Invention of Tradition in Colonial Africa." In *The Invention of Tradition,* 211–62. Edited by Eric Hobsbawm and Terence Ranger. Cambridge: Cambridge University Press.

Roseberry, William. 1989. *Anthropologies and History.* New Brunswick, NJ: Rutgers University Press.

Sahlins, Marshall. 1976. *Culture and Practical Reason.* Chicago: University of Chicago Press.

Sahlins, Marshall. 1981. *Historical Metaphors and Mythical Realities: Structure in the Early History of the Sandwich Islands Kingdom.* Ann Arbor: University of Michigan Press.

Sahlins, Marshall. 1985. *Islands of History.* Chicago: University of Chicago Press.

Sahlins, Marshall. 1993. "Cosmologies of Capitalism: The Trans-Pacific Sector of the World System." In *Culture/Power/History: A Reader in Contemporary Social Theory,* 412–55. Edited by Nicholas B. Dirks, Geoff Eley, and Sherry B. Ortner. Princeton: Princeton University Press.

Said, Edward. 1979. *Orientalism.* New York: Vintage.

Saunders, Thomas Bailey. 1968. *The Life and Letters of James Macpherson.* New York: Haskell House.

Stafford, Fiona J. 1988. *The Sublime Savage: A Study of James Macpherson and the Poems of Ossian.* Edinburgh: Edinburgh University Press.

Taussig, Michael. 1987. "History as Commodity in Some Recent American (Anthropological) Literature." *Food and Foodways* 2:151–69.

Taylor, Rev. William. 1858. *Catalogue Raisonée of Oriental Manuscripts in the Library of the (late) College.* Madras: At the Government Press.

Trevor-Roper, Hugh. 1983. "The Invention of Tradition: The Highland Tradition of Scotland." In *The Invention of Tradition,* 15–43. Edited by Eric Hobsbawm and Terence Ranger. Cambridge: Cambridge University Press.

White, Hayden. 1978. *Tropics of Discourse: Essays in Cultural Criticism.* Baltimore: Johns Hopkins University Press.

Williams, Raymond. 1977. *Marxism and Literature.* Oxford: Oxford University Press.

Wilson, H. H. 1828. *Catalogue of Oriental Manuscript of Col. Mackenzie.* Calcutta: Government Press.

Where Is Sociology after the Historic Turn? Knowledge Cultures, Narrativity, and Historical Epistemologies

Margaret R. Somers

In recent decades the human sciences have turned with enthusiasm to history. In anthropology, literature, and philosophy as well as in economics, sociology, and political science, much of the best work examines data from the past, studies processes over time, and approaches its subject matter through a variety of historical methods. This essay explores this "historic turn" in the social sciences and assesses its impact on social theory and sociology. Following the example of Barrington Moore, the essay asks—so what? What difference has the historic turn made?

My answer is qualified: on the one hand, substantively, the subfield has been an unqualified success. It would be hard to understate the importance of historical sociology in enlarging our understanding of the historical variations in class, gender, revolutions, state formation, religion, and cultural identity. Having recognized that a link such as that between social class and revolution, for example, changes historically, we are now able to see that causal propositions must vary with time. On the other hand, we have been less quick to examine how our fundamental categories such as "agency" and "structure," as well as our standards of knowledge themselves, have histories—histories of unending contestation—not unlike many of the subjects we study. We have paid scant attention to the link between history and the construction of sociological knowledge as such.[1] This neglect has led historical sociology into many of the same theoretical impasses that have troubled the social sciences since their inception.

Three of the most intractable of these impasses are the conundrums of *knowing, being,* and *asking.* The first of these concerns epistemology—the standards we use to *know* about the world and the grounds we use to legitimate these foundations of knowledge. Philosophers of science call this the *context of justification,* and it is addressed through debates over *methodologies.* The second concerns *ontology*—the problem of how to know the *character* of society or of the social agent. The conundrum of what we mean when we speak of society and action and how the two relate to each other has recently taken center stage for many social theorists (e.g., Alexander 1982, 1988, 1989). The third of the enduring conundrums is what philosophers of science call the *context of discovery* or what the French call the "problematique." What is the question being asked and the problem to be explained? In particular, this pertains to the relationship between the explanation on the one side and on the other the question to which the answer responds. The intractability of the problem of asking is reflected in the heated and ongoing debate among philosophers over the degree to which the context of discovery (the question-being-asked) influences, if at all, the context of justification (the answer). To our great loss, social theorists and social scientists have not shown a great deal of interest in the conundrum of asking (exceptions include Schuman [1981] and Zald [1990]). Its epistemological centrality is nonetheless not diminished and perhaps is even increased by our lack of attention.

In this essay I argue that two factors help explain the limitations of historical sociology. The first is that the historic turn in the social sciences has insufficiently explored the significance of *history* itself—not as subject matter or as extended longitudinal data but as *epistemology.* The second is that historical sociologists have failed to direct our historical focus to the very foundations of our own discipline—namely, *science* itself. Here I speak of science not in the parochial sense of the natural science disciplines such as biology or even physics but in the classical sense of science as *foundational knowledge* based on the certainties of nature. Remarkable developments in the sociology, history, and philosophy of science in recent decades have pointed increasingly to the *historicity* of scientific knowledge and practices.

I will approach these reflections through a "historical epistemology." The term is intended to contradict the assumed foundationalism of epistemology and standards of knowledge. Such epistemology presumes that all of our knowledge, our logics, our presuppositions, and our reasoning practices, are indelibly (even if obscurely) marked with the signature of time. They are "history laden."[2] The challenge of a historical epistemology is to appropriate and interpret histories of knowledge through a reconstruction of their making, resonance, and contestedness over time. I will do this by looking closely at the rootedness of certain theoretical categories and epistemological assumptions in what I will be calling *knowledge cultures.* A knowledge culture is constituted by the specific range of thinking, reasoning, and institutional practices *possible in a given historical time and space.* The concept should not be confused with a sociology of knowledge approach; a knowledge culture is not the "material" grounds underlying and "pressing upon" the "ideal" realm of ideas. Nor is it a single "hegemonic" set of beliefs or "truths." Rather than any specific truths, a knowledge culture frames what can be conceived of as "true-or-false."[3]

There are several reasons why considering knowledge, ontology, and discovery is essential to an evaluation of the historic turn. The first is rooted in the story of at least one of the paths by which the subfield of historical sociology emerged and developed.[4] The turn toward history began in the 1960s as a result of a perceived interrelationship between the prevailing methodologies of mainstream sociology and its substantive political conservatism (especially that of modernization and status-attainment theories). The intellectual inspiration for this perception was above all C. Wright Mills (1959), though Gouldner (1970) reinforced the same tendency. Mills's contribution was to have joined together issues of substance and epistemology by criticizing the political implications of "abstract empiricism" and "grand theory" (functionalist Parsonianism) alike. Most important, he argued convincingly that these implications were themselves inevitable consequences of the antihistoricalism characteristic of these approaches.

Mills's insights were complemented by the activism of the 1960s and early 1970s, which inspired general interest among a generation of graduate students and young faculty in social change and class analysis. Hardly new of course, these topics were central to modernization and status-attainment studies— arguably the two most prestigious areas of the social sciences in the 1960s and 1970s.[5] But in two respects these areas of interest were both newly appropriated and significantly transformed when they became the core of the new subfield of comparative historical sociology. The first was the historicizing of these themes, a process driven by the snowballing conviction among young sociologists that there was an inevitable connection between the political conservatism of modernization and status-attainment theories on the one hand and their methodologies—whether functionalist or empiricist—on the other. Following Mills, it seemed that the political stance toward "equilibrium" was in part an intellectual result of sociology's antihistoricalism (Calhoun 1990). This sparked a sudden sense of urgency in historical studies on the left.[6]

The second and much deeper reason why philosophical and epistemological criteria are both important for an evaluation of historical sociology is rooted in the character of the development, course, and consequences of the original social science project and its perduring conundrums: that is, eighteenth- and nineteenth-century social science was the product of an original fusion between a "revolutionary epistemology" on the one side and the eighteenth- and nineteenth-century discovery of "modern society" on the other. Sociology's philosophical foundations emerged from this particular rendering of a particular historical moment through a particular epistemological filter. That filter was the revolutionary social naturalism of the eighteenth century combined with a revamped seventeenth-century social ontology of the self. That moment was the social drama of the macrohistorical rupture between "tradition" and "modernity" as it was perceived by the historical sociologists who were the social theorists of the eighteenth and nineteenth centuries. Endowed with generality by nineteenth-century social thought, this highly particularistic historical narrative was then abstracted into the foundations of what we still know as social science. As a result, the core of those foundations consists of "frozen" fragments of that historical narrative distilled into theoretical presuppositions. Classical modernization theory was both the outcome and the great and lasting invention of this complex fusion of history and epistemology. Not merely a subfield in the social sciences, it has been its invisible epicenter (Somers 1992; Somers and Gibson 1994).

The historic turn and a historical epistemology thus need each other. Historical sociology needs to probe further into the epistemological foundations of our substantive arguments. This probing, however, must not be solely philosophical. Instead, we must recognize and reconsider many of the historical and empirical processes encoded in modern social science and theory. Our conceptual vocabularies and categories, our ways of constructing standards of knowledge, our definitions of significant problems, and our methods of justifiable explanation themselves all have histories. And because these histories have shaped and continued to shape the foundations of sociological knowledge, exploring them in some depth can potentially help us rethink some of the fundamental problems of social science.

The first section of this essay, "Social Science and Its Dilemmas," examines the roots and developments of social science reasoning and its original conundrums, the ongoing debates over these problems in the philosophy of the social sciences, and the reasons why the recent historic turns in both sociology and science have affected the terms of debate. The second section, "Knowledge Cultures: The Historicity of Reasoning Practices," is a discussion of the concept of a knowledge culture and its applicability to the social sciences. It forms a bridge to the third part, "Toward a New Historical Epistemology," in which I will explore those three dimensions of the social science knowledge culture that embody the fault lines of the discipline—the contexts of discovery, ontology, and justification—each of which will introduce the importance of the concept of *narrativity* in historical epistemology.

Social Science and Its Dilemmas

Like the remarkable fable that inaugurated its birth, the logic of modern social science has elements of the fantastic. Both were built from utopian fictions about society's emancipation from history. William Townsend, the late eighteenth-century English statesman, wrote a social parable about the isle of Juan Fernandez. The island (it had been made famous in England by the mythical Robinson Crusoe) was populated only by goats and dogs (men and women). According to reigning Hobbesian assumptions, these allegorical people should have had brutish, nasty, and very short lives. Townsend, however, endowed the island with natural harmony through a perfect balance of population and food. No state or artificial law was necessary to maintain the equilibrium. Townsend fashioned this tale by borrowing a revolutionary new metaphysics—the laws of nature—from a revolutionary new epistemology—natural science. In his general treatises, he combined these into a new "science of society" to conceptually liberate the social world from political or social authority. This minisociety flourished precisely because it was left to its natural laws freed from the chains of politics and religion.[7]

Classical social science was born of this revolutionary epistemology constructed upon a myth and a metaphor about a unified social system with its parts expressive of an autonomous logic. Many social thinkers of the late eighteenth century appropriated Townsend's anti-institutional naturalism as the core metaphor of a new science of society. For Hobbes, society needed a state because humans were *like* beasts; for Townsend, it seems that natural law sufficed because humans *were* beasts (Polanyi [1944] 1957). Liberated from the burdensome traditions of the past—elegant in its parsimonious simplicity—the revolutionary science of "society" had arrived.[8]

The three problems I referred to in the preceding—of knowing, of being, and of asking—were built into this naturalistic metaphor and its scientific foundations. The first problem resulted from the appropriation of scientific logic as the grounds for our knowledge about the social world. If science provides the criteria for knowledge and reveals objective laws of nature (now, of society) that exist independently of us, how can the fact that the subjects of study are social, rather than natural, beings be accommodated? Does it make a difference that the subjects have *consciousness?* Should this not affect our method for obtaining knowledge? Where does the capacity for human understanding fit into establishing knowledge? These were all problems of the foundations for social knowledge. Debates over these foundational questions primarily have taken the form of deep divides between so-called positivist and interpretative methodologies (e.g., Alexander 1982).

The second problem was ontological: what *is* society? what *is* a social actor? The problem was how laws of nature could be reconciled with people being moral agents. Here the perduring question has been: if society is made up of humans and humans have free will to act, how is the capacity for *agency* accounted for in a naturalistic ontology? Devised to solve the problem of how there could be any social order in a society comprised of autonomous individuals (the Hobbesian dilemma), the systemic solution created this yet more intractable problem, one that has since left the social sciences fundamentally divided over the relative import of action and order.

The third problem, that of asking, concerns the relationship between sociological explanation and sociological problematization. How do questions and problems find themselves on the sociological agenda in the first place? What effect does the "discovery" of certain problems have on the character of explanation? As I suggested above, the epistemological centrality of the problem of asking is evidenced in the duration and heatedness of the debate among philosophers of science over the degree to which the context of discovery (the question-being-asked) influences the context of justification (the answer).

From the extent of these divisions, it would appear that a science of society intended both to find laws of nature as well as interpretations of how people think has been inevitably stalemated in opposition on very first principles. But I want to argue that the stalemate actually rests on several deeper agreements. First, in saying how science can explain human action, positivism makes explanation and confirmation a matter of general laws and logical principles. The hermeneuticist also accepts and endorses this covering law model as both appropriate for and a correct definition of the natural sciences.

This is the first point of agreement: that scientific knowledge is in fact founded on the certainty of nature. The second point of agreement is deeper and more worrisome. Both approaches advocate generalizing and a priori rules of explanation once their respective criteria for truthful propositions have been fulfilled. For positivism this is more obvious: a true hypothesis need only be analyzed logically in relationship to that which is to be explained. For the hermeneuticists, the hypothesis is examined closely to discern whether it satisfies the test of principles of understanding and subjectivity. Both positions have fixed standards of judgment that are not subjected to historical reformulations. Both Weber and Parsons, for example, believed they could understand the relation between universalistic values and conduct in the same way in different historical circumstances.

A third (and seemingly paradoxical) point of agreement is that both positions reject process-based causal analysis (Hempel [1942] 1959, 1965). For positivist philosophers, this is because *on its own* causal explanation of processes is too historical; to be justified, any particular connection of cause to effect must be logically deduced as a subset from a logical and predictive proposition using a priori rules (Hempel and Oppenheim 1948). Causality and explanation in this process sense are not scientific or logical concepts in that they are not found in nature but in history. Causation thus tends to disappear into the "mechanisms" or "physical intuitions" that generate the covering laws in the mind of the scientist and thus are considered not a part of scientific epistemology but a part of the "genius" or "quirkiness" of discovery. Interpretivists similarly reject causality, ironically, precisely because they accept uncritically their opponents' redefinition of cause as an entailment of general law. Cause, by this definition, of course excludes the central interpretivist concerns—meaning, locality, and contextuality—and so must be rejected. Rejecting causality altogether, however, is deeply problematic. In its explicit absence, implicit and ad hoc "causes" inevitably sneak into arguments. And at the same time, the vacuum left from the explicit anticausalism is too often filled by residual implications of cultural stability that may actually resemble the logic of covering laws.

My main argument here is that when either positivism or interpretivism studies historical social patterns they must inevitably return to "mechanisms" or causal processes that vary over time and space. Yet neither epistemology has developed rules for developing knowledge of such historical processes.

The Historic Turn in the Philosophy of Science and Social Science

Like almost every other discipline, the philosophy of science and social science has taken a dramatic "historic turn" in recent decades. It began on a large scale in 1962, when Kuhn ([1962] 1970) published a book with a now famous first sentence: "History, if viewed as a repository for more than anecdote or chronology, could produce a decisive transformation in the image of science by which we are now possessed."[9] That image, he argued, is false; it presents as absolute and timeless its foundations for knowledge. He did not suggest that science presents as absolute any particular piece of knowledge but that this is conceived of by philosophy of science as an instrumental problem alone. In principle, the right method may ultimately generate truth on the grounds of logical foundations.

Among the gauntlets Kuhn threw down to the covering law philosophers, the most overarching was that knowledge only exists in time and is historical. This appeal to historicity also included the claims that data are "theory driven" (there can be no foolproof distinction between observation and theory); that science is not automatically cumulatively progressive in the sense that we do not get progess by better answers to the same questions but only when our questions get better; that science consists of paradigmatic "puzzle solving" in which theories are not refuted by anomalies but rather adjusted for "measurement problems"; and that scientific progress occurs largely through paradigmatic revolutions in communities of scientific practitioners. It is also this aspect of Kuhn's work that has been most criticized for its relativism (on the debate, see Hollis and Lukes 1982; Gutting 1980). He was accused of ascribing irrationality and "mob psychology" to the scientific community (Lakatos 1970).[10] Kuhn did not consider himself "irrational" because he was challenging only standard notions of how and why theories are accepted or rejected, not the theories themselves. Nor did he believe that because theory could not be separated from observation that that made all scientific observation, let alone scientific theories, useless.

But rather than discuss Kuhn here I will emphasize those points of the post-Kuhnian historic turn in epistemology directly relevant to my discussion of the historic turn in sociology: (1) the current foundations of scientific knowledge are historical rather than cumulative truths; (2) the ontologies of science, the conceptual entities whose behaviors constitute the questions of science, are also historical;[11] and (3) knowledge construction is a dual process, that is, the context of discovery—or how we ask questions about the world—is inseparable from that of justification. Before I take up the implications for sociology of this historic turn in science, let me address the historic turn in sociology.

The Historic Turn in Sociology

One of the hallmarks of the recent historic turn in sociology has been its own interest in reflecting on the project of constructing a historical and comparative methodology (e.g., Stinchcombe 1978; Tilly 1984, 1993; Skocpol 1984; Ragin 1987). It is thus all the more indicative of just how stubborn are the meta-theoretical impasses to note that there seems to be very little difference in the terms of epistemological debate between sociology before and after the historic turn (Abbott [1983, 1988, 1990], Stinchcombe [1978], and Tilly [1984] are the exceptions).[12] Despite the deepening of our knowledge of the past we in historical sociology have generally been caught in the same dichotomies—only now exported on to historical data.

Consider first "ways of being." Although historical sociologists tend to avoid explicit metatheoretical issues, debate over the relative import of agency versus structure in explaining social processes is always more or less implicit (Alexander 1982; Aminzade 1992).[13] The burgeoning of new discussion over the viability of rational choice analysis among historical sociologists (e.g., Kiser and Hechter 1991) indicates that the debates over the character of society and the social actor have remained virtually unchanged since the original social science logic: is society a systemic whole irreducible to its actors or is society an aggregate of individual actions and preferences? Is the social actor constituted collectively or as an individual who enters into society? What is notable about these discussions is not that they have not been resolved over the last two centuries. Rather, it is that the arguments and the terms of opposition are the same as when Marx wrote—to paraphrase—that men make history . . . but not under the conditions they choose. In this phrase he brilliantly summed up the perduring ontological fault line of social science before and since his time.

But it is debates over method that have predominated in historical sociological discourse. One way into the terms of this debate is through a self-critical glance at Skocpol and Somers (1980). There, three strategies of comparative historical sociology are distinguished: (1) "parallel comparisons"—the use of comparisons to demonstrate repeatedly evidence for a general theory (e.g., Wallerstein 1974); (2) "contrast-oriented"—the use of comparisons to highlight the unique and contextually meaningful features of each case (e.g., Geertz 1983); and (3) "macroanalytic"—the use of comparisons to explain different outcomes and regularities (e.g., Moore 1966; Skocpol 1979). Skocpol and Somers (1980) were explicit advocates of the macroanalytic approach, and it is to that position that most of the criticisms have been addressed.

The first set of criticisms came from the logic of statistical probability. They rejected the "imperfect empiricism" of the macroanalytic approach—it suffers from too small a sample and too large a universe of potential independent variables. These criticisms are anticipated most forcefully in Smelser 1976. It is arguable, however, that the problem is not that the sample is too small; it is that since the method creates causal configurations (comprised of different aspects of cases) even with a small number of cases the number of possible configurational "conjunctures" is potentially overwhelming (Ragin 1987). Moreover, Zeldich (1974) argues that any loss in scientific precision is more than compensated by the greater intelligibility resulting from deeper subject matter knowledge. It is precisely this concern with context that motivates the second set of criticisms from the interpretive and hermeneutic position. Because they want to stress the particularities and the meaning within each case, they reject the configurational strategy of macroanalyis. In principle, however, there is no reason why meaning should suffer from this strategy. Indeed, it is possible that this approach potentially could make culture and meaning *more* significant by identifying which specific aspects of a cultural and meaningful context can be more strongly linked than others to the patterns or outcomes under investigation (compare the analysis of German miners in Moore [1978]). The problem is that because the interpretive tradition in historical sociology rejects what they define as "causal analysis" in favor of using an ideal-typical methodology, we more often than not end up with arguments about "deviations" from the (ahistorical) ideal-type rather than explanations of *variation* between and among cases. Clearly, we must question the possibility of reconstructing any meaningful historical trajectories without the implicit or explicit use of causal argument about sequences and processes (Stinchcombe 1978).

I have reviewed this methodological debate at length for several reasons. First, I wanted to observe that the epistemological disagreements of social science seem fundamentally untouched by the fact that the substantive *content* of the scholarship is historical. Albeit in simplified form, the three approaches can still easily be identified as variants of the Popper-Carnap debate between deductivism (parallel comparisons) and inductivism (macroanalytic) on the covering law side and interpretivism or hermeneutic sociology (contrast-oriented) on the other. Consider the macroanalytic strategy: although using the adverb *analytic* and bearing few resemblances to Carnap, the method is a straightforward application of J. S. Mill's inductivist methods of difference and similarity (Skocpol and Somers 1980). Not surprisingly, it is similarly vulnerable to the same criticisms. The recent Kiser and Hechter (1991) position is an explicit recapitulation of Popper (with Lakatosian modifications) restating the case for primacy of a priori general theory and the subsumption of cause to an instance of the conditional proposition (see also Burawoy 1989). And the contextualists make the hermeneutic rejection of causal analysis on the assumption that causality entails general laws and thus precludes meaning as an empirical variable (in the law-of-nature view of the economy, for example, the objective maxims enter only as utilities obeying its laws, not as a historical variable we study to understand history). Second, each defense of macroanalysis entailed a move toward the third (previously rejected) position—thus sounding suspiciously interpretive. Yet to the interpretivists, such a move sounds suspiciously positivist, and to the deductivists, both suspiciously inductivist and interpretivist. Surely this is a sign of a deeper commonality. Third, I have tried to highlight the striking irony that it is in historical sociology itself that we seem to have been singularly untouched by the historic turn in the very exemplar for our discipline—science itself.

In light of these striking thematic continuities there is one overriding set of questions that call out to be answered: why, when we have turned to history in the hopes of working our way out of some of the intractable problems of social science logic, have the same fundamental oppositions over laws, realism, context, causality, variables, understanding, action, and order doggedly appeared nonetheless? Where are the epistemological identity crises we in historical sociology should be having?

Knowledge Cultures: The Historicity of Reasoning Practices

My argument is that the epistemological stalemate among historical sociologists stems from a common participation in a social science *knowledge culture*. The concept of a knowledge culture builds from the premise that all theories, epistemologies, ontologies, philosophical anthropologies, metatheories, questions, conceptual frameworks, methodologies, and data always bear within them the signature of their passage through time. Both theory and observation, and everything in between, is history laden; all thinking and all reasoning practices and all logic and all research takes place within time and space. The parameters of a given time and space constitute a knowledge culture. A close synonym is what Hacking has called a "style of reasoning" (a term he borrows from Crombie), but it misses the practical and organizational dimensions of a cultural environment.

The term *knowledge culture* refers to an environment with a broad spectrum of contested truths and falsehoods (theories of the world, beliefs about how to justify knowledge, problems-to-be-solved, and so on) that is nonetheless *delimited* by that culture's *ways of thinking and reasoning*. These parameters do not specify anything so narrow as "truth." What they do establish are the boundaries of what is conceivable within our historical imagination. In the above debate, this would mean that the fault lines and the contradictions of each position are shaped by the historicity of the reasoning processes we use to try to find solutions. As members of a shared culture of reasoning, our attempts to solve its internal conundrums inevitably reproduce them, and a defense of a position on either end of the continuum will move us only closer to the other end.

A knowledge culture is both a part of history and *has* a history. Various ones might include the Greeks' embeddedness in Euclidean thought, the seventeenth century's in experimental method, and the nineteenth century's discovery of statistical reasoning. Indeed, each of those were highly contested within each knowledge culture. The foundations of what were to become the parameters of social science's knowledge culture were first fought out in the seventeenth century when Hobbes and Boyle contested the legitimacy of experimental versus theoretical reasoning (Shapin and Schaffer 1986). Ultimately, these parameters were determined by a representational conception of knowledge and an autonomous conception of the knowing subject. In the late eighteenth century, these early scientific parameters were easily appropriated into the upstart new science of society. What binds these various examples together is not that each one had certain or distinct notions of truths, science, or even methodologies and epistemologies. Each of those were highly contested within their knowledge cultures. (Although there might well be what Foucault has called a "regime of truth" dominating a particular time or place that would nonetheless be an empirical question to be investigated; it is not inherent in the concept itself.) What is constitutive of a knowledge culture is the existence of a *spectrum of conceptual and practical possibilities* that establishes the parameters of what will be a candidate for reasoning practices at all. All knowledge cultures share the trait of being limited only by the range of what is to be considered at all for the question, "Is it true or false?" Or "shall we test this with statistics or fieldwork?" Or "is the modern self an alienated autonomous self or a communitarian one?" Or, to come at it from the other direction, the concept of a knowledge culture helps us to understand that certain problems would not exist, and so would not be subject to debate, if they did not exist within a historically given spectrum of reasoning.

The idea of a knowledge culture and its historical process can be seen in the following process. Thought operates within a knowledge culture—a way of thinking and reasoning that produces a capacious but delimited spectrum of conceptual possibilities. Knowledge cultures are products of history; every aspect of the culture is history laden. The conceptual imagination is limited by this spectrum, so the range of consideration about ontologies, philosophical anthropologies, and even our views of reality are historically contingent. This spectrum limits the conceptualization of propositions about what may be thought about as either true or false and what constitutes even a question to be asked. What is problematized is thus historically contingent. The range of possible ways of explaining problems and questions depends on a concept of explanation. Explanation too is thus historically contingent. Just how capacious is that culture or just how many rival interpretations of truth can coexist may be unknowable. What we do know is that there are certain things simply not in the running in any given knowledge culture. This does not necessarily mean that no one will think them. It only means that such thoughts do not go anywhere in the social field defined by the knowledge culture.

Let me be careful to say what I do not mean by the term *knowledge culture*. First, and for several reasons, a knowledge culture is not equivalent to popular conceptions of a paradigm. Paradigms are usually seen as tightly coherent constellations of theories, methods, and problems. This is too holistic to be a useful historical tool for understanding epistemologies and social ontologies that always cut across numerous theories and methods. Within a given knowledge culture, people may vehemently argue about what is true and never settle the issue. These people are unlikely to work together in a tight scientific community such as those that characterized Kuhn's paradigms. They agree, however, on those things even to be considered for the question of truth-or-falseness because they share a knowledge culture and a spectrum of conceptual possibilities.

A knowledge culture is also different from Kuhn's notion of paradigm in that while it cannot develop what, post hoc, we see as future conceptualizations, or even those that are part of unconnected knowledge cultures, it is very much tied up with previous ones. The past is not at all "incommensurable," in Kuhn's and Feyerband's expression. For a new knowledge culture to develop, it must not only have new and different ways of thinking and reasoning. It must also have a way of explaining both the original coherence and the current incoherence of the previous ways of thinking (MacIntyre 1980, 72). For Kuhn ([1962] 1970, 206), for instance, Einstein is closer to Aristotle than to Newton because of the former's ontology of mechanics. But it is more plausible that Einstein won acclaim because he provided an answer to the question of why "from the standpoint of an approach to truth" Newtonian mechanics is superior to Aristotelian. Why? Because regardless of how Aristotelianism might have developed, it is virtually impossible that its problems regarding time could have produced the questions to which relativity is the answer. A history that moved "from Aristotelianism directly to relativistic physics" is not an "imaginable history" (MacIntyre 1980, 72). To understand physics, we must treat it like all other forms of theory and method and truth—as embedded in history. Kuhn's historicity is limited to the sociological history of any given paradigm. We must look between paradigms for more than "incommensurability" and empty space to make sense. To imagine any conceptual schemata as changing historically to the point of incommensurability with the past assumes an untenable ontology—namely, that any reasoning practice could be context-free enough to call into question *everything* within its own culture. This is the fiction of Descartes's own story; its resonance still reflects the appeal of his underlying conception of the self as autonomous from the world. But we learn from Hume's story that such a belief is the ingredient not for philosophical breakthrough but for mental breakdown (Hume 1941, bk. 1, iv, vii, 267–69).[14]

A knowledge culture is also not a form of logic like induction or deduction. Logic entails the skill of jumping "from truth to truth" (Hacking 1982). Its goal is to justify already extant classes of propositions or to show that a new proposition was really hidden in the old all along. By contrast, a knowledge culture brings into being new classes within a spectrum of propositions, ontologies, questions, possibilities. And a knowledge culture is similarly distinct from Lakatos's "research programme" for it has no substantive "hard core" that perdures despite peripheral challenges. A way of thinking and reasoning is a practice, not an argument, and a practice can entail numerous substantive and even metaphysical principles. Finally, a knowledge culture is not a set of truths and meanings that makes two different cultures incommensurable until we learn each other's languages of truth and meaning. To communicate or to understand requires not a new vocabulary but to understand the practices and processes of reasoning characteristic of another culture. Thus, translation is not enough; it is conceivable that reasoning practices can be shared across different conceptual languages. Instead, we would need to understand how it is that other knowledge cultures come to problematize in their particular vocabularies.

This sequence of arguments about the historical contingency of thought, however, does not mean we may not have good reasons for having our own standards of truth and reason. To say that the existence of a spectrum of possibilities is historically contingent is not to deny but to affirm that within that spectrum many propositions may in fact be deemed true on the basis of evidence as evidence is conceived within that culture (Alexander 1991; Longino 1990). What it does suggest is a certain degree of agnosticism concerning foundations. A knowledge culture therefore makes epistemology historical rather than either strictly logical or subjective. A historical epistemology in turn explains why the spectrum of conceivable ontologies, the range of conceivable questions-to-be-asked and problems-to-be-solved, and the range of possible justifications for theories and propositions are all also historically contingent. The contingency is mutual as well: Hacking (1988) has shown how the emergence of statistics was the result of questions people came to ask at a particular time, only because at that time they had started to define society and the individual in certain ways. And that they had done this was because of a style of reasoning that had come into existence historically—and had not been there before.

The Knowledge Culture of Historical Sociology

The limits to sociology's historic turn are the limits of this shared knowledge culture. This claim can be supported in several ways. First, there are increasing attempts to join interpretation and positivist methods so that some degree of meaning is combined with some degree of science. This is done skillfully, for example, by both Zald (1990) and Ragin (1987). Reconciliations between action and order are evident in theoretical discussions of social ontologies. Hybrid terms such as *structuration* and *multidimensionality* now characterize the literature of historical sociology. A second support for the claim that historical sociologists share a common knowledge culture is that despite the differences and the vehemence of opposition, there are fundamentally shared assumptions among the positions. I have suggested that the epistemological foundations of both the inductivist and deductivist versions of the positivist as well as the hermeneutic traditions are both antihistorical in that they have a priori rules of justification and are both opposed to causality.

Similar shared assumptions exist in the debates over ontologies and ways of being. Regardless of which position one takes on the debate over the self, for example, communitarian and rational-actor perspectives both presuppose the existence of an essential human nature. They agree on what the entities are but disagree about how to find what is in them. Similarly, both perspectives on society—the aggregationist and the holistic—share the assumption that this social entity is analytically independent of its social agents and thus can be represented as an entity. In both cases "society" is a social fact not a historical one, and there is an essential "something" out there that exists prior to our categorization of it, regardless of whether that turns out to be meaning-centered, communal, individualist, and so on. It is important to note that I am not saying that these positions are right or wrong. What I am insisting on is the historicity of the reasoning practices embedded in the common conceptions of what counts as a social entity in the first place (to which attributes to be investigated are to be attached).

Toward a New Historical Epistemology

If this argument for the inherent limitations in social science logic and its alternatives is at all convincing, how might we begin to look differently at the issues at stake? How might the historic turn in sociology challenge the limits of its own epistemological environment? One answer to these questions lies in our having another look—albeit a critical one—at the historic turn in the very field that has been the model for so many of our persistent conundrums, the philosophy of science and even science itself. This historic turn deserves the attention of historical sociologists. It has implications for rethinking our most contested and stubborn problems of explanation, confirmation, and concept formation. In the rest of this essay I will develop the following arguments for rethinking the three central conundrums of the social science knowledge culture: (1) attention must be turned to the centrality of the context of discovery; (2) less attention should be directed to the claim that all data is theory laden and more to the claim that theory is history laden, and we need a new way of rethinking our conceptual frameworks based on the epistemological centrality of temporality; and finally (3) we need to develop a *causal narrativity*—a reclaimed notion of causality based on narrativity sequence and contingency rather than universality and predictive law.

The Context of Discovery

Philosophers of science make a fundamental distinction between the *context of discovery* and that of *justification* (Reichenbach 1947, 2). It is the latter, the context of justification, that most of us think and worry about most of the time—namely, the question of what best justifies and confirms our theories. Virtually the entirety of academic ire among scientists is exercised over questions of validity, verification, and justification: is it reasonable? supported by evidence? confirmed by experiment? corroborated by stringent testing? We in the social sciences then go on to argue about the value of quantitative versus qualitative methods, survey versus historical methods, and so on. The context of discovery, by contrast, is neglected. But it should not be. For it is the context in which we "discover" the questions we ask in our research, in which we define that which is considered problematic in the first place (or what is necessary to be explained), and in which we select our conceptual vocabulary to formulate that question. Discovery thus comprises the prehistory of theory construction.

The chief reason for this neglect is that one of the pillars of philosophical thinking has been the insistence on a rigid separation between discovery and justification. Popper ([1934] 1959), Carnap (1966), and Hempel (1965) alike charged that the context of discovery had nothing to do with the truth value of what was actually discovered, and to think otherwise was to commit the "genetic fallacy." It mixed up history with scientific logic. Whitehead's observation that getting the question right was half the way to the solution has still not led philosophers to ask how we can tell when we have the question right.

Questions are considered quirky, often born of "mere curiosity," of sociological, historical, or even psychological circumstances (such as Kepler's sun-worshiping habits). Because they are conceived to emerge from idiosyncratic and psychological interests, questions and conjectures cannot be located as part of scientific discourse. To be sure, if not for Kepler's peculiar commitment to sun-worshiping we would not have the scientific explanations that we do have. But according to this dogma the fundamental *logic* of Kepler's theory is untouched by its *history.* The randomness of interest and intrigue with mystery creates an equal randomness in how we problematize the questions we ask of the world. Logic, by contrast, can never be random. Because scientists cannot answer questions they are not ready to ask, this means that the actual existing body of knowledge that is logically proved contains answers *only* to those questions that have been asked in the first place.

It was Collingwood ([1939] 1970) who first challenged the claim for the autonomy of justification from discovery. He argued for the existence of a "question-answer" relationship between discovery and justification in both scientific and social explanation. He believed that any attempt at empirical explanation was doomed unless we know what question we are trying to explain. What it is that we are asking will determine where and how and on what grounds and with what evidence we look for an explanation. Just as importantly, it will determine what we leave out of the explanatory inquiry. In his most famous example, Collingwood demonstrates how a general question about a stalled car—"what is wrong with my car?"—looks inconsistent with respect to the answer we are most likely to give in the actual attempt to get the car started: "my spark plugs are fine." That answer, he points out, is a response to a more specific question: "are my spark plugs broken?" In this latter question hundreds of other potential causal variables are indeed neglected, but it can be argued that the answer is at least "true" for the question and the variables (spark plugs) about which guesses have been hypothesized. Collingwood used this "question-answer" epistemology to argue that explanatory statements exist only in relationship to particular questions. Before 1970, no one *asked* whether their oxygen detector was malfunctioning.

Kuhn dealt an even more serious blow to the separation of discovery from justification from within the history of science itself. Because for Kuhn science is in time and is essentially historical, there could be no epistemological separation of discovery from justification. He argued that scientific problems are hardly serendipitous. Rather, a standard set of problems are part of "normal science." According to Kuhn, what constitutes the essence of normal science is exactly its stable of scientific problems and "puzzles."

This brings us back to history in that the narrative of paradigmatic change—or the historical conditions under which normal science is overthrown and replaced by new versions—was of course the central focus of Kuhn's work on scientific revolutions. Influenced by Kuhn but wanting to preserve Popper, Lakatos (1970) has since perhaps most accurately explained why some questions are asked and not others—why scientific change is so difficult. Lakatos describes the scientific project not as a paradigm but as a "research program" comprised of a negative and positive heuristic. The "hard core" is not open to debate. It takes on the status of a metaphysic insulated by an outer, more malleable "protective belt." Although Lakatos believes scientific progress is about the transformation of the auxiliary belt—a transformation that develops out of new questions posed by anomalies—his description more accurately explains social scientific stability and the extraordinary durability of so many of our "hard-core" assumptions. *Homo economicus,* for example, certainly among the most perdurable of such assumptions, is assumed invariantly to be a person, to be able to form contracts, to be able to change the price of what he or she sells, and to be a legal adult. But these features are, of course, historically variable. Corporations, after all, became persons able to do all these things within historical memory.

Questions and Historical Epistemology

Historical sociologists' reflections on theory and method have been impoverished by the singular focus on justification and the nonrecognition of the importance of the context of discovery. We have not been epistemologically self-conscious enough about this dual nature of theory construction but can ill afford this antihistorical approach to theoretical development. We must recognize that questions are indeed epistemologically prior to answers and that they cannot be treated as residuals. There is no such thing as an explanation that does not contain within it a prior question. The very language, shape, and content of our explanations are forged by the questions that inform them. Indeed, explanations are only called into existence by prior questions.[15] Our research agendas are not shaped by method and data but by the formulation of the problem to be explained. If justification is so linked to discovery, one important avenue into a rethinking of our stubborn debates over method and justification would be to begin to look more closely at question formation. From this perspective, it begins to look as if attending to questions will give us a new and very different route into thinking about the dilemmas of social science logic—a route substantially more historical than through direct theoretical encounter.

There is another, even less apparent, implication of attention to the context of discovery. Questions at any given time reflect the explanations we are ready to give and to investigate. That is Kuhn's central point. But they also reflect what kinds of beings and entities we think there are in the world in the first place (whose behavior generates our questions). This is the link on the other side (the first being the answer) of question formation: that is, the conceptual and categorical ontologies that precede discovery. Following the history of discovery will, willy-nilly, lead us to the often hidden issues of ontology and being (action and order, for example). After all, if questions precede explanation, what precedes questions? Where do questions come from? Zald (1990) has recently argued one important and convincing answer, namely, that questions come from civilizational concerns. I think this is very much the case but through a rather more indirect route than this argument suggests.

Questions are born of historical and conceptual ontologies. Because they are historical, they lack coherence or stability and carry with them an inherent set of problems and conundrums. Moreover, these ontologies will be in ongoing competition or contestation with other ontologies—primarily over winning intellectual consensus over ongoing points of crucial difference among entities. These internal problems and external debates are wholly products of the conceptual frameworks and their assumptions. They are only considered problems because of the content of these ontologies. They exist within the parameters of their knowledge culture. Thus, these problems inevitably carry within them the assumptions, and the solutions, of their cultural environment. The questions we ask in social science are therefore inherently ontological, or to put it simply, contain a priori decisions about how we understand the social world to be constituted.

The shaping of problems by ontologies works in three ways: first, it is crucial to understand that ontologies of the world are not reflections of that world. Far more commonly, these ontologies and categorical knowledges are the movers and shakers of worldly development and social context. Adam Smith's social ontology, for example, was as powerful as any more "material" force in making history. So were Hobbes's, Boyle's, and Freud's (Shapin and Schaffer 1986; Miller 1987). Social ontologies are thus constitutive of the "worldly" things we take to be problems for research. Second, ontologies of the world will have shaped the ways that contemporaries framed their questions about their world. Because we inherit, and only rarely reframe, our questions from history, we inherit these ontologies and work within their parameters—often, albeit, unconsciously. Third, ontologies shape the conceptual vocabulary and the linguistic forms through which we frame our current questions and problems.

Problematizing Questions

Questions, then, are the linchpins of theory construction. On the one side, they lead us to answers, and on the other they flow from fundamental assumptions. The implications of this are that we must develop ways to mine the epistemological significance of the long neglected context of discovery. A crucial aspect of the pre-Kuhnian conception of science is that questions are random, a form of discourse devoid of history. But if conjectures are indeed so randomly conceived, there is no very convincing explanation for how certain questions become more or less dominant at different times or how certain questions are more or less legitimate at different times. Also lacking, certainly, is the necessary narrative of how knowledge is problematized over time. And if this is true, then we also have no way to judge the value of our questions, despite a new recognition of their crucial epistemological role in knowledge construction. We are thrown back to a focus only on logic, explanation, soundness of method, and justification—exactly where Popper and Carnap believed the focus should be.

But there is an alternative. A historical epistemology would begin by looking directly at questions, at problem formation and its history. A crucial task would be to explore how, when, and why questions change over time—one way to put it would be the "rise and fall of questions." Exploring why certain concepts become problematic at certain times (why the "discovery" of poverty, for example, in late-eighteenth-century England?), why certain questions once considered in the realm of ethics or theology are transformed into questions of economics or morality, demands not only a deep understanding of the context of these questions. More important, it demands understanding of the internal construction of our questions in order to know why their answers would resonate at certain times and not others, to certain authorities and not others. Looking at the rise and fall of questions will teach much about the rise and fall of answers and thus the construction of knowledge.

If an exploration of the rise and fall of questions is to have meaning, we would want to know how certain ontologies distinguish between relevant and irrelevant questions as well as between superior and inferior methods for answering them. In social science we distinguish between valid questions about empirical causality and invalid questions about normative causality. Educational achievement, for example, constitutes a standard explanatory variable in hypotheses about the causes of poverty. But we do not consider questions about the link between a society's level of, say, social justice to be a comparable hypothetical variable (as legitimate as we may agree it to be for philosophical inquiry). This distinction is not a judgment about whether people should be concerned about justice; indeed, that justice is an irrelevant criterion has no bearing on the normative implications for the discipline. There is instead a knowledge-culture reason why this question is ruled out: (1) justice cannot be measured; it cannot even be defined, so we cannot ask about it; (2) the history of the paradigm of social science has excluded issues of moral philosophy from its problematics. These assumptions determine the spectrum within which the problems of social science research operate.

Through the context of discovery history enters into the logic of both science and social science argumentation and into the conundrums of being and knowing and explaining. Because questions are so important and questions come from conceptual and ontological frameworks that carry within them ongoing problematics, the real challenge is to problematize our problems. I suggest this can be approached by deconstructing and historicizing our conceptual frameworks, categories, and vocabularies—our thinking about ways of being.

Ways of Being: The Historicity of Ontologies

Given that the goal of a historical epistemology is to explore the process by which those problems that have such a formative place in theory construction have gotten identified as such, the next step toward that end is to examine the cultural and social construction of conceptual ontologies as they unfolded historically and in turn to examine the internal logics of their categories and assumptions. The aim is not primarily to understand "why" in the sense of locating a sociological environment. It is more to understand "how" competing sets of ontologies of identity, political life, society, and so on gain currency and shape the empirical problems we encounter as historical sociologists. The idea of a knowledge culture suggests that the very ontologies that shape our questions are contingent and historical. This in turn suggests that our theoretical renewal cannot proceed without a historical one: we need to look at the encoding of category by history. Most of what we in sociology treat as abstract or "presuppositional" categories—subject and object, agent and structure, for example—carry within them frozen historical arguments that have been abstracted into our familiar general categories. To "unfreeze" requires an "undoing" and an "unthinking" (Wallerstein 1991) and that requires history. The theoretical task is thus a historical one: we cannot overcome the historicity of our theory without a new look at the history it encodes. But we cannot reread history without a new conceptual framework—at least a tentative one. Because each task requires the other, both must proceed at once.

From Hacking (1984, 1990), I lift the phrase "taking a look" to characterize this kind of project, one that joins history and epistemology through a genealogical accounting of conceptual configurations. The approach does not ask whether ideas are "true" or "false" but rather how and to what effect ideas and ontologies are even considered either true or false, how they gain and lose their currency and resonance. This means exploring the cultural, historical, and narrative construction of concepts (Calhoun 1990). What makes it narrative is that this kind of history is not a chronicle of events. The fact of its narrativity insists on an acknowledgment of the constructed nature of such a conceptual history. And like a narrative structure it tries to find those reasoning practices embedded in the conceptual constructions that allowed meaning and resonance over time.[16]

The whole premise of this approach is that knowing *how* we got to where we are will help to *analyze* and *clarify where* we are (Taylor 1989; Calhoun 1991). If we can understand what puts ideas and knowledges in place and what brings them into being—not a teleology but an account of contingencies and "might-have-beens"—we can hopefully better grasp the meanings and the effects of those ideas and their role in problem formation. This, to be sure, is what Popper ([1934] 1959) and Carnap (1966) dismissed as the genetic fallacy. But because the approach is explicitly nonteleological, I agree with Hacking (1990) that the accusation of committing the genetic fallacy is but name-calling produced by an overly great admiration for a priori logic.

Indeed, it is precisely this historical approach that has contributed so mightily to the recent challenges mounted by a new generation of post-Kuhnians to the antihistorical view of science. The works of Latour and Woolgar (1979), Pickering (1984), Shapin and Schaffer (1986) all demonstrate the power of genetic, contested, and constructivist accounts of knowledge. These works conclude that classifications, categories, and concepts of science are not "found" in nature but in time and are constructed through historical activities. They are not, let me emphasize, claiming that natural phenomena do not exist. What they are arguing is that entities only exist for scientific practice and knowledge in historical time. Quarks, for example, were only discovered recently. That does not mean that such a phenomenon in nature was not out there long before we named it a quark. Rather, it suggests that that phenomenon did not exist either historically or socially—that is, in time. Quarks had to be constructed before they could actually cause anything else or be affected by other entities. Nature is not, therefore, unreal or made up. Only the *theories* that categorize nature are made up. But the entities outlast the theories.

The point about this historical epistemology that must be emphasized is this: that what we know about natural entities is a product of historical reasoning does not diminish its value as truth or knowledge (Longino 1990; Alexander 1991). It is just that our foundational ideas about what constitutes "real" must take a more pragmatic turn with the onset of the historic turn. The "unthought" world, in Hacking's (1984, 11; 1990, 6) felicitous phrase, simply does not come premade in facts; the "factization" of the world is a human activity, and there is no reason to assume that scientific truth should or could be organized through anything but the same social, and historically variable, criteria as any other concerns. With a view to those processes and principles of historical construction the reasons why certain problems persist become much clearer (Gusfield 1980; Hacking 1988).

Action and Order Historicized

Taking a look at the historicity of apparently presuppositional categories of social thought also involves asking how the historical construction and transformations of a concept shaped and continues to shape its logical dimensions and its social meanings. Hacking (1990, 359; 1984, 110) calls this level of conceptual analysis looking at words in their "sites." It is another approach to historicizing by locating conceptual problematics not only in time but in conceptual space. Sites include "sentences, uttered or transcribed, always in a larger site of neighborhood, institution, authority, language" without which ideas would be just words, not concepts. Looking at the rise and fall of moral and social concepts as words in their sites and in time reveals their existence as historical—and thus contingent.

Let me exemplify this by returning to the ontological impasse of agency and structure in social science logic. We know that the conceptual framework of modern social science has a built-in tension between agency and order, a tension in part born of the revolutionary epistemology I described in the opening paragraph. But the problems of reconciling agency and order are not only a product of the logic of social science. Even more significantly they rest on the core of a historical metanarrative of modernity and the "transition from feudalism to capitalism" (Somers 1992, 1994a). The metatheoretical attempt to resolve the conundrum flounders on the unexplored historicity of its central categories.

Modern social theory was crafted out of epic moments in history. Plagues, wars, famines, and revolutions all play their parts. The Black Death, the English Civil War, the Reformation, the French Revolution, the Industrial Revolution—all figure as shadows in the heart of the metatheoretical and theoretical framework. The classical founders constructed a social theory based upon an appropriation of the historical and empirical world. Indeed, the very power and durability of sociological thought can only be explained by the substantive and empirical content of its core principles and the concepts to which it gave rise. Its principles thus emerged from—and so encoded—the macrosociological obsession that possessed them all, namely, how to explain the emergence and the nature of the modern world and its epochal break from "traditional society." The conundrums of modern sociology must be traced to more than an abstract explanatory logic and revolutionary naturalism. These were categories generated by a fusion of history and epistemology.

What were the consequences of this inextricable entanglement of the new social scientific naturalism of the historical transformations of the nineteenth century? Classical modernization theory (whether in its Marxist, Durkheimian, or Weberian expression)—the macrotheoretical schema aimed at describing and explaining the making of the modern Western world, its structural and its social dynamics—was the outcome, indeed the great and lasting invention, of this complex fusion of history and theory. The new theorists of society deployed the social scientific tools of Townsend's naturalism to carve out their views of the macroscopic transformation of the social world. In so doing, they abstracted from history to flesh out a victorious epistemological vision. They aligned themselves with the willful optimism of the revolutionary epistemology by propounding a most unique idea: if the nature of modern society could be conceived as being organized according to the systemic laws of nature, the emergence of modernity could be explained by an endogenous, rational, and progressive logic shed of the constraints of ethics and law, political authority, religion, and kinship. New concepts were unleashed, now guided by a set of "presuppositions": the social world was developmentally bifurcated between "tradition" and "modernity" and was driven by the relentless motor of technical rationality, which had the power to remake society, institutions, social life—even the drama of human intentionality itself—in its own image.

Modern sociological logic and the metanarrativity of Western modernization—an enmeshing of history and epistemology—are therefore ineluctably entangled. That these historical constellations have so long passed as universal truth is a major source of the continuing dualities and antinomies of sociological thought. Ours is a social theory comprised of both historical concepts and a conceptual history. What we know today as social theory and metatheory are the legacy of those historical fragments distilled into abstract ontological and scientific presuppositions. These essential categories of our frozen observation language—whether defined as agency and structure, subject and object—are presuppositional only in the degree to which they are universally defined as social scientific givens.

We may have arrived at one of the reasons for the enduring presence of the ontological impasse over agency and structure in historical sociology. Agency and structure are presuppositional and ontological concepts that were a creation of a particular historical narrative. It is their unexamined and deeply problematic historicity that is central to the ontological dilemma of social science. If the impasses of sociology are in the original fusion of macrohistorical analysis and epistemology and if the concepts we use to describe the world are historicized and limited, it follows logically that we must deconstruct the historicity of the concepts we use by means of a historical epistemology. Agency and structure in social theory must be reexamined in their origins and in relationship to classical modernization theory. We must indeed "take a look." In what follows, I offer brief, speculative conclusions based on analyses done elsewhere (see Somers 1992, 1994b; Somers and Gibson 1994).

Recall the epistemological template for the problem of action as expressed in Townsend's fantasia of the goats and the dogs on the isle of Juan Fernandez. This naturalism was one moment of the general revolutionary progressivism of eighteenth- and nineteenth-century science and politics. Faced with the dilemma that naturalism inevitably threatened to annihilate the subject, sociological theory did not bury a theory of action. Rather, it made an unlikely conjoining of naturalism with the philosophical counterpart to social structural progressivism—what I have called the "revolutionary idiom of action" (Somers and Gibson 1994). What made this view of the subject revolutionary was the conceptual transformation of social agency into an abstract individual driven by the motivation of "freedom from . . . " anything associated with a world caricatured as *Gemeinschaft* or traditional society. This was a modernized ontology of progressive autonomy. Although Marx, Weber, and Durkheim each had different notions of the autonomous actor, all three nonetheless appropriated the striving for autonomy. Consequently—and inevitably—they each built their theories on the dualities of subject and object, the individual and society. In this schema, the identity of the subject was abstracted from history; social relations and institutional practices—even collective memory—would exist as external objects of power and constraint.

As a result of the revolutionary idiom, much of the data of social action has been the subject of social science problematizing and is usually explained by recourse to some version of social determinism. Why? Because the dispossessed modern agent is "less liberated than disempowered." Indeed, the subject cannot—even heuristically or "analytically"—exist. To protect this idiom of agency, action that does not conform to its postulates must be explained by the external power of order or institutional constraint, be it norms and social laws, bureaucratic power, or economic forces. The idiom of the modern agent thus contains a built-in and paradoxical mechanism of self-extinction: it strives to assert moral agency against the determinism of the naturalistic logic of society, but its criteria for authentic agency forces structure, order, and society into an oppositional and external system of domination.

Aspiring to essentialize and freeze a universally autonomous modern subject has consistently problematized forms of moral agency that link autonomy to complex relationality and attempt to specify identity as variable and historical. The consequences of this problematization in sociology are usually dizzying tautologies about "internalized social norms." When action is in the final analysis defined as internalized social norms, the meaning of action becomes "oversociologized," a mere reflection of a stage in a developing social order. In this, agency is detached from history, time, and space while remade by the restless momentum of changing social conditions. The autonomy of action cannot survive this ontology of the subject, which can only explain agency by recourse to the external social order. Deprived of substance, action can only be a response to collective constraint or internalizations.

Alternative conceptions of ontologies might include "ontological narrativity" and "narrative identity" (Somers 1992, 1994a; Somers and Gibson 1994). On the face of it nonsociological expressions, they are nevertheless concepts capacious and historically sensitive enough to capture the presence of contested meanings of the self and agency. Narrativity suggests identities are not formed by interests imputed from a stage of societal development (be it preindustrial or modern) or by "experience" imputed from a social category (such as artisan, peasant woman, or factory laborer) but by one's contingent "place" in cultural settings comprised of (breakable) rules, (variable) practices and discourses, binding (and unbinding) institutions. Narrativity makes action not an event but an *episode*—one that is shaped by both memory and anticipation. Narrativity also eliminates the notion that certain actions are rational while others are irrational or "backward-looking"; the contexts that give meaning, contingency, and historicity to identity have no teleology. If identities are historically constituted, we cannot define absolutely the nature of agency. Narrativity makes identities both malleable and contested but nonetheless only intelligible through the more challenging exploration of the intersection of agency and history.

Ways of Explaining: Causal Narrativity and the Context of Justification

I turn now to the third conundrum of *explaining*. The term *causal narrativity* denotes a form of explanation that detaches cause from its alliance with prediction and a priori logic and restores to it its core constituents—narrativity, sequence, temporality, and contingency. This could be called the temporality thesis (following Aminzade 1992; Quadagno and Knapp 1992; and Hall 1978) as well as the narrativity thesis (following Abbott 1992a,b; Abell 1987; Griffin 1992; and Somers 1992, 1994a) because of its emphasis not only on time but on space, narrative relationality, and causal emplotment more broadly. The problem being addressed here is how to bring historicity and temporality into the method itself.

What would we want from a causal explanation after an epistemological historic turn? To get at what we would want and need from an adequate historical method entails inverting many of the problems we have identified with the prevailing methods. We would want a method that can identify cause and at the same time account for sequence and contingency of history. It would be a method that would step out of the dichotomy between cause and meaning—insisting that meaning can be a cause and that cause can be meaningful. And it would have to be a method that also refused to participate in the either/or of general covering law versus "just random history." For the issue is not a dichotomy between generality and "storytelling" but whether a *historically intelligible explanation* can be found (Stinchcombe 1978, 13–17; White 1992, 65–115, 287–316; Steinmetz 1992; Somers 1992; Tilly 1984). With these criteria so distinct from those of the covering law position, we might also assume that the means of achieving them would also be quite the opposite from those of the traditional model. This is indeed the case. We would want to separate cause from law. It is the conflation of the two that has made cause so antithetical to those who would pursue historicity and meaning. Making this separation will allow us to see that from a different angle causality is inherently narrative and historical. It can account for patterns that nonetheless exist within frames of contingency and indetermination.

To elaborate, I return to the three modes of inquiry and strategies of justification (Skocpol and Somers 1980) discussed previously. In the absence of an alternative model of explanation, attempts to incorporate historicity remain vulnerable to the charges of "naive inductivist empiricism." This is the charge issued most vehemently by Kiser and Hechter (1991) in their recent attack on historical sociology. Their charge is directed especially at "analytic inductivism"—the method of building arguments from historical research using analytic concepts to organize evidence. They lambaste historical sociology for its lack of universality and for not being "bold" enough in its scope and propositions. Where are we to look for adequate responses to these reaffirmations of antihistorical definitions of explanation? The macroanalytic alternative has itself been unable to make temporality a constitutive part of its causal strategy—reverting instead to an interactive model of converging variables rather than a contingent process of narrative sequence (Abbott 1994; Sewell, this volume). The hermeneutic alternative, accepting uncritically the covering law's narrow definition of cause, not only refuses a method that excludes a place for meaning but also dismisses as a goal altogether any form of causal explanation. Indeed, it is arguable that none of the three modes are capable of accounting for sequence, temporality, and contingency while still adhering to an explanatory goal. In light of this apparent stalemate, let us once again turn to science's historic turn to search for a model for the challenge of constructing a narrative causality.

A New Historic Turn

In the last decade, a new historic turn in the epistemology of scientific method itself has begun to emerge from a corner of the philosophy and sociology of science as well as from practicing scientists. It is one that has much to offer both the social sciences and the humanities. Most prominently, Miller (1987), and Gould (1988, 1989), all to greater or lesser degrees of explicitness, have rejected the covering law definition of causality and taken up the challenge of defending the historicity of the explanatory process. The keystone of their argument is a renewed—one could say *reclaimed*—definition of *cause.* They insist on the analytic detachment of cause from prediction and law, and in so doing they have provided a model for historicizing social explanation.

In order to highlight the novelty of their arguments, let us look briefly at existing models of cause. Take any historical narrative about which we want to explain a pattern of events across cases—say, revolutions. The models we have now require setting up a general conditional proposition about revolutions that analyzes the necessary and sufficient conditions for a revolution to occur. That means, given *C,* then when *X* happens, *Y*—say, the French Revolution—will follow. There are two ways of arriving at this explanation: (*a*) from deduction; (*b*) from induction. What is wrong with these approaches? The first problem is that they cannot accommodate what is different about trying to understand historical events as opposed to experimental phenomenon. The revolutions occurred in a particular temporal-historical sequence: they followed or were built on an accumulation of past events. The interaction of the conditional variables, however, says nothing about this sequence. The narrativity of the phenomenon to be explained becomes residual to the superior importance of the simple presence or absence of crucial variables. In Gould's (1989) phrase, it assumes that if we "ran the tape backwards," as long as the same variables eventually came together, a revolution would occur. The reason why these uses of causality cannot cope with this crucial aspect of narrativity and sequence has to do with the fundamental defining feature of the method, that is, the necessity for generality and for cause to have a uniform logical structure outside of any particular circumstance that would limit its applicability or testability.

Narrativity is excluded precisely because of its necessary contingency. Abbott (1992a) has shown this in an analysis of "what do cases do" in standard sociological analysis. Taking apart a few studies, he demonstrates that the typical sociologist's case begins with "mere existence" and then is constructed out of the relevant properties assigned to it by the investigator. This is true whether the case is, for example, a biological individual or a state. He finds that in order for the causal variable relations to hold across cases, all the cases must follow only one narrative sequence (even if they in fact do not). Variable analysis, in this model, thus means sacrificing the narrative order on the assumption that sequence and order would not affect the causal explanation. In Abbott's words (1992a, 7), "cases are not complex entities whose character is simplified in this model, but characterless entities 'complexified' by the variables that assign properties to them." In one study, the sociologist takes the stories of how workmen's compensation developed in forty-eight states in the United States and transforms these forty-eight narratives into 960 independent, one-step narratives by analyzing each state's process of developing the policy at twenty different time periods. This means that what for a historical case is the state of Massachusetts in the years 1912, 1913, and 1914, for example, is treated by this historical sociologist as three different cases—Massachusetts in 1912 is one case, Massachusetts in 1913 another, and so on. Contrast this with a historian's discourse in which a case is defined by both geography and temporality. For the sociologist, however, that any given event was constitutively connected to the past events on which its very existence depended or was contingent is extraneous to the scientific method.

An additional feature of this approach forces historical cases into stasis. Social transformations may be the object of explanation, but the explanatory process consists in assigning enduring—and not changing—variables to the case. Contrast this with a historical case in which, as Abbott (1992a, 15) points out, a case that began as one category may end up being an instance of another: a state becomes a nation, a craft becomes a profession, and so on. Refusing transformation within the case itself—as opposed to being the object of explanation—is another aspect of the inability of the standard approach to account for contingency.

Causality after the historic turn would, therefore, first and foremost gain autonomy from a priori structure, conditional propositions, and the necessity of prediction. In the absence of this a priori logic, Miller (1987, 80–88) specifically suggests the notion of a "core conception" that contains some varieties of classes that count as causes but which can be extended through intermediate cases. An adequate causal description then becomes empirical depending on context, subject matter, and the given state of subject matter knowledge. That alternative can be found in Gould's (1988, 1989) notion of contingency as the essence of history, in Miller's (1987) notion of causality as historical, comparative, and antigeneral, and in Abbott's (1992b) idea of narrative positivism or Cartwright's (1983) notion of causal stories. Each of these represents different angles for getting outside the dichotomous bind of determinism, a priori general logic, cause as a subset of prediction on one end of the Manichean opposition, and randomness, particularism, and noncausal chance events on the other. By contrast, they each represent the argument that meaningful cause can be detected and meaningful patterns can be explained, but that outcomes cannot be predicted from explanations. Each step of the pattern "proceeds for cause," but no finale is prepatterned into that cause. A change in an early event will produce a very different pattern of sequence.

Stinchcombe (1978), Aminzade (1992), Quadagno and Knapp (1992), and Griffin (1992) each make the temporality thesis central to their historical epistemologies of causal explanation. Aminzade (1992) develops a conceptual vocabulary of the temporality thesis even further. Abbott (1983, 1984, 1988, 1992a, 1992b) argues that processes over time have been ignored by the fixation on variables. Camic (1989) and Alexander and Smith (1993) demonstrate causal narrativity in theoretical analysis. Camic (1989) transforms the epistemological edifice in which Parsonian theory has long been encased. No longer Parsons's Cartesian invention, the universalist content of his social theory emerges as the central plot in Camic's story of the original Parsonian "Charter." Alexander and Smith (1993) show us how models of relational discourse determine the interpretation of events—not the events or the variables intrinsically but the relational patterns among modes. They use causal narrativity to show over time how concepts about modernity change with the variation in the relationality among the discursive dimensions of the structural space.

What all of these approaches share is a concept of cause and a concomitant concept of theory that is shaped by a historical epistemology. The moral is that in science as well as in sociology and history an explanation that actually depicts causal mechanisms is always told in narrative form. It is a set of sentences with transitive verbs. Cause implies narrative—it exists at the boundary of theory and nature. Cause is historically and socially constructed—like narrative. The historical and temporal dimension of comparative history is thus as important as its comparative component, for it entails explanatory narrative. It is narrative because the explanation is embedded in time and moves through time. Indeed, the success of any explanation resides in its accounting for temporality, contingency, and sequence.

NOTES

This paper was written while I was supported in part as a visiting fellow in the Department of Sociology, Princeton University, 1989–90. I am grateful to Marvin Bressler for making that support possible. It was originally presented at the University of Michigan conference on "The Historic Turn in the Human Sciences," October 5–7, 1990. I thank Val Daniels and Michael Kennedy for being discussants, as well as members of the conference's audience. For their generous interventions and comments on earlier drafts (always appreciated if not fully heeded), I thank Art Stinchcombe—who contributed so generously and critically to my thinking that I am tempted to blame him for its shortcomings as well—as well as Andy Abbott, Ron Aminzade, Elizabeth Anderson, John Hall, Clifford Geertz, Gloria Gibson, Terry McDonald, Matthew Price, Howard Schuman, Marc Steinberg, and Mayer Zald. Finally, I am grateful to the spirited intellectual camaraderie of "The Historic Turn" subgroup of the Program in the Comparative Studies of Social Transformations (CSST) out of which this conference emerged and in which many of my ideas received a critical hearing: Nick Dirks, Geoff Eley, Steven Mullaney, Sherry Ortner, Bill Sewell, and above all, Terry McDonald, our convener and relentless nudger.

1. Since this essay was written, the situation has begun to change radically. See especially Abbott (1990, 1992a, 1992b), Aminzade (1992), Griffin (1992), Quadagno and Knapp (1992), and Wallerstein (1991).

2. This phrase is meant to evoke, but also to escape, the constricting and Manichean dichotomy between "theory-laden" and "empiricist/positivist" conceptions of science and social science, which frames the terms of controversy within most social science theory. This is developed at length in the text that follows.

3. The difference between the absolute notion of truth and the historical question of what can be conceived within a given epistemological frame as even a question of "true or false" originates in Heidegger 1977.

4. The degree to which parts of this story of historical sociology are parochial and "Harvard-centric" has been argued recently by Andrew Abbott (1994).

5. One of the greater ironies of the Social Science Research Council's series on modernization was that it culminated in Tilly's (1975) edited collection, *The Formation of National States,* a landmark work in signaling the demise of the functionalist approach.

6. Barrington Moore's (1966) comparative historical analysis of the varying routes to the "modern world" and E. P. Thompson's (1968) magisterial story of English workers were the two exemplary texts setting the terms for sociology's recent historic turn. By problematizing variation rather than assuming deviance or "lags," Moore demonstrated how comparative historical methodology could be used to address issues of social change and class analysis to a very different effect from that of modernization theory. E. P. Thompson provided a model for how a historical approach could challenge both vulgar Marxist and empiricist approaches to class analysis by restoring agency and consciousness to the historical actors themselves. See Skocpol's (1984) edited collection on historical sociology for the best discussion of these influences.

7. A version of this and the following paragraph appears in Somers and Gibson (1994).

8. The potency of the parable was not dependent on its lack of empirical validity. Condorcet passed it on to Malthus and Malthus to Darwin. Yet both owed the success of their theories in large part to the anti-institutional impact on social policy that Townsend enjoyed. His injunction that "legal constraint is attended with much trouble, violence and noise; creates ill will, and never can be productive of good and acceptable service: whereas hunger is not only peaceable, silent, unremitting pressure, but, [is] the most natural motive to industry and labor [and] lays lasting and sure foundations for good will and gratitude" spurred the repeal of the English Poor Laws which had long supported the poor in periods of unemployment (Polanyi [(1944) 1957], chap. 7–10).

9. Kuhn, as is well known, built on the previous work of Michael Polanyi, Norman Hanson, and Alexander Koyre. Why it was Kuhn whose work made the breakthrough into mass academic consciousness is a question for the sociology of knowledge.

10. Lakatos himself reconstructed Kuhn's account of paradigms and covering law conceptions to eliminate their incompatibilities and the "mob psychology" he attributed to Kuhn's view of scientists.

11. This does *not* mean he believed that natural entities themselves are socially constituted. Natural entities are real. Long after the *theory* of photons and electrons has been surpassed, supermarket doors will still be opening automatically thanks to whatever reality the concepts of "electrons" and "photons" now represent (Hacking [1983]).

12. Even though the well-known dispute between E. P. Thompson and Louis Althusser is technically a dispute between nonsociologists, their respective arguments have been imperfectly echoed by a number of prominent historical sociologists.

13. MacIntyre ([1980], 64) has suggested that this view of ontological ahistoricity would make empiricism a disease and paranoia a reasonable epistemology because only the latter has a conceptual framework ("the world is out to get me") through which to experience the world.

14. One of my favorite illustrations of this comes from MacIntyre ([1981], 88): "Charles II once invited the members of the Royal Society to explain to him why a dead fish weighs more than the same fish alive; a number of subtle explanations were offered to him. He then pointed out that it doesn't."

15. Many of Foucault's (1972, [1970] 1973) investigations, Tilly's ([1984], chap. 1– 3) and Wallerstein's (1991) discussions of nineteenth-century social science, Taylor's (1989) and MacIntyre's (1981) work on the construction of the self could all serve as exemplars. See also Hacking (1988) and Gusfield (1980).

16. The next three paragraphs draw from Somers and Gibson (1994).

REFERENCES

Abbott, Andrew. 1983. "Sequences of Social Events: Concepts and Methods in the Analysis of Order in Social Processes." *Historical Methods* 16:129–47.

Abbott, Andrew. 1984. "Events Sequence and Event Duration: Colligation and Measurement." *Historical Methods* 17:192–247.

Abbott, Andrew. 1988. "Transcending General Linear Reality." *Sociological Theory* 6:169–86.

Abbott, Andrew. 1990. "Conceptions of Time and Events in Social Science Methods: Causal and Narrative Approaches." *Historical Methods* 23(4):140–50.

Abbott, Andrew. 1992a. "What Do Cases Do? The Place of Activity in Sociological Analysis." In *What Is a Case?*, 53–82. Edited by Charles Ragin and Howard Becker. Cambridge: Cambridge University Press.

Abbott, Andrew. 1992b. "From Causes to Events: Notes on Narrative Positivism." *Sociological Methods and Research* 20(4):428–55.

Abbott, Andrew. 1994. "History and Sociology: The Lost Synthesis." In *Engaging the Past: The Uses of History across the Social Sciences,* 77–112. Edited by Eric Monkkonen. Durham, NC: Duke University Press.

Abell, Peter. 1987. *The Syntax of Social Life.* New York: Oxford University Press.

Alexander, Jeffrey. 1982. *Theoretical Logic in Sociology.* Vol. 1 of *Positivism, Presuppositions, and Current Controversies.* Berkeley and Los Angeles: University of California Press.

Alexander, Jeffrey. 1988. *Action and Its Environments.* New York: Columbia University Press.

Alexander, Jeffrey. 1989. *Structure and Its Meaning.* New York: Columbia University Press.

Alexander, Jeffrey. 1991. "Sociological Theory and the Claim to Reason: Why the End Is Not in Sight." *Sociological Theory* 9 (2): 147–53.

Alexander, Jeffrey, and Philip Smith. 1993. "The Discourse of American Civil Society: A New Proposal for Cultural Studies." *Theory and Society* 22:151–207.

Aminzade, Ron. 1992. "Historical Sociology and Time." *Sociological Methods and Research* 20(4):456–80.

Bossy, John. 1982. "Some Elementary Forms of Durkheim." *Past and Present* 95 (May): 3–18.

Burawoy, Michael. 1989. "Two Methods in Search of Science: Skocpol versus Trotsky." *Theory and Society* 18:759–806.

Calhoun, Craig. 1990. "What Social Theory Needs from History Now: Culture and Action as Problems for Historical Sociology." Paper presented at the conference, "The Historic Turn in the Human Sciences," University of Michigan, Ann Arbor, October.

Calhoun, Craig. 1991. "Morality, Identity, and Historical Explanation: Charles Taylor on the Sources of the Self." *Sociological Theory* 9(2): 232–63.

Camic, Charles. 1989. "Structure after 50 Years: The Anatomy of a Charter." *American Journal of Sociology* 95:38–107.

Carnap, Rudolf. 1966. *An Introduction to the Philosophy of Science.* Edited by Martin Gardner. New York: Basic Books.

Cartwright, Nancy. 1983. *How the Laws of Physics Lie.* Oxford: Clarendon Press.

Collingwood, R. G. [1939] 1970. *An Autobiography.* Oxford: Oxford University Press.

Foucault, Michel. [1970] 1973. *The Order of Things: An Archaeology of the Human Sciences.* New York: Vintage.

Foucault, Michel. 1972. *An Archaeology of Knowledge.* New York: Pantheon.

Geertz, Clifford. 1983. *Local Knowledge.* New York: Basic Books.

Gould, Stephen Jay. 1988. "Mighty Manchester." *New York Review of Books,* October 27.

Gould, Stephen Jay. 1989. *Wonderful Life.* Cambridge: Harvard University Press.

Gouldner, Alvin. 1970. *The Coming Crisis in Western Sociology.* New York: Basic Books.

Griffin, Larry. 1992. "Temporality, Events, and Explanation in Historical Sociology." *Sociological Methods and Research* 20:403–27.

Gusfield, Joseph. 1980. *The Culture of Public Problems.* Chicago: University of Chicago Press.

Gutting, Gary, ed. 1980. *Paradigms and Revolutions.* South Bend, IN: University of Notre Dame Press.

Hacking, Ian. 1982. "Language, Truth, and Reason." In *Rationality and Relativism,* 48–66. Edited by M. Hollis and S. Lukes. Cambridge: MIT Press.

Hacking, Ian. 1983. *Representing and Intervening.* Cambridge: Cambridge University Press.

Hacking, Ian. 1984. "Five Parables." In *Philosophy in History,* 103–24. Edited by Richard Rorty, J. B. Schneewind, and Quentin Skinner. Cambridge: Cambridge University Press.

Hacking, Ian. 1988. "The Sociology of Knowledge about Child Abuse." *Nous* 22:53–63.

Hacking, Ian. 1990. "Two Kinds of 'New Historicism' for Philosophers." *New Literary History* 21:343–64.

Hacking, Ian. 1990. *The Taming of Chance.* Cambridge: Cambridge University Press.

Hall, John R. 1978. *The Ways Out: Utopian Communal Groups in an Age of Babylon.* Boston: Routledge and Kegan Paul.

Heidegger, Martin. 1977. "The Essence of Truth." In *Heidegger: Basic Writings.* Edited by David F. Krell. New York: Harper and Row.

Hempel, C. G. [1942] 1959. "The Function of General Laws in History." In *Theories of History.* Edited by Patrick Gardiner. Reprint, New York: Free Press.

Hempel, C. G. 1965. *Aspects of Scientific Explanation.* New York: Free Press.

Hollis, Martin, and Steven Lukes, eds. 1982. *Rationality and Relativism.* Cambridge: MIT Press.

Hume, David. 1941. *Treatise of Human Nature.* Edited by L. A. Selby-Bigge. London: Oxford University Press.

Kiser, Edgar, and Michael Hechter. 1991. "The Role of General Theory in Comparative-Historical Sociology." *American Journal of Sociology* 97:1–30.

Kuhn, Thomas. [1962] 1970. *The Structure of Scientific Revolutions.* 2d ed. Chicago: University of Chicago Press.

Lakatos, Imre. 1970. "Falsification and the Methodology of Scientific Research Programmes." In *Criticism and the Growth of Knowledge,* 91–196. Edited by I. Lakatos and A. Musgrave. Cambridge: Cambridge University Press.

Latour, Bruno, and Steve Woolgar. 1979. *Laboratory Life: The Social Construction of Scientific Facts.* Beverly Hills: Sage Publications.

Longino, Helen. 1990. *Science as Social Knowledge.* Princeton: Princeton University Press.

MacIntyre, Alasdair. 1980. "Epistemological Crises, Dramatic Narrative and the Philosophy of Science." In *Paradigms and Revolutions,* 54–74. Edited by Gary Gutting. South Bend, IN: University of Notre Dame Press.

MacIntyre, Alasdair. 1981. *After Virtue: A Study in Moral Theory.* South Bend, IN: University of Notre Dame Press.

Miller, Richard. 1987. *Fact and Method.* Princeton: Princeton University Press.

Mills, C. W. 1959. *The Sociological Imagination*. London: Oxford University Press.

Moore, Barrington, Jr. 1966. *Social Origins of Dictatorship and Democracy: Lord and Peasant in the Making of the Modern World*. Boston: Beacon Press.

Moore, Barrington, Jr. 1978. *Injustice: The Sources of Obedience and Revolt*. Cambridge: Harvard University Press.

Pickering, Andy. 1984. *Constructing Quarks*. Edinburgh: Edinburgh University Press.

Polanyi, Karl. [1944] 1957. *The Great Transformation*. Boston: Beacon Press.

Popper, Karl. [1934] 1959. *The Logic of Scientific Discovery*. New York: Basic Books.

Quadagno, Jill, and Stanley J. Knapp. 1992. "Have Historical Sociologists Forsaken Theory?: Thoughts on the History/Theory Relationship." *Sociological Methods and Research* 20(4):481–507.

Ragin, Charles. 1987. *The Comparative Method*. Berkeley and Los Angeles: University of California Press.

Reichenbach, Hans. 1947. *Experience and Prediction*. Chicago: University of Chicago Press.

Schuman, Howard. 1981. *Questions and Answers in Attitude Surveys*. New York: Academic Press.

Sewell, William H., Jr. 1985. "Ideologies and Social Revolutions: Reflections on the French Case." *Journal of Modern History* 57:57–85.

Shapin, Steven, and Simon Schaffer. 1986. *Leviathan and the Air Pump: Hobbes, Boyle, and the Experimental Life*. Princeton: Princeton University Press.

Skocpol, Theda. 1979. *States and Social Revolutions: A Comparative Analysis of France, Russia, and China*. New York: Cambridge University Press.

Skocpol, Theda. 1984. "Emerging Agendas and Recurrent Strategies in Historical Sociology." In *Vision and Method in Historical Sociology*, 356–91. Edited by Theda Skocpol. New York: Cambridge University Press.

Skocpol, Theda. 1985. "Cultural Idioms and Political Ideologies in the Revolutionary Reconstruction of State Power: A Rejoinder to Sewell." *Journal of Modern History* 57:86–96.

Skocpol, Theda, and Margaret Somers. 1980. "The Uses of Comparative History in Macrosocial Inquiry." *Comparative Studies in Society and History* 22:174–97.

Smelser, Neil. 1976. *Comparative Methods in the Social Sciences*. Englewood Cliffs, NJ: Prentice-Hall.

Somers, Margaret R. 1989. "Workers of the World, Compare!" *Contemporary Sociology* 18:325–30.

Somers, Margaret R. 1992. "Narrativity, Narrative Identity, and Social Action: Rethinking English Working-Class Formation." *Social Science History* 16:591–630.

Somers, Margaret R. 1994a. "Narrative and the Constitution of Identity: A Relational and Network Approach." *Theory and Society* 23:605–50.

Somers, Margaret R. 1994b. "Rights, Relationality, and Membership: Rethinking the Making and Meaning of Citizenship." *Law and Social Inquiry* 19:63–112.

Somers, Margaret R., and Gloria D. Gibson. 1994. "Reclaiming the Epistemological

'Other': Narrative and the Social Constitution of Identity." In *Social Theory and the Politics of Identity*, 37–99. Edited by Craig Calhoun. Oxford: Basil Blackwell.

Steinmetz, George. 1992. "Reflections on the Role of Social Narratives in Working-Class Formation: Narratives and Social Sciences." *Social Science History* 16:489–516.

Stinchcombe, Arthur L. 1978. *Theoretical Methods in Social History.* New York: Academic Press.

Taylor, Charles. 1989. *Sources of the Self.* Cambridge: Harvard University Press.

Thompson, C. P. 1968. *The Making of the English Working Class.* New York: Vintage.

Tilly, Charles. 1984. *Big Structures, Large Processes, Huge Comparisons.* New York: Russell Sage.

Tilly, Charles. 1993. "The Times of States." Center for Studies of Social Change Working Paper No. 172, New School for Social Research, New York.

Tilly, Charles, ed. 1975. *The Formation of National States in Western Europe.* Princeton: Princeton University Press.

Vallier, Ivan, ed. 1974. *Comparative Methods in Sociology.* Berkeley and Los Angeles: University of California Press.

Wallerstein, Immanuel. 1974. *The Modern World System.* Vol. 1. New York: Academic Press.

Wallerstein, Immanuel. 1991. *Unthinking Social Science: The Limits of Nineteenth-Century Paradigms.* Cambridge, UK: Polity Press.

White, Harrison C. 1992. *Identity and Control: A Structural Theory of Social Action.* Princeton: Princeton University Press.

Zald, Mayer. 1990. "Sociology as a Discipline: Quasi-Science and Quasi-Humanities." *The American Sociologist* 22(3–4):165–87.

Zeldich, Morris, Jr. 1974. "Intelligible Comparisons." In *Comparative Methods in Sociology*, 276–307. Edited by Ivan Vallier. Berkeley: University of California Press.

What We Talk about When We Talk about History: The Conversations of History and Sociology

Terrence J. McDonald

Introduction

As the epigraph for his enormously influential 1949 book *Social Theory and Social Structure* Robert K. Merton selected Alfred North Whitehead's statement that "a science which hesitates to forget its founders is lost." And both history and sociology have been struggling with the implications of that statement ever since. On the one hand, it was the belief that it was possible to forget one's "founders" that galvanized the social scientists (including historians) of Merton's generation to reinvent their disciplines. But on the other hand, it was the hubris of that view that ultimately undermined the disciplinary authority that they set out to construct, for in the end neither their propositions about society nor epistemology could escape from history.

Social and ideological conflict in American society undermined the correspondence between theories of consensus and latent functions and the "reality" they sought to explain. The belief in a single, scientific, transhistorical road to cumulative knowledge was assaulted by theories of paradigms and incommensurability. Marxist theory breached the walls of both idealism and the ideology of scientific neutrality only to be overrun, in its turn, by the hordes of "posts": postpositivism, postmodernism, post-Marxism, poststructuralism, and so on. In the deepest irony of all, many today believe that the oasis of epistemological peace shimmering on the horizon may be . . . history.

We work now in the twilight—but by no means the complete absence—of the authorities of that generation of historians and sociologists. Their inevitably timebound version of reality—both social and epistemological—is crumbling. The complaints of those who believe that the social sciences are losing their grip on "reality" are almost right: a certain version of reality containing propositions about society, history, and epistemology, is losing its grip on us. But we are still working today within, not beyond, the disciplinary relationships, both intellectual and institutional, constructed in that epoch. The deep interrelationships between all the disciplines reinvented in America after World War Two retain much power. For example, our referents for "sociology" or "history" and the metaphors of our own interdisciplinary projects—turns, boundaries, the attempt to "talk across" disciplines, to avoid the "retreat behind disciplinary walls," and the like—exist not in some transhistorical space but in the knowledge of disciplines and their interrelationships constructed in this era. It is only because of this shared knowledge of what these disciplines "are" that we can now talk about work that is "interdisciplinary," "multidisciplinary," or "metadisciplinary."

But this preexisting relationship is doubled edged. For while it permits us to talk it also tends to maintain the conversation within the safe boundaries of preexisting discourse. Should historians use theory? Should sociologists do archival research? These questions—and others like them focusing on issues of practice—have dominated the discourse between history and sociology because they protect and do not destabilize the currently operative relationship between these disciplines. Although these discussions are carried out with much heat at times—both within and across the disciplines—they serve only to prevent discussion of two more dangerous questions: shall history become an object of theory? Shall sociology become an object of history?

This essay proposes that particular but not obvious kinds of atheoretical history and ahistorical sociology sprang from the same post–World War Two moment in American intellectual history. The constitution of history as a discipline that borrowed theory saved it from the responsibility and potentially destabilizing effects of producing theory. Historians were authorized to borrow theory from sociology (and other disciplines) but not to generate, or even initially discuss, theory themselves. The constitution of sociology as a cumulating "science" developing theory for all times and places prevented that discipline from recognizing the historical contingency of its own discourse. Sociologists were able to use history (it is not correct to say borrow it) as long as they did not allow sociology itself to become an object of history. The condition of transformation, assuming that such is desired, is that each discipline embrace its deepest fear, that history accept the potentially destabilizing threat of theory and sociology accept the potentially destabilizing threat of history. But it is the advocates of interdisciplinary work themselves who, in maintaining these relationships in the way that they have been structured, fail to recognize this and thus prevent such transformation.[1]

To make this argument, I will examine, in turn, history's construction of its relationship with sociology and sociology's construction of its relationship with history. In the case of the former, my argument will be based on an analysis of statements about social science and history by historians as well as a case study of the sources of theory in one of the most important of the joint ventures between history and sociology, the so-called new urban and social history. In the case of the latter, I will similarly examine the historical context for and contents of statements about history in sociology, focusing in particular on a case study of the leading sources of historical theory in forty-eight articles by sociologists on historical sociology published between 1957 and 1990.

History's Sociology

In the years following World War Two, history drank deeply of the elixir of the new. Many of its leading figures identified themselves increasingly with the social sciences and with the help of the Social Science Research Council (SSRC) historians embarked on a highly successful transformation of their own discipline that would involve the demolition of the old scientific approach to history (with its view of a relatively unmediated relationship with the facts) and its replacement by a version of a new scientific approach to history (paralleling that of Merton and his counterparts in the social sciences), within which middle-range theory mediated the relationship between the historian and the facts both as source of hypotheses and guarantor of "objectivity."

At the level of epistemology, this transformation resulted in a permanent separation between the "actual" past, the "recorded" past, and the "written" past. At the level of historiography, this change ultimately produced a spate of "new" histories—for example, the "new" urban, labor, political, family, women's, and so on—that exploded into prominence in the 1960s and 1970s and that shared a theoretical orientation, some methodological sophistication, and a claim to be doing history "from the bottom up."

Most commentaries on these changes have failed to understand the connection between the first and the second, and have, therefore, misconstrued the second as essentially a methodological—not theoretical—change (Higham 1983; Novick 1988). In reality, the turn to the social sciences was not primarily methodological because it was necessitated by the destabilizing effects of the epistemological separation noted previously. Once the unmediated search for facts was attacked, both the danger of relativism and the prestige of science convinced many historians that it was time to look to the social sciences for a model of the disciplining role of theory. Advocates of this new relationship between history and social science rarely mentioned method. But they did not advocate a full-fledged relationship with theory either. In order for theory to do the job that was expected of it historians were to remain inferior to theory-producing disciplines. They were urged, therefore, to borrow theory but not to produce it or even understand it well.[2]

However, the necessity for a disciplining role for theory was far from the minds of Charles Beard and his allies as they wrote the text for the 1946 report of the SSRC's Committee on Historiography, *Theory and Practice in Historical Study*. Indeed, the report made only fleeting reference to the social sciences at all, noting that "significant advances in making the most comprehensive historical generalizations will require the close and constant cooperation of specialists in historical work with specialists in the social sciences and humanities," but also calling for coordination of the work of historians with the physical and biological sciences (SSRC 1946, 139–40).

Beard and his allies had other goals in mind. The first of these was to convince the historical profession of the tripartite distinction between history as actuality, as record, and as text, and the second was to put forward a theory of change in the text. At the very opening of the report, Beard laid down the definitions that would inform it. "History as actuality" referred to "all that has been felt, thought, imagined, said, and done by human beings as such. . . ," while "history as record" was "the documents and memorials pertaining to history-as-actuality on which written-history is or should be based." "History-as-written," therefore, became "the systematic or fragmentary narration or account purporting to deal with all or part of this history-as-actuality" (SSRC 1946, 5).

These separations between "history" as actuality, as record, and as text were repeated in the chapter on "Controlling Assumptions in the Practice of American Historians" and were further strengthened in the chapter on "Problems of Terminology," written by the philosopher Sidney Hook. Because of them, there was no history without what the report called a "frame of reference," which Hook defined "loosely" as "the set of principles which guides [the historian] in the selection of his problem, the organization of his materials, and the evaluation of his findings." The key question for historians, then, was how and why these frames of reference changed. The answer that the volume proposed through both its descriptive and prescriptive sections was a functional one. Historians wrote within a context "of a problem faced by men [in the present], of the causes of that problem, the means for its solution, and the course actually adopted." The frame of reference for history had been and always would be "functional" for the present. This argument was supported by an analysis purporting to demonstrate that changes in historiography in the twentieth century were brought about by the changing social and political agendas of American society, with, for example, the history of Turner and Beard influenced by the progressive reform movement, that of the 1930s by the "problems of capitalistic development," and that of the postwar years to be affected by a changed international situation (SSRC 1946, 5, 19, 51, 125).

The storm of protest that greeted this volume—amply treated by Peter Novick in his 1988 volume on American historiography, *That Noble Dream*— dealt primarily with this essentially political-functional and avowedly "presentist" theory of historiographical change, not the differences between history as actuality, record, and text. (Although because the report had both destabilized the fact/framework issue and offered this theory of change in the framework they were at times confused.) While most historians understood this difference—in theory at least—few were willing to surrender their ability to reconstruct the past "as it really was" to the claim that their frames of reference for doing this were fatally compromised by their presentist origins. The question that this report raised among its critics was, given this separation between history as actuality, record, and text, could there be a more disciplined source for these frames of reference?

The 1954 report of the SSRC's historiography committee (with mostly new membership) offered an argument that was to last for almost thirty years in its claim that social science theory would provide a stable—indeed "scientific"— source of ideas for these frames. This volume was the first of what would grow to be a large number of works by advocates of the social sciences in history published in the 1950s and 1960s, including, besides the SSRC volumes (1946, 1954, 1963), volumes of essays on the topic edited by Edward Saveth (1964) and Seymour Martin Lipset and Richard Hofstadter (1968) and other essays and volumes by H. Stuart Hughes (1960), Thomas Cochran (1964), and Robert F. Berkhofer Jr. (1969). These authors and volumes disagreed on many things, including, for example, how many and how much historians would use social science theory and methods, whether history should become a social science or merely use social science theory to clarify its generalizations, and whether the use of social science theory was simply to be an antidote to the "Beardian relativism" of the 1946 SSRC volume or the route to a cumulative historical knowledge gathered according to scientific principles. But they also agreed on many things, including the rejection of the Baconian belief that synthesis would emerge from the "facts," the priority of theory over method in the relationship between history and the social sciences, the role of theory as a guarantor of objectivity, the necessity and desirability of historians importing rather than generating theory, the preference for middle-range over "grand" theory, and the irrelevance of Marxism to this entire enterprise. A brief review of these areas of agreement will reveal the way in which historians helped to structure an essentially atheoretical relationship with the social sciences.

The rejection of Baconianism was an assumption so deeply rooted in these works that it was seldom given much consideration. Just as the 1946 volume of the SSRC committee denounced the view that historians could indefatigably collect "facts," the section on "objectivity, certainty, and values" in the 1954 report declared that "no one now supposes that past history in its totality is recoverable, and few believe that 'the facts speak for themselves'" (SSRC 1954, 19). Similarly, in 1969 Berkhofer admiringly quoted Carl Becker's condemnation of the old scientific history as "expecting to obtain final answers to life's riddles by absolutely refusing to ask questions— . . . the oddest attempt ever made to get something for nothing" (Berkhofer 1969, 23).

It was this belief in large part that steered these commentators away from discussion of method and toward theory. Obsession with method, after all, could become just another more sophisticated kind of Baconianism. More important were the sources and types of theory that would help to carry history beyond Baconianism. Faithfully reflecting the pecking order of the philosophy of science of their time, these authors agreed that history was not yet a science and, therefore, not yet capable of generating theory or even, for that matter, cumulative knowledge. For this reason, as H. Stuart Hughes put it, their works cast the historian "in a comparatively humble role—as a learner sitting at the feet of his colleagues in the social sciences" (Hughes 1960).

The 1954 report of the SSRC committee on historiography was the locus classicus of this approach. The report declared that history as social science "rests on the postulate that history can be more than entertainment and more than ideology" and that theory was the route beyond both. On the one hand, it was only via theory that history too could become a cumulative science. "It is," the report declared, "the use of theory that permits us to hope that in history, as in other sciences, the results of research may become increasingly cumulative." As importantly, on the other hand, it was theory that guaranteed objectivity. Contrary to what is sometimes believed by those "outside the scientific disciplines," the report declared that "a set of interrelated hypotheses is the best check against unconscious bias." Indeed, without such an explicit scheme, "the data are likely to be subconsciously selected, or catalogued on the basis of implicit or surreptitious assumptions not subject to a conscious process of analysis and rectification." Because of this, it was a high priority for this

report—and later commentaries—that "principles of selection and interpretation . . . be rationally chosen and rationally established; by making the theories
upon which it is based explicit and open to objective appraisal" (SSRC 1954,
90).

To facilitate this use of theory, the report's central section was a review of
"concepts and viewpoints in the social sciences" that might be useful to historians. This was a chapter by historian Thomas Cochran on the state of the
theoretical art in anthropology, sociology, demography, social psychology,
political science, and economics that still repays reading. However, the limits
of Cochran's plan for historical social science that were implicit in this Cook's
tour of theory were explicit in his opening declaration that "A little knowledge
may be a dangerous thing, but it is a necessary thing for the general historian"
(SSRC 1954, 34–85).

Indeed it was. For a generation that believed, as Berkhofer would write in
1969, that the "theoretical conceptions prevalent in his own society" define the
"limits of the historian's objectivity" a "little knowledge" might have even
been better than more (Berkhofer 1969, 25). Because the goal was a stabilized,
objective history, not a theorized history, a deeper encounter with theory might
have been counterproductive for it would inevitably have revealed the disputes
over theory that raged in some of the disciplines. Nowhere in the volume were
historians encouraged to test theory or even attempt to understand it thoroughly. Cochran noted somewhat lamely that "if the reader is not quite sure
that he understands the meaning of the terms and concepts mentioned in this
chapter, he is in no worse situation than other social scientists. Even leading
scholars in disciplines as closely related as sociology and social psychology
find difficulty in precise communication" (SSRC 1954, 34, 83).

One of the most popular guides to this relationship between history and
social science theory, the essay on "The Historian and the Social Scientist" by
H. Stuart Hughes that was published in the *American Historical Review* in
1960, suggested even less engagement. Hughes accepted wholeheartedly the
view that history would take its theory from other disciplines: "since history
has no generalizations of its own—since the only specifically historical
category is that of time sequence—it must necessarily borrow its intellectual
rationale from elsewhere." However, the way to apply this theory was quite
different in Hughes's scheme. For Hughes, even the phrase *application of
theory* was "too immediate and too concrete" to describe accurately what the
historian may most profitably do with the insights of his fellow workers in the
social sciences. He continued:

In many cases, perhaps in a majority of cases, he does not really "apply" them at all. He lets them remain in the back of his mind, without bringing them explicitly into the foreground of his historical writing. He does not parade his knowledge of social science theory; he simple permits his thought to be informed by it. To the unpracticed eye, his prose may remain just as untheoretical as in the past. But the new type of knowledge he has absorbed will actually have worked subterranean alterations in his whole mode of thought and expression. (Hughes 1960, 34)

There were those in this camp who disagreed with Hughes, most prominently David Potter in his contribution to the 1963 SSRC volume *Generalization in the Writing of History,* "Explicit Data and Implicit Assumptions in Historical Study." For Potter, the approach recommended by Hughes was precisely the use of "implicit theory" that he criticized. But the more frequent references to Hughes than to Potter among historians tell a tale of retrenchment along this front that was broader than just the essay by Hughes. The 1963 SSRC volume itself had pulled back considerably from the great expectations of the one in 1954, admitting that there were only some historians—the report called them the "theoretical historians"—who would use social science theory anyway and concluding weakly that "historians borrow ready-made generalizations whether they know it or not. If they were to borrow them knowingly, they might be in a stronger intellectual position" (SSRC 1963, 178–95, 209).

One source from which historians were not to borrow, though, was Marx. The utility of Marxism was so thoroughly discredited in the SSRC volumes that it was rarely even mentioned as a source for theoretical borrowing outside of them. In the 1954 report, Marxism was not classified as social theory at all but discussed along with a variety of conceptions and "misconceptions" of historical change, including evolutionary or theological theories and the works of Toynbee and Spengler (works already notorious among historians as merely speculative "philosophies of history"). According to this report, the Marxist interpretation lacked validity because of its "limited purview of operative forces and the factual fallacy in the labor theory of value." The "complex windings of Marxian dogma" did not result in cumulative knowledge "because it is of first importance in Marxian dialectics that each new proposition asserted to be true must be logically consistent with the words of the master; it is a secondary consideration whether or not the words have any empirical validity" (SSRC 1954, 140).

In the only essay in the 1963 volume that mentioned Marxism in general— that by William Aydelotte—Marx remained lodged among the "a priori" system-builders of the type with whom theoretically inclined historians were loath to be identified. Aydelotte was at some pains to distinguish the generalizations he urged upon historians from those of Toynbee, Spengler, and Marx, which some historians mistakenly confused as generalizations. While declaring that he did not advocate "ignoring the larger questions relating to the structure of society and politics that have always fascinated men," Aydelotte nonetheless argued that "the restriction of objectives, in history and the other social sciences, may be a sign not of degeneration, but of maturity." For him, as for so many of his generation, the preference was for those "middle-range" theoretical procedures recommended by sociologist Robert Merton (SSRC 1963, 145–77).

This reluctance to engage with theory—or even to recognize a broader menu of theory—has often been ascribed to the essentially atheoretical and methodological relationship between history and sociology. In this argument, theory was downplayed because historians—atheoretical to begin with—were really interested in the method of the social sciences. But this view is contradicted by analysis of the actual use of social science literature by the most popular and widespread of the "new" histories—the "new" urban and social history. For an earlier study, I undertook an analysis of every citation outside of history in 140 works (113 articles and 27 books) of American urban history published from 1940 through 1985. This has netted 1,543 such citations for analysis that reveal that this encounter between history and the social sciences was broad-based, overwhelmingly theoretical, primarily sociological, mostly middle range, and, unsurprisingly, only minimally Marxist.[3]

Of the 113 essays analyzed for this project only 16 (14 percent) contained no references to works outside of history while 71 (63 percent) had three or more. Only 39 (2.5 percent) of the 1,543 citations were explicitly methodological, and of these 39 the majority had to do with demographic calculations. Similarly, there were only 44 (2.9 percent) citations of the works of Marx or Marxists among all of these, and the bulk of those came after 1980, 24 in a 1983 collection of essays alone. However, the lack of attention to Marx himself was symptomatic of a broader turn away from most classical social theory and toward the "middle-range" theory under construction in the years after World War Two. References to almost all works of classical social theory begin to die out in these citations after about 1963, and only about 20 percent of all these citations were to works of any author published before 1950, classical social theorist or otherwise. Table 1, which lists the most frequently cited authors, reveals an overwhelmingly sociological bias with a special attention to—not surprisingly—urban sociology. But it also reveals the popularity of some of the

TABLE 1. Authors Cited Nine or More Times in Works of Urban History

Leo Schnore[a]	36
Robert Park[a]	28
Otis Duncan[a]	26
Louis Wirth	25
Lewis Mumford	18
Gideon Sjoberg	18
W. Lloyd Warner[a]	17
Adna Weber	17
Seymour Lipset[a]	16
Herbert Gans[a]	15
Robert Dahl	14
Robert and Helen Lynd	14
Brian Berry[a]	12
Amos Hawley	12
Max Weber	12
Robert Merton	11
Ernest Burgess	10
Stanley Lieberson	10
Homer Hoyt	9
C. Wright Mills	9

[a]Author or coauthor.

most important theorists of the middle range writing in the 1950s and 1960s, for example, Merton, Lipset, and political scientist Robert Dahl.

There was, however, almost no commentary on this theoretical development within the field. What was invoked instead of the authority of theory was the authority of the theory-producing discipline that produced it. In a famous article "introducing" urban "ecological" theory to the field of urban history, historian Eric Lampard devoted exactly one paragraph to exposition of the theory, noting that it was actually developed in sociology and was, therefore, "already at hand" (Lampard 1961, 60). When in 1967 Charles Tilly lamented that "no one [among urban historians] listens" to Lampard, he got it wrong, as table 1 reveals (Tilly 1967, 103, 104). Almost everyone was "listening" to urban sociological theory, ecological or otherwise.

The problem for historians was that no one was talking back to theory. Of more than forty essays on the state of the field of urban history published between 1963 and 1985, less than half even mentioned theory and only two produced very searching analyses of any part of it. As the rate of almost two definitional essays per year reveals, historians attempted obsessively to define and redefine the field on the terrain of historiography. But the problem went deeper than historiography because, whether they admitted it or not, the field was, to a great extent, theory driven.

One result of the inability to confront theory was a failure to rethink the relationship between history and sociology. Even the advocates of this convergence on the history side offered little that was new. The 1954 report of the SSRC committee boldly declared that the relationship between history and the social sciences was not to be merely "one-way" because historians could "teach much as well" (SSRC 1954, 16). But there were no sections on the contribution of historians to social science. Stephan Thernstrom offered little more than this in one of the very few essays by a historian ever published in the *American Sociological Review,* his 1965 essay "Yankee City Revisited: The Perils of Historical Naivete." Thernstrom pointed out rightly that communication between history and sociology had been "in the form of a monologue; with history on the receiving end." But his own article did little to challenge that relationship because the not unimportant brunt of his lengthy critique of W. Lloyd Warner's studies of Newburyport was that Warner didn't have his facts straight. Rather than proposing a new relationship between history and sociology, Thernstrom reinforced the old wherein sociology dealt with the theory and history with the facts. The choice that Thernstrom offered sociologists regarding history was identical to that offered in the 1964 report of the SSRC to historians regarding theory. According to Thernstrom, the student of contemporary society was not "free to take his history or leave it alone. . . . The real choice is between explicit history, based on careful examination of the sources, and implicit history, rooted in ideological preconceptions and uncritical acceptance of local mythology" (Thernstrom 1965).

For their part, allies on the sociology side offered little more than backhanded encouragement. Leo Schnore's important 1975 essay on "Urban History and the Social Sciences: An Uneasy Marriage" in the *Journal of Urban History* offered one paragraph under the subheading "Historians Can Help the Social Scientist" and eight-and-a-half pages on how "Historians May Benefit from Exposure to the Social Scientist." The subject of the one paragraph was the infamous—and, as Schnore admitted, essentially vacuous—notion of "historical perspective" (Schnore 1975, 398).

This passive and ultimately untenable role for the historian vis-à-vis the social sciences brought with it two positive—if unintended—consequences: a sharpened sense of disciplinary self-consciousness and greatly lowered boundaries between history and the other disciplines. By continuously attempting to resolve the theoretical problems of history on the terrain of historiography historians never lost a sense of the construction of their discipline in history. History is today, therefore, one of the most historically self-conscious of the disciplines thanks, in large part, to a series of theory-generated transformations of the discipline. Similarly, while it was wrong to engage theory too deeply, at the level of borrowing "everything was permitted." Historians have therefore continued to borrow massively from other disciplines, and their sources of theory have spread far beyond sociology into anthropology, literary theory, feminist studies, cultural studies, ethnic studies, and elsewhere.

Neither this heightened sense of history, however, nor this broadened base of borrowing can overturn the long-standing—and by now quite comfortable—relationship of inferiority between history and the social sciences. Historians did not fail to develop a discourse about theory because they were ignorant of it, opposed to it, or dumbfounded by it but because their relationship with theory was initiated in order to provide stability and prestige in a time of dangerous relativism. If to engage theory means to change this relationship, the silence may remain deafening.

Sociology's History

In the late 1930s the SSRC attempted to encourage interdisciplinary dialogue by selecting six leading works of social science that it then submitted to interdisciplinary panels for evaluation. To read the published transcripts of the discussions of these evaluation committees in the SSRC series *Critiques of Research in the Social Sciences* is to eavesdrop on the founding conversation about modern work across the disciplines, including history and sociology. The importance of this conversation for our purposes is that it reveals an attitude toward history in the social sciences generally and among sociologists in particular that would remain prevalent, in spite of dramatic changes in historical practice, down to the present day.

From history the SSRC selected for analysis historian Walter Prescott Webb's book *The Great Plains,* which had been published in 1931. The committee assigned another western historian, Fred Shannon, to prepare a critique that the committee would then discuss. Shannon produced two hundred pages of empirical criticism that included such things as the complaint that Webb's description of jackrabbit hunting was inadequate. Webb was so enraged by the evaluation and discussion of his work that he denied at the end that the book was a work of "history" at all. Much of the discussion by the interdisciplinary panel that met in September 1939 revolved around the proper relationship between facts and theory—or as it was referred to in the discussions, generalizations, hypotheses, or frames of reference. The evaluation committee included such giants of the social sciences of that epoch as Louis Wirth from sociology, Robert Redfield from anthropology, and Arthur M. Schlesinger and Roy Nichols from history, both of whom were strong allies of interdisciplinary work in history (SSRC 1940).

The historians on the committee clearly worked to minimize the bitterness between Webb and Shannon, and thus improve the potential reception of the exercise among historians, by adopting the position that there was room in the profession for all "types" of historians. Historian John D. Hicks argued that historians fell into two categories, "those who are interested in the woods as a whole and those who are interested in the trees, leaf by leaf." While each group antagonized the other, there would always be such divisions among historians (SSRC 1940, 192).

Wirth, in particular, however, held out for a more rigorous specification of the relationship between "facts" and "generalization" across all categories of history. According to Wirth, what historians, whether of the forest or trees, often failed to realize was that "facts are made; they are not just found." "You cannot just look the world in the face and expect to discover a fact," Wirth argued, because facts "are always made in the light of some hypotheses." Failure to recognize this relationship between facts and hypotheses was what Wirth identified as the major problem for historians: they "are not explicitly aware of the theories upon which they proceed and therefore naively conclude that they have none" (SSRC 1940, 189, 187).

Yet Wirth's own understanding of the relationship between facts and generalizations in general led him to send somewhat mixed messages to historians. At one point in the discussion he declared that "what we want, first of all, from the historians is authentic facts. Whether historians should generalize is a very complicated question. Their best service to social science, I think, is actually digging up the facts—bricks out of which some theoretic structure (generalization) may arise." Yet at another point he reminded them that historians, too, must work within a "frame of reference" to find the facts: "I hope historians will stick to the facts. Their concern should be to give us the facts—accurate, reliable facts. I realize, however, that nobody can get facts unless he has some frame of reference within which those facts appear" (SSRC 1940, 193).

As we have seen, historians themselves took up Wirth's call for the collection of "facts" within frames of reference beginning in 1946. Searching both for "science" and "objectivity," they borrowed massively from the social sciences—especially sociology—and transformed historical practice. Indeed, the works of the "new" urban and social history, while not producing a discourse on theory among historians, nonetheless effectively ended the epoch of purely "historical fact." Today in most subfields of history there are few "historical" facts that have not already been infused by (often sociological) theory.

But there has been little recognition of this momentous transformation in historical practice among sociologists supposedly friendly toward history. Thirty years after Wirth, during the high tide of history's construction of its sociology one of the major bridge figures in this effort, Seymour Martin Lipset, would make almost the same point as Wirth:

> History must be concerned with the analysis of the particular set of events or processes. Where the sociologist looks for concepts which subsume a variety of particular descriptive categories, the historian must remain close to the actual happenings and avoid statements which, though linking behavior at one time or place to that elsewhere, lead to a distortion in the description of what occurred in the set of circumstances being analyzed. (Lipset 1968, 23)

Even critics of Lipset's division of "theory" for sociology and "facts" for history have tended to reproduce similar distinctions between history and sociology. In one of the most frequently cited—and most thoughtful— discussions of the encounter between history and sociology, Charles Tilly's 1981 book *As Sociology Meets History,* Tilly rejects Lipset's division in prin- ciple but then reproduces it in his description of disciplinary practices. He notes, for example, that the authors analyzed by Arthur Stinchcombe in *Theo- retical Methods in Social History* are not "archive-mongering professional his- torians" and contrasts the effort of sociologists to "bring data to bear on two conflicting hypotheses" with the historian's imitation of the procedure of the "literary critic: moving . . . from reinterpretation to reinterpretation," with each reinterpretation producing "a new understanding of the place, time phenome- non, and underlying question under study" (Tilly 1981, 25). More recently, Theda Skocpol has similarly contrasted the "interpretive" sociology of a Clif- ford Geertz or an E. P. Thompson with the "analytical" sociology that she prac- tices. The former has the virtues of a "good Flaubert novel," while her brand of work analyzes the "facts" in search of "causal regularities" (Skocpol 1984).

According to Tilly, "an analysis is historical to the extent that the place and time of the action enter into its explanations." But for almost fifty years now, the "place and time of the action" between history and sociology have seemed irrelevant to sociological commentators on it. Why is it that sociologists repro- duce this "frozen" image of historical practice? The answer to this question requires analysis of sociology's experience with historical analysis and the theoretical sources for its construction of "history." But it also requires consideration of an issue that few advocates of historical sociology have considered: sociology's deep fear of becoming, itself, an object of history. For just as historians feared and avoided the destabilizing effects of a discourse around theory, sociologists have feared the threat from their own history, from the moment when their discourse of "science," " cause," "variable," and "analysis" is revealed, in its turn, to be historically contingent.

For all of the recent talk about sociology's "historical imagination," the discipline's encounter with history has, not surprisingly, been both relatively minimal and relatively recent. A survey of specialities of members of the American Sociological Association in 1959 (almost half of whom received their degrees before 1950) revealed only 0.2 percent who listed first a speciality in historical sociology or social history (Simpson 1961). And this lack of interest was reflected in articles published in the field's major journals. Analysis of the tables of contents for every year of the *American Journal of Sociology* (*AJS*) from 1895-96 through 1990-91 and the *American Sociological Review* (*ASR*) from 1936-37 through 1990-91 reveals a total of only thirteen articles in the former and eleven in the latter on the relationship between history and sociology and only ninety-five articles in the former and fifty-four in the latter with historical content. In the *AJS,* articles with historical content averaged about 5.5 percent of the total annually; in the *ASR* about 6.6 percent. In the *ASR,* this annual average is consistently above the mean only after the 1975-76 volume and in the *AJS* only after 1978-79. In the American case, at least, it is incorrect to say that sociology is rediscovering the "past," unless that means the past twenty years.[4]

Similarly, the sources upon which sociology is constructing its "history" are both relatively recent and overwhelmingly sociological. In table 2 I have listed (in order of frequency of citation) the authors of the most frequently cited (i.e., nine or more citations) sources of theory (of history and otherwise) in forty-eight programmatic essays by sociologists on historical sociology or history and sociology published between 1957 and 1990. The recentness of the references is explained by the recent appearance of most of the articles (listed in app. 1). The absence of historians among the most frequently cited is, of course, the striking thing about this list. In the top twenty-five authors cited there are only four historians: Gareth Stedman-Jones (seven citations), E. P. Thompson (seven), Ernst Bloch (five), and E. H. Carr (five). Both the theoretical legitimizers of historical sociology (e.g., Giddens and Stinchcombe) and the practicing commentators on it (e.g., Tilly and Skocpol) are sociologists,

TABLE 2. Authors Cited Nine or More Times in Essays on Historical Sociology

Charles Tilly	23
Theda Skocpol	17
Anthony Giddens	15
Arthur Stinchcombe	14
Randall Collins	10
Neil J. Smelser	9

with Skocpol having more than twice and Tilly more than three times the number of citations of the leading historians.

Is it safe for historical sociology to be constructed primarily by representatives from a discipline that, as Anthony Giddens has noted, has "repressed" history? In fact, it can be argued that at the core of sociology's "historical imagination" is a persistent attempt to imagine itself as exempt from history. To some extent, therefore, a battle on another front—between the forces of "presentism" and "historicism" in the history *of* sociology—helps to set the limits on history in sociology.

In the case of American sociology, at least, this ahistorical tendency in the history of sociology also springs from the fertile brain of Merton and his important distinction between the "history" and "systematics" of sociological theory. Merton's call for social science to "forget its founders" entailed not only the reinvention of disciplinary practice but also the end in any real sense of disciplinary history. His own words on this crucial issue in the 1949 edition of *Social Theory and Social Structure* bear repetition:

> The attractive but fatal confusion of utilizable sociological theory with the history of sociological theory . . . should long since have been dispelled by recognizing their very different functions. After all, schools of medicine do not confuse the history of medicine with current medical hypotheses, nor do departments of biology identify the history of biology with the viable theory now employed in guiding and interpreting biological research. Once said, this seems obvious enough to be embarrassing. Yet the extraordinary fact is that in sociology, this plain distinction between the history of theory and currently operating theory has in many places not caught hold. (3)

For Merton, the analogy between natural and social science was the crucial legitimation for the separation between history and theory. Therefore, "systematic sociological theory" represented "the highly selective accumulation of those small parts of earlier theory which have thus far survived the tests of empirical research." The history of theory included "also the far greater mass of conceptions which fell to bits when confronted with empirical test." Though "acquaintance" with "all this" (history) might be useful for sociologists, Merton believed that it was "no substitute for training in the actual use of theory in research." What he called the "prehistory of sociology" was "very far from cumulative," and, therefore, the contemporary sociologists were not—in the famous phrase of Newton's that Merton was to make so much of—"pigmies standing on the shoulders of giants." In fact, "the accumulative tradition is still so slight that the shoulders of the giants of sociological science do not provide a very solid base on which to stand" (Merton 1949, 3–5).[5]

This distinction—which Merton was to repeat and fortify—had two somewhat contradictory consequences within sociology. On the one hand, sociologists would cohabit with the "founders" (e.g., classical social theorists) to the extent that they had produced ideas that had not fallen to bits "when confronted with empirical test." On the other hand, they were implicitly forbidden to consider the historical context of transformations in sociological theory or practice, including their own. Invocations of the founders would be widespread both as inspiration and legitimation and "middle-range" operationalization and testing of their theories would be permitted, but historical analysis of the construction of sociology's modes of inquiry would be downplayed if not prohibited.

With the period before 1949 placed behind the "veil" of "prehistory," sociologists were spared the potentially unedifying sight of the triumph of recent tendencies in sociological theory and method and allowed to believe that the present development of sociological science was occurring "above" history. The historical development of such tools as "cause," "variable," or "general linear model" was ignored, as were the contemporary appropriation of dichotomies from philosophy and elsewhere (e.g., idiographic, nomothetic; context of discovery, context of justification; analytic, interpretive) that justified particular kinds of sociological practice. What history of sociology there was came increasingly to resemble the regnant "history" of science before Thomas Kuhn, which, as Kuhn has noted, worked for both pedagogic and persuasive—but not historical—ends by chronicling the "successive increments" of cumulative knowledge and the "congeries of error, myth, and superstition that have inhibited the more rapid accumulation of the constituents of the modern science text." (As we have seen, this was Merton's own description of the history of sociology.) Not surprisingly, sociology's self-image, rather than as a discipline constructed in a certain place and time, became that of a "science" developing principles (of both theory and practice) relevant for all places and all times (Kuhn [1962] 1970, 1–2).

This problem of sociology's historical self-consciousness has only recently (but increasingly) been noted by historians of sociology as the problem of "historicism" versus "presentism" in the history of sociology. This debate, as carried out by Stephen Seidman and others, revolves around the question of whether in the history of sociology it is legitimate to "interpret texts in relation to the current theoretical context" (the presentist position) or whether a genuine history of sociology must be anchored in the historical context (the historicist position). Although this debate is relatively recent in sociology—because post-Kuhnian history of sociology is only about a decade old—its terms portend significant changes in the relationship between history and theory within sociology. For the historicist argument is that presentist approaches result in a narrative of scientific progress and enlightenment that tends toward an ideological reconstruction aimed at legitimating current theoretical or methodological positions. Just as a new empirical (but historicist) history of science destabilized the philosophy of science (and social science), a new historicist history of sociology has the potential to relativize and destabilize current sociological practice (Seidman et al., 1985, 13–14).[6]

In this context, however, what I have called the "frozen" image of historical practice is doubly functional for mainstream sociology. For by trivializing "history" as unscientific the discipline is spared both the relativizing dangers of its own history and the potential threat to the mainstream from historical sociology. But this image is also functional for some historical sociologists who themselves exhibit little historical self-consciousness and consciously or not overemphasize the differences between their work and that of historians. To these historical sociologists the history practiced by historians must remain different from—if not inferior to—their own if historical sociology's claim to credibility with the sociological mainstream is to be taken seriously.

The variety of these tendencies among historical sociologists is exhibited in the programmatic statements of the four most frequently cited influences on historical sociology noted above: namely, Tilly, Skocpol, Giddens, and Stinchcombe. While all of these authors have produced works of great importance for all practitioners of history, there are, nonetheless, notable differences in their positions on the possibility of a unified "historical social science." On this point the two theorists of historical practice bracket the two practitioners. The more conventional empiricism of Stinchcombe links the historical sociology of the present more firmly to the "science" of the past and legitimates continuing separation between history and sociology, while the more radical "historicity" of Giddens leads to a critique of scientific "naturalism" in the past and thereby legitimates disciplinary convergence in the future.

Stinchcombe's somewhat idiosyncratic *Theoretical Methods in Social History* offers an unself-conscious empiricist plague on the houses both of history and theory that is delivered with little interest in (or apparent information about) the doings of professional historians. Stinchcombe's empiricism can be called conventional because it is anchored—like Merton's—in the analogy to the physical sciences: "It is not necessary to ignore the facts in order to have general concepts, as the example of the physical sciences shows. The argument of this book is that it is not only not necessary, it is also a bad idea." What he calls "epochal interpretations" (grand theories) ignore the facts by prematurely applying theory to them, "giving a specious sense that we understand the nature of the society we live in by providing a myth of how it came about—a myth illustrated with historical events." Narrative histories, on the other hand, "ignore the facts" by giving the false (linguistic) impression that the narrative is causal when in fact narratives must be broken down into "theoretically understandable bits" before causal analysis can proceed via his method of deep analogy. For Stinchcombe, the "theoretical method" in social history requires both detaching the narrative from its "naive epistemological moorings" and "tossing out the epochal (theoretical) garbage" (Stinchcombe 1978, 1–25).

At the other end of the spectrum stands Giddens whose characterization of the differences between the natural and social sciences and similarities between the latter and history distinguish him sharply from Stinchcombe. For Giddens there were three components of "mid-century" sociology (or what he calls the "orthodox consensus"): a description of "industrial" society, a set of theoretical propositions loosely called "functionalism," and a set of statements about similarities in the historical development and logical structure of the social and natural sciences that he calls "naturalism." While the rebellion against the first two is widespread, the predominance of the third remains less seriously challenged. It is, of course, the residue of this view that undergirds contrasts between (scientific) "analysis" and (discursive) "interpretation" and, therefore, "sociology" and "history" (Giddens 1979, 230–33, 234–59).

By rejecting this naturalism Giddens is able to argue that because of their shared theoretical problematics and methodological challenges there is no "intellectually defensible" division between history and social science. Elaborated most completely in *The Constitution of Society*, Giddens's argument recognizes both the transformation in historical practice and the interpretive nature of much of sociological practice. Agreeing with Philip Abrams that the "acknowledged masterpieces of the discipline of history have become increasingly theoretically explicit," Giddens argues that the problems of social theory and of agency, structure, and forms of explanation are "problems shared in general by all the social sciences." Furthermore, he contends that because most social science work is conducted "in and through texts" the methodological problems of making sense of texts are also shared by history and the social sciences (Giddens 1984, 355–63).

It would be wrong to say that the most frequently cited practitioners—Tilly and Skocpol—are ranged between Stinchcombe and Giddens because both are more closely linked to the former, and therefore to mid-century naturalism, than to the latter. For example, both Tilly and Skocpol cite Stinchcombe, but in their programmatic work through 1984, neither cited anything by Giddens. While both are undoubtedly critics of the mid-century orthodoxies that Giddens labels "industrial society" and "functionalism," neither totally rejects the naturalism that Giddens criticizes, and both, therefore, uphold the distinctions between "analysis" and "interpretation" that have replaced "theory" versus "facts" as the language of separation between sociology and history.

As we have seen, even in his rejection of the long-standing division of labor of "theory" and "facts" between sociology and history Tilly has reproduced the separation between the two on another level. Although his portrayal of the distinguishing features of the historical profession are quite similar to those of Giddens, Tilly has not called for a "general rapprochement" between history and sociology but "a highly selective shift of particular topics to historical analyses and historical materials." According to Tilly, historians group and gloss texts (the written residues of the past) in order to reconstruct past human behavior, and they consider "where, and especially when an event occurred to be an integral part of its meaning, explanation and impact." But sociologists are not turning into historians because "they are not learning to do archival research . . . taking their questions from the prevailing historical agenda, or suppressing their inclinations to explicit modeling, careful measurement, and deliberate comparison." In other words, they are not, to use his earlier terms, either mongering archives or succumbing to interpretation (Tilly 1981, 14, 43).

Skocpol has maintained a similar division, but incorporated it into sociology, in her 1984 essay "Emerging Agendas and Recurrent Strategies in Historical Sociology," in *Vision and Method in Historical Sociology*. While professing a buoyant methodological pluralism ("Surely it would be a mistake to tie historical sociology down to any one epistemological, theoretical, or methodological development") Skocpol leaves little doubt about her preference for "analytical" over what she calls "interpretive" historical sociology. In language deeply indebted to Stinchcombe, she describes the former branch of sociology as involving the search for "causal regularities" without an effort to "analyze historical facts according to a preconceived general model." Because good analytic history requires that the "unities of time and place be broken for the purposes of drawing comparison and testing hypotheses," analytical sociologists must neither be fazed by the demand of some historians that they use "primary sources" nor let their findings be "dictated simply by historiographical fashions that vary from case to case or time to time." Interpretive sociology, on the other hand (a very broad category that for her includes the work of both historian E. P. Thompson and anthropologist Clifford Geertz, among others), displays "an insouciance about establishing *valid* explanatory models" that, from the standpoint of those "concerned with causal validity" in their analyses, can be "misleading even when they are compelling." Interpretive works "seem extraordinarily vivid and full, like a good Flaubert novel," but their appeal is only to "others who share their sense of problems and their world views" (Skocpol 1984, 356–91).

But, of course, the same thing could be said of Stinchcombe and Skocpol themselves. For only those who share their sense of the untheorized historical "fact," the "garbage" of epochal theory, and the "naivete" of narrative will apparently be convinced by their analyses. Stinchcombe defends himself from the knowledge that historians produce only theorized facts by selecting for analysis only "historians"—Tocqueville, Trotsky, Bendix, and Smelser—who have not participated in the theoretical transformation of history. (And this, not their lack of "archive mongering" is, pace Tilly, the point.) By trivializing "historiographical fashions," Skocpol makes much the same mistake, ignoring the increasingly sophisticated discussions of historical practice in that literature over the last two decades.

Comparisons between Skocpol and Stinchcombe, on the one hand, and British sociologists like Abrams and Giddens, on the other, would seem to suggest that the former speak not in the universal language of "science" but in the provincial "scientistic" argot of American academe. In spite of overall similarities in the emergence and spread of professionalized sociology and history in the post–World War Two years in Britain and the United States, the British sociologists evince an almost complete absence of a rhetoric of "science" that justifies continuing differences between history and historical sociology. John Hall's 1989 article on historical sociology in Britain ("They Do Things Differently There") proposes some reasons for this difference: a preexisting body of sociological work on British social structure that led to a relative immunity to Parsonian functionalism, a favorable response in Britain to the earliest postwar American historical sociologists (e.g., Bendix, Lipset,

C. Wright Mills, and Barrington Moore) and an early and close intellectual and political partnership between sociologists and practitioners of "history from below" (e.g., E. P. Thompson, Raymond Williams, William Hoggart) (Hall 1989).

It is the failure to recognize the crucial point of this difference that detracts from what is otherwise without doubt one of the most brilliant recent analyses of historical sociology, Michael Burawoy's 1989 article "Two Methods in Search of Science: Skocpol versus Trotsky." This is a lengthy and searching critique of Skocpol's methodological pronouncements that discusses, among other things, her contradictory attempt to produce historical sociology while standing "outside" of history and that, therefore, challenges her positions on "facts," "historiography," and "theory." But because his discussion is conducted almost entirely in the language of a Popperian philosophy of science, Burawoy fails to realize that his own categories do not stand "outside" of history either. The unasked question is whether the prominence of these categories or the metaphor of the "research program" are not themselves worthy of historical analysis. If they are, then he has stopped his historical analysis just one step short of where it might have gone. In so doing, however, he has revealed the "hard core" of the research program for historical sociology that he and Skocpol share completely: that everything is an object of history except sociology itself (Buroway 1989).

The Future of the Past

In a comparison of the methods and agendas of historical sociology and social history Skocpol has compared them to the proverbial "two trains passing in opposite directions in the night." As this essay has pointed out, this metaphor of separation and opposition continues to reinvent the boundary between history and sociology even as it pretends to speak across it. In fact, substantial segments of both of these disciplines are moving on parallel tracks toward the same goal: a historical social science. Different obstacles, however, lay on each track (Skocpol 1987, 17–30).

For historians, the obstacle is a weak understanding of the relationship between history and theory. In 1963, at the dawn of the relationship between history and social science that we have just considered, the historian A. S. Eisenstadt wondered if, in a time of philosophical dismantling, "we do not take sides, we only take cover." From that day until this historians have tried to "take cover" by borrowing theory from other, allegedly more advanced disciplines with little or no commentary on the controversies over theory within those disciplines or the effects of theory within history. Until theory finds a fuller voice within history—and history therefore better understands the theoretical aspirations it shares with sociology—this track toward historical social science will remain blocked (Eisenstadt 1966, 110–25).

For sociologists, the tracks are blocked by a somewhat ironic lack of historical self-consciousness. Charles Tilly has noted that a "hidden" piece of history "roots most sociology in the present." And that "piece of history" is the piece that sociologists are currently living. For almost fifty years sociology has lived in an eternal present, free until quite recently from both its own "history" and from many practitioners of historical sociology. Because of this, unfortunately, its historical practitioners have little sense of the way that they have retained links with the traditions they think they have superseded. Until sociology is willing to face its own history—and therefore to understand better the "interpretive" tasks it shares with history—progress on its side will be slow (Tilly 1981, 214).

There is no reason to expect disciplinary convergence on these questions any time soon, but the current moment does seem to suggest intriguing possibilities. At least since the time of C. Wright Mills, the vision of a historical social science has been nurtured in the hobo jungles at the side of the mainstream disciplinary tracks. Today these jungles seem larger than at any time in the last forty years.[7]

APPENDIX 1: ESSAYS INCLUDED IN CITATION ANALYSIS OF ARTICLES ON HISTORICAL SOCIOLOGY

Abbott, Andrew. 1988. "Transcending General Linear Reality." *Sociological Theory* 6:169–86.

Abrams, Philip. 1980. "History, Sociology, Historical Sociology." *Past and Present* 87:3–16.

Aiken, Michael, Kenneth Land, James McCartney, and Martha Tienda. 1981. "Comment: Boundaries and Bridges—The Domains of Sociology." *Sociological Quarterly* 22:447–70.

Aminzade, Ronald. 1989. "What Is Historical about Historical Sociology?" History and Society Program Working Paper, University of Minnesota, Minneapolis.

Aronson, Sidney. 1969. "Obstacles to a Rapprochement between History and Sociology." In *Interdisciplinary Relationships in the Social Sciences,* 292–304. Edited by M. Sherif and C. W. Sherif. Chicago: Aldine.

Billings, Dwight B., and Kathleen M. Blee. 1986. "Bringing History Back in the Historicity of Social Relations." *Current Perspectives in Social Theory* 7:51–68.

Bock, Kenneth E. 1963. "Evolution, Function, and Change." *American Sociological Review* 28:229–37.

Bonnell, Victoria E. 1980. "The Uses of Theory, Concepts, and Comparison in Historical Sociology." *Comparative Studies in Society and History* 22:156–73.

Bulmer, Martin. 1974. "Sociology and History: Some Recent Trends." *Sociology: The Journal of the British Sociological Association* 8:138–50.

Burawoy, Michael. 1989. "Two Methods in Search of Science: Skocpol versus Trotsky." *Theory and Society* 18:759–806.

Cahnman, Werner J. 1976. "Historical Sociology: What It Is and What It Is Not." In *The New Social Sciences*, 107–22. Edited by B. N. Varma. Westport, CT: Greenwood Press.

Cahnman, Werner J., and Alvin Boskoff. 1964. "Sociology and History: Reunion and Rapprochement." In *Sociology and History: Theory and Research*, 1–18. Edited by Werner J. Cahnman and Alvin Boskoff. New York: Free Press.

Chirot, David. 1976. "Introduction: Thematic Controversies and New Developments in the Uses of Historical Materials by Sociologists." *Social Forces* 55:232–41.

Collins, Randall. 1985. "The Mega-Historians." *Sociological Theory* 3:114–22.

Collins, Randall. 1988. "The Micro Contribution to Macro Sociology." *Sociological Theory* 6:242–53.

Corcoran, Paul. 1989. "Godot Is Waiting Too: Endings in Thought and History." *Theory and Society* 18:495–530.

Erikson, Kai T. 1970. "Sociology and the Historical Perspective." *The American Sociologist* 5:331–38.

Goldstone, J. A. 1986. "How to Study History: The View from Sociology." *Historical Methods* 19:82–84.

Hall, John A. 1989. "They Do Things Differently There, or, the Contribution of British Historical Sociology." *British Journal of Sociology* 40:544–64.

Halpern, Ben. 1957. "History, Sociology, and Contemporary Area Studies." *American Journal of Sociology* 63:1–10.

Hawley, Amos. 1978. "Presidential Address: Cumulative Change in Theory and in History." *American Sociological Review* 43:787–96.

Hay, C. 1981. "History, Sociology, and Theory." In *Transaction of the Annual Conference of the British Sociological Association, 1980*. London: British Sociological Association.

Heller, Agnes. 1989. "From Hermeneutics in Social Science toward a Hermeneutics of Social Science." *Theory and Society* 18:291–322.

Jenkins, J. Craig. 1982. "Why Do Peasants Rebel? Structural and Historical Theories of Modern Peasant Rebellions." *American Journal of Sociology* 88:487–514.

Johnson, Bruce C. 1982. "Missionaries, Tourists, and Traders: Sociologists in the Domain of History." *Studies in Symbolic Interaction* 4:115–50.

Laslett, Barbara. 1980. "Beyond Methodology: The Place of Theory in Quantitative Historical Research." *American Sociological Review* 45:214–28.

Light, Ivan. 1974. "Reassessments of Sociological History." *Theory and Society* 1:361–74.

Lipset, Seymour Martin. 1958. "A Sociologist Looks at History." *Pacific Sociological Review* 1:13–17.

Lloyd, Christopher. 1989. "Realism, Structuralism, and History: Foundations for a Transformative Science of Society." *Theory and Society* 18:451–94.

McMichael, Philip. 1980. "Incorporating Comparison within a World-Historical Perspective: An Alternative Comparative Method." *American Sociological Review* 55:385–97.

Morawska, Ewa. 1989. "Sociology and 'Historical Matters.'" *Journal of Social History* 23:439–44.

Ragin, Charles, and David Zaret. 1982. "Theory and Method in Comparative Research: Two Strategies." *Social Forces* 61:731–54.

Roth, Guenther. 1975. "Socio-Historical Model and Developmental Theory." *American Sociological Review* 40:148–57.

Roy, William G. 1987. "Time, Place, and People in History and Sociology: Boundary Definitions and the Logic of Inquiry." *Social Science History* 11:53–62.

Schwartz, Mildred. 1987. "Historical Sociology in the History of American Sociology." *Social Science History* 11:1–16.

Skocpol, Theda. 1984. "Emerging Agendas and Recurrent Strategies in Historical Sociology." In *Vision and Method in Historical Sociology.* Edited by Theda Skocpol. Cambridge: Cambridge University Press.

Skocpol, Theda. 1987. "Social History and Historical Sociology: Contrasts and Complementarities." *Social Science History* 11:17–30.

Skocpol, Theda, and Margaret Somers. 1980. "The Uses of Comparative History in Macrosocial Inquiry." *Comparative Studies in Society and History* 22:174–97.

Smart, Barry. 1982. "Foucault, Sociology, and the Problem of Human Agency." *Theory and Society* 11:121–42.

Smelser, Neil J. 1974. "Sociological History." In *Essays in Social History,* 25–38. Edited by M. W. Flinn and T. C. Smout. Oxford: Clarendon Press.

Stinchcombe, A. L. 1978. *Theoretical Methods in Social History.* New York: Academic Press.

Sztompka, Piotr. 1986. "The Renaissance of Historical Orientation in Sociology." *International Sociology* 1:321–38.

Tilly, Charles. 1981. "Sociology, Meet History." In *As Sociology Meets History,* 1–52. Edited by Charles Tilly. New York: Academic Press.

Wolff, Kurt H. 1959. "Sociology and History; Theory and Practice." *American Journal of Sociology* 65:32–38.

Zaret, David. 1978. "Sociological Theory and Historical Scholarship." *The American Sociologist* 13:114–21.

Zaret, David. 1980. "From Weber to Parsons and Schutz: The Eclipse of History in Modern Social Theory." *American Journal of Sociology* 85:1180–1201.

NOTES

The research assistance of Victoria Getis was indispensable to this essay, and it was also improved by many conversations with her. My colleagues in the "Historic Turn" group of Comparative Studies of Social Transformation (CSST) will see that I have tried to steal as many of their ideas as possible for this essay.

1. This essay does not discuss the ways in which these tendencies became institutionalized in professional cultures, university departments, and so on. General works that do this include, for history, Higham (1983) and Novick (1988), and for sociology Halliday and Janowitz (1992).

2. For an argument on this point similar to mine, see Tyrell (1986).

3. For details of this analysis see McDonald (1994).

4. Data on articles are from my own survey.

5. It is, of course, somewhat ironic that this view of the utility of history for sociology was written by a man whose own dissertation involved the history of science in seventeenth-century England. For an analysis of Merton that makes a useful distinction between his "substantive" and "discipline building" works, see Crothers (1987).

6. The terms of this debate were originally laid out for the social sciences more generally in Stocking (1965).

7. One of the most important contributors to—and historians of—this work at the side of the tracks is sociologist Andrew Abbott, who has both thoughtfully probed the ahistorical scientism of sociology's method and carefully analyzed the convergence between history and sociology (Abbott 1988, 1994).

REFERENCES

Abbott, Andrew. 1988. "Transcending General Linear Reality." *Sociological Theory* 6:169–86.

Abbott, Andrew. 1994. "History and Sociology: The Lost Synthesis." In *Engaging the Past: The Uses of History Across the Social Sciences,* 77–112. Edited by Eric H. Monkkonen. Durham, NC: Duke University Press.

Aydelotte, William O. 1963. "Notes on the Problem of Historical Generalization." In *Generalization in the Writing of History,* 144–77. Edited by Social Science Research Council, Committee on Historical Analysis. Chicago: University of Chicago Press.

Berkhofer, Robert F., Jr. 1969. *A Behavioral Approach to Historical Analysis.* New York: Free Press.

Burawoy, Michael. 1989. "Two Methods in Search of Science: Skocpol versus Trotsky." *Theory and Society* 18:759–806.

Cochran, Thomas C. 1964. *The Inner Revolution: Essays on the Social Sciences in History.* New York: Harper and Row.

Crothers, Charles. 1987. *Robert K. Merton.* London: Tavistock Publications.

Eisenstadt, A. S. 1966. "American History and Social Science." In *The Craft of American History* 2:110–25. Edited by A. S. Eisenstadt. New York: Harper and Row.

Giddens, Anthony. 1979. *Central Problems in Social Theory.* Berkeley and Los Angeles: University of California Press.

Giddens, Anthony. 1984. *The Constitution of Society.* Berkeley and Los Angeles: University of California Press.

Hall, John A. 1989. "They Do Things Differently There, or, the Contribution of British Historical Sociology." *British Journal of Sociology* 40: 544–64.

Halliday, Terrence C., and Morris Janowitz, eds. 1992. *Sociology and Its Publics: The Forms and Fates of Disciplinary Organization.* Chicago: University of Chicago Press.

Higham, John. 1983. *History: Professional Scholarship in America.* Baltimore: Johns Hopkins University Press.

Hughes, H. Stuart. 1960. "The Historian and the Social Scientist." *American Historical Review* 66:20–46.

Kuhn, T. S. [1962] 1970. *The Structure of Scientific Revolutions.* Chicago: University of Chicago Press.

Lampard, Eric E. 1961. "American Historians and the Study of Urbanization." *American Historical Review* 67:49–61.

Lipset, Seymour Martin. 1968. "History and Sociology: Some Methodological Considerations." In *Sociology and History: Methods,* 20–59. Edited by Seymour Martin Lipset and Richard Hofstadter. New York: Basic Books.

Lipset, Seymour Martin, and Richard Hofstadter, eds. 1968. *Sociology and History: Methods.* New York: Basic Books.

McDonald, Terrence J. 1990. "Faiths of Our Fathers: Middle Range Social Theory and the Remaking of American Urban History." Unpublished paper prepared for conference on "Modes of Inquiry for American City History," Chicago Historical Society, Oct. 25–27, 1990.

Merton, Robert K. 1949. *Social Theory and Social Structure: Toward the Codification of Theory and Research.* Glencoe, IL: Free Press.

Novick, Peter. 1988. *That Noble Dream: The "Objectivity Question" and the American Historical Profession.* New York: Cambridge University Press.

Potter, David M. 1963. "Explicit Data and Implicit Assumptions in Historical Study." In *Generalization in the Writing of History,* 178–95. Edited by Social Science Research Council, Committee on Historical Analysis. Chicago: University of Chicago Press.

Saveth, Edward N., ed. 1964. *American History and the Social Sciences.* New York: The Free Press of Glencoe.

Schnore, Leo F. 1975. "Urban History and the Social Sciences: An Uneasy Marriage." *Journal of Urban History* 1:395–408.

Seidman, Stephen, et al. 1985. "The Historicist Controversy: Understanding the Sociological Past." *Sociological Theory* 3:13–28.

Simpson, Richard L. 1961. "Expanding and Declining Fields in American Sociology." *American Sociological Review* 26:458–66.

Skocpol, Theda. 1984. "Emerging Agendas and Recurrent Strategies in Historical Sociology." In *Vision and Method in Historical Sociology,* 356–91. Edited by Theda Skocpol. Cambridge: Cambridge University Press.

Skocpol, Theda. 1987. "Social History and Historical Sociology: Contrasts and Complementarities." *Social Science History* 11:17–30.

Skocpol, Theda, ed. 1984. *Vision and Method in Historical Sociology.* Cambridge, UK: Cambridge University Press.

Social Science Research Council, Committee on Historical Analysis. 1963. *Generalization in the Writing of History.* Chicago: University of Chicago Press.

Social Science Research Council, Committee on Historiography. 1946. *Theory and Practice in Historical Study: A Report of the Committee on Historiography.* New York: Social Science Research Council.

Social Science Research Council, Committee on Historiography. 1954. *The Social Sciences in Historical Study: A Report.* New York: Social Science Research Council.

Social Science Research Council. 1940. *Critiques of Research in the Social Sciences III: An Appraisal of Walter Prescott Webb's* The Great Plains: *A Study in Institutions and Environment.* New York: Social Science Research Council.

Stinchcombe, Arthur L. 1978. *Theoretical Methods in Social History.* New York: Academic Press.

Stocking, George W. 1965. "On the Limits of 'Presentism' and 'Historicism'" in the Historiography of the Behavioral Sciences." *Journal of the History of the Behavioral Sciences* 1:211–18.

Thernstrom, Stephan. 1965. "'Yankee City' Revisited: The Perils of Historical Naivete." *American Sociological Review* 30:234–42.

Tilly, Charles. 1967. "The State of Urbanization." *Comparative Studies in Society and History* 10:103–4.

Tilly, Charles. 1981. *As Sociology Meets History.* New York: Academic Press.

Tyrell, Ian. 1986. *The Absent Marx: Class Analysis and Liberal History in Twentieth-Century America.* Westport, CT: Greenwood Press.

Webb, Walter Prescott. 1931. *The Great Plains.* Boston: Ginn and Company.

Science, Non-Science, and Politics

Rogers M. Smith

The canon of major works on politics includes a considerable number that claim to offer a new science of politics or a new science of man that encompasses politics. Aristotle, Hobbes, Hume, Publius, Comte, Bentham, Hegel, Marx, Spencer, Burgess, Bentley, Truman, Easton, and Riker are among the many who have claimed, more or less directly, that they are founding or helping to found a true political science for the first time. This aspiration has usually been expressed via criticism of earlier "unscientific" approaches. Thus, William Riker, advocating rational choice theory as the basis of political analysis, once dismissed "traditional methods—i.e., history writing, the description of institutions, and legal analysis" as able to produce only wisdom and neither science nor knowledge. "And while wisdom is certainly useful in the affairs of men, such a result is a failure to live up to the promise in the name political science" (Riker 1962, viii).

Despite Riker's considerable influence, many political scientists refused to abandon such methods. Recently, many more have been turning to methods very much like them—that is, to the study of institutions and ideas, usually in historical perspective, and to historical patterns and processes more broadly. Some excellent scholars believe this turn is a disaster. It has been termed a "grab bag of diverse, often conflicting approaches" that does not offer anything like a scientific theory (Chubb and Moe 1990, 565).[1]

In this essay I will argue that the turn or return to institutions and history is a reasonable response to two linked sets of problems. First, the dominant pluralist and functionalist approaches to political science had major descriptive and normative limitations that were exposed by political events of the 1960s and 1970s. Second, a more fundamental tension has characterized the enterprise of political inquiry since its inception. This basic tension is between convictions that politics, and human agency in politics, really matter, usually on the assumption of some sort of human free will, and desires to explain politics and political decisions almost inevitably in terms of exogenous, impersonal forces that may then seem far more important than "mere" politics, if not indeed fully deterministic.[2] All studies of human conduct confront such conflicting pulls between trying to explain human agency and trying to preserve its intrinsic significance. The problem is, however, particularly acute for political scientists. They generally believe political decisions are especially influential over virtually all spheres of human life. Yet they are particularly prone to analyze those decisions in terms of "nonpolitical" forces, such as economic imperatives, psychological drives, or the largely prereflective social beliefs, customs, and "transcripts" that constitute a "culture." The unresolved, perhaps unresolvable, tension between depicting political decisions as architectonic "first causes" and explaining their causes has perennially prompted political analysts to seek better approaches. I will argue that reflection on how we might deal with this tension suggests not only why a turn to history makes sense but also how political scientists can do so most fruitfully.

I nonetheless believe that the critics who regard the recent historical-institutionalist efforts as "non-science," if not nonsense, are correct in one respect. It is true that those efforts do not now offer, or hold out much hope of offering, any grand predictive causal theory to guide a new science of politics. Some believe that inquiry without such a unified guiding theory is not yet science. To be sure, the enterprise of seeking that theory is well worth continuing and improving. But the critics are quite wrong to believe that the study of politics should be confined to such efforts or that only this work deserves the name "science." Historical-institutionalist inquiries can, I will suggest, be fully scientific in their basic methodology. That is, they can and should develop falsifiable hypotheses suggested by broader accounts or theories, and then examine evidence for those hypotheses in accordance with the traditional logic of scientific method. To identify science only with the working out of some single causal theory encompassing all human political behavior would not only prove, in all probability, quixotic. It would almost certainly also involve the assumption that some ultimately deterministic explanation is correct, thus eclipsing the question of the character and significance of human political agency. To be intellectually honest, political science should adopt methods and a self-understanding that acknowledge that these fundamental questions are still very much open ones, unsettled by all past and present efforts to found a true political science.

For if it is not altogether wrongheaded, it is surely premature to treat any particular version of such theory, or even the quest for a unifying scientific theory per se, as the one legitimate claimant to the throne of "true political science." There is no rightful heir apparent; our potential princes are all still frogs if they are not frauds. The most we can hope for at present is to achieve some shared sense of how we can pursue different sorts of approaches to the study of politics in ways that help us to compare them, roughly but usefully— especially in regard to the enduring question of how we can understand human political action. As I have argued elsewhere, I think the historical-institutionalist turn in political science does suggest how the discipline might achieve this (Smith 1988, 1992). It suggests not a single grand theory but an inclusive general approach to scientific studies of politics. If widely embraced, this approach would promote meaningful accumulation of knowledge via comparison of different explanations for the things that most concern most students of politics: the purposive political decisions that seemingly must shape our lives, if human beings are able consciously to shape them at all.

The Fundamental Tension

Let me begin with the more fundamental source of the recent turns to history in political studies. To my knowledge, virtually everyone who has written about politics has or at least once had the conviction that the decisions made by persons in power matter a great deal. This is particularly true of persons possessed of governmental power, but also of those able to resist such power. Their decisions alter their own lives and those of most others for good or ill but in any event significantly. Aristotle believed those who legislated for a polis had great influence on the character and endurance of its shared life, so that politics was "the most sovereign and most comprehensive master science" (*Ethics,* 1094a). Hobbes was moved to write, at least in part, by the incessant civil "disorders" of his era, for which he held its political leaders partly responsible (1971, 728). Even Marx, who stressed the determining character of economic relations in much of his work, granted politics important autonomy in his historical writings and even more in his praxis. The various masters of American political science, from James Madison to Charles Merriam to Robert Dahl, all analyzed politics with a view to enhancing, not denying, the efficacy of democratic statesmanship and citizenship (Seidelman and Harpham 1985).

There the tension arises. How do we enhance the efficacy of political decision making and (to be sure) the prestige and influence of teachers of politics and (perhaps more deeply) enhance at the same time our ability to cope with the curiosities and fears about major political actions that we all feel at times, sometimes quite acutely? One obvious answer is to seek for reliable, even predictive, explanations of how political matters regularly work and how they can be expected to go if decision makers do Z instead of A. Natural scientists seem, after all, to have learned much by examining the physical and biological world in these ways. In political analysis, such explanations usually trace conduct back to other factors, such as economic interests; personal, group, or institutional power or status ambitions; the functional imperatives of social or political systems; religious, ethnic, nationalistic, republican, socialist, or other ideological commitments; psychic longings based on repressed trauma or eros; or simply human nature. These factors can best do the explanatory work we expect from them, moreover, if they are themselves relatively fixed and enduring, not subject to frequent fluctuation or political alteration, instead regularly exerting their shaping influence on the political landscape. Hence, most modern analysts of politics, at least, have offered explanations emphasizing just such enduring factors.

Yet without more, these explanations are all at least implicitly reductionistic and deterministic.[3] They suggest that political decisions are relatively predictable products of constellations of forces, be they economic concerns, systemic needs, ambitions, ideologies, or erotic egos, that could not really be different than they are. Thus, the decisions come to seem, in themselves, not all that interesting or momentous. They are not causes but effects, not "first things" but "epiphenomena," dogs wagged by their truly telling tails.

It is true that much mainstream political analysis presents itself as making only probabilistic, not deterministic, judgments, particularly when it is statistically based. These studies might therefore be thought to leave room for unexpected acts of human political creativity. Many political scientists would undoubtedly insist that, although they naturally emphasize explanatory causal factors beyond the control of political actors, they do not regard them as so powerful as to obviate all meaningful human agency.

These quite genuine attitudes on the part of researchers do not, however, erase what Stephen Krasner has termed the "connotative," as opposed to the "denotative," meaning of their research (Krasner 1990, 37). His contrast is between the message a study predominantly conveys to most readers—its "connotative" meaning—and its precise "denotative" content, visible only upon careful analysis. The understandable stress many studies place on causal factors that seem to explain the variance in some observed political behavior means that these analyses say little if anything about conduct that does not seem to be accounted for by such factors. The existence of unexplained variance can easily be chalked up to inherent but random unpredictability in the phenomena, akin to the ineradicable uncertainty in quantum physics about the exact location of a specific electron at any particular time.[4] Even if they do not endorse such explanations for residual variance in the behavior they study, very few self-consciously "scientific" works in the discipline develop any explicit accounts of autonomous human agency that might illuminate this "residual" political conduct.[5] Hence, the basic message they convey is that scientifically explicable political behavior is determined by such causes, while that which is not so explained remains a "black box," outside the scope of scientific analysis, at least until further causes are discovered.[6]

Perhaps one day some such explanatory theory will be judged essentially true. But at present, for a host of reasons, reductionist-deterministic explanations do not satisfy. First, so far they mostly fail on their own terms. Most are difficult to express in well-specified, coherent theoretical models of measurable political behavior that can be tested in replicable experiments, and those experiments often leave deterministic assumptions "empirically falsified" though not abandoned (Ricci 1984, 250–58; Almond and Genco 1990, 36). Marxist accounts of class struggle find the modern kaleidoscopic array of relationships to the means of production difficult to capture. Structural-functionalist analyses have difficulty coping with the survival of structures that are not really functional. Group models of politics have trouble modeling the behavior of all those who belong to several groups and even more in finding a place for those ascribed membership in "latent," unorganized groups.

And even when they seem theoretically elegant, as in the best rational choice models, contemporary scientific analyses of politics fail to explain more than a narrow range of political behaviors. Game theory cannot easily be extended to "games" involving more than two parties. For games extending over time or involving more than minimal information, there are so many possible equilibrium outcomes that formal modeling yields only indeterminacy. Auxiliary assumptions about preferences, which introduce a "thick," interpretive element into "thin," purely formal theories, are required (Tsebelis 1990, 579; Ferejohn 1991, 282, 284–85). Neither have rational choice theories displayed any great predictive capacity for major real-world political choices. Indeed, all past efforts at grand explanatory theories of politics and history that make predictions at all, from Marx to recent American "modernization" theories, have gone wildly astray. Few such theorists expected religious fundamentalism or absolutism to resurge in today's world, for example.[7]

The current proponents of historical-institutionalist approaches in political science have particularly, and appropriately, hammered on one descriptive failure of many prevailing brands of political science: namely, they tend to take their independent variables, be they class, group interests and resources, ideology, and so on, as "fixed" or unchanging and as "exogenous," external and impervious to political choices (March and Olsen 1984, 735–38; 1989, 6; Wendt 1987, 356; Smith 1988, 94, 100). That treatment is convenient, perhaps even necessary, for elegant scientific explanations, but it just seems false. Such factors do shape political decisions, but political decisions also seem to shape *them,* often producing quite fundamental political transformations. All accounts that fail to capture those complex interactions are likely to fail in important ways to explain politics. Elegance is not worth that price.

That point leads to the reasons the existing "sciences of politics" appear inadequate to persons outside the enterprise of scientific inquiry, who rely on perspectives born of lived human experience. To most such persons political decisions—to tax and spend; launch wars or end them; redistribute crops or burn them; build roads, schools, hospitals, sometimes churches, or close them—all seem to matter very much, and they do not seem to be simply epiphenomenal to anything else. Of course, many elements feed into such decisions, and a lot clearly involve coercion. Yet processes of mutual persuasion and deliberative reflection that appear far from predetermined, yet quite decisive, are also sometimes present. To persuade people that all these decisions are actually dictated by factors outside the actors' conscious control a heavy burden of proof must, quite appropriately, be met.

After all, our own daily experiences of making choices do not seem reducible to exogenous single-factor or even multifactor deterministic explanations. We feel that we, as mysteriously but meaningfully autonomous agents, have some independent causal role to play in shaping our choices. To tell us that we do not may be true, but it doesn't ring true with personal experience. Deep down, almost no one believes it. And in this court of appeal to personal experiences, which often influences our governing judgments more than scientific demonstrations, it does not help the case for deterministic accounts that, logically, they give us no real basis to decide how we should act. They simply deny that we really can decide. Thus, they can make the whole absorbing if often agonizing human condition of endlessly trying to shape our lives for the better seem a pointless farce. Because a conception of our condition as farcical threatens to foster nihilistic depression and moral irresponsibility, especially in politics, most people rightly refuse to grant it veracity very readily.

There are, then, good normative reasons for calling explicitly and implicitly deterministic accounts of human conduct into question and seeking methods of study that at least leave open the possibility of discovering that our commonsense feelings of genuine agency are right. Yet there are also good reasons why the appeal of implicitly deterministic scientific explanations is enduring, fundamental, and profound. We wish to understand and explain anything that affects us as greatly as politics seems to do. The task of explanation itself, moreover, seems to require the identification of some sorts of enduring causes, at least if explanations are to be precise, rigorous, and general enough to be compelling and useful. Indeed, strictly from the standpoint of complete understanding, we may hope to find causal explanations that fully account for the phenomena in question, leaving no possibility that the actions of agents might have been other than they were.

The strength of this pressure is visible when quite sophisticated "humanistic" accounts boldly strive to be explanatory without being deterministic and fail. Scholars influenced by Gramsci, for example, often stress that political and legal ideologies are at least relatively autonomous from their material preconditions, providing sources of meaning that can prompt political decisions in conflict with what otherwise appear to be imperatives dictated by those material conditions. Yet when ideologies are thus used to explain and predict behavior, the resulting accounts often treat them as so hegemonic that they can prevent political participants from recognizing that they might act other than they do—and so, on these accounts, political actors cannot really do so. Ideologies then become as much "iron cages" of human behavior as the material circumstances that were sometimes claimed to "cage" them in cruder versions of Marxism.[8]

To avoid this, we might insist firmly on the independent, autonomous importance of human choices, particularly political decisions; on their irreducibility to explanation by exogenous factors; and on their role in reshaping all such factors. But then we are in danger of giving up the possibility of explaining political decisions in any rigorous way. The nature of this autonomous agency is and perhaps must be mysterious, requiring as it does that we see ourselves as socially and biologically constituted but as somehow self-determining causes. Political analyses stressing such agency seem quickly to be limited to recounting how a number of apparently important decisions came to be made and what followed, in the manner of a devoutly antitheoretical narrative historian concerned to lay down events as they happened without any attempt to build more general explanations of politics out of those materials.

The most such histories promise is that we may gain some prudence from immersion in past experience (though we may also be misled, like the architects of the Maginot Line). But they typically fail to capture our frequent perceptions of recurring patterns in political decisions that appear traceable to forces that transcend any particular sequence of events. And apart from possibly bestowing a rather ineffable prudence, political history told as one damn thing after another also fails to give us any very concrete, reliable sense of what we can do to understand and control our collective political lives better. So we may well feel compelled to shift back to explanatory theories that are, at least implicitly, reductionist and deterministic if they have clear content at all.

If this abstract account of the problem of deciding on how to conduct inquiry into politics is correct, then we should expect political analysts to oscillate between approaches closer to the deterministic, quantifiable models of causality in (some of) the natural sciences and approaches that lean rather toward the tales of unpredictable, at best translucent, human agency found in narrative histories. At this point the reader will expect me to claim to perceive precisely this deep dynamic at work in the recent turn to history and institutions in political science. I will not disappoint. But I am not offering a single-factor causal theory. There have been other, more proximate causes at work, to which I now turn.

The Failures of Dominant Political Science Paradigms

A revealing aspect of the recent trends in political science has been an intensified concern with the history of the profession itself. Histories, and debates over histories, of part or all of American political science and public administration turned from a trickle to a gushing stream in the 1980s.[9] These studies vary considerably, but one near-universal theme is the tale of how American political science originated with aspirations to be both truly scientific and a servant of democracy, aspirations abetted by deep faith that these two enterprises went hand in hand.

There were partial exceptions, of course. John Burgess's comparative, historical political science adjoined a sharply limited conception of democracy underpinned by Darwinian views of nationalistic and racial struggle (Burgess 1890, vi, 3–4; Somit and Tanenhaus [1967] 1982, 28). Woodrow Wilson, a seminal figure in modern American political science, at times denied that political studies could really amount to "science," although public administration could. He did so precisely because he believed there was an ineradicable element of autonomous creativity in statesmanship (but not in "neutral" bureaucratic work) that no science could capture. Wilson really differed only in emphasis from the outlook of many of his counterparts, however. Like them, he believed that scholars of politics could provide democratic citizens and statesmen with the knowledge about institutions, issues, and alternatives that was absolutely necessary if democracy was to be feasible (Wilson 1911; Somit and Tanenhaus [1967] 1982, 78; Seidelman and Harpham 1985, 41; Fesler and Kettl 1991, 17–19).

Unfortunately, this faith in the joint destiny of science and democracy has proved hard to sustain. For in American political science, the more basic tension between asserting the importance of political agency and providing scientific explanations for it has especially been manifest in one way. It appears as a tension between desires for research that affirms and assists meaningfully democratic self-governance, taken to be the fullest realization of political agency by all citizens, and desires for research that develops full causal accounts of politics, usually on the model of natural sciences that deny any conscious agency to the phenomena they study. Despite this tension, political science has in many ways provided insights useful for democratic deliberations. Often, however, it has seemed to discredit or even threaten democratic authority. The most influential scientific accounts have sometimes made democratic commitments appear foolish by stressing the ignorance of voters and the apparently ineradicable power of economic, military, and professional elites, as well as structures and forces beyond conscious human control. They have also implied that effective governance, if possible at all, requires scientific knowledge beyond the grasp of most citizens. Hence, the assignment of extensive governmental powers to experts might well seem preferable. These positions have also frequently been advanced in highly technical language impenetrable to most citizens, who may thereby be led to believe that politics is indeed beyond their comprehension.

Recurringly, this tension has fostered an ironic arc to the career of leading political scientists, from Arthur Bentley, Charles Beard, and Charles Merriam to Harold Lasswell, David Easton, Gabriel Almond, and Robert Dahl. Early in their careers, these scholars all criticized previous forms of political science for being both naive about democracy and primitive and inadequate as science and consequently incapable of contributing greatly to the conduct or reform of American democratic institutions. Each helped promote new efforts to create a true science of politics, explicitly or implicitly confident that it would help make more sophisticated forms of democracy possible. Subsequently, however, each became dissatisfied with the results and methods of their intellectual progeny. Those works often disparaged the feasibility of democracy, however construed, in professional jargon inaccessible to ordinary citizens. Thus, late in their careers, these leading figures all turned away from emphasizing the pursuit of a truly "scientific" political science to stressing the vindication and advancement of effective human political agency via a more truly democratic politics. Such later works frequently have been judged, in turn, naive and unscientific by younger proponents of yet another new science of politics.

This cyclical pattern has been significantly modified by a secular linear one.

Whereas Beard and to a lesser degree Merriam came to denounce excessive "scientism" in politics, and even the possibility of a political science altogether, the later figures have not issued such explicit denunciations. Instead, the self-understanding of political scientists as members of a disinterested profession pursuing scientific knowledge for its own sake has become more entrenched (a phenomenon to which I will return). Furthermore, from the time of Lasswell onward, the concerns to aid democratic politics by political scientists like David Truman, V. O. Key Jr., David Easton, and Robert Dahl in the 1950s increasingly came to center on the provisions of tools and insights to managerial "democratic" elites. To be sure, from the late 1960s on Easton, Almond, Dahl, and Charles Lindblom, among others, reinstantiated the older pattern by moving from an early emphasis on scientific analyses (of systems, group politics, and incrementalist decision making, respectively) to explicitly normative efforts to further democracy, often by criticizing the power of corporations and experts and promoting a better informed democratic citizenry. Generally, however, such figures have neither been quite so dismissive of political science as Beard came to be nor so optimistic about the real possibilities for democratic improvements as Merriam seems to have remained.[10]

William Riker's writings dramatize how the cyclical pattern of moving from an emphasis on science to democracy has been tempered by increased commitment overall to the study of politics as a scientific pursuit and the inevitability of elite predominance even in democratic politics. Since turning to social choice theory, Riker never abandoned his confidence that it is the right candidate to guide a truly scientific politics. He tried, however, to show that although traditional democratic ideals were unscientific and naive (and particularly blind to cycling problems), an admittedly more elite-dominated version of democratic theory can be developed and defended (Riker 1962, 1982). He also wrote a more popular work edifying citizens about the "heresthetic art" of democratic statesmanship, an art "free men use to control their surroundings." "Heresthetics" includes creative elements that the science of rational choice can explicate but not generate or predict (1986 ix–x). Thus, Riker to some degree retraced the intellectual path of Beard and Merriam but now with science and an elite theory of democracy more firmly in command. Many other contemporary political scientists are much more skeptical about both science, particularly in the form of rational choice theory, and democratic elitism, as we shall see. But Riker probably typifies the modern profession's predominant trajectory on these issues prior to the recent turns to history and institutions and perhaps still today.

I will not try to review here the specific objections each successive "new scientist of politics" raised against his predecessors or the exact elements of the new version of science each offered. To keep things manageable, let me instead pick up the story with the approaches to politics that became dominant after World War Two. These are the forms that recent scholars have tried to transcend.

Most historians of the discipline agree that the postwar era offered multiple incentives for political scientists to identify themselves exclusively as professional pursuers of objective scientific knowledge on the model of the more successful natural sciences. The relative consensus on political ends and the desirability of liberal democratic political institutions during the cold war, leading to claims of "the end of ideology," made technical questions of means seem more salient than debates over purposes or first principles. Enhanced faith in science and technology stemming from their military contributions reinforced the already enormous prestige of "scientism." More concretely, government and foundations offered massive new support for certain sorts of "scientific" higher education and research. The Rockefeller Foundation made the national election studies of the Michigan Survey Research Center possible. The Ford Foundation sponsored the Center for Advanced Study in the Behavioral Sciences at Palo Alto (Dahl 1961a, 765–66). Researchers ever since have found that in applying for funds at federal sources like the National Science Foundation, projects that have had "the appearance of hard science have had the inside track" (Almond and Genco 1990, 46). The discipline was able to grow as never before during these years but only by presenting itself both as more of a purely academic profession and more as a science (Purcell 1973, 237–40; Somit and Tanenhaus [1967] 1982, 145–47, 167–72, 183–94; Ricci 1984, 112–13, 126–27; Seidelman and Harpham 1985, 151–59).

The now familiar label for the new science of politics of the 1950s was "behavioralism," but behavioralism meant many things. It usually indicated predilections for focusing on observable actions of political persons rather than formal institutions or those persons' public rhetoric and self-understandings ("study what they do, not what they say"). When "content analysis" was attempted, it often amounted to classifying statements according to the researchers' rather simplified categories rather than trying to grasp interpretively the subjects' own categories and perspectives. Indeed, with but a few exceptions, such as presidential studies, relatively little attention was paid to actual particular individuals involved in politics or holding political views. Behavioralists also favored questions of description and causal explanation rather than quests to define moral standards and normative ideals. To address these favored "empirical questions," many tacitly or explicitly endorsed Carl Hempel's "covering law" model of science, in which particular events are "explained" when they are shown to be instances of more general behavioral regularities. The prevalence of these features should not, however, be inflated. Most commonly, behavioralism simply renewed rather sensible calls for a scientific methodology of hypothesis formulation and empirical testing. The behavioralist "mood," to use Dahl's label, was thus compatible with a range of outlooks on the primary phenomena of politics and with no clear general outlook at all, only narrower hypotheses about specific aspects of political conduct.[11]

Many believed that if political science were truly to be a science, such scientific methods were not enough. The discipline needed an "operationalizable" guiding theory of what the primary factors in politics were and how they worked, from which more particular hypotheses could be deductively derived. It needed, in short, what Kuhn would call a dominant "paradigm" (albeit one that might prove timeless in a way that Kuhn's understanding of paradigms called into question). It is generally agreed as well that two (connectable) would-be paradigms especially came to the fore as foundations for the new "behavioral" science of politics: the pluralist group theory of Truman and Dahl, harkening back to Bentley (and John Dewey), and the structural or systems functionalism of Easton and Gabriel Almond, derived from the sociology of Talcott Parsons and the anthropology of the 1920s.[12] These perspectives each stood in opposition, above all, to frameworks derived from Marx. In the bipolar cold war world, Marxian analysis overhung the discourse of American political scientists even though there were few highly prominent proponents (and perhaps no great grasp) of it in the discipline (particularly in McCarthy's 1950s).

The response of the new American political scientists was largely to show that contemporary politics did not meet Marxian and other descriptions of class or elite domination. True, groups and systems were often driven by economic interests, as Madison well knew. But they had a range of other interests as well. Relationships to the means of production were not all-determining. Moreover, modern American politics, at least, was too porous and multiply populated for any particular economic group or interest to prevail all the time. This pluralism often provided both the opportunity and the necessity for political leaders to shape how things got done. But their actions were often portrayed simply as the intersections of pressures from social groups with the leaders' own interests in officeholding. Thus, groups more than leaders still set the public agenda.

Generally, because of their contemporary focus, behavioral political scientists responded less directly to Marxian accounts of history. But when they sketched accounts of historical development, as in Dahl's review of New Haven's history or V. O. Key's theory of realigning elections, they tended to write as if group struggle was a timeless model for politics, with a gradual broadening of the groups involved combined with a tendency for religious and racial cleavages to give way to "rational," compromisable socioeconomic interests over time. Almond's elaborations of structural-functionalist systems analysis into a model of economic and political development also served as an alternative theory of history in which systemic adaptation and acquisition of some type of "modern," Western-style political and economic institutions replaced class struggle and the ultimate triumph of the proletariat. In so arguing, both pluralists and system analysts seemed to regard their models of politics and of a set pattern of development as applicable to virtually all times and places, with truncated historical or Third World versions destined to flower into modern forms. Thus, to critics, pluralist and modernization theories appeared to be imposed on history rather than informed by it.[13]

And there were always many critics of the new behavioral science of politics, advocates of a wide range of alternative modes of analysis and political perspectives, from surviving exponents of the older historical-institutional approaches to conservative advocates of classical natural right to leftist scholars influenced by the Frankfurt School. Scholars agree that the tumultuous politics of the late 1960s and 1970s strengthened the voices and the credibility of these varied critics, particularly those decrying not only behavioral methods but the character and institutions of American political life. The race riots, the politics of poverty, the ferocious protests over Vietnam that were met by sometimes violent repression, and the mushrooming of the counterculture, followed in the 1970s by Watergate and the relative decline of the United States's global economic and political status after OPEC's embargo and the Vietnam withdrawal—all challenged prevailing political science portraits of American and world politics. They now appeared both descriptively inadequate and ideologically attuned to preservation of a particular, unsatisfactory status quo.

Insofar as they really existed, pluralist group politics did not seem so benign because groups like blacks and the poor might be harshly excluded. Nor did such politics seem so transparently likely to endure. The "state" seemed more real and significant than "pure" pluralist theory allowed, for it appeared at once capable of initiating redistribution and of stifling popular protest movements. It could also falter internationally with dangerous consequences at home and abroad. Notions that Western states might altruistically lead others toward liberal democratic "modernization" seemed naive. Politics, moreover, did not appear so fundamentally nonideological nor moral questions so obsolete. Thus, in a conflict-ridden, often topsy-turvy era, political science could persuasively be accused of offering only static, complacent, ethnocentric models that did not simply fail to produce any behavioral "laws," or to predict, explain, or provide effective social guidance concerning the startling events occurring. To an embarrassing extent, the political science literature also failed even to discuss these topics.[14]

The support that events gave to critical perspectives in political science during these years ushered the discipline into what some have called the "postbehavioral" era. But that label can mislead. For one, much of political science continues much as it did before. Furthermore, the various protests swept together by the label have little in common beyond some enemies. Hence, even though many of the critics emphasized the importance of history, as we shall see, they cannot plausibly be lumped together as part of a single "turn to history." "Postbehavioralism" is best understood as describing a time period not an intellectual school or approach (Somit and Tanenhaus [1967] 1982, 230–33; Ricci 1984, 188–90; Seidelman and Harpham 1985, 192–200).

In fact, in the 1970s, the leading professional response to the perceived failings of behavioral political science probably was increased interest in the leading new candidate for providing a true science of politics—namely, rational (or social, or public) choice theory, in all its main variants: models of individual decision making aimed at preference maximization, systems of aggregating preferences, and game theory. Since the mid-1970s, virtually all the nation's leading departments have competed vigorously to recruit the leading scholars in rational choice. Their work has, to be sure, evolved in ways that are partially responsive to criticisms of earlier forms of behavioralism. Most notably, Riker and others have abandoned their previous disparagement of institutional analysis to champion a rational choice form of "new institutionalism" or "neoinstitutionalism." These analyses involve efforts to model how institutional rules and structures affect the expression and aggregation of preferences, empowering some actors and at times resolving cycling problems by inducing a single, stable equilibrium. Because many political actors realize that institutional structures have these features, moreover, the politics through which institutions come to be adopted or reshaped can and has been made subject to more or less formal rational choice modeling.[15] Riker and others have also shown how rational choice theory can illuminate the behavior of political actors, legislative bodies, and electoral systems in different historical periods (Riker 1980, 1986; Cox 1987; Shepsle and Weingast 1987).[16]

From the standpoint of nonrational choice proponents of a turn history and to institutions, however, such modeling does not really succeed in capturing the most important things that the various strands of behavioralism missed. It still assumes that the substance of political actors' preferences are fixed by forces impervious to political transformation. It also analyzes alternative institutions only in terms of their effects on actors' efforts to maximize such preferences, including their decisions about which preferences to express and pursue (Noll and Weingast 1991, 239–43). If there were any common denominators to the antibehavioral protests, however, they probably were the complaints that in describing "mature" political reality as group competition within "modern" systems, political scientists had dismissed the possibility of meaningful alternatives to such systems and such a politics. Many critics insisted that insofar as the behavioralists' (and rational choice) versions of "reality" were true, they should instead be seen as recent products of major transformations in quite different past political worlds and as potentially subject to major, possibly radical transformation in the future (or even the present). Such transformations might not only involve the reconstitution of basic institutions but also of the basic values and indeed the very identities of political actors.

For some, these broader-ranging concerns called for a renewal of speculative political theory. But for many, they gave reasons for more genuine turns to history than rational choice could by itself provide. As Sheldon Wolin argued at the height of the assault on behavioralism, the history of political regimes and of political theory was a superb storehouse of alternative political visions that might suggest diagnoses and new possibilities for the present. Furthermore, history might reveal the transforming forces that helped craft the politics of the present, forces that must be understood if the character and prospects of that politics were to be fully comprehended (Easton 1969, 1058; Wolin 1969, 1077; Ricci 1984, 278, 311–12).

Despite these protests, there was no overwhelming rush to the study of historical processes or the history of political ideas in the 1970s or 1980s. The recent attention to the history of the discipline itself may be a sign that scholars are still searching to identify how and why political science has fallen short of its practitioners' aspirations. Nonetheless, some "turns to history" were made that have steadily grown more influential. In history of ideas, the investigations of Bernard Bailyn, Gordon Wood, and especially the sometime political scientist J. G. A. Pocock have seemed to a wide variety of scholars to have actually uncovered an alternative political vision that might be of some use in the present. Their accounts of "civic humanism" or "republicanism" have suggested that Americans are heirs to a neglected nonliberal legacy of more communitarian, virtuous, perhaps even participatory, politics. Some political scientists have subsequently joined the historians' quest to shed light on modern politics by discovering how and how far republicanism became liberalism in America. Others are engaging in speculation about how the desirable features of early republicanism can be recaptured today (Bailyn 1967; Wood 1969; Pocock 1975; Lienesch 1980; Hanson 1985; Sandel 1984; Sunstein 1990).

Especially since the mid-1970s, political theorists and historians of political ideas have also offered the discipline another sort of "turn to history" of mounting influence: the "hermeneutical turn," inspired largely by postmodernist European critical theory and radicalized in more recent postmodernist variants. Those labels refer to an imposingly large and quite varied body of work by scholars like Hans-Georg Gadamer, Jürgen Habermas, Michel Foucault, Paul Ricoeur, and Jacques Derrida. Their work was then expounded and extended in American political science by such theorists as Alasdair MacIntyre, Charles Taylor, William Connolly, and Michael Shapiro and reinforced by the qualified advocacy of leading historians of political ideas, notably Quentin Skinner (Skinner 1969; MacIntyre 1971; Taylor 1985a, 1985b; Connolly 1974; Derrida 1976; Foucault 1977; Habermas 1979; Ricoeur 1981; Shapiro 1981; Gadamer 1982).

These bodies of work are far too complex and diverse to be summarized here, but two frequently visible themes are particularly pertinent. First is an emphasis on the interpretive character of all human knowledge: far from ever discovering objective laws about politics or indeed any other facet of our world, hermeneutical thinkers stress how all accounts are only controversial, partial interpretations stitched together largely from other such interpretations and often unified only by the interpreter's quest to impose on phenomena a sense and meaning that the interpreter values. Second, however, in more radical postmodernist writers this apparent focus on "the interpreter" is often undercut by an insistence that "the interpreter" and her senses of meaning are effectively constituted by preexisting languages, interpretations, and discourses that have been both spawned in and formative of a wide range of social contexts. Thus, all "interpreters" (that is to say, all human beings) may be understood as no more than particular congeries of interpretations emerging out of the complex pageant of preceding human history.[17] In that unfolding drama, moreover, some perspectives have been forced into the wings, often brutally.

Hermeneutically minded scholars give these points very different specifications and weight, and they certainly do not concur on what all this implies for understanding human beings. But most agree that the task involves, at least in part, grasping more fully the traditions, contexts, and languages that have at least partly constituted particular persons or groups. That task is pursued largely by taking the discourse and actions of such persons as "texts" and unfolding (or "deconstructing") their constitutive elements to approach, not a full grasp of the human world in which they emerged, but, in Gadamer's term, the "effective-historical" world they can project for us. Some postmodernist scholars rest with such deconstructive readings. But many others enrich their interpretations via similar engagement with other "texts" comprising and comprised by the historical contexts of the scholars' primary interests. These sorts of historical inquiries may help scholars see, for example, the manner in which one language (of, say, professional psychology) has delegitimated others (such as forms of political, cultural, and sexual radicalism). For such postmodernists, the quest for a positive, causal social science gives way to, or is at most a transitional moment in, interpretive empirical inquiries into historically constituted "texts" that encompass human political action. Although still more avant-garde than mainstream and still more centered on theoretical expositions than concrete explorations, hermeneutical works and postmodern works are proliferating in the discipline and are increasingly concerned with substantive interpretations of, for example, American political thought and culture (e.g., Hanson 1985; Norton 1986; cf. Ricci 1984, 275–88).

Until recently, however, republican revisionism and hermeneutics were of interest almost exclusively to political theorists, not to empirically minded political scientists. They were more impressed by perhaps the most influential assault on pluralist complacency, Theodore Lowi's *The End of Liberalism.* That work stressed the contention that the pluralist politics of the 1950s and 1960s were far from timeless. Pluralism was instead the genuinely modern product of historical forces, particularly the rise of a (deplorable) new public philosophy of "interest group liberalism" embodied in a (corrupt) "Second Republic" of the United States. On the whole, Lowi's work remained quite contemporary, with only the most broadly sketched historical arguments. Thus, it only raised the questions of how American politics had been changed over time and what forces might change them in the future. But its success helped renew the receptivity of the discipline to studies that explored how institutions (like the presidency) had altered through history, in ways partly traceable to different historical conceptions of their purposes. Many of those studies have been more historical than Lowi's work (Lowi [1969] 1979, 1985; Ceaser 1979; Tulis 1987; Skowronek 1993).[18]

In 1973, the dean of the study of comparative politics in the United States, Gabriel Almond, issued an even more explicit call for his subfield to seek "a cure in history." Almond first conceded to his critics that the "system functionalism" of the 1960s had tended to underestimate "the dynamic and conflictual aspects of social systems" and to be too "deterministic" and negligent of "acts of human decision and choice" that "by themselves have causal value."

Functionalist works had wrongly postulated fixed stages and sequences of development that often simply did not capture actual historical struggles. To do better, Almond and several colleagues undertook a number of historical case studies in which they applied the various theories of development Almond had critiqued (system functionalism, social mobilization theory, rational choice theory, accounts of leadership) and evaluated how well, singly and in combination, they served to explain certain historical events. This synthetic enterprise, Almond thought, showed the way to "a general theory of politics" (Almond 1973, 7, 13, 27). The book was less imitated than its authors hoped, and that general theory has remained elusive. But Almond's arguments have been invoked as legitimating authority by recent advocates of new institutionalist analyses in comparative politics (e.g., Krasner 1984, 225).

The turn to history that has probably been most widely noted as such in the discipline appeared in these new institutionalist writings. Their authors identified themselves in the first instance, however, as turning to institutions, specifically to the importance of "the state." Calls to "bring the state back in," which quickly attracted numerous supporters and critics in the late 1970s and early 1980s, were traceable to the protests of a few years before against the failure of prevailing behavioral accounts to comprehend what was then going on in the world. For example, Theda Skocpol's influential argument that state structures conditioned the character and fate of the world's major modern revolutions was sparked by a concern to understand the obstacles to revolutionary change facing movements in America and elsewhere during her student days. Those obstacles (in, for example, South Africa) emphatically seemed to include the role of states. She and others arguing for the importance of state structures and institutions have nonetheless typically come to that perspective through extensive immersion in history. More importantly, their arguments about how institutions shape behavior, which then reshapes institutions, have to be made via history, through discussion of fairly long periods of time. Most stress that institutions make historical development "path dependent," influenced by previous institutionally conditioned decisions that open up certain further lines of development while closing off others (Skocpol 1979, xii–xiii, 1985; Skowronek 1982; Krasner 1988, 67, 72; Karl 1990, 7–8; Sewell 1990).[19]

The reasons why the recent turn to institutions also involves turning to history can further be seen by considering the most ambitious effort so far to "theorize" a new institutionalism not limited to rational choice modeling, namely, James G. March and Johan P. Olsen's *Rediscovering Institutions* (1989). The book expands their earlier, exceptionally influential *American Political Science Review* article (March and Olsen 1984).[20] March and Olsen acknowledge as I have here that the new institutionalism does not offer any general guiding theory as rational choice does. They also agree that new institutionalist studies are driven by certain linked intellectual dissatisfactions with the models of politics that have prevailed in social science in the postwar era, including both behavioralism and rational choice.

First, in March and Olsen's account, those models did indeed treat politics as "epiphenomena," affected by, but not significantly affecting, elements like "class, geography, climate, ethnicity, language, culture, economic conditions, demography, technology, ideology, and religion." Second, extending that point, the older models treated the "preferences and powers" of political actors as "exogenous . . . depending on their positions in the social and economic system" and not alterable by political deliberations, decisions, institutions, or processes. Third, but also an aspect of the same reductionism, behavioralist and rational choice theories have treated symbols, ideologies, and political visions as essentially all political "devices" wielded on behalf of political actors' socioeconomic self-interests, not as matters of intrinsic value and importance. And fourth, this persistent dismissal of the causal importance of political life has generally been made credible by assuming that economic and social systems are functionally "efficient." Less productive and stable modes are assumed to be weeded out over time one way or the other. So if we know what constitutes a more efficient economic or social system (e.g., liberal market systems), we can expect that socioeconomic (and thus political) systems will evolve toward such institutions in the long run, however politicians may choose in the short run (March and Olsen 1989, 3–4, 7–8, 48–52).

In place of these views, March and Olsen suggest that political actions and political institutions shape their environments even as they are shaped by them; that persons' resources and very preferences are often constituted by past political actions and institutions, which shape the meanings persons find in their lives; that these efforts to craft and preserve meaning are, as hermeneuticists often contend, as much moving forces in political behavior as economic or social and political status imperatives; and finally, that as a result the actors and concerns that shape history are so multiple and complex that historical processes cannot be captured by models of evolutionary efficiency. Socioeconomically inefficient structures and behavior do occur and endure, for other sorts of reasons.

Those are all propositions that most new institutionalists want to defend. But to defend them, they must turn to history. They cannot otherwise show how past actions and institutions constitute the powers and preferences of agents in contemporary politics nor can they discern any actual patterns of historical evolution that may exist even though sequential stages of efficient evolution do not. Thus, while some new institutionalist studies focus primarily on the present, the agenda of the institutionalist turn means that on the whole, if political scientists accept these arguments, historical inquiries must proliferate.

We have now reached the multifaceted recent turn to history in political science by way of its proximate causes. As the road has been rather long, let me summarize here why I believe these causes can legitimately be understood in terms of the deeper tension I initially described as dissatisfaction with a political "science" that failed to capture how politics seems so much to matter. The "postbehavioral" critics had to combat the powerful professional incentives noted earlier that pressed scholars to develop and empirically investigate causal theories similar to those in the natural sciences, without much regard to how well these works responded to the political problems of the day. The critics were aided by increasingly widespread beliefs that contemporary political events were so important as to render a political science negligent of them morally and intellectually indefensible. The quests for political alternatives that these events triggered had as implicit premises beliefs that political actors can make meaningful choices of the sorts of political worlds they work for and that their choices have some real chance to reshape the world. Moreover, because many critics also identified themselves with the vindication of a more genuinely democratic politics than the American status quo of the late 1960s and 1970s, the critical assaults also frequently manifested the more particular tension in American political science between working out a true science of politics and doing scholarship that legitimates and assists democratic self-governance.

The rise of rational choice since the 1960s might seem to belie these claims. But although its growth is traceable to the continued appeal of a science of politics more than an affirmation of agency, rational choice models did at least portray actors as rational calculators and instrumental choosers, even if their ends appeared to be beyond their choosing.[21] The renewed attentions to administrative institutions; to historical revolutions and lesser transformations as well as to "the state"; and to the history of political ideas, public philosophies, and political culture even more clearly expressed the sense that sometimes our central political institutions, and even our beliefs about politics, do make a difference. All of March and Olsen's arguments, moreover, clearly rest on the belief that politics matters and that socioeconomic reductionisms are inadequate because politics reshapes other aspects of our social world, including our powers, preferences, and very senses of meaning, and hence it affects all historical development. The various turns to history and to institutions in political science, then, do seem to manifest the basic tension between developing deterministic causal explanations of politics, which much of behavioralism ardently tried to do even if it failed, and vindicating our sense that the conscious decisions of political actors matter, which behavioralism at least implicitly minimized. And for many American proponents of these turns, the politics that they most wished to matter remains democratic, at least in aspiration.

But, thus far, the various schools of revisionist scholars cannot boast of any great progress in resolving either of these profound tensions. Their works often suggest, however ruefully, that even if politics matters, democracy as anything more than a means of "throwing the rascals out" (to be replaced by others) appears unattainable. Rational choice theorists, again, have explicitly concluded that only a quite elitist version of democracy is possible. Thus, Riker's more popular work edifies about democratic statesmanship, not citizenship. Similarly, Almond's historical studies give much more support to the agency of leaders than democratic citizens. Many advocates of republicanism have instead hoped for a more truly democratic, participatory polity. Often postmodernist critical scholarship also promises to democratize human affairs by debunking the truth claims of dominant views and showing the insights in marginalized ones. Lowi has repeatedly called for a more truly democratic "juridical democracy," and writers like Skocpol and Skowronek have clearly wished to probe ways that stronger but more fully democratic states can be achieved. But these same scholars tend to suggest instead that if classical republicanism was ever present, it is irretrievably lost in the privatistic, commercial, inegalitarian modern world; that prevailing forms of political interpretation and culture are unalterably hegemonic; that, in particular, the dominance of self-seeking and unequal interest groups over American institutions cannot be broken; and that Americans are not likely to achieve a much stronger state unless it is much less democratic.

It has, moreover, not been possible to sketch the new approaches without already indicating that much in them still minimizes not just democracy but human agency itself, perhaps as much as previous explanations did. Rational choice models limit us to questions of means, not ends. Basic political preferences are beyond the realm of conscious human alteration. And to keep their models manageable in design and determinate in outcome, rational choice theorists often take a narrow view of what the unalterable preferences of agents are. Many scholars simply assume that political actors are motivated chiefly by wealth and power or status, apparently as a result of relatively unchangeable human biological and psychological structures.

In an important essay, John Ferejohn has suggested that rational choice theorists should instead use interpretive historical works to judge what sorts of interests and preferences political actors actually possessed in particular contexts. Thus, agents can be portrayed as having a more varied array of goals. But those portrayals are tacked on to the rational choice view of agency. They do not flow from it. Insofar as rational choice analyses turn to history in this way, they simply admit the limited distinctive contribution of the "science of rational choice" to political analysis. That limitation could be overcome if theorists could show how the historical formation of preferences and values can be grasped in rational choice terms. But if values are shaped by forces other than calculations of how best to pursue preexisting preferences (such as, for example, noninstrumentalist normative reflection), then rational choice cannot hope to do so. Its view of agency places all such forces outside the realm of rational human decision making (Ferejohn 1991; discussed in Smith 1992).[22]

All the other perspectives I have noted represent more genuine "turns to history." They are all trying to explain how the character and preferences of political agents are developed and changed through historical processes rather than to merely feed the results of such processes into an ahistorical model. But they not only conceive of those processes in significantly different ways. All of their accounts also contain features threatening the attribution to agents of meaningful control over both their means and ends. At the other end of the current intellectual spectrum from rational choice, hermeneutical scholars tend to portray agents as constituted primarily by historically evolving languages and traditions that offer standards of intrinsic meaningfulness and therefore give the conduct of agents a dimension not captured in models of instrumental rationality on behalf of economic or status interests. Scholars of republicanism and the rise of modern "interest group liberalism" similarly stress the role of changing public ideologies in shaping agency, action, and outcomes, at least implicitly. They generally have greater faith, however, that they can portray the interactions between traditions of public philosophy and "external" socioeconomic developments than do pure hermeneuticists, who see languages only as self-referential systems of signs. Yet in all these accounts, ideologies, public philosophies, prevailing interpetations, and languages all sometimes either seem still to be puppets of socioeconomic forces or they are themselves prisons of consciousness that do more to limit than to empower political actors.

The various historical new institutionalists, in turn, are willing to encompass languages and ideologies as kinds of structures or institutions, but through the mid-1980s, at least, they often placed most emphasis on the determining role of political organizations as traditionally understood, especially state bureaucracies (e.g., Skocpol 1979; Skowronek 1982; Krasner 1984). In some of these works, "state structures" often came close to being reified as autonomous entities that severely constrained if they did not altogether displace "voluntarist" features of political life.[23] Recognizing that those accounts may have unduly minimized personal human agency, new institutionalist writers like March and Olsen, Theda Skocpol and Terry Karl have increasingly called for "interactive" approaches that give due weight to both sides of the "dialectic of meaningful actions and structural determinants" (Skocpol 1984, 4; March and Olsen 1989, 45, 52; Karl 1990, 1). But just how one does that remains very problematic. Hence, these approaches are only beginning to suggest some ways meaningful actions can reshape structural contexts and to compare differing accounts of such historical human agency.

The embryonic character of these efforts and the great difficulties they face explain why some believe recent developments have only exacerbated the splintering of a troubled discipline. Many responded to Gabriel Almond's characterization in 1988 of political science as a profession marked by increasing balkanization, with devotees of true social "science," especially rational choice, ever more greatly polarized from the assorted "historical approaches" reviewed here as well as from more traditional behavioralisms. Others fear that the historical approaches, moreover, sacrifice scientific rigor in favor of fuzzy belletristic "explanations," while providing nothing that can really advance either the evidence for, or the exercise of, effective human agency, particularly within democratic politics. Hence, we are now hearing the gloomy indictments of the new institutionalist turn to history cited at the outset (Skocpol 1984, 4; Almond 1988; Smith 1988, 92–101; March and Olsen 1989, 16, 46).

A Possible Future for History

It seems to me that the new institutionalism has much more promise than its critics allow. Although I hold out little hope that it will generate a definitive predictive and explanatory theory for all politics, it may lead to an increasing approximation of the fullest understandings that subject permits. This potential is important because I do not think political science will flourish best if it continues as it on the whole does now. Political scientists often complacently answer doubts by invoking the desirability of a pluralistic discipline and suggesting that over time, the competition of ideas will automatically winnow out better from poorer accounts of politics. Others suggest virtually all approaches will be seen to capture truths at different but compatible "levels," such as the scientific "level" of physical causality and the hermeneutical "level" of symbolic meaningfulness.[24]

A sort of competition surely occurs, but it is usually not one in which persons attentive to all forms of political analysis choose the types that prove most powerful. The discipline is already so fragmented that its different schools of thought rarely compete directly, offering rival accounts of the same phenomena to the same audience. Instead, adherents of different outlooks write and judge largely among themselves. Their relative professional status is greatly influenced by the extent to which they find prestigious like-minded audiences in other corners of the intellectual world outside the discipline, such as economics, philosophy, or literary theory. There is no guarantee that the most intellectually powerful forms of political science will find proportionately influential external audiences; nor does this form of competition encourage cross-fertilization among different approaches. Occasional suggestions that we embrace almost all approaches as illuminations of truth at different "levels," moreover, risk being fatuous. Often, various approaches are advancing sharply opposed views of the basic character and driving forces of human action that imply different predictions for behavior in particular circumstances. If they can somehow be shown to be compatible, substantial careful argumentation, not a genial tolerance, is required.

This survey suggests, however, that the multiple flavors of political science do have certain things in common. Although those things are quite general, I believe the discipline can build upon them. As I have tried to show, all political scientists are inescapably concerned to offer accounts, explicitly or implicitly, of human political agency and its relationship to political outcomes. Their accounts differ greatly, however, in what they take the character of human political agency to be, and these differences are not adequately explored. Thus, much progress might be made by comparing the power of different accounts and by accumulating the evidence for particular conceptions that those comparisons provide. To do so, researchers would have to reformulate their work to put these issues center stage, in the ways many new institutionalist writers have suggested. They would present as their basic units of analysis different types of structures or institutions that, they hypothesize, constitute political actors and their environments in important ways, endowing actors with specifiable constraints or capabilities, or both.[25]

Virtually everything that might reasonably be postulated as influencing or contributing to human political conduct could be studied as such constitutive structures, including the biological and genetic systems that give people their physical capacities; the sets of emotional affects toward political parties, nations, and the like that are fostered in childhood socialization; and the kinship networks, structures of ethnic and racial relations, and religious organizations and practices that shape these affects and indeed constitute actors' senses of their personal identities and purposes; and so on. Structures would also include the economic relationships and the routinized work practices that shape actors' opportunities and interests, the particular political agencies and strategic situations they confront, the more basic set of political institutions in their constitutional systems, and much more. The possibilities are endless, especially insofar as many combinations of structures or institutions would also have to be explored.[26]

Those expansive possibilities are appropriate because the proposed framework is designed to encompass, not exclude, existing forms of research and to promote systematic comparisons of alternative theories of political action, not to privilege any particular one. Investigators would ordinarily begin by treating structures as independent variables, hypothesized to cause or shape certain kinds of actions in specified ways. For many, this would at first blush amount to minor relabeling, as they continued to consider, for example, whether racist emotional affects are more or less present than in the past, whether the separation of powers in the United States makes it harder to pass legislation than in parliamentary systems, how the division of authority over issues may enable a committee system to produce stable outcomes, and many other familiar topics.

But moving to this conception of the political science enterprise would have some significant consequences both for what is studied and how it is studied. Students of politics have notoriously different conceptions of what forms of political action are most important, indeed of what counts as "political" action. For some, it is decisions of elected officials, for others workplace struggles, and for still others forcible establishment of gender roles and hierarchies within families. And there are many other views as well. But proponents of each particular position are implicitly committed to explaining at least some of the actions others emphasize, if only to show that they are not independently significant. Decisions of lawmakers, judges, and administrators affecting industrial and familial relations, for instance, must be related to the struggles in those arenas regardless of which ways an investigator believes the causal arrows should point. If researchers saw themselves as sharing a common enterprise of illuminating political action, or even if they were simply concerned to refute claims of rival views, they would consciously construct their studies to encompass actions that adherents of conflicting theories recognize as important.

Researchers working in these ways would then clarify whether the structures they are taking as independent variables are hypothesized to constrain an actor to take specific actions or whether they are instead thought to enable the actor to adopt any of a specified *range* of possible courses.[27] The latter sort of hypotheses will be favored whenever researchers doubt that an ultimate external determinant for an actor's choices can be found. If political scientists still choose to adopt the first kind of hypothesis, which is the pattern in much existing work, they would be making clear their supposition of deterministic views of human agency, at least in regard to the conduct studied. Researchers' choices to specify ranges of behavior instead might, in turn, result either from their crediting agents with powers of strategic choices within a set of interest-maximizing options or from attributing to them capabilities to define their interests in any of several different ways.[28]

Investigators adopting the second sort of hypotheses, that is, suppositions that we can at best define a range of possible actions agents might choose from, would then have a further stage of analysis open to them. The choices of the political actors they examine, once discovered, would have to be treated subsequently as independent variables, which would sometimes reshape the structures that influenced or even constituted those political actors in the first place. Such reshaping might well be pivotal for future political developments. To keep their tasks manageable, analysts usually would not in all probability pursue these interactive historical paths very far. But those advancing these sorts of agency-sympathetic hypotheses would be committed to presenting their accounts as parts of such paths.[29]

If scholars complied with these precepts, then the discipline as a whole might be better able to accumulate some knowledge of how well models emphasizing different causal structures account for the same political decisions and actions; of how agency-sympathetic theories fare in comparison with more deterministic ones; of where political scientists have found behavior that simply does not seem well captured by any deterministic account; and of how those relatively autonomous actions, in particular, have affected the political world. Political scientists would also be better positioned to pursue an array of even more complex and intriguing questions.

For example, if certain structures appear to do most of the important explanatory work in some situations, while others matter in different ones, investigators could move toward more general propositions about when different structural contexts are most salient and how they interact. Some might even be tempted to devise a grand theory of historical development that indicates when particular structures are most influential and why, though most new institutionalists believe the complexities of historical processes and the unpredictability of human political choices make such a theory quite improbable.[30] Perhaps most significantly for a political science relevant to political practice, investigators could also study what structures appear to broaden actors' capacities for meaningful agency in important ways. I have elsewhere offered some preliminary evidence that the rise of a new discourse in a political culture can enable actors to redefine their political identities and goals in ways that were not previously likely by suggesting alternative conceptions of self-interest (Smith 1992). New opportunities and new obstacles for coalition-building and policy formation then emerge. A political science that shed more light on what political actors can reasonably hope to do to solve the political and social problems they confront would obviously be of great value.

A concern for agency would also prompt researchers to pay more attention to instances of political conduct they find that do not seem explicable in terms of imperatives derived from the structures that constitute the actors in question or their situations. Some conduct may not even fall within the range of actions the investigators believe their subjects were capable of undertaking.[31] When they examine what the actors in such situations did, analysts may find that their hypotheses misconstrued the constraints and capabilities provided by the structures in question, or they may argue that they have found evidence for the impact of a structure previously neglected. Sometimes, however, it may appear that actors have drawn on the resources available to them to redefine their own objectives, or to persuade others to redefine theirs, in ways that were extraordinarily difficult to imagine, much less predict, in advance. James Madison's famed redefinitions of "republican" as opposed to "democratic" governments in *Federalist* paper no. 10 might be an example (Rossiter 1961, 81–82). His novel account of forms of government was strategically designed to purge republicanism of its natural affinities for the Anti-Federalist position. But it was also a substantive attempt to work out the political vision Madison wished to define as well as defend.

If this and many other such examples stood up to close examination over time, the discipline would collectively document a portrait of political agency as involving both skill in instrumental rationality, indeed genuine strategic creativity, and also true human originality in conceiving what human societies and their goals might be. Such capacities would be explicable but not reducible to the actors' constitutive elements and contextual circumstances. The actors themselves would indeed also be independent variables. Political science would then include accounts of politics in which the central phenomena we study—political actions—would clearly matter very much indeed.

I do not wish to deny that these sorts of hypotheses and arguments are visible in political science at present. Ours is a prolific discipline. But I do think many researchers are not adequately attentive to the assumptions about human political action they are making and what their research shows about the plausibility of those assumptions. Hence, I think reformulation of existing types of work to attend more explicitly to issues of the character and relative autonomy of political action is feasible and that such a reformulation would prove conducive to greater communication among different approaches than now occurs. And communication, not consensus, is probably the only sort of unity the discipline can or should hope for, at least at present.

Political science was once unified, at least to some degree, by shared familiarity with the traditional canon of great works in political philosophy, and some readers may wonder how such texts would fit into the sort of discipline I am describing. I believe they would be central to it in at least two ways. First, great works of political theory arguably craft or at least articulate memorably structures of political ideas that may themselves be causal factors in political developments, a possibility that can be explored through a combination of careful textual readings and empirical historical inquiries. Second, by presenting powerful alternative views of politics, the canon of great works can serve as an invaluable guide for significant hypotheses about how politics actually operates and what alternate arrangements might be feasible, thus helping empirical investigators and theoretical innovators to avoid both reinventing wheels or wallowing in trivia. As I have argued elsewhere, these hypotheses could well include notions about the existence and influence of any ultimate moral reality that may exist, as well as about more mundane factors.[32]

Few will be persuaded of all this, however, without more clarification of the obvious ambiguities and difficulties in the conception of political science I have sketched. Many will want more specification of what counts as "politics," "political actors," "political actions," "structures," "institutions," and so on. I have consciously resisted offering the sorts of precise definitions here that I would provide in defending particular substantive hypotheses of my own. My concern at present is to call for a discipline that is open to all remotely plausible candidates to fill out such terms. Empirical research should then be the means for deciding which definitions should receive the most scholarly attention in the long run. That criterion sets few restrictions on researchers other than the admonition to seek ways of doing their work that make its relevance as apparent as possible to the views of political agency advanced by as wide a variety of scholars as possible. Thus, research designs should include whenever possible types of structures, institutions, and conduct that other scholars are likely also to examine when testing rival hypotheses and explanations.

"Political actors" or "agents" should similarly be defined broadly to include possible collective actors like classes, state agencies, nations, and the like. But if the scope of human action is to be fully illuminated, then scholars should strive to explain how the conduct of such collective actors is related to, though not necessarily reducible to, the decisions and actions of individual human beings. Every account should at least aspire to helping us see the operations of the factors it stresses from the standpoint of our worlds of lived experiences, which are always worlds of people.

In the same vein, scholars should strive to make their hypotheses, and the evidence they take to be consistent with them, as clear as possible to those with opposing explanations, even when they are engaged in the sorts of interpretive inquiries that have usually eschewed the scaffolding of hypothesis formulation and testing. As I have argued elsewhere, there is no deep hostility between sensitive interpretation and this basic logic of scientific methods (Smith 1992). Implicitly or explicitly, hermeneutical accounts also begin with hypotheses about what particular symbols, texts, customs, or rituals signify, and then analysts modify those suppositions in light of how far they are sustained by empirical evidence. Scholars who appear to be fighting over "causal-scientific" versus "interpretive" methods are often really opposed over their substantive views of human action. Rather than indulging in methodological ostracism, the challenge is to find ways to explore and debate these more substantive differences more constructively.

Finally, I should underline that, however ecumenical my recommendations may sound, scholars cannot really adopt this sense of the tasks of political science without taking what Almond called "the historical cure." Individual studies, to be sure, might still focus on modeling contemporary politics to explore specific points manageably. But once the profession's agenda includes investigations not only of how various structural contexts constitute political agents with certain capabilities and constraints but also how far those agents reconstitute their contexts, analyses will more typically have to encompass Krasner's chains of events of "structures to decisions to structures" (Krasner 1984, 225; 1988, 72). Moreover, such historical analyses are well advised to attend not only to "normal politics" within various regimes but also to the "extraordinary" politics that occur in periods of revolution and new foundings. Even though many transformational decisions occur in "routine" eras, scholars are most likely to find political actors altering not only their strategies but their very senses of political identity and purpose in such "extraordinary" times. And the decisions taken then often dramatically reorder the lives of many others for years thereafter.

At this point, many readers may wish to ask not whether such a political science involves a turn to history but whether it is not indeed the abdication of political science in favor of narrative history. I do not think that is the case. The discipline I am projecting would still employ standard scientific methods of hypothesis formulation and fair empirical testing aimed at identifying decisive causal forces, whether external to agents or attributable to the agents themselves. It would involve full examination of how far structural factors can explain political decision making, not any a priori emphasis on the unpredictable decisions of autonomous agents, although it would be self-consciously attentive to the possibility that such decisions exist and can matter a great deal.[33] If the body of work built up by such a political science ended up stressing the contingent choices of political actors more than any other factor, and therefore resembled some types of narrative history, that would represent not a surrender but a culmination of the methods of social science. It is also, at this point, a quite premature worry. Political scientists have plenty of structural determinants to explore, some with explanatory power that seems if anything all too massive in comparison with effective human agency.

In any case, the crucial question is not whether the most fruitful way to study human affairs involves choosing between "history" or "science," a dichotomy that all the foregoing analysis puts into question. The real issue is how scholars can study politics in ways that promise to give people greater insight into what the driving forces in their affairs have been and how they can hope to influence them more constructively, when and if they can influence them at all. It is that sort of inquiry that I believe scholars can promote by focusing on questions of human political agency. They will do so especially if they are explicitly open to the possibility that, through political decisions and actions that are truly their own, people can actually make a difference in their world.

NOTES

This essay is a greatly revised version of "The New Non-Science of Politics: On Turns to History in Political Science," prepared for the 1990 Comparative Studies of Social Transformations (CSST) Conference and subsequently issued as CSST Working Paper No. 59. I am indebted to more people than I can list for comments on that draft. Peter A. Hall and Alex Wendt deserve special thanks. Also extraordinarily helpful were Steven Brint, Robert Dahl, James Fesler, Donald Green, Victoria Hattam, Stephen Macedo, David Mayhew, Terry McDonald, Adolph Reed, Bruce Russett, Ian Shapiro, the late Judith Shklar, Stephen Smith, and Richard Zinman. The remaining flaws are due to my prejudices.

1. In this context, John Chubb and Terry Moe are defending the theoretical superiority of economistic models, which they and others use as part of a rational choice

variety of "new institutionalism" or "neo-institutionalism." I discuss this sort of work and its limitations subsequently in the text and, more fully, in Smith (1992).

A Marxist scholar, Paul Cammack, has argued against Theda Skocpol's historical and institutional sociology in a way that parallels Chubb and Moe. Her sort of work leads, Cammack says, to abandonment "of any kind of coherent theoretical framework at all, in favour of middle-level enquiries into a multiplicity of issues in a multiplicity of settings in the hope that something will turn up. Studies pitched in the middle of nowhere are not likely to lead anywhere" (Cammack [1989], 287). Here I suggest instead that studies pitched, not "nowhere," but in a number of theoretical places, all trying to account for common experiences, are more likely to be fruitful than staking all on one grand theory in advance.

2. I use "deterministic" here to refer to accounts that explain the behavior of political actors *entirely* in terms of factors outside the actors' conscious control. I therefore do not mean that all causal accounts are deterministic. For example, propositions that agents are affected though not wholly determined by external physical causes, that their actions may be caused by what they take to be good reasons, and that their acts are themselves physical causes of other events are not deterministic in this sense.

3. Almond (1973), 6, 12–13; Almond and Genco (1990), 32, 45. Almond and Genco argue that the "elements of the implicit logic that informs much of political science research today appear to imply a substantive model of the political world which closely resembles the deterministic 'clock model' outlined by Popper" (45).

4. For example, in 1973 Gabriel Almond was still saying that if structural functionalism "falls short of explanation in the tight sense of experimental science then it suffers the difficulties encountered by all science 'that nature is capricious at the quantum level' and that 'the order of systems emerges as a statistical reality out of the disorder of particles'" (6). The remainder of that important essay focused on the importance of human political choices but did not really treat them as so random as this quotation implies. And Almond explicitly disavowed "the quantum-jump model" as a mischaracterization of "rational human behavior" in Almond and Genco (1990).

5. For instance, further in his coedited 1973 volume, Almond admitted that he and his coworkers had dealt with the political choices of leaders only "impressionistically." Thus, "leadership phenomena tend to be treated residually," even though Almond believed leadership choices to be "the sufficient explanation of a specific outcome" in most cases (Almond and Mundt [1973], 621, 648–49).

6. Almond and Genco similarly argue that although political scientists do not "actually see" the political world deterministically and often give more complex pictures in their detailed empirical analyses, the "meta-methodological principles and procedures" they have "borrowed from the physical sciences—or more correctly, from a certain philosophical perspective on the physical sciences" have come to the discipline "with an array of substantive assumptions," committing it to a "research program designed to strip away the . . . purposive aspects of political reality in order to expose its 'true' clocklike structure" ([1990], 45).

7. Some readers have suggested that the prediction of major complex events is too demanding a test, noting that seismologists did not predict the 1989 San Francisco earthquake. But they did predict that major earthquakes would occur at some point in the relatively near future, and they can provide persuasive retrospective accounts of past earthquakes. Most modern political science (including Marxian analyses) suggested instead that revivified religious absolutism on a large scale, as in Iran and elsewhere, was unlikely. We are, moreover, far from achieving generally persuasive "postdictive" accounts of these phenomena.

I do *not* take these facts as proof that we will never reach a more mature and powerful science of politics, only as evidence that we are, at best, still far from such a thing.

8. For relevant discussions, see Takaki (1979); Gordon (1984). Charles Taylor has made a similar criticism of followers of Derrida, whose emphasis on the constitutive role of self-referential languages can render "the code as ultimate, dominating the supposedly autonomous agent" (Taylor [1985b], 11). Some new institutionalists, such as Meyer, Boli, and Thomas (1987), argue explicitly that they see "action as the enactment of broad institutional scripts rather than a matter of internally generated and autonomous choice, motivation and purpose" (13).

9. Cf., e.g., Crick (1959); Somit and Tanenhaus ([1967] 1982); Kress (1973); Karl (1974); Blondel (1981); Gunnell (1983); Collini, Winch, and Burrow (1983); Higgot (1983); Ricci (1984); Ward (1984); Seidelman and Harpham (1985), Seidelman (1990); Natchez (1985); Janos (1986); Farr (1988a, 1988b, 1990); and Dryzek and Leonard (1988, 1990).

10. The preceding three paragraphs are chiefly distilled from the overviews provided by Crick (1959); Purcell (1973); Somit and Tanenhaus ([1967] 1982); Ricci (1984); Seidelman and Harpham (1985); and Farr (1988a). Easton's noted critique of the profession, which still defends its scientific character, is his presidential address (1969). Almond's progression from early works outlining structural-functionalist social science to advocacy of a focus on purposive human choices while critiquing functionalist and other approaches as "deterministic" can be traced by comparing Almond and Coleman (1960); Almond and Powell (1966); Almond (1973); and Almond and Genco (1990). The later works of Dahl and Lindblom, which more elaborately pursue aspirations to inform citizens and combat obstacles to democracy that have been visible throughout their careers, include Dahl (1985, 1989) and Lindblom (1977, 1990).

11. Dahl (1961a), 765–69; Purcell (1973), 240; Somit and Tanenhaus ([1967] 1982), 173–83; Ricci (1984), 134–44; Seidelman and Harpham (1985), 151–53; and Almond and Genco (1990), 40–46. These works review the leading attempts to define "behavioralism."

12. There were important differences between focusing on "groups" and "systems," but the two modes of analysis could be linked, as Almond did, by treating "interest articulation" as a systemic function performed by various sorts of interest groups (Almond and Coleman [1960], 33; Almond and Powell [1966], 73–127). Much other

influential work, such as the numerous analyses of voting behavior, could be read as identifying existing political groups and mapping their interests and electoral behavior, even when pluralist theory was not explicitly invoked.

13. The preceding three paragraphs rely chiefly on Key (1955, 1958); Almond and Coleman (1960); Almond and Powell (1966), especially 34–51, 299–332; Almond (1973), 13, 22–23; Dahl (1961b), especially 34–36, 59; Purcell (1973), 242, 260–66; Somit and Tanenhaus ([1967] 1982), 188–89; Ricci (1984), 124–25, 136, 149, 155–57, 169–71, 214–17, 282–83; Skocpol (1984), 2–3, (1985), 4–5; Krasner (1984), 227–29; Seidelman and Harpham (1985), 178–83, 193; and McDonald (1989), 19–22.

14. Easton (1969); Purcell (1973), 267; Somit and Tanenhaus ([1967] 1982), 213–17; Ricci (1984), 175–78; Skocpol (1984), 3–4, (1985), 6–7; Seidelman and Harpham (1985), 188–98.

15. See, e.g., Shepsle (1979, 1986); Shepsle and Weingast (1981, 1984); McCubbins, Noll, and Weingast (1989). Writing less formally, Terry Moe has evaluated and contributed to this body of work in a number of significant essays (see, e.g., Moe [1989, 1990a, 1990b] and references therein).

16. Shepsle has also claimed at times that formal theory is beginning to grasp "the ways in which preferences are induced or molded," although his examples really show only how certain institutions and relationships affect how interests are "channeled, expressed, and revealed" (see Shepsle [1986] 51, critiqued in Smith [1992]).

17. Cf. the comments by Taylor and by Meyer, Boli, and Thomas cited at note 8 above.

18. Much of my own work falls under this rubric (Smith [1985; 1996]).

19. Terrence McDonald has analyzed the influential urban politics literature by such scholars as Amy Bridges, Ira Katznelson, and Martin Shefter that similarly brings "the state" back in in the form of the urban "machine" (McDonald [1989]).

20. Although March and Olsen are perhaps most frequently cited by American advocates of a historical new institutionalism (see, e.g., Krasner [1988], 68; Smith [1988], 90; Karl [1990], 8), notice should also be taken of the prolific writings on "structuration" of Anthony Giddens, who has influenced March and Olsen and many others (see, e.g., Giddens [1984]).

21. For more extended discussions of this attraction of rational choice theory, as well as its limits, see Almond (1973), 14–16; Almond and Genco (1990), 48; and Smith (1992).

22. Despite their other virtues, Almond's essays calling for attention to the choices of political actors display the same limited focus on purely instrumental, strategic agency. In 1973, for example, he indicated that the "freedom of choice" of leaders was limited to the "logically possible coalitions" that could be formed, given the existing array of preferences. He did not contemplate transformations in preferences, even though his leading example, the Mexican leader Cardenas, in fact fostered a coalition "outside" the set suggested by such preexisting preferences (Almond and Mundt [1973], 637–38). Almond and Genco also discuss political choices essentially in terms of the

"constraints and opportunities" for pursuing their existing interests that agents face as well as their efforts at "strategic coping" ([1990], 35, 58).

23. Skocpol's initial methodological manifesto explicitly called for "nonvoluntarist structural" perspectives, although she has subsequently stressed "the interplay of meaningful actions and structural contexts" ([1979], 14; [1984], 1; critiqued in Dunn [1985], 74–78).

24. For perhaps the best argument for the compatibility of understanding human actions as physically caused and as expressive of intentions grounded on reasons, see Davidson (1990), especially 207–44.

25. Such broader new institutionalist views include Skocpol (1984); Giddens (1984); Wendt (1987), 337–39; Krasner (1988); March and Olsen (1989); Karl (1990). Anthony Giddens's arguments for "structuration" are similar enough that a clarifying note seems advisable. My aim is to sketch a framework for designing research projects that can enable quite different hypotheses about structure and agency to be explored. Giddens's primary concern is to offer a set of such hypotheses. Although they are certainly ones that should be examined in the ways I am endorsing, I share Michael Taylor's concern that, by heavily stressing the "mutually constitutive" character of structures and agents, Giddens's position makes it hard to draw causal arrows (Taylor [1989], 117–18).

26. Some new institutionalist writers have, indeed, begun to offer classifications of different types of basic institutions and the differing capabilities of actors, including capabilities for change, they provide (Krasner [1988], 74). Most nonetheless prefer as I do to describe a research approach that permits all candidates for significant structures and agent capabilities to be explored. Thus, Skocpol calls generally for examining "the interplay of meaningful actions and structural contexts ([1984], 1) and Terry Karl, for "an interactive approach that seeks explicitly to relate structural constraints to the shaping of contingent choice" (Karl [1990], 1).

27. For similar suggestions, see Almond (1973), 637, and especially Karl (1990), 7–8.

28. Admittedly, such choices also might only reflect beliefs that agents behave randomly.

29. Krasner (1988), 67, 72, makes this point in just these terms, and like most new institutionalists, stresses the "path-dependent" character of the analyses that result. See also Karl (1990), 7; and Sewell (1990), 16.

30. Thus, two leading writers, Stephen Skowronek and Karen Orren, argue powerfully that particular structures may display largely independent paths of development and interact with others in "multi-layered" ways that can only be grasped retrospectively and not predicted (Skowronek [1990]; Orren and Skowronek [1994]).

31. As noted above, Almond and Mundt (1973), 637–38, describe such an unanticipated discovery.

32. The discipline should also continue to encompass many forms of normative inquiry and argument. All such efforts inevitably take some stance on the character and

significance of political agency, but I would not burden normative theorists with the duty of providing empirical support for their assumptions in every work. For debate over whether the sorts of descriptive work I am advocating can actually assist normative inquiry, as I believe, see Smith (1988), 105–6, (1989), 74–87; and Barber (1989), 56–73.

33. Cf. William Sewell's similar defense of Traugott's work as an "*evenemential sociology*" but one that "remains an evenemential *sociology*" (Sewell [1990], 21).

BIBLIOGRAPHY

Almond, Gabriel A. 1973. "Approaches to Developmental Causation." In *Crisis, Choice, and Change: Historical Studies of Political Development,* 1–42. Edited by Gabriel A. Almond, Scott C. Flanagan, and Robert J. Mundt. Boston: Little, Brown.

Almond, Gabriel. 1988. "Separate Tables: Schools and Sects in Political Science." *PS: Political Science and Politics* 21:828–42.

Almond, Gabriel A., and James S. Coleman. 1960. *The Politics of the Developing Areas.* Princeton: Princeton University Press.

Almond, Gabriel A., with Stephen Genco. 1990. "Clouds, Clocks, and the Study of Politics." In *A Discipline Divided: Schools and Sects in Political Science,* 32–65. Edited by Gabriel A. Almond. Newbury Park, CA: Sage Publications.

Almond, Gabriel A., and Robert J. Mundt. 1973. "Crisis, Choice, and Change: Some Tentative Conclusions." In *Crisis, Choice, and Change: Historical Studies of Political Development,* 619–49. Edited by Gabriel A. Almond, Scott C. Flanagan, and Robert J. Mundt. Boston: Little, Brown.

Almond, Gabriel A., and G. Bingham Powell. 1966. *Comparative Politics: A Developmental Approach.* Boston: Little, Brown.

Aristotle. 1962. *Nicomachaean Ethics.* Translated by M. Ostwald. Indianapolis: Bobbs-Merrill.

Bailyn, Bernard. 1967. *The Ideological Origins of the American Revolution.* Cambridge: Harvard University Press.

Barber, Sotirios A. 1989. "Normative Theory, the 'New Institutionalism,' and the Future of Public Law." *Studies in American Political Development* 3:56–73.

Blondel, Jean. 1981. *The Discipline of Politics.* London: Butterworths.

Burgess, John W. 1980. *Political Science and Comparative Constitutional Law.* Boston: Ginn & Co.

Cammack, Paul. 1989. "Review Article: Bringing the State Back In?" *British Journal of Political Science* 19:261–90.

Ceaser, James W. 1979. *Presidential Selection: Theory and Development.* Princeton: Princeton University Press.

Chubb, John E., and Terry M. Moe. 1990. "Controversy: Should Market Forces Control Education Decision Making?" *American Political Science Review* 84:558–67.

Collini, Stefan, Donald Winch, and John Burrow. 1983. *That Noble Science of Politics: A Study of Nineteenth-Century Intellectual History.* Cambridge: Cambridge University Press.

Connolly, William E. 1974. *The Terms of Political Discourse.* Lexington, MA: D.C. Heath.

Cox, Gary W. 1987. *The Efficient Secret: The Cabinet and the Development of Political Parties in Victorian England.* Cambridge: Cambridge University Press.

Crick, Bernard. 1959. *The American Science of Politics: Its Origins and Conditions.* Berkeley and Los Angeles: University of California Press.

Dahl, Robert A. 1961a. "The Behavioral Approach in Political Science: Epitaph for a Monument to a Successful Protest." *American Political Science Review* 55:763–72.

Dahl, Robert A. 1961b. *Who Governs? Democracy and Power in an American City.* New Haven: Yale University Press.

Dahl, Robert A. 1985. *A Preface to Economic Democracy.* Berkeley and Los Angeles: University of California Press.

Dahl, Robert A. 1989. *Democracy and Its Critics.* New Haven: Yale University Press.

Davidson, Donald. 1990. *Essays on Actions and Events.* New York: Oxford University Press.

Derrida, Jacques. 1976. *Of Grammatology.* Baltimore: Johns Hopkins University Press.

Dryzek, John S., and Stephen T. Leonard. 1988. "History and Discipline in Political Science." *American Political Science Review* 82:1245–60.

Dryzek, John S., and Stephen T. Leonard. 1990. "Controversy: Can Political Science History Be Neutral?" *American Political Science Review* 84:587–607.

Dunn, John. 1985. *Rethinking Modern Political Theory.* Cambridge: Cambridge University Press.

Easton, David. 1969. "The New Revolution in Political Science." *American Political Science Review* 63:1051–61.

Farr, James. 1988a. "The History of Political Science." *American Journal of Political Science* 32:1175–95.

Farr, James. 1988b. "Political Science and the Enlightenment of Enthusiasm." *American Political Science Review* 82:51–69.

Farr, James. 1990. "Controversy: Can Political Science History Be Neutral?" *American Political Science Review* 84:587–91.

Ferejohn, John. 1991. "Rationality and Interpretation: Parliamentary Elections in Early Stuart England." In *The Economic Approach to Politics: A Critical Reassessment of the Theory of Rational Action.* Edited by Kristen Renwick Monroe. New York: HarperCollins.

Fesler, James W., and Donald F. Kettl. 1991. *The Politics of the Administrative Process.* Chatham, NJ: Chatham House.

Foucault, Michel. 1977. *Discipline and Punish: The Birth of the Prison.* New York: Vintage Books.

Gadamer, Hans-Georg. 1982. *Truth and Method.* New York: Crossroad.

Giddens, Anthony. 1984. *The Constitution of Society: Outline of the Theory of Structuration.* Berkeley and Los Angeles: University of California Press.

Gordon, Robert W. 1984. "Critical Legal Histories." *Stanford Law Review* 36:57–125.

Gunnell, John G. 1983. "Political Theory: The Evolution of a Subfield." In *Political Science: The State of the Discipline,* 3–45. Edited by Ada W. Finifter. Washington, D.C.: American Political Science Association.

Habermas, Jürgen. 1979. *Communication and the Evolution of Society.* Translated by Thomas McCarthy. Boston: Beacon Press.

Hanson, Russell L. 1985. *The Democratic Imagination in America: Conversations with Our Past.* Princeton: Princeton University Press.

Higgot, Richard A. 1983. *Political Development Theory.* London: Croom-Helm.

Hobbes, Thomas. [1651] 1971. *Leviathan.* Hammondsworth, UK: Penguin Books.

Janos, Andrew C. 1986. *Politics and Paradigms: Changing Theories of Change in Social Science.* Stanford: Stanford University Press.

Karl, Barry D. 1974. *Charles E. Merriam and the Study of Politics.* Chicago: University of Chicago Press.

Karl, Terry Lynn. 1990. "Dilemmas of Democratization in Latin America." *Comparative Politics* 23:1–21.

Key, V. O., Jr. 1955. "A Theory of Critical Elections." *Journal of Politics* 17:3–18.

Key, V. O., Jr. 1958. *Politics, Parties, and Pressure Groups.* 3d ed. New York: Crowell.

Krasner, Stephen D. 1984. "Approaches to the State: Alternative Conceptions and Historical Dynamics." *Comparative Politics* 16:223–46.

Krasner, Stephen D. 1988. "Sovereignty: An Institutional Perspective." *Comparative Political Studies* 21:66–94.

Krasner, Stephen D. 1991. "Global Communication and National Power: Life on the Pareto Frontier." *World Politics* 43:336–67.

Kress, Paul F. 1973. *Social Science and the Idea of Progress: The Ambiguous Legacy of Arthur F. Bentley.* Urbana: University of Illinois Press.

Lienesch, Michael. 1980. "The Constitutional Tradition: History, Political Action, and Progress in American Political Thought, 1787–1793." *Journal of Politics* 42:1–30, 47–48.

Lindblom, Charles E. 1977. *Politics and Markets: The World's Political-Economic Systems.* New York: Basic Books.

Lindblom, Charles E. 1990. *Inquiry and Change: The Troubled Attempt to Understand and Shape Society.* New Haven: Yale University Press.

Lowi, Theodore J. [1969] 1979. *The End of Liberalism.* 2d ed. New York: W. W. Norton.

Lowi, Theodore J. 1985. *The Personal President.* Ithaca: Cornell University Press.

MacIntyre, Alasdair. 1971. *Against the Self-Image of the Age.* New York: Schocken Books.

March, James G., and Johan P. Olsen. 1984. "The New Institutionalism: Organizational Factors in Political Life." *American Political Science Review* 78:734–49.

March, James G., and Johan P. Olsen. 1989. *Rediscovering Institutions: The Organizational Basis of Politics.* New York: Free Press.

McCubbins, Matthew D., Roger G. Noll, and Barry R. Weingast. 1989. "Structure and Process, Politics and Policy: Administrative Arrangements and the Political Control of Agencies." *Virginia Law Review* 75:431–82.

McDonald, Terrence J. 1989. "The Burdens of Urban History: The Theory of the State in Recent American Social History." *Studies in American Political Development* 3:3–29.

Meyer, John W., John Boli, and George M. Thomas. 1987. *Institutional Structure: Constituting State, Society, and the Individual.* Newbury Park, CA: Sage Publications.

Moe, Terry M. 1989. "The Politics of Bureaucratic Structure." In *Can the Government Govern?* 267–329. Edited by John E. Chubb and Paul E. Peterson. Washington, D.C.: Brookings Institution.

Moe, Terry M. 1990a. "The Politics of Structural Choice: Toward a Theory of Public Bureaucracy." In *Organization Theory: From Chester Barnard to the Present and Beyond,* 127–87. Edited by Oliver E. Williamson. New York: Oxford University Press.

Moe, Terry M. 1990b. "Political Institutions: The Neglected Side of the Story." Paper presented at the "Organization of Political Institutions" conference, Yale Law School Program in Law and Organization, New Haven, April 27–28.

Natchez, Peter B. 1985. *Images of Voting/Vision of Democracy.* New York: Basic Books.

Noll, Roger G., and Barry R. Weingast. 1991. "Rational Actor Theory, Social Norms, and Policy Implementation: Applications to Administrative Processes and Bureaucratic Culture." In *The Economic Approach to Politics: A Critical Reassessment of the Theory of Rational Action,* 237–58. Edited by Kristen Renwick Monroe. New York: HarperCollins.

Norton, Anne. 1986. *Alternative Americas: A Reading of Antebellum Political Culture.* Chicago: University of Chicago Press.

Orren, Karen, and Stephen Skowronek. 1994. "Beyond the Iconography of Order: Notes for a 'New Institutionalism.'" In *The Dynamics of American Politics: Approaches and Interpretations.* Edited by Lawrence C. Dodd and Calvin Jillson. Boulder, CO: Westview Press.

Pocock, J. G. A. 1975. *The Machiavellian Moment: Florentine Political Thought and the Ancient Republican Tradition.* Princeton: Princeton University Press.

Purcell, Edward A. 1973. *The Crisis of Democratic Theory: Scientific Naturalism and the Problem of Value.* Lexington: University Press of Kentucky.

Ricci, David M. 1984. *The Tragedy of Political Science: Politics, Scholarship, and Democracy.* New Haven: Yale University Press.

Ricoeur, Paul. 1981. *Hermeneutics and the Human Sciences: Essays on Language, Action, and Interpretation.* Cambridge: Cambridge University Press.

Riker, William H. 1962. *The Theory of Political Coalitions.* New Haven: Yale University Press.

Riker, William H. 1980. "Implications from Disequilibrium of Majority Rule for the Study of Institutions." *American Political Science Review* 74:432–46.

Riker, William H. 1982. *Liberalism against Populism: A Confrontation between the Theory of Democracy and the Theory of Social Choice.* San Francisco: W. H. Freeman.

Riker, William H. 1986. *The Art of Political Manipulation.* New Haven: Yale University Press.

Rossiter, Clinton, ed. 1961. *The Federalist Papers.* New York: New American Library.

Sandel, Michael J. 1984. Introduction to *Liberalism and Its Critics.* Edited by Michael J. Sandel. Oxford: Basil Blackwell.

Seidelman, Raymond. 1980. "Controversy: Can Political Science History Be Neutral?" *American Political Science Review* 84:596–600.

Seidelman, Raymond, and Edward J. Harpham. 1985. *Disenchanted Realists: Political Science and the American Crisis, 1884–1984.* Albany: State University of New York Press.

Sewell, William H., Jr. 1990. "Three Temporalities: Toward a Sociology of the Event." Comparative Study of Social Transformations, Working Paper No. 58, Ann Arbor.

Shapiro, Michael J. 1981. *Language and Political Understanding: The Politics of Discursive Practices.* New Haven: Yale University Press.

Shepsle, Kenneth A. 1979. "Institutional Arrangements and Equilibrium in Multi-Dimensional Voting Models." *American Journal of Political Science* 23:27–59.

Shepsle, Kenneth A. 1986. "Institutional Equilibrium and Equilibrium Institutions." In *Political Science: The Science of Politics,* 51–81. Edited by Herbert F. Weisberg. New York: Agathon Press.

Shepsle, Kenneth A., and Barry R. Weingast. 1981. "Structure-Induced Equilibrium and Legislative Choices." *Public Choice* 37:503–19.

Shepsle, Kenneth A., and Barry R. Weingast. 1984. "When Do Rules of Procedure Matter?" *Journal of Politics* 46:206–21.

Shepsle, Kenneth A., and Barry R. Weingast. 1987. "The Institutional Foundations of Committee Power." *American Political Science Review* 81:85–104.

Skinner, Quentin. 1969. "Meaning and Understanding in the History of Ideas." *History and Theory* 8:3–33.

Skocpol, Theda. 1979. *States and Social Revolutions: A Comparative Analysis of France, Russia, and China.* Cambridge: Cambridge University Press.

Skocpol, Theda. 1984. "Sociology's Historical Imagination." In *Vision and Method in Historical Sociology,* 1–21. Edited by Theda Skocpol. Cambridge: Cambridge University Press.

Skocpol, Theda. 1985. "Bringing the State Back In: Strategies of Analysis in Current Research." In *Bringing the State Back In,* 3–37. Edited by Peter B. Evans, Dietrich Rueschemeyer, and Theda Skocpol. Cambridge: Cambridge University Press.

Skowronek, Stephen. 1982. *Building a New American State.* Cambridge: Cambridge University Press.

Skowronek, Stephen. 1990. "Remarks on Periodization." Paper presented at the UCLA conference on "American Politics in Historical Perspective," Los Angeles, May.

Skowronek, Stephen. 1993. *The Politics Presidents Make.* Cambridge: Harvard University Press.

Smith, Rogers M. 1985. *Liberalism and American Constitutional Law.* Cambridge: Harvard University Press.

Smith, Rogers M. 1988. "Political Jurisprudence, the 'New Institutionalism,' and the Future of Public Law." *American Political Science Review* 82:89–108.

Smith, Rogers M. 1989. "The New Institutionalism and Normative Theory: Reply to Professor Barber." *Studies in American Political Development* 3:74–87.

Smith, Rogers M. 1992. "If Politics Matters: Implications for a New Institutionalism." *Studies in American Political Development* 6:1–36.

Smith, Rogers M. 1996. *Civic Ideals: Conflicting Visions of Citizenship in American Public Law.* New Haven: Yale University Press.

Somit, Albert, and Joseph Tanenhaus. [1967] 1982. *The Development of American Political Science: From Burgess to Behavioralism.* 2d ed. Boston: Allyn & Bacon.

Sunstein, Cass. 1990. *Beyond the Rights Revolution.* Cambridge: Harvard University Press.

Takaki, Ronald. 1979. *Iron Cages: Race and Culture in Nineteenth Century America.* New York: Oxford University Press.

Taylor, Charles. 1985a. *Human Agency and Language.* Cambridge: Cambridge University Press.

Taylor, Charles. 1985b. *Philosophy and the Human Sciences.* Cambridge: Cambridge University Press.

Taylor, Michael. 1989. "Structure, Culture, and Action in the Explanation of Social Change." *Politics and Society* 17:116–61.

Tsebelis, George. 1990. "Controversy, Crime, and Punishment: Are One-Shot, Two-Person Games Enough?" *American Political Science Review* 84:576–86.

Tulis, Jeffrey K. 1987. *The Rhetorical Presidency.* Princeton: Princeton University Press.

Ward, James F. 1984. *Language, Form, and Inquiry: Arthur F. Bentley's Philosophy of Social Science.* Amherst: University of Massachusetts Press.

Wendt, Alexander E. 1987. "The Agent-Structure Problem in International Relations Theory." *International Organizations* 41:335–70.

Wilson, Woodrow. 1911. "The Law and the Facts." *American Political Science Review* 5:1–11.

Wolin, Sheldon. 1969. "Political Theory as a Vocation." *American Political Science Review* 63:1062–81.

Wood, Gordon S. 1969. *The Creation of the American Republic, 1776–1787.* Chapel Hill: University of North Carolina Press.

Discursive Forums, Cultural Practices: History and Anthropology in Literary Studies

Steven Mullaney

In his 1986 presidential address to the Modern Language Association, J. Hillis Miller noted with some alarm a recent and pervasive transformation of literary studies: "As everyone knows, literary study in the past few years has undergone a sudden, almost universal turn away from theory in the sense of an orientation toward language as such and has made a corresponding turn toward history, culture, society, politics, institutions, class and gender conditions, the social context, the material base . . . , conditions of production, technology, distribution, and consumption" (Miller 1987, 283).[1] Miller's list of unhappy developments is generous enough to encompass a great many recent trends in the field, among them new historicism, cultural materialism, feminism, various forms of revisionary Marxism, and cultural studies. It is also general enough, I suspect, to resonate with analogous developments in other disciplines—with the heterogeneous movements we are here regarding, under the rubric of an unlikely singularity, as *the* historic turn. Whatever affiliations and alliances we do discover within and between disciplines, the general reorientation of literary studies to which Miller refers has indeed been an emergent force in my own field. Not everyone "knows" this reorientation, however, in terms of the trajectory Miller describes—as a universal turn away from theory.

Because I am writing here as something of an anthropological informant, mediating between the literary native's point of view and the social scientist's, a bit of local knowledge might help to explicate Miller's hypostatized invocation of theory. As in the other disciplines we are considering here, the turn toward history in literary studies is a recent development within (and not away from) poststructuralist theory, although the direction this development has taken—toward greater dialogue and even some assimilation with Marxist, feminist, and other modes of social and cultural analysis—is clearly not a road Miller regards as well chosen, or even on the map. In describing "theory" as "an orientation toward language as such," Miller in fact stakes out a decidedly parochial domain, one identified with certain reduced and strictly American versions of deconstruction—what amount, in fact, to rather faulty translations of Derrida as he was incorporated into formalist modes of literary analysis in the United States. Derrida's emphasis on the overdetermined structures of certain hierarchized binary oppositions in Western culture is highly fraught with implications for the study of social, political, and ideological formations, and has provided a useful tool for cultural analysis, not only for literary critics but also for some historians.[2] In the strand of American literary deconstruction that Miller himself has promoted, however, Derridean *overdetermination* becomes a linguistic and rhetorical *indeterminacy* of meaning; Derrida's famous and much misunderstood statement that "there is nothing outside of the text" (*il n'y a pas de hors-texte*) becomes instead an assertion, endlessly reiterated in close readings of canonical literary works, that there is no way of *getting* outside the (literary) text, due to its tropological *aporias* of meaning. Miller's "theory" can stand in opposition to "history, culture, politics, institutions, class and gender conditions" only because, as Louis Montrose has suggested, Miller radically polarizes the discursive and the social. "The prevailing tendency across cultural studies," Montrose notes, "has been to emphasize their reciprocity and mutual constitution: on the one hand, the social is understood to be discursively constructed; and on the other, language-use is understood to be always and necessarily dialogical, to be socially and materially determined and constrained" (Montrose 1989, 15).

What Miller misrepresents as a turn away from theory is, however, a genuine and decisive departure from his *own* theories of textuality and linguistic indeterminancy, a difference that needs to be stressed because it is not always registered when readers from other disciplines survey the current literary scene.[3] Although the various modes of sociopolitical and historical criticism that have emerged in recent years are diverse in their theoretical origins and assumptions and sometimes at apparent, if not fundamental, odds in their ideological agendas, they are generally in accord in their efforts to redraw the boundaries of literary studies, to reconceive, in terms of a mutually constitutive and open-ended dialectic, the relationship between literary and other cultural discourses, the discursive and the social. Although neither as sudden nor as universal as Miller hyperbolically suggests, such a reorientation does challenge and has begun to alter some traditional paradigms and practices of literary criticism. For example, the aesthetic analysis of literary texts, regarded

as relatively self-contained linguistic artifacts, is being displaced by the ideological analysis of discursive cultural practices, including but not restricted to
the literary, and nondiscursive practices as well. The interpretation of literature
within a strictly *literary* history, a diachronic sequence of canonical texts in
dialogue with one another but otherwise relatively autistic, is being opened up
to a less teleological but decidedly more heteroglossic interpretation of the
social, political, and historical conditions of possibility for literary production
and of the recursive effects of literary production and dissemination upon those
conditions. The literary is thus conceived neither as a separate and separable
aesthetic realm nor as a mere product of culture—a reflection of ideas and
ideologies produced elsewhere—but as one realm among many for the negotiation and production of social meaning, of historical subjects, and of the
systems of power that at once enable and constrain those subjects.

This emphasis on the literary as both a form of and a forum for cultural
practice and on literary analysis as a vehicle rather than an end in itself—that
is, a means of gaining access to other cultural forums and to the complex and
heterogeneous processes through which social meaning and subjects are
produced—bears obvious relationships to developments in anthropology and
sociology over the last fifteen years (Ortner 1984). It is also a prominent feature
of what has come to be known as the new historicism, which I intend to
examine in some detail here. It was in 1982 that Stephen Greenblatt first spoke
of a "new historicism" that was noticeably reshaping the study of English
Renaissance literature, and although few of those centrally associated with the
movement were happy with the label,[4] it definitely caught on. Raised or reified
to capitalized status and shorn of its inverted commas, new historicism is now
used to describe a wide range of historically oriented work in other periods of
literary studies and has also become strongly associated with the multidisciplinary scholarship published, since its inception in 1983, in the journal
Representations. Although neither originary in its emphasis on cultural practices and production nor an entirely unified or fully cohesive movement, new
historicism has consequently been the subject of a great deal of debate and
discussion in recent years, in both academic journals and the popular press. It
has been characterized by Edward Pechter as a Marxist "specter . . . haunting
criticism," although Pechter's sense of what unites and defines various Marxisms is, it must be said, decidedly curious ("they all view history and contemporary political life as determined, wholly or in essence, by struggle, contestation, power relations, *libido dominandi*" [Pechter 1987, 292]); conversely, it
has been viewed as a politically evasive, essentially liberal movement com-
plicit in the structures of power and domination it purports to analyze, although

in terms that come close to equating any critical analysis of a dominant power structure *with* such complicity (see Porter 1988). Some see it as part of a pernicious conspiracy, allied with feminism and ethnic studies, bent on perverting immortal literature and timeless, universal values (see Montrose [1989, 29], citing an editorial in the *San Diego Union*); certain feminists, however, would deny the alliance, viewing new historicism as a largely male appropriation, displacement, and/or erasure of feminist concerns and critical practices (Newton 1989; Boose 1987; Neely 1988).[5] From other shores or disciplines, it has sometimes been viewed as a climatic phenomenon, the latest Californian cult or fad (Kermode 1989),[6] while to others it has seemed in danger of becoming a new and far from localized orthodoxy (Montrose 1986); it has been characterized as a break from and critique of the various pre- and poststructuralist formalisms that have dominated literary studies (Greenblatt 1982, 1989), and as the latest manifestation of such formalism (Liu 1989; Montrose 1989). Given the lack of consensus within literary studies about new historicism—what it is, what it is not, and what any right- (or left-) thinking person is to think about it—a general caution is in order: no survey, the present one included, is to be entirely trusted.

This essay, then, is a partisan account of new historicism, written from within the movement but not, I hope, uncritically so. It is also necessarily partial, in the sense that it does not profess to give a complete or synoptic view of the current state of literary studies in general. New historicism is by no means the only example of a "historic turn" in literary studies, and the contradictory views briefly chronicled above suggest that it is far from representative, exemplary, or definitive in its approaches to sociohistorical analysis. Nonetheless, the issues it has raised, the debates it has provoked, and the methodologies and theories with which it is associated resonate powerfully with other arguments and issues and movements—not only in literary studies but also in history, anthropology, sociology, and other disciplines. In the discussion that follows, I have tried to focus on those aspects of new historicism that are at once most fundamental to it, most controversial, and (partly as a consequence) most often misrepresented, but they are also aspects most germane to recent debates in the social sciences. From its early focus on the relationship between cultural forms and structures of state and institutional authority, new historicism has been an inquiry, or rather a series of not always harmonious inquiries, into the power such forms and structures have to determine ideas and ideologies, historical subjects and their actions, and cultural practices and their potential for either reinforcing or contesting that power and those structures.

Unlike other disciplines, literary studies have traditionally been oriented toward the examination of a specific canon of texts, often conceived as relatively autonomous cultural artifacts. Even when such study has been in some sense historical, the relationship between literature and history has customarily been constrained by the reflectionist model implicit in the binary opposition of literary text and historical context. Early definitions of new historicism emphasize its departure from such approaches. Thus Greenblatt speaks of literary works as "fields of force, places of dissension and shifting interests" rather than "as a fixed set of texts that are set apart from all other forms of expression . . . or as a stable set of reflections of historical facts that lie beyond them." Such an approach "challenges the assumptions that guarantee a secure distinction between . . . artistic production and other kinds of social production" and shifts analysis from the literary in itself to the role that literary production plays in the larger social formation: "These collective social constructions on the one hand define the range of aesthetic possibilities within a given representational mode and, on the other, link that mode to the complex network of institutions, practices, and beliefs that constitute the culture as a whole" (Greenblatt 1982, 6). Such a shift shares certain assumptions with recent developments in British Marxist literary studies, characterized by its practitioners as a form of cultural materialism. Although not avowedly Marxist in terms of its politics, new historicism is strongly indebted in its theoretical orientation to the work of Raymond Williams (from whom the phrase *cultural materialism* derives) and especially to his articulation of the nature and functioning of hegemonic culture.[7] In Williams's development of Antonio Gramsci's concept, hegemonic culture is neither singular nor static, nor is hegemony synonymous with cultural domination. On the contrary, the culture of any given historical period is conceived as a heterogeneous and irreducibly plural social formation and as a dynamic process of representation and interpretation rather than as a fixed ensemble of meanings and beliefs. In such a view, culture is an ongoing production, negotiation, and delimitation of social meanings and social selves, composed through both discursive and nondiscursive means and in various and competing forums. Moreover, as Williams reminds us, the dominant culture of any given period is never either total or exclusive, never an accomplished fact but rather an ongoing process that "has continually to be renewed, recreated, defended, and modified" because it is being "continually resisted, limited, altered, challenged by pressures not at all its own"—by marginal, residual, and alternative cultures that, together with the dominant, comprise the hegemonic (Williams 1978, 112).

In calling for a cultural as opposed to a historical materialism, Williams did not of course intend to suppress history but rather to move away from overly teleological models of history associated with classical Marxism and to displace the economic as the final ground of materialism by focusing historical analysis instead upon what might be called the symbolic economy of any given period.[8] This entails, to my mind, a methodological shift toward a form of cultural or anthropological criticism that has not been adequately reflected in British cultural materialism of the last decade. Jonathan Dollimore's *Radical Tragedy* (1984), for example, combines the findings of relatively traditional historians of ideas with familiar Marxist modes of ideological analysis to examine explicit antihumanist ideological debate on the Jacobean stage. The study is a powerful one, and cultural materialism in general has proved a necessary and salutary corrective to certain tendencies in new historicism, especially in its more deterministic variants; but historical and cultural speci-ficity tend to escape the grasp of ideological analysis conducted on such a level, especially insofar as such specificity relates to the diverse, heterogeneous, and often nondiscursive cultural practices and processes of the social formation— what Williams called the "internal dynamic relations" of hegemonic cultures, and whose dynamics he seemed principally concerned to open up to a more broadly conceived ideological-cultural analysis.

The "historic turn" in new historicism has a great deal of cultural or anthro-pological torque to it, supplied in part by cultural historians such as Natalie Davis, Robert Darnton, and Carlo Ginzburg and symbolic and Marxist an-thropologists and sociologists such as Marshall Sahlins, Mary Douglas, and Pierre Bourdieu. The most prominent signatures on the movement, however, are those of Clifford Geertz and Michel Foucault. In his anti-Burckhardtian study of the social construction of and constraints upon Renaissance selves, Stephen Greenblatt aligns his own project, which he calls a "poetics of culture" (Greenblatt 1980, 5), with Geertz's loosely semiotic model of cultural systems of meaning: "Culture is best seen not as complexes of concrete behavior patterns—customs, usages, traditions, habit clusters— . . . but as a set of control mechanisms—plans, recipes, rules, instructions . . . for the governing of behavior" (Geertz 1973, 44). Others have emphasized Geertz's approach to cultural practices as interpretive forms or "cultural performances" (Mullaney 1988) or his focus upon the symbolic dimensions and construction of the real (Goldberg 1983).

But as Geertz himself has acknowledged, his semiotic model of culture is hardly original to him or, in its general outlines, unique to his own brand of symbolic anthropology. As Montrose suggests, the more telling Geertzian influence on new historicism is a methodological one, an adoption and adaptation of the ethnographic practice Geertz described (Geertz 1973, 3–30) as "thick description":

> Geertz's work offered to literary critics and cultural historians not so much a powerful *theory* of culture as an exemplary and eminently literary *method* for narrating culture in action, culture lived in the performances and narratives of individual and collective human actors. . . . "Thick description" might be more accurately described as "interpretive narration": it seizes upon an event, performance, or other practice and, through the interrogation of its minute particulars, seeks to reveal the collective ethos of an alien culture. (Montrose 1992, 399)

Geertzian "thick description" is indeed easy to align with the literary practice of providing an intensive "reading" of a text or set of texts and is "eminently literary" in this relatively neutral or at least strictly methodological sense. Geertz's work is also, however, clearly invested in a particular ideology of form that is itself strongly associated with certain approaches to art and literature. His analyses tend to aestheticize the political and ideological domain,[9] explicating and even celebrating the cohesion of cultural meanings rather than analyzing their fragmentary and contested production, treating texts, events, and practices as collective *expressions* of a cultural essence or ethos rather than as ideological *constructions* of the collective or the essential. Describing man as "an animal suspended in webs of significance he himself has spun" (1973, 5), Geertz traces the semantic intricacy of the web with extraordinary skill and verve but pays scant attention to the social, political, or ideological intricacies—and inequities—that allow the web to be spun. "Cultures are webs of mystification as well as signification," as Roger Keesing comments. "We need to ask who *creates* and who *defines* cultural meanings, and to what end" (Keesing 1987, 161–62). When Geertz describes ethnographic events as "texts," he invokes not only a semiotic but also an aesthetic model, and the aesthetics informing much of his work seem close to the formalism of literary New Criticism, which was still dominant in literary studies in the late 1960s and early 1970s (when the essays collected in *The Interpretation of Cultures* were written). The Balinese cockfight is an "art form" (Geertz 1973, 443), and at times in Geertz's explication and appreciation of its nuances it resembles nothing so much as a literary work in the hands of a New Critic: a complex, ambiguous, but ultimately unified and coherent expression of cultural (or literary) sensibility. In this regard, Keesing's critique of Geertz echoes new historicist concerns with such formalism, New Critical and poststructuralist, in literary studies; both are

. . . silent on the way cultural meanings sustain power and privilege . . . blind to the political consequences of cultures as ideologies, their situatedness as justifications and mystifications of a local historically cumulated status quo. Where feminists and Marxists find oppression, symbolists find meaning. (Keesing 1987, 166)

Like a great many anthropologists indebted to Geertz but critical of such tendencies, new historicists—many, like myself, equally indebted—attempt to "synthesize cultural and Marxist (or at least politically informed) analyses" (Biersack 1989, 84), to combine, however successfully, a poetics with a politics of culture.[10]

As Marxist critics especially have noted, however, new historicist analyses of the processes through which cultural meanings are produced, systems of power and privilege sustained, negotiated, or contested, operate primarily within a synchronic field or cultural system rather than on a diachronic axis. Thus, while registering its similarities with Marxism, Walter Cohen also stresses, as a fundamental difference, that "new historicism describes historical difference, but it does not explain historical change" (1987, 33). The focus upon historical difference is not a superficial trait, although it is reflected in new historicism's characteristic penchant for the unusual, uncanny, and even bizarre historical detail—sometimes narrated as a paradoxically illustrative anecdote, often subjected to full analysis as part of a broader cultural pattern or logic. Nor is the delineation of historical difference absolute. As in Foucault's later work, new historicist practices of defamiliarization are often strategic efforts to displace traditional accounts of the past in order to clarify both similarities and differences with the present—to open up perspectives, however partial and incomplete, upon the production of historical subjects in the present and "to experience facets of our own subjection at shifting internal distances—to read, as in a refracted light, one fragment of our ideological inscription by means of another" (Montrose 1992, 414; see also Mullaney 1988, xii).

Even when a considerable historical span is studied, however, as in Peter Stallybrass and Allon White's impressive and influential *The Poetics and Politics of Transgression,* an account of the forces that precipitate or structure historical change is not forthcoming. Differences in the dynamics of the bourgeois imagination or political unconscious are adeptly analyzed within historical periods ranging from the Renaissance to the modern, but as relatively discrete moments of what Norbert Elias called the "civilizing process." Needless to say, the problem is not unique to new historicism nor are the solutions proffered by recent critics unproblematic in themselves. In a recent essay, for example, Elizabeth Fox-Genovese characterizes new historicism as one of many movements in various disciplines in which "the preoccupation with structure has given way to the preoccupation with system" (1989, 218), a displacement that in her terms precludes the analysis of historical causation and change. What she means by the recent "preoccupation with system" in new historicism and other movements, however, is marred by an all-too-familiar confusion of radically different fields of poststructuralist theory. In new historicism, she finds such a preoccupation in what she claims is an adherence to a "notion of textuality in the large sense," thereby tarring new historicism with the brush of American deconstruction as wielded by figures such as J. Hillis Miller, with whom I began. For Miller and others like him, textuality "in the large sense" is indeed a narrow linguistic field, so narrow that it would be fair to say that "extratextual considerations defy proof and, accordingly, relevance" (Fox-Genovese 1989, 218). But such terms are not merely inaccurate in relation to new historicism; they are antithetical to its entire project, and Fox-Genovese's incapacity to distinguish such radically different and even opposed critical movements robs her critique of much if not all of its usefulness. What she means by "structure" is also less than clear and, more importantly, the easy and stable distinction she asserts *between* structure and system is to my mind quite problematic. At times in the essay, "structure" serves as an analytic *concept* that allows one to "take account of past and present politics" (218); at other times but in a very short space, it seems to be synonymous *with* politics. Both draw boundaries (which a preoccupation with system somehow denies) and both govern the same forms of cultural production by means of such delineation. Thus, "structure . . . governs the writing and reading of texts," but (and?) "politics draws the lines that govern the production, survival, and reading of texts and textuality" (218). However, history is also to be "understood as structure," although here structure is not a governing or boundary-drawing principle or force but rather an aggregate phenomenon, understood not as politics but as "sets or systems of relations of superordination and subordination" (221)—among which I, and I assume most new historicists, would locate politics. The problem is not, however, merely one of confused usage and/or reception. As Anthony Giddens suggests, functionalist emphases on structure over system require a stable distinction between the two, a distinction impossible to maintain where social systems are concerned:

The "structure" of an organism exists "independently" of its functioning in a certain specific sense: the parts of the body can be studied when the organism dies, that is, when it has stopped "functioning." But such is not the case with social systems, *which cease to exist when they cease to function:* "patterns" of social relationships only exist in so far as the latter are organised as systems, reproduced over the course of time. Hence in functionalism also, the notions of structure and system tend to dissolve into one another. (Giddens 1979, 61–62)

In Giddens, structure is more closely related to an Althusserian notion of ideology than to Fox-Genovese's "politics": it is set of structuring properties "understood as rules and resources, recursively implicated in the reproduction of social systems . . . [but] temporally 'present' only in their instantiation, in the constituting moments of social systems" (1979, 64). These structuring properties or rules or resources are distinct from Althusserian ideology, however, in their recursivity, the distinguishing characteristic of Giddens's concept of structuration:[11]

The concept of structuration involves that of the *duality of structure,* which relates to the *fundamentally recursive character of social life, and expresses the mutual dependence of structure and agency.* . . . the structural properties of social systems are both the medium and the outcome of those social systems. The theory of structuration, thus formulated, rejects any differentiation of synchrony and diachrony or statics and dynamics. The identification of structure with constraint is also rejected: structure is both enabling and constraining. (1979, 69)

I dwell upon Giddens in part because he and other social theorists have recently entered into some new historicists' efforts to theorize their own practices and methods (see Montrose 1989, 33 n. 12 and 1990, 35–36) and in part because Giddens's emphasis on the constraining *and* enabling force of collective social structures has been a consistent focus of new historicist work yet has been consistently ignored or marginalized in accounts of that work.

According to such accounts, which range over a wide political spectrum, from the "red scare" tactics of Pechter (1987) to the Marxist overview of Cohen (1987), new historicism achieves a certain unanimity despite its heterogeneity. The charge is not that it revels in thickly described meaning but that it finds oppression, or cultural determination, everywhere and denies the possibility of collective or individual agency. According to such accounts of literary studies in the 1980s, where others would find subversion, new historicists find containment.

In a 1981 essay entitled "Invisible Bullets: Renaissance Authority and Its Subversion," Stephen Greenblatt introduced the not-quite-binary opposition of containment and subversion. He argued that the dominant culture of early modern England did not merely *allow* certain forms of unruliness or discontent or subversive thought to be manifested; rather, "the very condition of power" for the Tudor state rested in its capacity to *produce* forms of resistance and subversion, both in order to contain them and to use them to its own ends. Although he did not say that any and all acts of resistance or subversion are merely apparent, are either the ruse and effect of power or the register of how fully contained the subjects of that power are—even when they think they are resisting it—he *did* suggest that much of what we embrace as subversive or radical in the period is, when examined more closely, not only "contained by the power it would appear to threaten . . . [but also] the very product of that power" (1985, 23–24).

The essay was revised and expanded for two subsequent anthologies and most recently was included in *Shakespearean Negotiations* (Greenblatt 1988). It immediately prompted considerable debate and counterargument among both new historicists and cultural materialists. The reaction of the latter was interesting, given the stakes involved for British Marxists in making their own critical practice a form of political and ideological resistance. In the introduction to *Political Shakespeare* (1985), which includes an updated version of the "Invisible Bullets" essay, Jonathan Dollimore accepts Greenblatt's general criticism of previous approaches, namely, that apparent radicalism in the period has often been too unquestionably embraced as genuine. He finds Greenblatt's account of the production of subversion persuasive at times—especially in the extended analysis of Thomas Harriot's colonial encounters in Virginia, from which the title is taken[12]—but questions the scope and efficacy of such ideological management and manipulation of subjects in the period. Quite rightly, he faults the impossibly monolithic power structure that allows Greenblatt to push his argument to the extreme (Dollimore and Sinfield 1985, 12) and which Greenblatt has subsequently clarified (Greenblatt 1988, 2–3, 65). Generally speaking, the reaction of other new historicists has been the same: ideological containment can be seen to operate in such a paradoxical and cunning fashion in some local and historically specific instances, perhaps in a great many, but not as a generalized condition of power.

The essay attempts to describe certain characteristics of early modern power in operation, not to provide a general theory of such power—although many responses to it project such a goal onto Greenblatt's argument. And as the reaction of other new historicists should suggest, neither is the essay a manifesto of new historicism, in the sense that principles, attitudes, or arguments associated with it can fairly be abstracted and attributed to the movement in general. Greenblatt himself addresses both points in a recent essay in which he contrasts his own argument in "Invisible Bullets" with the version of that argument disseminated by critics of new historicism:

> I did not propose that all manifestations of resistance in all literature (or even in all plays by Shakespeare) were co-opted—one can readily think of plays where the forces of ideological containment break down. And yet characterizations of this essay in particular, and new historicism in general, repeatedly refer to a supposed argument that any resistance is impossible. A particularizing argument about the subject position projected by a set of plays is at once simplified and turned into a universal principle from which contingency and hence history itself is erased. (Greenblatt 1990, 75)

I feel the need to dwell on this particular essay at some length because it has indeed served, in distorted and simplified form, as a template through which all too many commentators have viewed new historicism in general. Although such distortion is hardly unprecedented in scholarly debate, an emphatic *caveat lector* is especially in order here.[13]

What the controversy provoked by "Invisible Bullets" has also failed to register, moreover, is the powerful and altogether salutary effect Greenblatt's essay, like his work in general, has had on the nature of Renaissance literary criticism and the level at which it has subsequently been conducted. Like any genuinely seminal work, Greenblatt's has introduced new topics and parameters for subsequent analysis, new terms for debate and discussion. Greenblatt's critics, like Geertz's, sometimes fail to acknowledge the degree to which their differences depend, for their very articulation, upon the transformation of the field that Greenblatt (and others) made possible. But while Greenblatt is without question one of the founding figures and ablest practitioners of new historicism, not all aspects of his work are accepted uncritically by other new historicists. To my mind, for example, Greenblatt's approach to a "poetics of culture" tends, in its application, to obscure or homogenize a politics of culture, even when the heterogeneity of cultural forms, institutions, and practices is his primary focus. Thus, in his recent study of the Shakespearean theater, focused upon the forms of cultural capital produced when objects, ideas, ceremonies, and cultural practices were displaced or otherwise transferred from one cultural realm to another, his emphasis is upon a generalized "social energy" and, in the case of the stage, the *aesthetic* empowerment produced by such circulation and negotiation. The potential ideological force of such displacements from the proper to the improper is largely ignored; circulation and acquisition are key metaphors, but appropriation is not (1988, 10–11). The category of the aesthetic in regard to Renaissance popular drama—even, perhaps especially, Shakespeare's—is itself quite problematic given the fact that such drama was not accorded the dignity or propriety to qualify as literature or "poesy" in the period. Greenblatt also tends to aestheticize the sites occupied by the popular playhouses—areas outside the city walls known as the Liberties—describing them as "carefully demarcated playgrounds" (120) where the stage was "marked off openly from all other forms and ceremonies of public life precisely by virtue of its freely acknowledged fictionality" (116). Rather than neutral zones, however, the Liberties were complexly inscribed domains of cultural contradiction, ambivalence, and license. The emergence of popular drama in them was not the escape of an art form to a sheltered retreat or preserve but rather a forceful, and forcefully felt, appropriation of a highly volatile zone in the city's spatial economy—which is indeed how the city viewed the emergence of the popular theater (see Mullaney 1988, 1–59; Agnew 1986). Moreover, in the sixteenth century, the emergence of popular drama, as a burgeoning but far from official social phenomenon and institution, produced a sudden and explosive expansion of the discursive domain within which knowledge was produced and circulated—a domain that was at once a relatively closed system and one that was not strictly governed by issues of literacy. The boundary between oral and literate cultures was highly permeable, such that ideas and ideologies were disseminated not only by direct access to the printed word but also by diverse processes of representation and re-presentation in official and unofficial forums, ranging from the pulpit to the tavern, the juridical scaffold to the home or shop. Any significant expansion of this relatively closed discursive economy, any significant difference in the *degree* to which ideas and attitudes could be disseminated, threatened to become a difference in *kind* as well—altering the structure of knowledge by redefining its boundaries, contributing to the historical pressures that were forcing a transition from a relatively closed to a radically open economy of knowledge and representation. And unlike other significant expansions of the symbolic economy of the period, such as the rapid evolution of print culture and the concomitant vernacular translations of the Bible, literacy was not the price of admission to the theater, which gave the stage a currency and accessibility that was rivaled only by the pulpit.

To what degree such an expansion was or could be controlled, and by what apparatuses of a far from unified or centralized state, raises the issue of power in its ideological dimension. Although a key term in new historicist work, power is also less than adequately theorized in that work. An undeniable reliance upon Foucault's concept of power as "the multiplicity of force relations" (1978, 92) in society, not primarily repressive but productive and acutely focused upon the construction of subjects and subjectivities, has led to charges that new historicists, like Foucault, foreclose all possibility of social struggle or contestation. Focusing on Greenblatt but generalizing about new historicism and Foucault, Frank Lentricchia argues that

> [Greenblatt's] description of power endorses Foucault's theory of power, preserving not only the master's repeated insistence on the concrete institutional character of power, its palpability, as it were, but also his glide into a conception of power that is elusively and literally indefinable—not finitely anchored but diffused from nowhere to everywhere, and saturating all social relations to the point that all conflicts and "jostlings" among social groups become a mere show of political dissension, a prearranged theater of struggle set upon the substratum of a monolithic agency which produces "opposition" as one of its delusive political effects. (1989, 235)

Although Lentricchia's account is clearly informed by Greenblatt's "Invisible Bullets," that essay is not mentioned in an otherwise comprehensive critique. Rather, it supplies the terms, or exaggerations thereof, that Lentricchia folds back into significantly different work, and this procedure produces some less than accurate characterizations, for example, of the critique of humanist notions of an autonomous self that structures *Renaissance Self-Fashioning* (1980).[14] Lentricchia's version of Foucault, however, is a more telling distortion, based on a distressingly common selective (mis)reading. He not only associates Foucauldian power with a monolithic agency, which amounts to a full inversion and perversion of "the master's repeated insistence," but he also ignores Foucault's repeated assertions that a relational and contingent theory of power implies a relational and contingent theory of resistance:

> Where there is power, there is resistance, and yet, or rather consequently, this resistance is never in a position of exteriority in relation to power. Should it be said that one is always "inside" power, there is no "escaping" it, there is no absolute outside where it is concerned, because one is subject to the law in any case? Or that, history being the ruse of reason,

power is the ruse of history, always emerging the winner? This would be to misunderstand the strictly relational character of power relationships. Their existence depends on a multiplicity of points of resistance: these play the role of adversary, target, support, or handle in power relations. These points of resistance are present everywhere in the power network. Hence there is no single locus of great Refusal, no soul of revolt, source of all rebellions, or pure law of the revolutionary. Instead there is a plurality of resistances, each of them a special case . . . . by definition, they can only exist in the strategic field of power relations. But this does not mean that they are only a reaction or rebound, forming with respect to the basic domination an underside that is in the end always passive, doomed to perpetual defeat. Resistances do not derive from a few hetero-geneous principles; but neither are they a lure or a promise that is of necessity betrayed. (Foucault 1978, 95–96)

Any operation of power produces a site of potential resistance, and while Foucault emphasizes here what might be called the *tactical* dynamics of both—their highly volatile, localized, partial, and transitory manifestation within the social formation—these dynamics are in neither case either dispersed or dissipated. Like power, resistance comes from below, and al-though there is no "source of all rebellions," resistance does achieve *strategic* force as well: "it is doubtless the strategic codification of these points of resistance that makes a revolution possible, somewhat similar to the way in which the state relies on the institutional integration of power relationships" (Foucault 1978, 96).[15] Foucault deconstructs the notion of autonomy rather than agency; Lentricchia and others like him fail to recognize the crucial distinction between the two.

Criticizing traditional concepts of power for their emphasis on a centralized and repressive force operating from above, Foucault once suggested that "we have still not cut off the head of the king" (1978, 88–89). Working in a period when the sovereign corpus was still quite literally intact, Renaissance new historicists have necessarily but sometimes too exclusively focused upon mo-narchical power, often relying on Foucault's argument that an "economy of visibility" structured the power of the sovereign (1977, 187) to emphasize that royal power existed only insofar as it manifested itself, that it was, in a sense, theatrically conceived, produced, negotiated, and maintained. To what degree the royal aura created and projected in monarchical processions, rituals of authority ranging from coronation ceremonies to public executions, and the carefully managed dissemination of royal portraits and proclamations succeeded in fostering "an effective internalization of obedience" (James 1988, 358), and how such efforts were enhanced or contested in unofficial discursive and representational forums, has been the subject of wide opinion and disagreement. Greenblatt suggests that dramatic representations of monarchy on stage were, however corrosive or subversive in appearance, implicated in and contained by "the English form of absolutist theatricality" which structured monarchical power (1988, 65). However, this view has been criticized for conflating distinctly different manifestations of Renaissance "theatricality." Royal pageantry and ritual relied upon the *presentation* of authority, the unique royal presence, rather than its *representation;* or rather, to borrow Robert Weimann's terms (Weimann 1988), who is representing and what is being represented need to coincide in the figure of the monarch, and the proper interpellation of the subject depends upon the aura generated by this carefully preserved and controlled synthesis of image and identity. Theatrical representation, however, radically splits image and identity. Working with sixteenth-century theories of the monarchical corpus—the king's two bodies—some have even argued that even in apparently royalist plays the effect of bringing a monarch on the dramatic scaffold, a royal figure played by a lower-class actor in borrowed robes, was inherently corrosive—that theatrical representation dismantled and derogated the carefully maintained and quasi-mystical aura of monarchical power, not simply by reproducing it but by rendering it reproducible (Moretti 1982; Kastan 1986; Mullaney 1989).

If it is misleading to collapse theatrical representation into the "theatricality" of sovereign power, it is equally misleading to take at face value the pretensions and mystifications of sovereign presentation. In his study of the politics of literature in Jacobean England, Jonathan Goldberg draws on both Derrida and Foucault to examine the enabling contradictions of rule under James I and the degree to which poets and playwrights appropriated the radically equivocal style of Jacobean absolutism to position and sustain themselves both within and outside of the court patronage system (Goldberg 1983). The poetics and politics of Elizabethan rule have been richly and influentially examined by Louis Montrose in a series of essays that in many ways stand as exemplary instances of new historicist methodology and practice. Drawing on a wide variety of materials ranging from royal processions and proclamations to the fantasies and dreams of Elizabethan (male) subjects, Montrose provides a richly nuanced account of ways in which Elizabeth maintained her tenuous position as the female ruler of a patriarchal state by eliding the vulnerability of her own power with the vulnerability of gender and turning them both to her own advantage; styling herself as the unattainable, hence endlessly pursued,

Virgin Queen; and appropriating aspects of the Marian cult and the conventions of pastoral romance to restructure and manage the shape of her subjects' sexual as well as political desires. The analysis of the symbolic forms of mediation Elizabeth managed so dexterously does not preclude but rather implies and opens the way for Montrose's examination of the social, political, and material realities mystified in the process (see especially Montrose 1980a, 1983a, 1983b, 1986b). Elizabethan literary works are viewed as integral and active forces in a complex process of cultural production, engaging in sometimes contestatory negotiations with and productions of Elizabethan culture, often in a manner that clarifies the male anxieties that structure and motivate traditional and historically conjunctural gender hierarchies (Montrose 1983a). Drawing explicitly on Raymond Williams's cultural theory, Montrose argues for a notion of ideology that is "heterogeneous and unstable, permeable and processual" (1989, 22) and for a relationship between structure and subject that is both dynamic and recursive, a mutually constitutive process in which agency is neither foreclosed nor unconstrained. What he calls the "process of subjectification" is an equivocal one, "on the one hand, shaping individuals as loci of consciousness and initiators of action—endowing them with *subjectivity* and with the capacity for agency; and, on the other hand, positioning, motivating, and constraining them within—*subjecting them to*—social networks and cultural codes that ultimately exceed their comprehension or control" (1989, 21). For Montrose, this process of subjectification is also inescapably gender-specific, an *en-gendering* of historical subjects and subjectivities. His work with the figure of Elizabeth and the attendant cultural materials he brings to bear upon her reign have charted terrain that is in many ways crucial to a historically informed analysis of the Renaissance sex-gender system.[16]

   Although issues of gender have been a recurrent concern in new historicism, the relationship of the movement to feminist literary criticism is at best an evolving one. Its emergence to a position of some prominence in the early 1980s was viewed by some feminist critics with understandable alarm and suspicion. At a moment when feminists had begun to carve out a niche for themselves within the academy, a new movement was being embraced by the profession as something like the latest fad, threatening to displace and marginalize feminist studies and reconstruct them, in retrospect, as a passing fashion as well. That the movement in question tended to subordinate questions of feminism to those of gender and questions of gender to those of power only exacerbated suspicion. In Renaissance studies in the early 1980s—that is, the period(s) of new historicism's emergence—feminist literary criticism was itself in a state of significant transition, or rather on the verge of such a transition.

In 1980, the two most significant publications in Renaissance studies were Stephen Greenblatt's *Renaissance Self-Fashioning* and *The Woman's Part,* a collection of feminist essays on Shakespeare edited by Carolyn Lenz, Gayle Greene, and Carol Neely that in many ways put the feminist study of Shakespeare on the map of literary studies. The theoretical ferment of Marxist, poststructuralist, and feminist theory in the mid- to late 1970s is not significantly reflected in *The Woman's Part,* however. Centered on the interpretation of images of women in plays and strongly psychoanalytic in its approach to them—and influenced by American rather than French variants of psychoanalytic theory—the volume codified the advances of the first wave of feminist criticism in this country but at a time when a second wave was already developing (see Cohen 1987, 22–26; Erickson 1985). British materialist feminists were in particular critical of what they viewed as an ahistorical approach to Renaissance women and dramatic characters, of a tendency to treat the latter as though they were the former, and of the essentializing model of the self applied to both (see Jardine 1983). A more materialist and historically informed feminist criticism has been emerging in this country in recent years, partially in reaction to such critiques and partially as a separate evolution of feminist literary criticism. It is evident in the work of scholars such as Jean Howard, Karen Newman, Laura Levine, and others. Such work by American, British, and Third World feminists (see especially Belsey 1985; Callaghan 1989; McKluskie 1989; Loomba 1989) has been influenced by new historicism and has also provided salutary and influential critiques of certain new historicist tendencies. Gender in such work is historically situated and not subordinated to an amorphous concept of power (as early versions of new historicism tended to be) but no longer the exclusive or central category of analysis (as early feminist critiques of new historicism insisted it should be). Rather, in such work, gender is increasingly inscribed within a complex nexus of class, gender, and race hierarchies.

New historicism has not become, as some feared, the latest orthodoxy, nor has it died away. To my mind, the record of recent years suggests it has been part of a productive, polyvocal, far from harmonious but necessary dialogue with materialist feminism, cultural materialism, and other participants in the broader field of cultural studies.

The need for a more materialist apprehension of historical heterogeneity confronts new historicism as well. In one of the more cogent critiques of the movement, James Holstun (like many others) records his dissatisfaction with the various manifestations of a "will-to-totalization" in new historicist approaches to culture. Unlike others, however, he neither attributes such totalizing tendencies to a submerged metaphysical or political agenda nor does he pretend to offer or have in his own pocket a model of cultural criticism that does not "explicitly or implicitly work from some model of cultural totality" (Holstun 1989, 198). Rather, he suggests that new historicism attributes an overly *logical* structure to culture—as do, I would add, both Geertz and Foucault, albeit in very different ways—that licenses its persistent return to canonical literary works, situated as privileged texts where cultural pressures, forces, and practices are more complexly and revealingly coded than elsewhere. The problem is not that new historicism totalizes culture, but that it

> totalizes prematurely by arguing that all cultural conflicts, all exercises of power and resistance necessarily register themselves inside canonical cultural artifacts. This sort of argument assumes that culture is a *logical* structure that can be captured by an artwork forming a structure homologous to it. A view of culture as a *material* entity, on the other hand, studies the relation between the way a subculture articulates itself and the way it is articulated by another subculture. (Holstun 1989, 198–99)

Holstun is concerned in particular with the radical pamphlet literature of the English Revolution and the lack of attention devoted to such material, taken as evidence of "oppositional collective self-fashioning" (1989, 209) by new historicists, despite all their talk of subversion or resistance or containment. He returns us to Raymond Williams, as it were, with a little help from Christopher Hill.

New historicism can hardly be accused of ignoring noncanonical texts, literary or otherwise, or of translating oftentimes compensatory articulations of dominant ideologies into the worldview of a period. Nor has it been blind to the fundamental problematics that confront any sociohistorical analysis. History is accessible to us only in the textual traces recorded and preserved in the past, whether those traces take the form of a play or a poem, a medical treatise or political pamphlet, a census of births and deaths, or a register of litigation. The process of recording and preservation is at once incomplete and partial in a different, ideological sense of the term. Even when one acknowledges that the historical archive is incomplete and fragmentary, reading documents from that archive merely as records or reflections of past reality raises the danger of reinscribing and reproducing the ideological agendas served by their original preservation. Such documents, as Dominick LaCapra has suggested, "are themselves historical realities that do not simply represent but also supplement the realities to which they refer, and a critical reading of them may provide insight into cultural processes" (LaCapra 1985, 62). In its efforts to gain such insights, new historicism has not restricted itself to the articulate and articulated consciousness of the culture in question but has sought to combine the critical analysis of such discursive records with the interpretive reconstruction, however fragmentary and even hypothetical, of more implicit, less codified modes of thought and action—to attend, in Anthony Giddens's terms, to both the *discursive* consciousness of the period (defined as that "knowledge which actors are able to express on the level of discourse") and to the more heterogeneous realm of its *practical* consciousness (understood as those "tacit stocks of knowledge which actors draw upon in the constitution of social activity" [Giddens 1979, 5]). However, it has tended to homogenize the latter, and here Holstun's critique is especially apt, and appropriate not only for the period of the English Revolution.

Given the nature of the Reformation in sixteenth-century England and what we know of the combinatory (il)logic with which people processed the various and competing knowledges available to them, we should be especially wary of prematurely imposing an order upon those traces of practical consciousness we can derive from recorded events and documentary evidence of whatever kind. The English Reformation progressed, if that is the right term, in a manner more conducive to cultural schizophrenia than to unquestioned political and religious orthodoxy. A man or woman reaching maturity in Henry VIII's early reign and fully accessible to ideological interpellation might well have been confused in his or her identity: In the course of relatively few years, he or she would have been a loyal Roman Catholic, a Henrician Catholic, a Protestant—first moderate and then more radical in Edward's later reign—then a Catholic again (and a "bloody" one to boot), then some variety of Anglican or Elizabethan Protestant. For that presumably significant portion of the population that did not embrace each succeeding state religion with equal fervor, the displacement of one orthodoxy by another, each claiming unrivaled status as absolute truth, must have decentered and destabilized the very notion of the absolute, producing a skeptical if not cynical relativism even among the lower classes. "What manner of religion we have in England I know not," declared William Binkes, a tailor from Finchingfield, in 1577, "for the preachers now do preach their own inventions and fantasies, and therefore I will not believe any of them" (Emmison 1970, 46). Such frank and radical religious skepticism needs to be coupled with evidence that occasionally surfaces in court records of the inventive delight taken, especially by the lower classes, in appropriating fragments of knowledge from discrete and quite different discursive realms and combining them to produce their own *bricolage* theories of state and church, God and man (or woman). Working from records of the Italian inquisition, Carlo Ginzburg has provided a rich account of such an irreverent appropriation and assimilation of orthodox and heterodox ideas in the case of a Friulian miller named Menocchio (Ginzburg 1980). Although Ginzburg's study does not provide the evidence he claims, of a primordial, oral, popular culture that is fully autonomous from dominant or ruling hegemonies, it does provide a rather full view of a practice of ideological *bricolage* that we catch partial glimpses of elsewhere, and one that we should be wary of folding back into an ordered cultural logic, whether the period's own or one we have artfully and thickly described.

"In a quite literal sense," as Jean and John Comaroff have wryly observed, "hegemony is habit forming" (Comaroff and Comaroff 1991). But while the historical analysis of cultures needs to clarify the processes through which habits, ideas, meanings, and subjects are indeed formed to fit the needs of hegemony, such analysis must also recognize that the fit is never certain and must attune itself to the fault lines and contradictions of social determination as well. Even where official manifestations of royal power are concerned, there is ample evidence that what might be called the intended illocutionary force of such power in operation could have an unintended illocutionary effect. Lacking the bureaucracy necessary for the policing and surveillance of its populace, early modern England was forced to rely upon a system of exemplary justice, of public and oftentimes spectacular punishment, that sought to instill the proper degree of awe and fear in the minds of its subjects. Even so eminent a figure as Sir Edward Coke was forced to recognize, however, that such a system was at best inadequate to the task—if not contrary to it: "We have found by wofull experience that it is not frequent and often punishment that doth prevent like offenses. . . . Those offenses are often committed that are often punished, for the frequency of the punishment makes it so familiar as it is not feared" (cited in Skulsky 1964, 157). Punishment makes familiar both the crime and its consequences, but with a crucial difference. Frequent punishment advertises the taboo or the forbidden as a common occurrence, and at the same time inures its audience to the spectacle of the law taking hold of and inscribing itself upon the body of the condemned. Exemplary power not only fails to deter, it even produces and promulgates the very transgressions it acts upon— by the sheer fact that it must act upon them, giving them a currency or circulation they would not otherwise possess. What Coke confronts is not a general "undecidability" of meaning or juridical effect but rather a paradoxical unpredictability and overdetermination of affect, and one that suggests a fundamental constraint upon *any* effort to control the production of historical meaning and subjects.

Although not as bleakly deterministic as some of its critics have charged, new historicism would do well to recall Coke's history lesson, to combine its analysis of the historical constraints upon individual agency with a fuller awareness of the limits, potential or actualized, of any hegemonic power. It would do well, in fact, to follow Roger Chartier's lead and "reformulate the notion of appropriation and place it at the centre of a cultural historical approach" (Chartier 1990). Such a move would allow it to realize, more fully perhaps than it has, that cultural production is never a one-way street. Exemplary displays of power, official and unofficial disseminations of ideas and images, even what registers as "facts," enter into a cultural economy that is inherently dialogical; once placed into circulation, any cultural practice, text, or representation is available for and subject to appropriation, for both licit and illicit ends.

NOTES

1. An early version of this essay was first presented as a response to Miller in a talk given in 1987 at The Modern Language Association. For another response to Miller, also in the context of new historicism, see Montrose (1989, 1992).

2. For example, see the recent work of Joan Wallach Scott (1988) as well as the essay by Nicholas B. Dirks in the present volume.

3. This is to some degree true of Elizabeth Fox-Genovese's recent essay (1989), which I discuss later in the text. It is decisively the case in Spiegel (1990), where the assumptions of American literary deconstruction are projected onto an incredible range of authors, including Foucault, Geertz, Jameson, and Williams.

4. For representative early works, see Jonathan Goldberg (1981), Louis Montrose (1980a, 1980b), Steven Mullaney (1980), Stephen Orgel (1975), and Leonard Tennenhouse (1982), as well as Greenblatt's own seminal book *Renaissance Self-Fashioning* (1980).

5. Although there has been a tendency by some to situate new historicism and feminism as antagonistic movements, as in conference panels entitled "Feminism vs. New Historicism," there has also been a great deal of salutary influence in both directions, and a significant amount of work by male and female critics alike that would be difficult to categorize as one or the other. In a recent conference address, Jean Howard provided an astute ideological critique of the institutional and disciplinary pressures that induce divisive and exclusionary positioning of such movements in the American academy and stressed the need to resist those pressures and to pursue instead the

mutually productive affiliations between various forms of cultural study. For a fuller discussion of feminist and new historicist literary criticism, see the later sections of this essay.

6. In an uncharacteristically splenetic moment at the 1986 Modern Language Association Convention—the occasion, as well, of Miller's presidential address—Dominick LaCapra described the movement as a "West Coast Foucauldianism of infantile desire," or so my transcription of his remarks reads. For a more considered discussion, see LaCapra (1989).

7. Although Williams is not often cited by Greenblatt, he is one of the central and often unrecognized influences on the latter's work. For others explicitly indebted to Williams, see Mullaney (1988) and the extensive series of essays by Louis Montrose.

8. For the phrase "symbolic economy" in this context, see Mullaney (1988, 41–47, 96–97).

9. Geertz himself acknowledged this danger, warning that interpretive anthropology could all too easily become a kind of "sociological aestheticism" out of touch "with the hard surfaces of life—with the political, economic, stratificatory realities within which men are everywhere contained" (1973, 30).

10. I think it is crucial to distinguish, as I have tried to do, between Geertz's method and the formalist aesthetic ideology that dictates the application of that method, and I think it is entirely possible and legitimate to do so. Vincent Pecora suggests that such a distinction is impossible in his otherwise astute analysis of the Indonesian political realities effaced in Geertz's work. Pecora's charge is that new historicism inevitably performs analogous effacements, due to its methodological borrowings from Geertz. At the same time, however, Pecora seems to regard his critique as an indictment of *all* anthropology, whether indulging in thick description or not. See Pecora (1989).

11. For an analysis and critique of Giddens, see Sewell (1989).

12. To explain the massive and unprecedented sickness and death that visited them along with the English, the Algonkians explained their strange fatalities by analogy to the equally strange and impressive weapons of the English and with Harriot's encouragement attributed both the "invisible bullets" that were decimating their tribe and the visible ones the English had at their disposal to the power of the English God.

13. Although many of the misreadings have been outrageous enough to seem willful and raise questions about their motivations, some of the terms that structure Greenblatt's analysis have contributed to the slipperiness of the essay. "Subversion," for example, is a curiously loaded term, at once highly abstract and narrower in scope than one might imagine, for it apparently does not include rebellion, especially from below (Greenblatt 1988, 47). As James Holstun notes, "The very concept of subversion is unsatisfactory for describing resistance or revolution. 'Subversion' is more likely to be the fantasy of someone inside a dominant subculture, whether he is eager to 'identify' it and root it out, or to identify with it. . . . In a sense, the debate over subversion and containment is a nondebate, since 'subversion' is already included in 'containment'" (Holstun 1989, 198).

14. Like other critics of Greenblatt's argument—namely, that apparently subversive forces are not so much illusory as complex, sometimes serving to reinforce the dominant culture in the process of contesting it—Lentricchia seems oblivious to the extensive body of Marxist analysis that argues much the same point and clearly without the defeatist message Lentricchia attributes—falsely, as far as I am concerned—to Greenblatt (see Bloch et al. 1980).

15. I am using *tactical* and *strategic* in the sense developed by Michel de Certeau (1984, xviii–xx).

16. Judith Lowder Newton, for example, while critical of certain occlusions of the material realm in the work of Catherine Gallagher, Nancy Armstrong, and Mary Poovey, finds that Montrose has begun to integrate the material and the symbolic realms. See Newton (1989).

REFERENCES

Adelman, Janet. 1987. "'Born of Woman': Fantasies of Maternal Power in *Macbeth*." In *Cannibals, Witches, and Divorce: Estranging the Renaissance,* 90–121. Edited by Marjorie Garber. Baltimore: Johns Hopkins University Press.

Agnew, Jean-Christophe. 1986. *Worlds Apart: The Market and the Theater in Anglo-American Thought, 1550–1750.* New York: Cambridge University Press.

Belsey, Catherine. 1985. *The Subject of Tragedy: Identity and Difference in Renaissance Drama.* London and New York: Methuen.

Biersack, Aletta. 1989. "Local Knowledge, Local History: Geertz and Beyond." In *The New Cultural History,* 72–96. Edited by Lynn Hunt. Berkeley and Los Angeles: University of California Press.

Bloch, Ernst, et al. 1980. *Aesthetics and Politics.* Translated and edited by R. Taylor. London: Verso.

Boose, Lynda E. 1987. "The Family in Shakespeare Studies; or—Studies in the Family of Shakespeareans; or—The Politics of Politics." *Renaissance Quarterly* 40:707–42.

Bourdieu, Pierre. 1977. *Outline of a Theory of Practice.* Translated by Richard Nice. Cambridge: Cambridge University Press.

Callaghan, Dympna. 1989. *Woman and Gender in Renaissance Tragedy: A Study of "King Lear," "Othello," "The Duchess of Malfi," and "The White Devil."* Atlantic Highlands, NJ: Humanities Press International.

Certeau, Michel de. 1984. *The Practice of Everyday Life.* Translated by Steven F. Rendall. Berkeley and Los Angeles: University of California Press.

Chartier, Roger. 1990. *Cultural History: Between Practices and Representations.* Translated by Lydia G. Cochrane. Ithaca: Cornell University Press.

Cohen, Walter. 1987. "Political Criticism of Shakespeare." In *Shakespeare Reproduced: The Text in History and Ideology,* 18–46. Edited by Jean E. Howard and Marion F. O'Connor. New York and London: Methuen.

Comaroff, Jean, and John L. Comaroff. 1991. *Of Revelation and Revolution: Christianity, Colonialism, and Consciousness in South Africa.* Vol. 1. Chicago: University of Chicago Press.

Darnton, Robert. 1984. *The Great Cat Massacre and Other Episodes in French Cultural History.* New York: Basic Books.

Dollimore, Jonathan. 1984. *Radical Tragedy: Religion, Ideology, and Power in the Drama of Shakespeare and His Contemporaries.* Chicago: University of Chicago Press.

Dollimore, Jonathan, and Sinfield, Alan. 1985. *Political Shakespeare: New Essays in Cultural Materialism.* Ithaca: Cornell University Press.

Emmison, F. G. 1970. *Elizabethan Life: Disorder.* Colchester, UK: Cullingford and Co.

Erickson, Peter. 1985. Review of *The (M)other Tongue: Essays in Feminist Psychoanalytic Interpretation,* edited by Shirley Nelson Garner, Claire Kahane, and Madelon Sprengnether. *Hurricane Alice: A Feminist Review* 3:6–7.

Erickson, Peter. 1987. "Rewriting the Renaissance, Rewriting Ourselves." *Shakespeare Quarterly* 38:327–37.

Ferguson, Margaret W., Maureen Quilligan, and Nancy J. Vickers, eds. *Rewriting the Renaissance: The Discourses of Sexual Difference in Early Modern Europe.* Chicago: University of Chicago Press.

Foucault, Michel. 1977. *Discipline and Punish: The Birth of the Prison.* Translated by Alan Sheridan. New York: Pantheon.

Foucault, Michel. 1978. *The History of Sexuality, Vol. 1: An Introduction.* Translated by Robert Hurley. New York: Random House.

Fox-Genovese, Elizabeth. 1989. "Literary Criticism and the Politics of New Historicism." In *The New Historicism,* 213–24. Edited by Aram H. Veeser. New York and London: Routledge.

Gallagher, Catherine. 1989. "Marxism and the New Historicism." In *The New Historicism,* 37–48. Edited by Aram H. Veeser. New York and London: Routledge.

Geertz, Clifford. 1973. *The Interpretation of Cultures: Selected Essays.* New York: Basic Books.

Geertz, Clifford. 1980. *Negara: The Theatre State in Nineteenth-Century Bali.* Princeton: Princeton University Press.

Geertz, Clifford. 1983. *Local Knowledge: Further Essays in Interpretive Anthropology.* New York: Basic Books.

Giddens, Anthony. 1979. *Central Problems in Social Theory: Action, Structure, and Contradiction in Social Analysis.* Berkeley and Los Angeles: University of California Press.

Ginzburg, Carlo. 1980. *The Cheese and the Worms: The Cosmos of a Sixteenth-Century Miller.* Translated by John and Anne Tedeschi. Baltimore: Johns Hopkins University Press.

Goldberg, Jonathan. 1981. *Endlesse Worke: Spenser and the Structures of Discourse.* Baltimore: Johns Hopkins University Press.

Goldberg, Jonathan. 1982. "The Politics of Renaissance Literature: A Review Essay." *English Literary History* 49:514–42.

Goldberg, Jonathan. 1983. *James I and the Politics of Literature.* Baltimore: Johns Hopkins University Press.

Greenblatt, Stephen J. 1980. *Renaissance Self-Fashioning: From More to Shakespeare.* Chicago: University of Chicago Press.

Greenblatt, Stephen J. 1985. "Invisible Bullets: Renaissance Authority and its Subversion." In *Political Shakespeare: New Essays in Cultural Materialism,* 18–47. Edited by Johathan Dollimore and Alan Sinfield. Ithaca: Cornell University Press.

Greenblatt, Stephen J. 1988. *Shakespearean Negotiations: The Circulation of Social Energy.* Berkeley and Los Angeles: University of California Press.

Greenblatt, Stephen J. 1989. "Towards a Poetics of Culture." In *The New Historicism,* 1–14. Edited by Aram H. Veeser. New York and London: Routledge.

Greenblatt, Stephen J. 1990. "Resonance and Wonder." In *Literary Theory Today,* 74–90. Edited by Peter Collier and Helga Geyer-Ryan. Ithaca: Cornell University Press.

Greenblatt, Stephen J., ed. 1982. *The Power of Forms in the English Renaissance.* Norman, OK: Pilgrim Books.

Holstun, James. 1989. "Ranting at the New Historicism." *English Literary Renaissance* 19:189–225.

Howard, Jean E. 1986. "The New Historicism in Renaissance Studies." *English Literary Renaissance* 16:13–43.

Howard, Jean E. 1987. "Renaissance Anti-Theatricality and the Politics of Gender and Rank in *Much Ado About Nothing.*" In *Shakespeare Reproduced: The Text in History and Ideology,* 163–87. Edited by Jean E. Howard and Marion F. O'Connor. New York and London: Methuen.

Howard, Jean E., and Marion F. O'Connor, eds. 1987. *Shakespeare Reproduced: The Text in History and Ideology.* New York and London: Methuen.

James, Mervyn. 1988. *Society, Politics, and Culture: Studies in Early Modern England.* Cambridge: Cambridge University Press.

Jardine, Lisa. 1983. *Still Harping on Daughters: Women and Drama in the Age of Shakespeare.* Brighton, UK: Harvester Press.

Kastan, David Scott. 1986. "Proud Majesty Made a Subject: Shakespeare and the Spectacle of Rule." *Shakespeare Quarterly* 37:459–75.

Keesing, Roger M. 1987. "Anthropology as Interpretive Quest." *Current Anthropology* 28:161–76.

Kermode, Frank. 1989. "The New Historicism." *New Republic,* February 29, 31–34.

LaCapra, Dominick. 1985. *History and Criticism.* Ithaca, NY: Cornell University Press.

LaCapra, Dominick. 1989. *Soundings in Critical Theory.* Ithaca, NY: Cornell University Press.

Lentricchia, Frank. 1989. "Foucault's Legacy: A New Historicism?" In *The New Historicism,* 231–42. Edited by Aram H. Veeser. New York and London: Routledge.

Lenz, Carolyn Ruth Swift, Gayle Green, and Carol Thomas Neely, eds. *The Woman's Part: Feminist Criticism of Shakespeare.* Urbana: University of Illinois Press.

Levine, Laura. 1986. "Men in Women's Clothing: Anti-Theatricality and Effeminization from 1579 to 1642." *Criticism* 28:121–43.

Liu, Alan. 1989. "The Power of Pluralism: The New Historicism." *English Literary History* 56:721–71.

Loomba, Ania. 1989. *Gender, Race, Renaissance Drama.* Manchester and New York: Manchester University Press.

McKluskie, Kathleen. 1989. *Renaissance Dramatists.* Atlantic Highlands, NJ: Humanities Press International.

Miller, J. Hillis. 1987. "Presidential Address 1986. The Triumph of Theory, the Resistance to Reading, and the Question of the Material Base." *PMLA* 102: 281–91.

Montrose, Louis Adrian. 1980a. "'Eliza, Queene of Shepheardes' and the Pastoral of Power." *English Literary Renaissance* 10:153–82.

Montrose, Louis Adrian. 1980b. "The Purpose of Playing: Reflections on a Shakespearean Anthropology." *Helios* n.s., 7:51–74.

Montrose, Louis Adrian. 1983a. "Shaping Fantasies: Figurations of Gender and Power in Elizabethan Culture." *Representations* 2:61–94.

Montrose, Louis Adrian. 1983b. "Of Gentlemen and Shepherds: The Politics of Elizabethan Pastoral Form." *English Literary History* 50:415–59.

Montrose, Louis Adrian. 1986a. "Renaissance Literary Studies and the Subject of History." *English Literary Renaissance* 16:5–12.

Montrose, Louis Adrian. 1986b. "The Elizabethan Subject and the Spenserian Text." In *Literary Theory/Renaissance Texts,* 303–40. Edited by Patricia Parker and David Quint. Baltimore: Johns Hopkins University Press.

Montrose, Louis Adrian. 1989. "Professing the Renaissance: The Poetics and Politics of Culture." In *The New Historicism,* 15–36. Edited by Aram H. Veeser. New York and London: Routledge.

Montrose, Louis Adrian. 1992. In *Redrawing the Boundaries: The Transformation of English and American Literary Studies,* 392–418. Edited by Stephen Greenblatt and Giles Gunn. New York: Modern Language Association.

Moretti, Franco. 1982. "'A Huge Eclipse': Tragic Form and the Deconsecration of Sovereignty." In *The Power of Forms in the English Renaissance,* 7–40. Edited by Stephen J. Greenblatt. Norman, OK: Pilgrim Books.

Mullaney, Steven. 1980. "Lying Like Truth: Riddle, Representation, and Treason in Renaissance England." *English Literary History* 47:32–48.

Mullaney, Steven. 1983. "Strange Things, Gross Terms, Curious Customs: The Rehearsal of Cultures in the Late Renaissance." *Representations* 3:40–67.

Mullaney, Steven. 1988. *The Place of the Stage: License, Play, and Power in Renaissance England.* Chicago: University of Chicago Press.

Mullaney, Steven. 1989. Review of *Shakespearean Negotiations: The Circulation of*

Social Energy in Renaissance England, by Stephen Greenblatt. *Shakespeare Quarterly* 40:495–500.

Neely, Carol Thomas. 1988. "Constructing the Subject: Feminist Practice and New Renaissance Discourses." *English Literary Renaissance* 18:5–18.

Newman, Karen. 1986. "Renaissance Family Politics and Shakespeare's *The Taming of the Shrew.*" *English Literary Renaissance* 16:86–100.

Newman, Karen. 1987. "'And Wash the Ethiop White': Femininity and the Monstrous in *Othello.*" In *Shakespeare Reproduced: The Text in History and Ideology,* 143–62. Edited by Jean E. Howard and Marion F. O'Connor. New York and London: Methuen.

Newton, Judith Lowder. 1989. "History as Usual?: Feminism and the 'New Historicism.'" In *The New Historicism,* 152–67. Edited by Aram H. Veeser. New York and London: Routledge.

Orgel, Stephen. 1975. *The Illusion of Power: Political Theater in the English Renaissance.* Berkeley and Los Angeles: University of California Press.

Ortner, Sherry B. 1984. "Theory in Anthropology since the Sixties." *Comparative Studies in Society and History* 26:126–66.

Pechter, Edward. 1987. "The New Historicism and Its Discontents: Politicizing Renaissance Drama." *PMLA* 102:292–303.

Pecora, Vincent P. 1989. "The Limits of Local Knowledge." In *The New Historicism,* 243–76. Edited by Aram H. Veeser. New York and London: Routledge.

Porter, Carolyn. 1988. "Are We Being Historical Yet?" *South Atlantic Quarterly* 87:743–86.

Sahlins, Marshall. 1975. *Culture and Practical Reason.* Chicago: University of Chicago Press.

Sahlins, Marshall. 1985. *Islands of History.* Chicago: University of Chicago Press.

Scott, Joan Wallach. 1988. *Gender and the Politics of History.* New York: Columbia University Press.

Sewell, William. 1989. "Toward a Theory of Structure: Duality, Agency, and Transformation." Comparative Studies of Social Transformations (CSST) Working Paper No. 29.

Skulsky, Harold. 1964. "Pain, Law, and Conscience in *Measure for Measure.*" *The Journal of the History of Ideas* 51:147–68.

Spiegel, Gabrielle M. 1990. "History, Historicism, and the Social Logic of the Text in the Middle Ages." *Speculum* 65:59–86.

Stallybrass, Peter. 1986. "Patriarchal Territories: The Body Enclosed." In *Rewriting the Renaissance: The Discourses of Sexual Difference in Early Modern Europe,* 123–44. Edited by Margaret W. Ferguson et al. Chicago: University of Chicago Press.

Stallybrass, Peter, and Allon White. 1986. *The Politics and Poetics of Transgression.* Ithaca: Cornell University Press.

Tennenhouse, Leonard. 1982. "Representing Power: *Measure for Measure* in Its Time." In *The Power of Forms in the English Renaissance,* 139–56. Edited by Stephen J. Greenblatt. Norman, OK: Pilgrim Books.

Veeser, Aram H., ed. 1989. *The New Historicism.* New York and London: Routledge.

Wayne, Don E. 1987. "Power, Politics, and the Shakespearean Text." In *Shakespeare Reproduced: The Text in History and Ideology,* 147–67. Edited by Jean E. Howard and Marion F. O'Connor. New York and London: Methuen.

Weimann, Robert. 1988. "Bifold Authority in Shakespeare's Theatre," *Shakespeare Quarterly* 39:401–17.

Williams, Raymond. 1978. *Marxism and Literature.* Oxford: Oxford University Press.

Woodbridge, Linda. 1984. *Women and the English Renaissance.* Urbana: University of Illinois Press.

Part 2. Making Histories

Is All the World a Text? From Social History to the History of Society Two Decades Later

Geoff Eley

History to the defeated may say Alas but cannot help or pardon.

—W. H. Auden

There is no document of civilization that is not simultaneously a record of barbarism.

—Walter Benjamin

History will teach us nothing.

—Sting

In the Beginning

In 1971 Eric Hobsbawm called it "a good moment to be a social historian" (1971, 43).[1] Ten years later this was still the case, despite a certain fractiousness and the readiness of some to find a crisis in the field. The main thing was the continuing growth of activity (the proliferation of journals, conferences, subdisciplinary societies, international networks, curricular initiatives, and dissertations, despite the contraction of history graduate programs), and in light of such expansion conflicts of direction were perhaps the normal signs of diversification and growth. That social historians could argue over theory and method was evidence of vitality more than ill health, and only those with narrow or sectarian views of social history's proper orientation could be upset by conflict as such.[2]

Ten years further on, though, such confidence is harder to sustain. I am not the only person to have detected a general discursive shift in the rhetoric and practice of the profession from "social" to "cultural" history, effected via what we have become accustomed to calling the "linguistic turn." Clearly this observation needs to be elaborated and specified, but a good barometer of the change in historiographical sensibility has been Gareth Stedman Jones. From his invigorating polemic against the liberal complacencies and positivistic assumptions of the British historiographical tradition in 1967 to a variety of critical and substantive essays in the mid-1970s, Stedman Jones developed a project of "non-empiricist" and "theoretically informed history" that was Marxist, open to other forms of social theory, and naturally materialist, as the unifying problematic of contemporary social history then took that to mean.

For many social historians, therefore, it was very disconcerting when in 1983 Stedman Jones seemed to embrace a form of linguistic analysis that was decidedly nonmaterialist in the classical sense and seemed to call the given assumptions of social history into doubt. Moreover, since that time things have moved fast. Stedman Jones's own rather cautious formulations have been left behind, disappearing in a more radical polarity of so-called deconstructionists and unrepentant materialists.[3] Of course, the social history that emerged from the 1960s was never a unitary project. But some notion of social determination, conceptualized on the ground of material life, whether in demographic, political-economic, labor-process, class-sociological, or class-cultural terms, generally provided a tissue of common assumptions. From a vantage point at the end of the 1980s, by contrast, a rough division seems to have opened within this "broad church" between those who have been rethinking their assumptions to the point of radically subverting the determinative coherence of the category of the social and those who continue defending the particular social-historical materialism that formed them.

In this respect, social history has become one site of a general epistemological uncertainty that characterizes large areas of academic-intellectual life in the humanities and social sciences in the late twentieth century. This flux is perhaps more extensive in some places than in others (in the sense that it pervades more disciplines more completely) and more central to disciplinary discussion in, say, literature and anthropology than in, say, sociology and the "harder" social sciences. Not by accident, the most radical and influential discussions have been occurring in areas that lack the constraining power of disciplinary traditions—especially women's studies and the emerging field of cultural studies. A valuable map of this uncertainty is provided by Peter Novick's concluding chapters in *That Noble Dream,* which usefully remind us of its more-than-French origins, building their account around Kuhn, Rorty, Fish, and Geertz rather than Foucault, Lacan, Barthes, and Derrida. But Novick also assimilates the debates too easily to the binary framework of "objectivism"/"relativism." While he is undoubtedly correct to find the dissolution of "history" as a professionally centered disciplinary project during the last three decades, he focuses too heavily on the ever more elaborate process of academic specialization and understates the impact of "contemporary continental thought." In fact, so far from having "little positive resonance within the historical profession, and practically none outside the sub-discipline of European intellectual history," figures like Hayden White and Dominick LaCapra have become the advance guard of a much broader intellectual phenomenon. By 1990, I would argue, interest in Foucault and Derrida extends far beyond a few "professionally marginal historians whose primary allegiance was to interdisciplinary communities with membership made up largely of literary theorists, cultural critics, and philosophers" (Novick 1988, 605).

It is difficult to periodize this movement with any precision. In retrospect, the first wave of polemical stocktaking essays, which are usually cited as marking a "crisis" of social history in the second half of the 1970s—those by Fox-Genovese and Genovese (1976), Stedman Jones (1976), Stone (1977), and Judt (1979)—were indeed remarkably innocent of the poststructuralist theory whose absence Novick detects in the discourse of historians. Moreover, these essays mostly stood their ground on an extremely unproblematic kind of materialism. I could make a similar point from a variety of other programmatic statements—including the founding editorials of new journals like *Social History* (*SH*) and *History Workshop Journal* (*HWJ*), both launched in 1976, or the omnibus survey of U.S. historical writing edited by Michael Kammen for the American Historical Association (AHA), *The Past before Us,* whose essays were commissioned in 1977–78 in an intellectual conjuncture also defined by the mid-1970s. In other words, this earlier moment of stocktaking belongs far more to the period of social history's dramatic post-1960s expansion than to the current period of uncertainty and flux, proceeding on the basis of the former's materialist assumptions rather than bringing them into doubt. Moreover, a systematic survey of more established social history journals—like *Past and Present* (*P&P*), *Journal of Interdisciplinary History* (*JIH*), or *Journal of Social History* (*JSH*), let alone more mainstream journals that also carry social history writings, like *Journal of Modern History* (*JMH*) or *American Historical Review* (*AHR*)—would also, I suspect, show a similar lack of interest in literary or linguistic theoretical influences. And whereas *AHR* and *JMH* have begun noticing these influences through review essays and forums, the older social history journals have kept their distance right down to the present, as has another journal that was very much in the vanguard of the exchange in the

1960s between history and social science, *Comparative Studies in Society and History* (*CSSH*).[4]

My own sense is that things began to change around 1980 and that the shift could be usefully traced through the newer journals like *HWJ, SH,* and *Radical History Review* (*RHR*). For instance, one might juxtapose the original editorials of *HWJ* on "Feminist History" and "Sociology and History" (1, spring 1976, 4–8) and another early one on "British Economic History and the Question of Work" (3, spring 1977, 1–4), which are firmly continuous with the critical materialist departures of the 1960s (and still connected to the older influences of Edward Thompson, Eric Hobsbawm et al.), with the editorial on "Language and History" several years later (10, autumn 1980, 1–5), which marked some distance from this founding materialism. The trajectory could then be further described: *HWJ*'s renaming itself a "Journal of Socialist and Feminist Historians" and simultaneous publishing of a guide to "Foucault for Historians" by Jeffrey Weeks (14, autumn 1982, 1, 106–19); an editorial on "Culture and Gender" (15, spring 1983, 1–3); the arrival of the new feminist literary criticism in review essays by Mary Poovey and Joan Scott (22, autumn 1986, 185–92); the gradual entry of psychoanalysis, through essays by Sally Alexander (17, spring 1984, 125–49), Laura Mulvey and T. G. Ashplant (23, spring 1987, 1–19 and 165–73), and then a full-blown special feature of four articles on "Psychoanalysis and History" (26, autumn 1988, 105–52), with a follow-up response by Jacqueline Rose (28, autumn 1989, 148–54); another special feature on "Language and History," including a very severe article by Peter Schöttler on "Historians and Discourse Analysis" (27, spring 1989, 1–65); and, most recently, a special feature on the French Revolution that is heavily "culturalist" in the current literary-cum-linguistic sense (28, autumn 1989, 1–87).[5]

To a great extent, I want to argue, this reflects a process of complex generationally internal revision. The launching of journals like *HWJ, SH,* and *RHR* and the strengthening and refurbishing of others, like *International Labor and Working-Class History* (*ILWCH*), marked the arrival of a particular generation (that trained in the 1960s and early 1970s) and their claiming of a distinct institutional space under the sign of a restlessly aggrandizing social history. The turn to linguistically conceived forms of cultural history by the end of the 1970s, moved by a combination of changing political contexts and autonomous theoretical engagement, most sharply registered in feminism and women's history, marked the fracturing of the same broad generational consensus. To some extent, these tensions expressed themselves in early conflicts over theory per se, as in the acrimonious attacks on "structuralist Marxism," which dominated left intellectual life in Britain for much of the later 1970s.[6] Moreover, the salience of this particular generation and its disagreements was magnified by the drastic reduction in the number of graduate historians in the later 1970s and early 1980s. Mainly for that reason, the succeeding generation has had little opportunity to declare its own distinctive voice—by contrast (one might guess) with the one qualifying in the later 1980s and early 1990s, which will have a great deal to say in the areas of gender history and cultural studies.

My choice of a particular moment to dramatize this generational flux would be an intense daylong discussion held at the University of Michigan around the theme "Whence and Whither Social History?" in October 1979. I choose this occasion partly for its local resonance and partly for personal reasons, because it marked my own introduction to social history discussions in North America.[7] But it also nicely encapsulated the dilemmas—and incipient dispersal—of a generational cohort previously united by certain shared assumptions about the methodological and substantive purposes of the social-historical project. Convened by Louise and Charles Tilly to take advantage of the local presence of various participants in the first North American Labor History Conference at Wayne State University, it brought together a number of representative and influential voices, including James Cronin, David Levine, John Merriman, Joan Scott, William Sewell, and Edward Shorter. Organized into three consecutive sessions, the meeting was invited to address precisely the four stocktaking essays referred to above (Fox-Genovese and Genovese, Stedman Jones, Stone, and Judt), although it quickly became clear that much of the momentum came from (justified) ire at the personal polemics of Tony Judt. As the day went on, there was much talk of the insufficiencies of "vulgar Marxism," by which seemed to be meant the quantitative study of everyday experience and material life, and the need instead for a "more sophisticated kind of cultural history." There was also much reference to European theory and British theoretical debate (which, as it happened, was about to reach one particularly unpleasant and chastening climax several weeks later at the thirteenth History Workshop in Ruskin College, Oxford, in December 1979). Such reference was focused partly on the interventions of the anthropologists present (Michael Taussig and Bernard Cohn) and partly on those of the present writer. And while the theory concerned was generally taken to be Marxist or Marxist-feminist, it was actually the imprint of a partially digested and still emerging antireductionist critique, which over the longer term was in the process of dissolving the Marxist problematic as we then knew it. Finally, although the discussions had been generally conducted in a spirit of openness and generosity, with much constructive positioning and clarification, the day ended with an angry intervention by Charles Tilly (directed against certain statements by William Sewell), in which he reasserted in no uncertain terms the primacy of "the harder-edged sociological work" the conference had apparently been called to defend.[8] Important things were clearly at stake.

Looking back, this was an extremely pregnant occasion. Within the year, William Sewell's *Work and Revolution in France* had appeared; Joan Scott had moved to Brown where she began a systematic poststructuralist encounter; and Charles Tilly continued to hold the line. Simply to mention these names is to register the change—attached to Tilly in the 1960s, the former under an SSRC Training Fellowship, Scott and Sewell were probably the leading progeny in European history of the union of history and sociology in the 1960s but were now arguing that the new social history was itself not enough. The discourse of social historians was beginning to disobey, outgrowing the present disciplinary containers, and spilling across the boundaries its practitioners had thought secure. As Couvares said in his written statement for the Tilly symposium (with a curious choice of language): "The new harlots of cultural anthropology, 'thick description', and semiotics threaten daily to shift the focus, to alter the terms of the discourse" (Couvares 1980, 675).

Yet the documentary trace of the occasion betrays virtually nothing of this emerging intellectual history. Thus, Charles Tilly notes the challenge of "anthropological work, . . . the study of *mentalités,* and . . . more rigorous marxist analyses" but then seems to believe that the existing project—"collective biography, quantification, social-scientific approaches, and rigorous studies of everyday behavior"—could continue much as before. The trick was simply connecting it better to "the established historical agenda" in language other historians could understand. As far as it goes, Tilly's description of social history's "two callings" is unexceptionable: "asking how the world we live in came into being, and how its coming into being affected the everyday lives of ordinary people; asking what could have happened to everyday experience at major historical choice points, and then inquiring how and why the outcomes won out over other possibilities" (C. Tilly 1980, 681). But as long as the cultural construction of these processes is ignored (and categories such as "everyday experience" and "ordinary people" not put into question), the formulation will continue to dissatisfy. Similarly, Louise Tilly's problematizing of "work" ("to talk about changes in women's work over time, more rigorous definitions, words, categories are needed") and "politics" ("Politics must be reconceptualized so we can talk about the politics of those without formal rights") as such is all to the good (L. Tilly 1980, 67). But it is also clear that the reconceptualizing is to proceed on a particular sociological ground. In that sense, *Women, Work, and Family* and *Gender and the Politics of History* are separated by far more than a matter of years.[9]

So we have entered "new times." What is striking to me, in this conjuncture, is the degree to which historians have been willing to become their own theoreticians. This seems to me not to have been as true of the 1960s, when social history declared its presence via a more eclectic and dependent turn to sociology (and sometimes anthropology), and the most self-conscious appropriations of social science focused on methodology (as in demography, family history, mobility studies, urban history, and so on) rather than theory per se. To that extent, Stedman Jones's essays of 1967–76, which called on historians to emancipate themselves from a junior relationship to social science and begin producing theory of their own, bespoke an accurate reading of the relationship.[10] In the meantime, in fact, some historians have been taking Stedman Jones at his word. In the 1970s this happened partly through a return to Marx, both directly via *Capital,* the *Grundrisse,* or political writings like *The Eighteenth Brumaire,* and indirectly via appropriation of heterodox theorists like Gramsci. It also happened through more self-conscious critiques of historians' sociological usage, by locating particular concepts (like "social control" or "community") in their originating problematic and unpacking the accumulated meanings that might compromise their present use (Stedman Jones 1976; McDonald 1985; Calhoun 1980; Gatrell 1982). A turning to anthropology rather than sociology (one of the specific bugbears of the Tillys) was certainly part of this overall process, one that was already visible in the rethinking that produced Sewell's *Work and Revolution in France* and became the more important as anthropology itself became "historicized" during the 1980s (Sewell 1980; also Cohn 1980, 1981; Medick 1987).

But the most salient sites of such independent theorizing, I would argue, are ones where uncritical borrowing is harder because of the absence of an existing practice to rationalize, as well as the paucity of relevant theory to use—where innovation, initiative, and interdisciplinarity have been inscribed more centrally in the very conditions and processes of knowledge production from the start, one might say—namely, the new and "un-disciplined" fields of feminist theory/women's history and cultural studies. Of course, no theory is ever conjured out of nothing, and it might be objected that historians in these latter areas are no less dependent on external theory than their predecessors (or previous incarnations) as new social historians. It is simply that a different *kind* of theory, literary rather than social-scientific, is in play. But it is no accident that several of the key influences in this domain, such as Michel Foucault or Stuart Hall, are distinguished precisely by their disobedience to conventional disciplinary classification (was Foucault a historian, or what?). And it does seem to me that historians (Joan Scott and Richard Johnson would be perfect respective examples) have become far more active participants in this new theoretical conversation than in the old.[11]

Despite Peter Novick's skepticism, therefore, there is some evidence that historians at large have been fruitfully interacting with the rich recent tradition of French poststructuralist theory and its British-American interpreters. It is significant that this reception has recently extended beyond the pages of journals like *HWJ* and *RHR* to the central organs of the North American profession. In different ways, both *AHR* and *JMH* have given generous space to the developing debates around the impact of the "linguistic turn."[12] To an extent, this exposure has featured the disagreements of intellectual historians, that is, those most immediately concerned with language and textuality in the stronger formal sense. But there is no doubt that the ideas are now circulating far more extensively, influencing the intellectual practice and certainly the rhetoric of large areas of social and political history. Thus, the modern German field (to cite one more example) has not been distinguished by its methodological and theoretical radicalism during the last three decades, even though there may have been groups of radicals within it. Indeed, one notable attempt to break through the conservatism with an ambitious theoretical argument about the collapse of the Weimar Republic was quickly silenced.[13] The "official" organ of North American Germanists, *Central European History* (*CEH*), has been a useful outlet for monographic and field-specific research but has seldom surpassed a reliable middle-of-the-road solidity. Apart from a couple of reviews and perhaps a few articles, there were no articles of an explicitly Marxist orientation until the publication of the Feldman-Abraham exchange in the seventeenth year of the journal's existence, and then the purpose was to delegitimize it. Apart from a now classic article by Renate Bridenthal in 1973 and three other articles dealing empirically with women, there were no articles with an explicitly feminist orientation until the journal's sixteenth year, when there were two, by Jean Quataert and Deborah Hertz (in the intervening five years there has been only one other, by Quataert again). And even under the most generous definition, the journal's social history content has averaged around one article a year during the first twenty years (1967–87).[14]

But in the meantime the ground has been shifting beneath our feet. The existence of the German Women's History Study Group on the East Coast since the 1970s has been one sign of this. The culmination of this was a conference at Rutgers in April 1986 on "The Meaning of Gender in German History," which sought to disturb and reshape the general thinking of the field.

By the end of the decade the linguistic turn had also arrived. A conference on "Re-evaluating the Third Reich" at the University of Pennsylvania in April 1988 managed to keep such influences at bay, but by 1989–90 a series of events registered the change: namely, a small symposium in Chicago in October 1989 on interdisciplinary influences on German history ("Postmodern Challenges in Theory and Methodology"); a major stocktaking conference on the *Kaiserreich* at the University of Pennsylvania in February 1990, which was organized to a great extent around questions of gender and the implications of the linguistic turn; another major conference in Toronto in April 1990 on "Elections, Mass Politics, and Social Change," where much of the same discussion continued; and a big event at UCLA in the same month on representations of Nazism and the Final Solution ("On the Limits of Historical and Artistic Representation"), at which Derrida personally arrived in German history. In fact, *CEH* was to be relaunched in the 1990s by a special issue containing the position papers from the Chicago symposium.[15]

The Current Landscape

In his 1971 essay, Hobsbawm suggested that most interesting social history was clustered around six complexes of questions:

1. Demography and kinship
2. Urban studies in so far as these fall within our field
3. Classes and social groups
4. The history of "mentalities," or collective consciousness, or of "culture" in the anthropologists' sense
5. The transformation of societies (for example, modernization or industrialization)
6. Social movements and phenomena of social protest. (Hobsbawm 1971, 12)

In reviewing this list two decades later, it is hard simply to add to the topical inventory because (as I am arguing) the main change is an underlying shift of perspective rather than the opening up of new areas.[16] The first three of Hobsbawm's categories are clearly alive and well. Thus, the machinery of historical demography continues to grind out its findings, often with the barest relationship to broader questions but at its best with a meticulous grounding in the classical materialist problematic of social change—usually from an eclectically sociological perspective.[17] Likewise, while, theoretically, urban history remains too loose and ill defined a category, the urban community study has become the main practical medium for investigating class formation.[18] The historiography of class has also unfolded to a great extent within parameters outlined by Hobsbawm, and to the research on the working class may now be added a burgeoning literature on peasants and a more recently developing one on the bourgeoisie and the petite bourgeoisie/lower middle class.[19]

But as a descriptive framework for "the actual practice of social history," Hobsbawm's list no longer serves. This is partly because new topical clusters need to be added—recent growth areas of social history include crime and punishment, medicine and public health, sexuality, popular religion, work, and popular memory, while social policy and education are older ones perhaps oddly missing from Hobsbawm's original list. More to the point, though, the entire construction of social history as a (sub)disciplinary field has been shifting during the last decade, so that a body of discussion has developed parallel to the existing research in a way that calls into question the conventionally constituted social-historical knowledge—with profound implications for all six of Hobsbawm's categories. Rather than just elaborating a longer inventory of topics, therefore, it is important to mention certain aspects of the surrounding flux.

(a) First, it needs to be said straight away that gender theory is transforming the basis on which we think about history. Whether as a dimension of analysis or an area of empirical work, women's history is absent from Hobsbawm's account, and to read older accounts such as his is to be reminded of how radical a change has occurred since the 1960s.[20] However, we should not exaggerate the rapidity of that change. The four critiques referred to earlier in this essay (Fox-Genovese and Genovese 1976; Stedman Jones 1976; Stone 1977; Judt 1979) are almost as indifferent to the transformative consequences of the new women's history, and indeed it was not until the later 1970s that a substantial body of monographic literature started to appear. Even then, quite aside from the political process of surmounting the prejudices inscribed in the structures of the profession and its disciplinary regime, much of the new work was somewhat self-neutralizing in its effects, either because of its adoption of a "separate spheres" type of framework or because it subsumed women within the history of the family. This is true par excellence of Carl Degler's essay in *The Past before Us,* but something of the same syndrome also befalls Tilly and Scott's *Women, Work, and Family* (Degler 1980; Tilly and Scott 1978).

While this move remains controversial, it is only more recently, with the conceptual shift from the history of women to the historical construction of sexual difference, that the protected central spaces of the discipline have started to give way. Of course, a large amount of work is being done on sexual representations as such. But major areas, like the history of work,[21] class formation,[22] citizenship and the public sphere (Landes 1988; Pateman 1988; Outram 1989; Catherine Hall 1985), and the study of popular culture[23] are all being reshaped by the application of a gender perspective. The latter also promises to recast understandings of nationalism and fascism, although some of the emerging work on masculinity tends to settle too easily into the study of men alone rather than in their relations with women.[24] We should not paint too optimistic a picture, of course. For instance, the core of historical demographers and historians of the family have remained remarkably resilient in their defense of an older-defined project.[25] But the insistent pressure for a recognition of gender as a "useful category of historical analysis" is only likely to become more intense (Scott 1988, 28–50).

(b) It is important to note the now pervasive influence of Foucault. It would be a mistake to exaggerate retrospectively the instigating centrality of Foucault's ideas to the departures we are discussing, and in practice they have achieved their resonance only within the broader universe of thinking I will be dealing with subsequently. Nor can the speed of his reception be overstated. The works themselves were actually available in translation quite early. But Foucault was completely absent from the pioneering works in the social history of crime, the law, and imprisonment in the 1970s, and at that time his English-language reception was conducted around the margins of official academic life—in journals like *Telos* and *Partisan Review* in the United States and by a self-conscious avant-garde of post-new left journals like *Economy and Society, Radical Philosophy, Ideology and Consciousness,* and *m/f,* in Britain.[26] It was only by the early 1980s that historians were explicitly beginning to take note (Weeks 1982; Harrison and Mort 1980). Since that time, work on sexuality (particularly the late-nineteenth- and twentieth-century constructions of sexual categories), on prisons, hospitals, asylums and other institutions of confinement, on social policy and public health, and on the history of science and the academic disciplines has been shot through with Foucault's formative influence.

Moreover, aside from directing attention in this way to new areas of research, Foucault's reception has had some vital theoretical effects. It has fundamentally redirected the understanding of power away from conventional, institutionally centered conceptions of government and the state and from the allied sociological conceptions of class domination, toward a dispersed and decentered conception of power and its "microphysics." It has sensitized us to the subtle and complex forms of the interrelationship between power and knowledge, particularly in the latter's forms of disciplinary and administrative organization. It has delivered the extraordinarily fruitful concept of discourse as a way of theorizing both the internal rules and regularities of particular fields of knowledge (their "regimes of truth") and the more general structures of ideas and assumptions that delimit what can and cannot be thought and said in particular contexts of time and place. It has radically challenged the historian's conventional assumptions about individual and collective agency and their bases of interest and rationality, forcing us to see instead how subjectivities are constructed and produced within and through languages of identification that lie beyond the volition and control of individuals in the classical Enlightenment sense.

(c) For much of the 1970s the history of *mentalités* functioned as a new panacea for a considerable number of social historians. It seemed a compelling alternative to the high-cultural, canonical, and formalistic-exegetical kind of intellectual history; it promised access to popular culture in the past; it provided ground for the application of quantitative methods and the appropriation of anthropology; and, of course, it was animated by the enticing vision of a "total history." For awhile the translation and reception of the major *Annales* works, orchestrated by a few well-placed individuals, was virtually uncritical. As one of them said, "social history seemed to turn around the *Past and Present-Annales* axis and to be sweeping everything before it" (Darnton 1980, 332). However, for some years the history of mentalities seems to have been in recession. The tone of the symposium that inaugurated the journal *Review* in 1978 was still largely celebratory, but by the mid-1980s a series of searching critiques had appeared—Stuart Clark in *P&P;* Samuel Kinser in *AHR;* Gregor McLennan in *Marxism and the Methodologies of History;* Michael Gismondi in *SH;* more ambiguously, Patrick Hutton in *History and Theory;* and finally Roger Chartier and Dominick LaCapra in the contexts of (largely successful) attempts to reaffirm the importance of a more textually based form of intellectual history (Clark 1983; Kinser 1981; McLennan 1981; Gismondi 1985; Hutton 1981; Chartier 1982; LaCapra 1985).

There can be no doubt that these critiques, together with the general unwillingness of the *Annalistes* to theorize their understanding of culture, have exposed the reductionisms and unspecified determinisms at the heart of Braudel's and Ladurie's work. Likewise, the meticulous critiques by Chartier and LaCapra leave little doubt that intellectual history has recovered the ground it seemed to have ceded in the 1970s. Neither of these developments compromises the achievements of Marc Bloch and Lucien Febvre or precludes the continuing production of cultural history in an *Annales* mode—suitably rethought in light of the intervening discussions. But this has yet to happen. On the whole, historians' discussions of culture have moved elsewhere, either outside the main early-modern location of *Annales*-influenced history or onto the ground of language where the running is being made by feminist theorists and intellectual historians, either untouched by the *Annales* paradigm or directly critical of it.[27] Moreover, the more interesting uses of Bakhtin are tending to come not from social historians such as Natalie Davis and Bob Scribner, who set the pace in the 1960s and 1970s, but from literary critics (compare Davis [1975] and Scribner [1981] with Bennett [1979], Stam [1988], and Stallybrass and White [1986]). In retrospect, the triumphal codification of *Annales'* achievement, *La Nouvelle Histoire,* now looks more like its epitaph, certainly at least in the history of mentalities as we encounter it in the previous decades. Andre Burguiere's discussion, which implies the past tense, seems tacitly to recognize this (Burguiere 1982).

(*d*) Another body of cultural analysis, contemporary cultural studies, has produced relatively little historical work so far. A still emergent cross-disciplinary formation, cultural studies comprises a varying miscellany of influences—sociologists, literary scholars, and historians in Britain (but not anthropologists) and mass communications, literary theory, and, potentially, reflexive anthropology in the United States. Strong existing traditions (e.g., in critical ethnography, cultural anthropology, and ethnomethodology) have worked preemptively against cultural studies in the social sciences in the United States, outside departments of communications, while their relative weakness in Britain allowed greater corresponding space for cultural studies to emerge. Thus, so far the main U.S. initiatives have come more from the humanities (e.g., the Unit for Criticism and Interpretive Theory at Illinois-Urbana or the Program in Comparative Studies in Discourse and Society at Minnesota), whereas the proliferating interdisciplinary programs and institutes in the social sciences have shown very little interest. On the other hand, feminist theory has played a key part in both Britain and the United States, as has the post-Saidian critique of colonial and racist forms of thought. Again, individual influences will vary (e.g., Gramsci or psychoanalytical approaches in Britain), but the linguistic turn, together with the fascination with postmodernism, has been common to both.

For our purposes we may note that most concrete work has so far been strongly located in the present. In one sense, that doesn't matter, as the "long present" of cultural studies is essentially the period since 1945, that is, almost half a century of historical time that badly needs historians' attention. But given the excitement currently surrounding a number of areas—for example, cultures of consumption, economies of pleasure and desire; the growth of serious work on the visual technologies of film, photography, video, and TV and on commercial media like advertising, comic books, and magazines; the relationship of women in particular to popular reading genres (romances, gothic novels, family sagas), TV (soap operas, detective series, situation comedies), and film (film noir, horror, science fiction, melodrama); the use of autobiography and the personal voice; postcolonial cultural critique; and the general reopening of debates around high/low/popular culture—we may expect more historical work increasingly to accrue (for introductions, see Punter [1986]; Hall et al. [1980]; Jackson [1989]; Brantlinger [1990]). Work on popular memory and representations of the (usually national) past already forms a particular genre in this way (Colls and Dodd 1986; Wright 1985; Lumley 1988; Bromley 1988; Niethammer 1983, 1985, 1986; Passerini 1987).

(e) I would like to end this series of observations with a paradox. On the one hand, the earlier ambition of a "total history," of writing the history of society in some integrated and holistic way, has come radically into question. In one of my own less memorable essays published over a decade ago, I argued that the most interesting feature of social history at the end of the 1970s was "its new totalizing potential." Now, it is possible to maintain some version of this claim still (e.g., the possibility of considering all phenomena and practices in their social dimensions), but the stronger form of the argument—"attempting to understand *all* facets of human existence in terms of their social determinations," as I put it—has become very problematic (Eley 1979, 55 f). As I will argue in the following, the confident materialist conception of social totality— "society" in its Marxist and non-Marxist sociological forms—has for many social scientists and cultural theorists ceased to be the natural organizing belief.

But, on the other hand, a considerable body of historical sociology continues to be written much as before, that is, organized within the established problematics of state-making, the rise of capitalism, comparative political development, revolutions, and so on (e.g., Tilly 1990; Wallerstein 1988). More than that, in fact, there has developed a new genre of world histories, extending literally from Mesopotamia to the global confrontation of the twentieth century, produced by leading British sociologists, seeking presumably to recapture the memories of their grammar school (or perhaps public school) history syllabus, essentially an attempt to rebuild social theory by writing the history of the world (Giddens 1981, 1985; Mann 1986; John Hall 1985). This creates an interesting juxtaposition. On the one hand, the radical diagnoses of the "postmodern condition" are proclaiming the demise of all master narratives; on the other hand, the most ambitious historical sociologists are defining their project by producing . . . a new range of grand narratives.

This essay has presented a truncated and selective survey of current developments, necessarily limited by the practical range of my own expertise. When considering the trajectory of social history since the 1970s there is no doubt that much could be said in relation to major fields of production that I know only very imperfectly—such as most U.S. social history, the social history of slave and postemancipation societies in the Americas, African social history, the study of colonial and postcolonial societies in the Third World, and so on. But I have tried to pick out certain aspects of the present context that may provide a useful basis for discussion.

All the World's a Text

Surveying the intellectual landscape of the social sciences at the end of the twentieth century then, it is hard not to be impressed by the power and popularity of literary theory, linguistic analysis, and related forms of theoretical address. Whether we look to the revival of intellectual history and the influence of Dominick LaCapra, to the potential convergence of intellectual historians with literary critics in a "new historicist" mold, to the enormous impact of Edward Said and now Gayatri Spivak on intellectuals writing in and about the Third World, to the interest of Joan Scott and other feminists in theories of gender and language, to the pull of reflexive anthropology toward the narrative ordering of the experienced world, to formal analysis of the "rhetoric" of economics and other apparently nonliterary disciplines, or simply to the common currency of terms like *discourse* and *deconstruction*—in all of these areas there seems to be no escape.

In many ways, Hayden White is the patron saint of this development for at an early stage (1973) his *Metahistory* problematized the boundaries between the humanities and the social sciences and showed how works in the latter are also constructed around particular narrative and rhetorical strategies, even when bound at their most rigorous and single-minded to the rules of evidence and scientific methodology. Moreover, White mounted this challenge from the older resources of literary criticism and his own original and idiosyncratic imagination, confronting "objectivist" history with the moral and aesthetic principles that order and inform its production (White 1973, 1978). In the meantime, the transformation of literary studies by the impact of (among others) Derrida and De Man has radicalized the challenge. The complexities of reading (and writing) have brought the category of the text and the work of interpretation into question. From focusing on authorial intention and the text's single attainable meaning (a chimera that obscures the indeterminacy and necessary openness of the text, its "undecidability," its multiplicity of meanings), literary theory has sharpened the practice of reading to a point of technical sophistication where meanings can seemingly be endlessly disclosed. For outsiders it has often been hard to break into this magic circle without devoting oneself full-time to learning a new language of cleverness and gesture, and sometimes it has seemed that a reprofessionalizing of literature and an authorizing of the theorist—a technocracy of the word—has been precisely the point.

Yet such suspicions cannot occlude the actual influence of such theory beyond its immediate domain. For some modified appropriation of deconstruction's basic program—at its simplest, "a reading which involves seizing upon [texts'] inconsistencies and contradictions to break up the idea of a unified whole" (*HWJ* editors 1980, 1)—has become very commonplace. For the social historian in particular, some notion of externality, what Derrida has called "the diachronic overdetermination of the context" or Raymond Williams's notion of determination as the setting of limits, is bound to loom as important (Derrida 1988, 606). Probably this means focusing on two kinds of moves—back, to the contexts of the text's production, and out, to the ways in which its meanings get constructed. Rather than what the text "means," in fact, it may be more fruitful to understand how it "works." As Tony Bennett puts it, with the characteristic Gramscian inflection on British cultural studies: "the text is a site on which varying meanings and effects may be produced according to the determinations within which the work is inscribed—determinations that are never single and given but plural and contested, locked in relations of struggle" (Bennett 1982, 235). Moreover, this mode of analysis has been increasingly extended from written texts in the more conventional sense to all manner of documents, and indeed to experience, behavior, and events as well. From assailing the transparency of the text in the discourse of literary criticism, textuality has become a metaphor for reality in general.

Interestingly, the turn to literary theory as such within the social sciences has a longer history. Two of the major influences in cultural studies in Britain and the United States—Raymond Williams and Clifford Geertz—were formed in this way, Williams by his own disciplinary background in English literature in the late 1940s and 1950s, Geertz by an appropriation of literary critical method in the time of his initial impact between the late 1950s and mid-1960s. At one level, Geertz's seminal 1973 essay, "Ideology as a Cultural System," affords a remarkable snapshot of U.S. social science at the peak of its postwar self-confidence, frozen just at the moment in the mid-1960s when all hell is about to break loose. The main referential context is still set by Talcott Parsons and the Harvard Department of Social Relations, but it has also reached the point of incipient dissolution. Geertz's footnotes read like the epitaph for a vanished discourse, and in this sense the essay is a fascinating intellectual document, poised at the cusp of a transition and heavily laden with its own moment. The interesting thing is that when Geertz breaks free to formulate his theory of symbolic action, he does so in the direction of philosophy and literary criticism. And, of course, the philosophy and literary criticism he uses are precisely the ones available in the United States of the 1950s (Geertz 1973a, 1973b).

When we turn to Raymond Williams and his equally seminal *Culture and Society* (1958) and *The Long Revolution* (1961), which were produced in roughly the same period, we find an intellectual formation locked just as firmly in its own national context, though here one that now lacked the power resources of an expanding metropolitan culture, resources that by contrast were carrying U.S. social science to the four corners of the world. In Williams's case the immediate context was a very English dialogue with the criticism of F. R. Leavis and I. A. Richards and a political engagement with the problem of democracy and high culture. But one of the remarkable features of Williams's subsequent career—right up to his tragically early death in 1988—was his ability to move with the times—not in the limited sense of following fashions but by consistently facing and assimilating the challenges of new theory. If we consider the fullness of his writing since the late 1960s, in fact, we find all the major theoretical influences that have been transforming understandings of culture and ideology since Geertz elaborated his first proposals—with the striking exception of Geertz himself and the wider corpus of U.S. cultural anthropology, to whose existence Williams seemed largely indifferent. (The indifference remained mutual.) Beginning with Central European aesthetics and philosophy (Lukács, the Frankfurt School) and continuing through the French lineage of structuralisms and poststructuralisms, the appropriation of Gramsci, and the discovery of Voloshinov and Bakhtin, Williams both registered the reception of continental European theory and worked the latter into his own distinctive contribution. The essay "Base and Superstructure in Marxist Cultural Theory" (1973) was one of the first installments in this process, anticipating the book-length *Marxism and Literature* (1977) and subsequent writings. Moreover, the openness of Williams's thinking was exemplary, and it would have been fascinating to have had his considered reflections on the emergent discourse of postmodernism in the later 1980s.[28]

Not the least of Williams's role and achievements during the 1970s and 1980s was to have mediated the impact of literary theory in wider areas of social, cultural, and political discourse, and also—a point of connection more lacking perhaps in the United States than in Britain—in a wider political domain. For behind the theoretical discussions referred to above lies a more political challenge—that is, the unresolved agenda of the post-1968 intellectual radicalism that spawned the rich profusion of Marxisms and feminisms that have done so much to shape the outlook of the affected generations of scholars in the last quarter of the twentieth century. Of course—and this is the departure point of my own reflections—since the heady days of the 1960s, when forms of "social" explanation carried all before them and grounded the imagination in the determinant causalities of an axiomatic materialism, a veritable flood has passed beneath the bridge. Moreover, the main current of the latter, despite the materialist beginnings just alluded to, has been an unrelenting antireductionism.

At first, the new diffusion of Marxism—which for the first time established a broad presence in the universities of the English-speaking world—seemed to uphold the classical commitments of the tradition, whether in Althusser's "antihumanist" separation of the mature from the young Marx, the more general structuralist stress on mode of production and an economically centered concept of class, the revival of Marxist economics, Braverman-inspired studies of the labor process, or the feminist domestic labor dispute. *Capital* became reinstated as the starting point. Yet, at the same time, these discussions defined themselves in no uncertain terms as departures, as critical advances on the older forms of economistic theory. The "base/superstructure" model of social determination, with its assignment of logical priority to the economic, came under particular attack. The efforts of Althusser and Poulantzas blew a gaping hole in such orthodoxies, through which an army of mainly French influences—Lacanian psychoanalysis, Saussurian linguistics, the philosophy of science of Bachelard and Canguilhem, the aesthetics of Macherey, semiotics and theories of film, and so on—was then able to rush. This freeing of politics and ideology for "relatively autonomous" analysis, anchored to the economy via "structural causality" and "determination in the last instance," opened the whole domain of the "noneconomic" to Marxist view—aesthetics, literature, the arts, theories of knowledge and the disciplines, intellectual life, popular culture, sexuality, and so on—in short, "culture," as a convergent strain of

British dissenting Marxism, was coming to define it (Hall et al. 1980; Benton 1984; Eley 1984; Lovell 1990).

The excitement of those days, the sense of participating in a continuous and unsettling process of revision, is worth remembering. And while the voice at this point is clearly personal (with a British accent), it is also worth recognizing this as a remarkable generational achievement, which both internationalized (or at least Europeanized) a previously parochial intellectual culture, wrenched it into an openly theorized mode of exchange, and simultaneously problematized the latter's terms of address. At the same time, there is also a danger of presenting this process as more unified, coherent, and logically continuous than it was (or could have been), so that one move followed rationally on another, causally inscribed in the contradictions and insufficiencies that preceded it. Yet intellectual histories are seldom as rationally constructed as this; and the process of revision was divisive rather than harmonious, instigated by conflicts and disruptions as much as by its own logical momentum.

Feminism is by far the most important influence of this kind, and the reader may have noticed its regular reappearance in my text—not quite as a disruption, as my understanding of its importance is too controlled for that, but not quite as a fully integral primary theme either. I have puzzled over what to do about this, and perhaps this accurately captures the relationship of feminist to general theory or social historical discussion (always assuming that "general" in this context is more than a synonym for androcentrism). Better, that is, to keep the sense of relative apartness and ability to disturb the narrative and logical coherence of the account than to be smoothly assimilated to its structure (which would also be a dishonesty of its own). On the one hand, as Terry Lovell observes, contemporary feminist writing shows a trajectory that is recognizable in the terms I am using:

The journey begins with Marxist- or socialist-feminist writings (in history, social science *and* cultural studies), seeking to uncover the material conditions of women's oppression under capitalism; it advances with the recognition that certain aspects of that oppression do not yield very readily to Marxist categories and that a more adequate account of feminine subjectivity is required for an understanding of the ways in which that oppression is *lived,* which might be sought in psychoanalysis rather than Marxism. Then, via Lacan and modern theories of language, the journey continues into the "poststructuralism" and "deconstructionism" whose luminaries include Foucault, Derrida and Kristeva. Some travellers continue beyond feminism itself, into a "postfeminism" and "postmodernism" which understand both Lacanian psychoanalysis and Marxism to have been mere staging-posts along the way. (Lovell 1990, 21 f.)

On the other hand, it is still necessarily apart. As Sally Alexander puts it in an essay that is still rather notable among social historians for its willingness to engage theoretically with this issue:

> If feminism has been only one of the detonators of "crisis" in marxist thought and practice it has been the most insistently subversive because it will not give up its wish to speak in the name of women; of women's experience, subjectivity and sexuality. . . . We were asking the impossible perhaps. As a feminist I was (and still am) under the spell of those wishes, while as a historian writing and thinking in the shadow of a labour history which silences them. How can women speak and think creatively within marxism when they can neither enter the narrative flow as fully as they wish, nor imagine that there might be other subjectivities present in history than those of class (for to imagine that is to transgress the laws of historical materialism)?[29]

Over the longer term, such discussions have played havoc with the received forms of Marxist and more general materialist understanding. For many, the logic of the antireductionist turn (as we might summarize the developments since the late 1960s) has been overpowering, leading eventually to the unanticipated embrace of a "post-Marxist" field of address and the more predictable counterreaction of those uncomfortable with such an apparent "retreat from class" (Wood 1986). But what for some has been the feared Pandora's box of uncontrollable heterodoxies remains for others a bottomless bag of tricks, which contains not only the antireductionist possibilities mentioned above but the more daring options of postmodernism and the linguistic turn. This restless probing of the limits shows no signs of coming to a halt. Shibboleths have fallen one by one. By now, the further pursuit of the antireductionist logic during the 1980s—through increasingly sophisticated readings of culture and ideology via Gramsci, Foucault, Voloshinov and Bakhtin, French poststructuralism, cultural studies in Britain, and the still diversifying field of feminist theory on both sides of the Atlantic—has left the earlier intellectual moment of the 1960s far behind, to the point of bringing the original materialist inspirations badly into doubt.

As the hold of the economy has been progressively loosened, and with it the determinative power of the social structure and its causal priorities, therefore, the imaginative and epistemological space for other kinds of analysis has grown. In fact, for many who have gone this route, the classical materialist connection has been broken once and for all. "Society" as a unitary object can no longer be maintained. There is no structural coherence deriving easily from the economy, from the functional needs of the social system and its central values, or from some other overarching principle of order. Particular phenomena—an event, a policy, an institution, an ideology, a text—have particular social contexts, in the sense of conditions, practices, sites, which conjoin for an essential part of their meaning. But there is no underlying given structure to which they can necessarily be referred, as its essential expression or necessary effects. In other words, the major casualty of this intellectual flux has been the confidence in a notion of social totality in its various Marxist and non-Marxist forms.

The commitment to grasping society as a whole, to conceptualizing its underlying principles of unity—which is now conventionally described as the specifically "modern" or Enlightenment project—has passed into crisis. For Marxists and others on the left this is also connected to a complex of political experiences, including the numerical decline of the historic working class and its traditions; the crisis of Keynesianism, the welfare state, and statist conceptions of socialism; the economic, political, and moral bankruptcy of communist systems; the catastrophe of the environment and of the scientific mastery over nature; and the declining purchase of straightforward class-political forms of address. As Lyotard says, the postmodern moment begins with an "incredulity with regard to master narratives." History, in this sense, has lost its way. The grand ideals that allowed us to read history in a particular direction, as a story of progress and emancipation, from the Industrial Revolution and the triumph of science over nature, to the emancipation of the working class, the victory of socialism, and the equality of women, no longer persuade. All bets are off. "[T]here is no single right way to read history. Indeed history becomes a narrative without a teleology," a story without an end (Lyotard 1984, xiii f.; Ellis 1989, 38).

Thus, the last two decades have seen a dizzying intellectual history. We have moved from a time when social history and social analysis seemed to be capturing the central ground of the profession and the force of social determinations seemed axiomatic to a new conjuncture in which "the social" has come to seem ever less definite and social determinations have surrendered their previous sovereignty. The road from "relative autonomy" and "structural causality" (the hard-won gains of the 1970s) to the "discursive character of all practices" (the poststructuralist axiom of the 1980s) has been rapid and disconcerting, and the persuasiveness of the antireductionist logic has been extraordinarily hard to withstand (rather like an up escalator with no way down).

But if "society" as a totalizing category is dissolving, does that mean that social explanation as such has lost all independent efficacy? There is a sense in which the reception of Foucault and subsequent poststructuralisms has collapsed the distinction between the social and the cultural altogether (where the latter becomes a summary description for the entire discursive domain), so that the social formation (and hence the bases of interconnectedness) becomes redefined agnostically as the aggregate of "discursive practices"—as "equivalent to the non-unified totality of these practices" or as "a complex, overdetermined and contradictory nexus of discursive practices" (Hall 1978, 12). In that case, if social reality is only accessible via language (in the constitutive theoretical sense as well as in the commonsense descriptive one that most would accept) and "the social" is only constituted *through* discourse, then what place is left for specifically social determinations at all?

This is the point that I take the discussion to have reached. A relatively small number of historians have taken the train to the end of the line, through the terrain of textuality to the land of discourse and deconstruction, to a radical epistemology that "relativizes the status of all knowledge, links knowledge and power, and theorizes these in terms of the operations of difference" (Scott 1988, 4). This can be alternately *empowering,* in that its revelation of the "nonfixity" of meaning shows how social and political definitions may be questioned and how the terms of the given are always in play and therefore susceptible to challenge, in the present no less than the past, and *disabling,* to the extent that the critique of epistemology in its most radical forms undermines the idea of historical knowledge as such and reduces the historian's task to more or less elaborate forms of historiographical critique (history not as the archival reconstruction of what happened but as the continuous contest over how the past is approached or invoked). A much larger group of social historians continues much as before, generally aware of what is happening but uninterested in the theory behind the linguistic turn and essentially wishing that it would go away. And then there are the rest of us, partly there for the ride, partly curious to see where it goes, and not at all sure we'll stay very long at the destination.

Now, this intermediate place (I hesitate to call it the "middle ground" because it certainly involves accepting the basic usefulness and interest of poststructuralist theory to begin with—that is, being willing to get on the train in the first place) is in my view a very good one to be in. It has some important virtues, pluralism chief among them. But it also has some real costs. It means giving up the claim to a distinct form of historical knowledge, let alone the aggrandizing and oft repeated claim to being somehow the "queen of the disciplines." History in the sense of the (mostly unreflected) practice of many or most historians does tend to a definite epistemology, which usually amounts to some brand of empiricism—that is, the belief in a knowable past, whose structures and processes are able to be distinguished from the forms of documentary representation, conceptual and political appropriations, and historiographical discourses that construct them. By now, I take the epistemological critique of this naive practice (or, more radically, the critique of epistemology per se as "a theoretical domain that tries to state a mechanism of correspondence between a discourse and objects existing outside discourse which can be specified and made the measure of it") to be basic (Hirst 1985c, 138).

But this does not mean that history becomes pointless or undoable. On the one hand, rejecting a correspondence theory of truth does not mean that doing history becomes completely arbitrary, that the historian can somehow invent documents at will, or that rules of evidence become irrelevant (fears typically voiced by the opponents of the linguistic turn). It does mean that criteria of truth have to be thought very differently. Knowledge is as "good" or "bad" as the quality of questions that constitute it: "Historical knowledge works by posing, re-posing and displacing questions, *not* by accumulating 'evidence' independently of them. Facts are not given, it is only relative to a question that we can begin to assess the value of those materials which are to constitute evidence for the answer to it" (Hirst 1985b, 54). As Stedman Jones said in his 1976 article, "history like any other 'social science' is an entirely intellectual operation which takes place in the present and in the head" and "The fact that the 'past' in some sense 'happened' is not of primary significance since the past is in no sense synonymous with history." In fact, the "real" past is beyond retrieval. Instead, the historian both evaluates documentary residues by the technical procedures of the profession and assigns them relevance via the construction of a significant problem. Accordingly, the common distinction between "history" and "theory" makes no sense: "The distinction is not that between theory and non-theory, but between the adequacy or inadequacy of the theory brought to bear" (Stedman Jones 1976, 296, 297). Moreover, the test of history's knowledge (its "truth") is not some general notion of epistemological validity ("truth-in-general") but the particular criteria of adequacy and appropriateness that history, no less than other particular fields (from biblical scholarship to automobile mechanics), has tended to devise (and which will always themselves be subject to varying degrees of consensus and disagreement).

On the other hand, history is simply unavoidable. It is constantly in play at the level of both everyday understanding and the formal discourses affecting social, economic, cultural, and political exchange. It is invoked and appropriated as a matter of course either implicitly or explicitly in order to make arguments. And for such arguments to be made (or countered) effectively, appropriate attention to the evidentiary conventions of the history profession will often need to be paid. But such conventions should not be mistaken for a viable epistemological claim. History's value is not as an archive or a court of "real experience." It is as a site of difference, a context of deconstruction— partly because it is *de facto always* being fought over (i.e., invoked and appropriated in contestatory ways) and partly because it affords the contexts in which the ever seductive unities of contemporary social and political discourse, the naturalizing of hegemonies, can be upset. History is different not in the sense that it reveals earlier stages in our own story or as an unapproachable realm of the exotic but in the sense that the very notion of a single coherent and unified story can be unpicked: "If [history] does not consist merely in the vindication of our own views of ourselves or in triumphalist accounts of modernity, it is because some historians can recognize that the past is different, not merely an earlier stage of our 'story,' but a means of unsettling ourselves and investigating, however partially, what we *are.*"[30]

Turning to History

Of course (the hard-bitten realists of the profession will say, patrolling their practice against these suggestions), such theory is all very well, but what difference does it really make? Worse, all this endless theorizing, the self-sustaining industry of critique, deflects one from more concrete and extended engagements with the past (whose pursuit, after all, remains the mundane justification for separate and specialized departments of history). Such attacks have become a familiar rhetorical move, intended to preempt, rather than to consider seriously, the theory concerned. But in an innocent form the complaint does contain a reasonable request. If the earlier assumptions of social history no longer hold and the older notions of social totality and social determination cannot suffice, then how can the practical project of a critical social history—in dissertation and monographic form, as opposed to essay-critique—be reaffirmed? Some exemplary answer to this question, in however indicative a form, is clearly owed.

There are no ready-made solutions to the conundrum, but one extremely fruitful response to current uncertainties has been to historicize the category of "society" itself by specifying the terms of its own social, political, and intellectual history—that is, by looking at the terms under which "the social" first became abstracted into an object of theory-knowledge, a target of policy, and a site of practice, so that the material context in which society could be convincingly represented as an ultimately originating subject became gradually composed.[31] Here "the social" refers not to the global analytical category of "society" in some unproblematic social science sense but to the historically located methods, techniques, and practices that allowed such a category to be constructed in the first place. The impetus for such a perspective is unmistakably Foucault.

Foucault's concept of the disciplinary society is concerned directly with this process. At one level, it profoundly shifts our understanding of politics, carrying the analysis of power away from the core institutions of the state in the national-centralized sense toward the emergence of new individualizing strategies "that function outside, below and alongside the State apparatuses, on a much more minute and everyday level" (Foucault 1980a, 60). But at another level, it is precisely through such individualizing strategies that *society* ("the social" or the "social body") became recognized, constituted, and elaborated as the main object of science, surveillance, policy, and power. Population (fertility, age, mobility, health), economics, poverty, crime, education, welfare became not only the main objects of government activity but also the measure of cohesion and solidarity in the emerging nineteenth-century social order. If we are to understand the latter, it is to the new social science and medico-administrative discourses, their technologies, and effects that we must look— to the new knowledges "concerning society, its health and sickness, its conditions of life, housing and habits, which served as the basic core for the 'social economy' and sociology of the nineteenth century" (Foucault 1980b, 176). In the late nineteenth- and early twentieth-centuries, the repertoire of power-producing knowledges then further expands—through psychiatry and psychology, social work and the welfare state, youth policy, industrial relations, public health, social hygiene, eugenics, and so on. As Donzelot and others have argued, the family becomes a particular object of such interventions and expertise. Moreover, as feminist scholars and Foucault's own final works have shown, sexuality provides an especially rich field for showing such power relations under construction (Donzelot 1979; Mort 1987; Copley 1989).

This "discursive" move—from the assumption of an objective "society" to the study of how the category of "the social" was formed—may be taken as paradigmatic for a variety of areas, and here I want to consider briefly two in particular, the process of working-class formation and the growth of citizenship ideals in the early nineteenth century, both of which have attracted some attention in this respect.[32] Since Thompson it has been harder and harder to present the process of working-class formation as the logical unfolding of an economic process and its necessary effects at the levels of social organization, consciousness, and culture. But nor can we conduct the alternative analysis simply as a process of empirical disaggregation, so that a fuller grasp of the working class's compositional complexities (its sectional variety across industries; its internal differentiation by hierarchies of seniority, status, and skill; and its cultural segmentation along lines of gender, religion, ethnicity, and race) and the time scale of its coalescence can emerge. To understand class as a political factor, in fact, we have to go further and accept the intractable methodological and theoretical difficulties of analyzing working-class politics (the rise of labor movements and socialist parties) as the causal expression of an economically located class interest and social structural position, indeed the futility of ever achieving historiographical consensus to this effect (quite apart from the epistemological problems with such a notion of social causality as I have been describing them).

In this sense, class as a political and cultural *postulate* (the assertion of a particular model of social identity) was just as crucial to the process of class formation as the existence of class as a demonstrable social fact (the creation of new social positions defined by the relationship to the means of production or some other material criteria). The *ideology of class,* the insistence that class was the organizing reality of the emerging capitalist societies and the growth of specific practices and organizations around that insistence (like trade unions and socialist parties), is arguably a better starting point for the study of class formation than the classical one of economics and social structure because it was at this discursive level that the operational collectivity of class—who got to be included, who set the tone, and who received the recognized voice—was defined. In these terms, the history of a class is inseparable from the history of the category. Class emerged as a set of discursive claims about the social world seeking to reorder that world in terms of itself.

A move of this kind helps us free analysis from the teleology of a class consciousness thought to be inscribed in the structures of class interest and class-collective experience—and from the need to find special explanations when that class consciousness is imperfectly, if at all, achieved. Indeed, it converts the notion of "interest" itself into a problem, a discursive effect of complex histories rather than a given, coherent, and agreed basis for action that is causally prior. Rather than asking which working-class interests were reflected in which organizations and forms of action (so that working-class consciousness becomes expressively derived), we should start asking how the prevailing understandings of working-class interest were produced, how particular practices and institutions encouraged or hindered particular constructions of working-class interest, and how one specific set of images of what the working class was came to be entrenched. From this perspective, "interest" is far more an effect than a cause.

Focusing on the construction of class as a structuring and motivating category in this way gives us better access to the partialities and indeterminacies of class formation and to the processes of exclusion on which its solidarities grew. And in exploring the always incomplete process of construction that thus defines class as an operative phenomenon, we should concentrate less on uncovering an underlying coherence in the languages of class than on understanding their lines of fracture and difference. As Robbie Gray observes, reflecting on Stedman Jones's intervention, such language is "multi-layered, complex, fractured, composed of incoherences and silences, as well as the smooth flow of would-be authoritative public discourses," and as such it must be read for its exclusions as well as for its unifying appeals (Gray 1986, 367). The most important and continuous of such exclusions has concerned women and is ordered along lines of gender.

The positive identity of the working class as it became elaborated during the nineteenth century—the ideal of the skilled male worker in industry—rested on powerfully dichotomous assumptions about what it meant to be a man or woman. Those assumptions were ordered into a pervasive dualism that aligned men with the worlds of work and the public domain of politics and women with the home and the private realm of domesticity—the one a site of control and rationality, the other a site of affect and subordination. Inscribed in the language of class were definite notions of masculinity and femininity that limited "women's access to knowledge, skill and independent political subjectivity" (Alexander 1984, 137). Consequently, the importance of gender, sexuality, and family cannot be bracketed from an account of the politics of working-class formation. On the contrary, the social construction of sexual difference in such a way that it did work to separate the private sphere of family from the worlds of work and class—the gendering of class formation—actually had a powerful impact on how working-class identity came to be understood. Moreover, the fixing of class identity in this way presupposed the suppression of alternative possibilities. Such a fixing presumed, indeed required, the silencing of alternative meanings that threatened to outgrow its terms. In the case of "class," the discourse marginalized the role of women through the fixity of its assumptions in this way. It seems to me enormously important to uncover such structures and their operation and convert the assumed meanings of class into a problem. It is vital, in other words, to upset the unity of meaning.

In fact, we need an opposing conception of identity that stresses its nonfixity and sees it as an unstable ordering of multiple possibilities whose provisional unity is managed discursively through language and is only ever constituted through incompletely ordered factors of difference. If the purpose is to understand the ways in which processes and structures of exclusion have ordered historical constructions of class, then overcoming such exclusions means recognizing the indeterminate multiplicity of identity. How we see ourselves as a basis for action and how we are addressed in the public arena are not fixed. We recognize ourselves variously—as citizens, as workers, as parents, as consumers, as enthusiasts for sports or hobbies, as religious believers, and so on. Those recognitions are inflected with power relations of different kinds, and they are heavily gendered by assumptions defining us as women or men. At one level, this complexity and nonfixity of subject positions is a banal observation. But the important thing is that politics is usually conducted *as if* identity is fixed. The issue then becomes: on what bases, in different places and at different times, does identity's nonfixity become temporarily fixed in such a way as to enable individuals and groups to behave as a particular kind of agency, political or otherwise? How do people become shaped into acting subjects, understanding themselves in particular ways? In effect, politics consists of the effort to "domesticate the infinitude" of identity (Mouffe 1989). It is the attempt to *hegemonize* identity, to order it into strong programmatic commitments. If identity is decentered, politics is about the *attempt to create a center.*

To return to the question of working-class formation, the power of the socialist tradition between the late nineteenth century and the 1930s (reaching a long denouement in our own time) was its ability to harness popular identities to a strong conception of the working class—that is, to construct popular political agency around the discourse of class in its classical gendered, skilled, nationally bounded, industrial sense. Now, in all periods and places such parties were always more complex in their sociology than this, whether in membership, support, or appeal. They mobilized workers, even in the restrictive definition, highly unevenly. And they always integrated wider sections of the populace around the male, skilled, religious, and ethnic core, whether these other constituencies were working class in the fuller sociological sense (e.g., women, the unskilled, national minorities, etc.) or not working class at all as that was classically understood (like dissenting intellectuals, certain sections of the professions, clerical and other white-collar workers, shopkeepers and other small businesspeople in working-class neighborhoods, and so on). Moreover, socialist parties were always active in "nonclass" ways, working through the public rhetoric of democratic citizenship, social justice, and egalitarianism as much as through the language of socialism per se.

But programmatically, the centering of their practice around the notion of class is clear enough. And concentrating identity in that way has its costs. It involves a reduction *to* class. It involves exclusions and neglects. The positive orientation toward the working class presumed a negative orientation to others—and not just to other classes but to other kinds of workers too (e.g., the unorganized, the rough and unrespectable, the criminal, the frivolous, the religiously devout, the ethnically different, and of course the female) and to other elements of subjectivity, in effect all the aspects of identity that could not be disciplined into a highly centered notion of class-political agency. More-over, the neglect of that space—the space defined by these "other" identities—provides opportunities for other labors of construction to occur, coming from the state, political competitors, the churches, commercial entertainment, and so on.

Thus, the "unity" of the working class, though postulated through the analysis of production and its social relations, is a never attainable object of construction, a fictive agency, a contingency of political action. Moreover, notions of citizenship can be similarly deconstructed, particularly if we push these back to the ideal of the rationally acting individual subject usually located in the traditions of thought descending from the Enlightenment. It has become a commonplace of feminist critique that modern political thought is highly gendered in its basic structures, particularly in the Enlightenment context of the later eighteenth century when the key elements of liberal and democratic discourse were first composed. In other words, the constitutive moment of modern political understanding was itself constituted by newly conceived or rearranged assumptions about woman and man: this was not only visible in constitutions, legal codes, and political mobilizations, but it also ordered the higher philosophical discourse around the universals of reason, law, and nature, grounding this in an ideologically constructed system of differences in gender.

The new category of the "public man" and his "virtue" was elaborated via a series of oppositions to "femininity," which both drew upon older notions of domesticity and women's place and rationalized them into a set of formal claims concerning woman's "nature." At the most fundamental level, specific constructions of "womanness" defined the quality of being a "man," so that the *natural* identification of sexuality and desire with the feminine allowed the *social* and *political* construction of masculinity to take place. In this sense, modern politics, among other things, was constituted "*as* a relation of gender" (Landes 1988, 204). In the rhetoric of the 1780s and 1790s reason was counterposed conventionally to "femininity, if by the latter we mean (as contemporaries did) pleasure, play, eroticism, artifice, style, politesse, refined facades, and particularity" (Landes 1988, 46). Then, in the concentrated circumstances of the French Revolution, women were to be silenced to allow masculine speech—in the language of reason—full rein. Together with others (class, race, ethnicity, religion, age, etc.), gender and sexual identity were the powerful exclusions from which the modern political subject became formed—indeed, which allowed that idea of rational subjectivity first to emerge.

There is no need to explicate this further. The point is to suggest how particular discursive formations—whose emergence and elaboration can be carefully located historically—are themselves centrally implicated in social history, in constituting the basic categories of understanding and therefore the social, cultural, and political environment in which people acted and thought rather than being predicated on "experience" or following unproblematically from a social cause. The nineteenth-century discourse of citizenship, no less than the related conceptions of class-collective identity, were immensely complex and powerful formations of this type, which finely ordered the social and political world and structured the possibilities of what could and could not be thought. Gender was crucial not only to the patterning and containment of one's class identity but also to the endowment and delimitation of one's political capacities. Recent feminist theory has acutely sensitized us to the procedures and assumptions that regulate access to a political voice. On the one hand, there is the synthesizing critique of patriarchy as a continuous figure of European political thought from Hobbes through Locke to the Enlightenment and beyond. In the latter, women are essentially confined within the household: "Within this sphere, women's functions of child-bearing, child-rearing and maintaining the household are deemed to correspond to their unreason, disorderliness and 'closeness' to nature. Women and the domestic sphere are viewed as inferior to the male-dominated 'public' world of civil society and its culture, property, social power, reason and freedom" (Keane 1988, 21). But on the other hand, the beauty of recent work is that it has shown how this pattern of subordination was reformulated and recharged in the midst of that major political cataclysm—the French Revolution—through which the ideal of human emancipation was otherwise radically enlarged. In other words, the emerging liberal model of rational political exchange was not just vitiated by persisting patriarchal structures of an older sort. The very inception of the liberal public sphere was itself shaped by a new exclusionary discourse directed at women.

In highlighting the exclusionary treatment of women, such work is also subverting the existing terms of the story—enabling not just the retrieval of a previously neglected aspect but a set of insights that fundamentally reconstructs our sense of the whole. There are now rich demonstrations in a variety of fields to this effect. Thus, Davidoff and Hall (1987) have shown how classical bourgeois society and politics no less than the nineteenth-century working-class presence were also produced by gendered processes of class formation. They stress *both* the constitutive importance of gender (i.e., the historically specific structuring of sexual difference) in the ordering of the middle-class social world via particular patterns of family and domesticity and particular styles of consumption *and* the reciprocal interactions between this private sphere and the public sphere of associational life and politics, in which the latter both reflected and actively reproduced the gendered distinctions of class identity generated between home and work. The remarkable associational activity of the early nineteenth century strictly demarcated the roles of women and men via a mobile repertoire of ideologies and practices, which consistently assigned women to a nonpolitical private sphere, "having at most a supportive role to play in the rapidly expanding political world of their fathers, husbands and brothers" (Catherine Hall 1985, 11). Moreover, this separation of spheres—between the masculine realm of public activity and the feminine realm of the home, which certainly did not preclude (and was finely articulated with) relations of interconnectedness between business/occupation and household and engendered a particular conception of the public and the private for the emergent ninteenth-century bourgeoisie—was replicated in the situation of the working class, as work on Chartism and nineteenth-century socialist movements as well as the social history of the working class has amply shown (Alexander 1984; Rose 1991).

Conclusion

In this essay I have tried to take stock of the last twenty years not to provide an accurate inventory of recent work but to provide a sense of current direction. However, while the 1970s were still characterized by a sense of forward movement, borne by the unlimited power of social explanation, the 1980s have seen far more a mood of uncertainty and flux. As I have suggested, this is partly a generational story, as one part of the social history cohort of the 1960s has detached itself from the previous materialist consensus (as we can minimally call it) to pursue the antireductionist logic of structuralist and poststructuralist theory, leaving another part (probably the majority) in considerable disarray—some dogmatically reaffirming older positions (which I have tended to call "classically materialist"), some opting for a more eclectic and anthropologically oriented cultural history, and many more continuing in their hard-won social-historical practice of the 1970s. At the risk of oversimplifying, I tend to see two main tributaries among English-speaking social historians to the linguistic turn: one is the large corpus of British post-Althusserian Marxism/post-Marxism (including a separate but convergent feminism) and the other is the remarkable North American impact of deconstructive literary theory, increasingly mediated through specifically feminist discussion. (Where this leaves the specifically anthropological contribution is less clear.) At this point, the radical pressure of feminist theory seems to me to be primary.

Critics of the so-called linguistic turn from the left (and the more mischievous ones from the right) happily reduce it to a particular kind of social project—as the self-indulgent acrobatics of left intellectuals who have lost their way, constructing seductive but self-serving rationalizations for their own ivory tower isolation, seeking a substitute for the working class that refuses their ministrations, and losing their nerve for the well-tried yet difficult radical projects (Wood 1986; Palmer 1990). In response, the constructive relationship between the theoretical perspectives I have been exploring and the chances of articulating a politics more adequate to the diverse and complex bases of collective identity at the end of the twentieth century is one I would—on the contrary—readily affirm. Moreover, the social and political histories of the last quarter century—in the so-called real world—that have induced such widespread skepticism about more traditional ideas of class-political agency among their putative bearers—as a primary and sufficient basis for understanding and acting on the world—certainly inform the appeal of those perspectives for those socialists such as myself who would like to reelaborate some viable basis of left-wing politics from the contemporary wreckage of the state-socialist traditions. There is also an available social analysis—of post-Fordism, postmodernity, and the transnational restructuring of the global capitalist economy—that can begin to ground the conditions of possibility for a politics of "new times." But such a social analysis of the intellectual history I have been recounting is not necessary to the theoretical and epistemological challenge it contains. It certainly can't be invoked as some kind of normalizing materialist move.

Indeed, the exact relationship between intellectual life—in this case a specific shift of theory and its effects in the doing of history—and general social and political conditions is anything but clear, and one of the purposes of my essay has been to point to the difficulties of bringing them causally together. It would be perverse—an act of materialist faith—to call the argument back to an older conception of the social and thereby to make harmless the very questions it is trying to raise. At all events, social history in its amorphous but aggrandizing form of the 1970s has ceased to exist: it has lost its coherence as an intellectual project (which derived, I suggested, from the sovereignty of social determinations within a self-confident materialist conception of social totality, both of which have been subjected to compelling critique) and it has lost its prestige as the natural location for the more radical, innovative, and experimental intellectual spirits in the profession, particularly in the generations currently being recruited. The "new cultural history" or cultural studies is currently taking its place.

I do not see this as a crisis or a cause for regret. But there is certainly no shortage of voices that do. In the most recent—and book-length—example, Bryan Palmer denounces the linguistic turn as "unmistakably an adversary maneuver" directed against historical materialism and social history. It represents a "hedonistic descent into a plurality of discourses that decenter the world in a chaotic denial of any acknowledgment of tangible structures of power and comprehensions of meaning"; a "reduction of analysis and theory to the puns and word games of scholastic pretension"; and "a messianic faddism" that has disastrously captured the imagination of social historians (Palmer 1990, 188). Palmer's is truly a bizarre book, oscillating abruptly between sympathetic exegeses of poststructuralist contributions and constructive appropriations on the one hand and wild condemnations on the other. In the end, the linguistic turn for Palmer has resulted straightforwardly in " . . . *crap,* a kind of academic wordplaying with no possible link to anything but the pseudo-intellectualized ghettoes of the most self-promotionally avant-garde enclaves of that bastion of protectionism, the University" (Palmer 1990, 199). Against this kind of intellectual police action ("These are refusals that must be made, and made clearly"—but according to what authority?), which is depressingly reminiscent of the worst excesses of Edward Thompson's *The Poverty of Theory* and the surrounding debate, *we* should insist on the need for pluralism. And that is the note on which I prefer to end. Whether individually we decide to take the linguistic turn or not, there will remain a diversity of histories in the profession, and as in practice there is no way of finally resolving these debates short of driving the opponents from the field and burning their books, the best we can ask is openness and intellectual seriousness in the exchange. Understanding advances through conflict and the polemical clarification of difference. But in the end it is the differences that have to remain.

NOTES

This essay was written during the summer of 1990 and reflects both the state of disciplinary discussion and my own thinking at that time. During the intervening years an enormous amount of publication, debate, and clarification has occurred, though arguably not a huge change in the basic epistemological landscape my essay describes. More historians have begun to explore the excitement of the new perspectives, but probably an equal number continue to rail against the pernicious effects of a demonized "postmodernism," and the field of difficulty continues much as before. Rather than trying to bring my citations up to date (an entire project in itself), I've left the text and footnotes in their original form, as a kind of snapshot of a history still in motion. On the other hand, the subsequent publications of Kathleen Canning and Peggy Somers deserve to be acknowledged, as they reflect earlier discussions that helped shape my own arguments about class formation. See Kathleen Canning, "Gender and the Politics of Class Formation: Rethinking German Labor History," *American Historical Review* 97 (1992): 736–68; "Feminist History after the Linguistic Turn: Historicizing Discourse and Experience," *Signs* 19 (1994): 368–404; *Languages of Labor and Gender: Female Factory Work in Germany, 1850–1914* (Ithaca, 1996); and Margaret R. Somers, "Workers of the World, Compare!" *Contemporary Sociology* 18 (1989): 325–30; "Narrativity, Narrative Identity, and Social Action: Rethinking English Working-Class Formation," *Social Science History* 16 (1992): 591–630. More generally, I would like to thank my friends and colleagues in the Program for the Comparative Study of Social Transformations (CSST), who provided the context of intellectual generosity and exploration that allowed this essay to be written. I owe a particular debt to Nick Dirks, Mike Kennedy, Sherry Ortner, Bill Sewell, and Peggy Somers, but especially Terry McDonald, who organized the conference from which this volume derived, and whose intellectual friendship and intelligence has been a vital part of my Michigan years. For an indication of developments since 1990, readers may wish to consult the Introduction to Nicholas B. Dirks, Geoff Eley, and Sherry B. Ortner, eds., *Culture/Power/History: A Reader in Contemporary Social Theory* (Princeton, 1994): 3–45; and Geoff Eley, "Playing It Safe. Or: How Is Social History Represented? The New Cambridge Social History of Britain," *History Workshop Journal* 35 (1993): 207–20.

1. The bibliographical context for this essay is potentially huge. Rather than cluttering the text itself with absurd numbers of citations or multiplying the footnotes, I have tried to indicate this context by citing only one or two representative titles on each occasion while collecting the full references in the bibliography at the end. Thus, the bibliography is intended to provide a reasonably full guide to the wider reading on which the argument of the essay is based.

2. Several essays from the later 1970s have been repeatedly cited for these polemical disagreements: Fox-Genovese and Genovese (1976); Stedman Jones (1976); Stone (1977); Judt (1979). They were followed by Stone (1979); and Eley and Nield (1980).

3. See the following of Stedman Jones's essays: 1972, 1975, 1976, 1977a, 1977b. The essay on language was Stedman Jones (1983b), in a volume that also republished several of the earlier essays. The best guide to the trajectory of his thinking is the introduction to that volume, together with an interview conducted by Stuart Macintyre (Stedman Jones [1977c]).

4. In *CSSH,* poststructuralist perspectives have begun to enter to some extent via anthropology. My comments refer to the specifically historical component of the journal's contents, where the main orientation remains heavily social science. The review essays are a partial exception to this.

5. Note also the ten-year retrospective editorial "Ten Years After" (20, autumn 1985, 1–4), which situates the development politically in relation to Thatcherism. A similar shift could be described in *RHR,* from the theme issue on British Marxist history (19, winter 1978–79), through one on "The Return of Narrative" (31, 1985) to one on "Language, Work, and Ideology" (34, 1986). Interestingly, the theme issue of "Sexuality in History" (20, spring-summer 1979) contains relatively little evidence of the new perspectives. One key article was Donald Reid's discussion of Jacques Rancière, "The Night of the Proletarians: Deconstruction and Social History," *RHR* 28–30 (1984): 445–63.

6. See Thompson (1978) and the coinciding debate around Johnson (1978). Other contributions include Anderson (1980), and the debate between Stuart Hall, Richard Johnson, and Edward Thompson at the Thirteenth History Workshop in Oxford in December 1979 and published in Samuel (1981). (A fourth, feminist, speaker withdrew from the History Workshop debate on the grounds that the tone and terms of the proceedings made her presence inappropriate. My favorite among the many subsequent commentaries is Magarey [1987]).

7. My reasons are also partly mischievous. The brief position papers produced for this occasion were published by the Tillys as "Problems in Social History: A Symposium" in *Theory and Society* 9 (September 1980): 667–81, including those by Louise Tilly, Edward Shorter, Francis G. Couvares, David Levine, and Charles Tilly. The only such paper not solicited for the published symposium (as I discovered when it appeared) was my own, presumably on grounds of quality.

8. None of the intensity or concluding explosiveness of these discussions is hinted at in the published account.

9. The first of these titles was coauthored by Louise Tilly and Joan Scott; the second collects Joan Scott's intervening essays and documents the striking intellectual distance.

10. See especially Stedman Jones (1972, 1976). For a particular case, see McDonald (1985). The best general illustration of the point is *P&P* between the late 1950s and late 1960s, when the generation of British Marxists who mainly left the communist party in 1956–57 turned to non-Marxist social theory to help their general rethinking. Philip

Abrams and Eric Hobsbawm were key in the exchange with sociology; Jack Goody, Peter Worsley, Keith Thomas, and Hobsbawm again in that with anthropology.

11. See Scott (1988) and Johnson (1978, 1979a, 1979b, and more recently 1986–87). Both began their careers in the 1960s in the more dependent relationship criticized by Stedman Jones, cultivating their analyses in the sun of sociology—Scott in a classic of the new social history, Johnson as a historian of education within a perspective of social control. See Scott (1974) and Johnson (1970).

12. See the articles by Toews (1987); Harlan (1989), with response by Hollinger and Appleby; Matthews (1990); Childers (1990); Chartier (1985); Darnton (1986); LaCapra (1988); and Fernandez (1988).

13. See Abraham (1981), and the exhaustive exchange between Abraham and his main persecutor, Gerald D. Feldman (1984). There is a good presentation of this affair in Novick (1988), 612–21.

14. See Bridenthal (1973); Quataert (1983); Hertz (1983); Quataert (1987). This judgment is based on the cumulative index to vols. 1–20 (1968–87) in *CEH* 20 (September–December 1987).

15. A good example of the change would be Koshar (1986), which is among other things an excellent exploration of the historical uses of resource mobilization theory. By the time of the conferences of 1989–90 listed previously in the text Koshar had re-emerged as probably the most radical poststructuralist among the participants. See, for instance, his unpublished papers for Chicago, "Representations, Symbols, Monuments," and Philadelphia, "The Kaiserreich as Ruin: Notes on Constructing the Popular Culture of Imperial Germany." *CEH* was relaunched with vol. 24 (1991), but the special issue preceded this, as "German Histories: Challenges in Theory, Practice, Technique," vol. 22, (September–December 1989). Similar shifts might be traced in the French field, juxtaposing the current work of figures like William Sewell, Lynn Hunt, and in France Francois Furet with the kind of social history they apparently stood for in the late 1960s and early 1970s. In France itself the political referents of the shift have been different and extremely national-specific, deriving from the extraordinary anti-Marxism of contemporary French intellectual life. Thus, in Furet's case the advocacy has moved away from social history to intellectual and political history but hardly toward gender or language in the more radical sense. At the same time, the detailed picture in France remains more diverse: for an indication, see Godelier (1980); Achard (1980); and more recently, Schöttler (1989).

16. This is reflected in the introduction to Thane and Sutcliffe (1986), which is consciously framed to update Hobsbawm's survey, but which presents a rather disorganized mélange of topics and trends. Ultimately, a general shift from "class" to "culture" in the organizing categories of British social history seems to be their overriding theme.

17. The apogee of achievement is Wrigley and Schofield (1981). The launching in 1986 of a new journal, *Continuity and Change. A Journal of Social Structure, Law and*

Demography in Past Societies, may presage a broadening of vision. In the meantime, see Levine (1987); Seccombe (1983); and Hochstadt (1982).

18. Specific urban phenomena naturally retain their importance, in contrast to urban history's claims of constituting a coherent field in itself. Urban planning, the fiscal dimensions of the local state, Third World urbanization since the 1960s, the city as the cultural ideal of modernism—these and other themes come readily to mind. It is the exaggerated expectations invested in urban history as a subdisciplinary specialism that seem to have come aground.

19. The literature on peasants may be best approached through the *Journal of Peasant Studies,* founded in 1973–74. For the petite bourgeoisie, see Blackbourn (1985); and Crossick and Haupt (1984). The most elaborate recent project on the bourgeoisie has been German-centered with extensive comparative ambitions and was coordinated by Jürgen Kocka at the University of Bielefeld. See especially Kocka (1988); and for an English-language collection in counterposition, Blackbourn and Evans (1990). There is also much activity in Italy, for which see the reports in the *Bollettino di informazion a cura del gruppo di studio sulle borghesie del xix secolo* (1985—). The role of gender in bourgeois class formation has also received important attention. See especially Davidoff and Hall (1987); Ryan (1981); Frevert (1988).

20. On the other hand, Hobsbawm was well aware of the importance of matters like the sexual division of labor or women's political emancipation, and his labor history writings showed both the relative strengths and the blindnesses of the communist political tradition in this respect. The difference can be gauged by considering someone of a similar generation whose lack of awareness was genuinely crass: Perkin (1981).

21. For work on Britain, see Alexander (1976, 1984); Rose (1986, 1991); Freifield (1986); John (1986); and the special issue of *Social History* on "Gender and Employment" (1988). Similar lists could be given for Germany, France, and the United States. But progress should not be overestimated: astonishingly, one recent imposing handbook of international research, Tenfelde (1986), contains among its *twenty* mainly thematic essays not a single entry on women.

22. Here the influence of Scott (1988) is obviously important, together with works such as Ryan (1981), and Davidoff and Hall (1987). I should also acknowledge the work on gender and class formation in Germany by my colleague Kathleen Canning. Again, the impact on more orthodox discussions of class formation, even where these profess innovation, should not be overstated. See Katznelson and Zolberg (1986), where gender relations are glaring in their absence (apart from a lamely exculpatory footnote on the second page of the introduction, 4).

23. This has become an area of great activity, most of which is strongly present-based and can be found in a range of new journals, including *New Formations* (1987—); *Block* (1979–89); *Cultural Studies* (1987—); *Social Text* (1982—); *Cultural Critique* (1985—); *Representations* (1983—); *Media, Culture, and Society* (1978—); and the women's studies journals. Key works would include: Mulvey (1989); William-

son (1986); Coward (1984); Gamman and Marshment (1988); Radway (1984); Modleski (1982); and Kaplan (1987). Conceptually, such work can be used by historians to excellent effect. For two examples relating to film, see Petro (1989); and Kuhn (1990). For an older genre, excellent in its kind, that treats film as a source of social commentary but from which both women as such and the new cultural theory are absent, see Stead (1989). Stead's book falls within the 1960s/1970s problematic of left-inclined British social history, doubly influenced by Thompson (1963) and Williams (1958), with all the virtues and limitations, which include the by-now-familiar innocence on questions of gender. See Swindells and Jardine (1990). Historical discussion within the newer cultural perspectives can be found in the film journals, *Screen* (1959—) and *Jump Cut* (1974—).

24. See Bridenthal, Grossmann, and Kaplan (1984); Macciocchi (1979); Caplan (1979); and Theweleit (1987, 1988). A good way into current work on masculinity is Chapman and Rutherford (1988), and review essays by Tosh, Roper, and Bristow in Roper (1990).

25. For an example of the continuous reduction of family history to the technical and procedural parameters of a demographic problematic, however compelling those imperatives in their own terms, see the response of Houston and Smith (1982) to Chaytor's dissenting article (1980). For indications of how recent theory might allow the history of the family to be (de/re)constructed, see Barrett and McIntosh (1982), and Riley (1983). Barrett and McIntosh (95–105) also provide a useful critique of an influential post-Foucauldian text, Donzelot (1979).

26. The first of Foucault's works to be translated was 1965, followed by 1970 and 1972. The other works rapidly followed, until by the end of the 1970s all were available (apart from volumes 2 and 3 of *The History of Sexuality,* yet to be published in French), including three collections of interviews and essays, the best of which is Gordon (1980). Remarkably, in retrospect, the rush of social-historical works around crime, law, and punishment in the 1970s seems to have been innocent of Foucault's influence: for example, Hay, Linebaugh, and Thompson (1975); Thompson (1975); Gattrell, Parker and Lenman (1980); Ignatieff (1978); Cockburn (1977); Brewer and Styles (1980); Bailey (1981); Donajgrodzki (1977). For a later collection that partially registers the intervening impact of Foucault, see Cohen and Scull (1983). On the other hand, two recent collections in non-British fields, pioneering interventions in empirical terms, manage to preserve their innocence: Evans (1988); and Snyder and Hay (1987). For one early text that did register Foucault's influence, via the French history and philosophy of science, notably that of Gaston Bachelard, see Tribe (1978); and for a more recent direct response, O'Brien (1989).

27. See the discussion in section (*d*) in the following text and in note 23 to section (*a*). See also Joyce (1987); many of the essays in Kaplan and Koepp (1986); Reddy (1987); Vincent (1990); and Hunt (1989). The impact of LaCapra and the current writings of Chartier are strong signs of this change: see Kramer (1989); and Chartier (1989). The four-way discussion in *JMH* between Chartier (1985), Darnton (1986),

LaCapra (1988), and Fernandez (1988) referred to in note 12 is also symptomatic. Interestingly, Burke (1987) falls much short of poststructuralist understandings of language, with the exception of Outram (1987). (Burke was a principal advocate of *Annales* history in the English-speaking world in the 1970s.) For an overview of the turn to culture among social historians in Germany, see Eley (1989).

28. Many further references may be added from Williams's voluminous bibliography: 1971 (an earlier engagement with continental literary theory); 1981 (a survey of the influences listed above); 1986 (on the specific legacy of the Vitebsk school of Soviet linguistic theorists from the 1920s—P. M. Medvedev, V. N. Volosinov, M. M. Bakhtin). Williams (1989) was reconstructed by Fred Inglis from lecture notes. But the verdict attributed to Williams on postmodernism—"Postmodernism for him was a strictly ideological compound from an enemy formation, and long in need of this authoritative rebuttal" (48)—does not at all characterize the text itself, which is silent on postmodernism per se, and should not be allowed to stand.

29. Alexander (1984), 127. The same passage is quoted by Swindells and Jardine (1990), 93, and by the introduction to Lovell (1990), 25, where the Alexander essay is also reprinted. I have always thought that there is a kind of presumption in male historians trying to speak for women's history. Yet the alternative of more incidental forms of reference cannot escape the effect of tokenism. There is no easy solution. For some useful thoughts, see Todd (1988), 118–34.

30. Hirst (1985c), 28. Hirst's essays, mostly produced between the late 1970s and early 1980s, are a useful guide through these questions. See also the following comment from Hirst (1979), 21:

We would argue that discourses and practices *do* employ the criteria of appropriateness or adequacy (not of epistemological validity) but these are specific to the objectives of definite bodies of discourse and practice. None will pass muster as a general criterion of validity, but there is no knowledge process *in general* and, therefore, no necessity for such a criterion. Techniques of criticism of biblical texts are of no use in garage mechanics. Questions of priority and relation in the Gospels, of the state of wear of a gearbox elicit different types of tests and disputes about them. The referents and constructs, Gospels, motor cars, depend on conditions which differ, so do criteria and tests. Tests, etc., develop within the discourses and practices to which they relate and are subject to dispute. *As tests* they are radically different, they seek to establish or challenge different things according to the objectives and circumstances of the practice in question.

31. Whereas this approach derives strongly from Foucault, it has affinities with the "keywords" method of Raymond Williams and with the work of Reinhart Koselleck and the West German tradition of *Begriffsgeschichte*. See Williams (1983); Brunner, Conze, and Koselleck (1972–89); Tribe (1989).

32. For important work in a similar direction, see Somers (1989, 1992) and Canning (1992, 1994).

REFERENCES

Abraham, David. 1981. *The Collapse of the Weimar Republic: Political Economy and Crisis.* Princeton, NJ.

Abraham, David. 1984. "A Reply to Gerald Feldman," and "On Professor Feldman's Insistence: Some Closing Remarks," *CEH* 17:178–244, 268–90.

Achard, Pierre. 1980. "History and the Politics of Language in France: A Review Essay." *HWJ* 10:175–83.

Alexander, Sally. 1976. "Women's Work in Nineteenth-Century London." In Juliet Mitchell and Ann Oakley, eds., *The Rights and Wrongs of Women,* 55–111. Harmondsworth, UK.

Alexander, Sally. 1984. "Women, Class and Sexual Difference." *HWJ* 17:125–49.

Allen, Robert C., ed. 1987. *Channels of Discourse: Television and Contemporary Criticism.* Chapel Hill, NC.

Anderson, Perry. 1980. *Arguments within English Marxism.* London.

Anderson, Perry. 1983. *In the Tracks of Historical Materialism.* London.

Angus, Ian, and Sut Jhally, eds. 1989. *Cultural Politics in Contemporary America.* New York.

Applewhite, Harriet B., and Darline G. Levy, eds. 1990. *Women and Politics in the Age of the Democratic Revolution.* Ann Arbor.

Baehr, Helen, and Gillian Dyer, eds. 1987. *Boxed In: Women and Television.* London.

Bailey, Victor, ed. 1981. *Policing and Punishment in Nineteenth-Century Britain.* London.

Barker, Francis, Peter Hulme, Margaret Iversen, and Diana Loxley, eds. 1982. *Europe and Its Others.* Vol. 1. Colchester.

Barker, Martin. 1984. *A Haunt of Fears: The Strange History of the British Horror Comics Campaign.* London.

Barrett, Michele, and Mary McIntosh. 1982. *The Anti-Social Family.* London.

Batsleer, Janet, Tony Davies, Rebecca O'Rourke, and Chris Weedon. 1985. *Rewriting English: Cultural Politics of Gender and Class.* London.

Bennett, Tony. 1979. *Formalism and Marxism.* London.

Bennett, Tony. 1982. "Text and History." In Peter Widdowson, ed., *Re-Reading English,* 223–36.

Bennett, Tony, Susan Boyd-Bowman, Colin Mercer, and Janet Woollacott, eds. 1981. *Popular Television and Film.* London.

Bennett, Tony, Colin Mercer, and Janet Woollacott, eds. 1986. *Popular Culture and Social Relations.* Milton Keynes.

Benton, Ted. 1984. *The Rise and Fall of Structural Marxism: Althusser and His Influence.* London.

Blackbourn, David. 1985. "Economic Crisis and the Petite Bourgeoisie in Europe during the Nineteenth and Twentieth Centuries." *SH* 10:95–104.

Blackbourn, David, and Richard J. Evans, eds. 1990. *The German Bourgeoisie.* London.

Brantlinger, Patrick. 1990. *Crusoe's Footprints: Cultural Studies in Britain and America.* New York.

Brennan, Timothy. 1989. *Salman Rushdie and the Third World.* New York.

Brewer, John, and John Styles, eds. 1980. *An Ungovernable People: The English and Their Law in the Seventeenth and Eighteenth Centuries.* London.

Bridenthal, Renate. 1973. "Beyond *Kinder, Küche, Kirche:* Weimar Women at Work." *CEH* 6:148–66.

Bridenthal, Renate, Atina Grossman, and Marion Kaplan, eds. 1984. *When Biology Became Destiny: Women in Weimar and Nazi Germany.* New York.

Bromley, Roger. 1988. *Lost Narratives: Popular Fictions, Politics, and Recent History.* London.

Brunner, Otto, Werner Conze, and Reinhart Koselleck, eds. 1972–89. *Geschichtliche Grundbegriffe.* 5 vols. Stuttgart.

Burguiere, Andre. 1982. "The Fate of the History of Mentalities in the *Annales*." *CSSH* 24:424–37.

Burke, Peter, and Roy Porter, eds. 1987. *The Social History of Language.* Cambridge.

Calhoun, Craig J. 1980. "'Community': Toward a Variable Conceptualization for Comparative Research." *SH* 5:105–29.

Canning, Kathleen. 1992. "Gender and the Politics of Class Formation: Rethinking German Labor History." *AHR* 97:736–68.

Canning, Kathleen. 1994. "Feminist History after the Linguistic Turn: Historicizing Discourse and Experience." *Signs* 19:368–404.

Caplan, Jane. 1979. "Introduction to Macciocchi:'Female Sexuality in Fascist Ideology.'" *Feminist Review* 1:59–66.

Carr, Helen, ed. 1989. *From My Guy to Sci-Fi: Genre and Women's Writing in the Postmodern World.* London.

Carter, Dale. 1988. *The Final Frontier: The Rise and Fall of the American Rocket State.* London.

Chapman, Rowena, and Jonathan Rutherford, eds. 1988. *Male Order: Unwrapping Masculinity.* London.

Chartier, Roger. 1982. "Intellectual History or Socio-Cultural History? The French Trajectories." In Dominick LaCapra and Steven L. Kaplan, eds., *Modern European Intellectual History: Reappraisals and New Perspectives,* 13–46. Ithaca.

Chartier, Roger. 1985. "Text, Symbols, and Frenchness." *JMH* 57:682–95.

Chartier, Roger. 1989. "Texts, Printings, Readings." In Lynn Hunt, *New Cultural History,* 154–75. Berkeley and Los Angeles.

Chaytor, Miranda. 1980. "Household and Kinship: Ryton in the Late Sixteenth and Early Seventeenth Centuries." *HWJ* 10:25–60.

Childers, Thomas. 1990. "The Social Language of Politics in Germany: The Sociology of Political Discourse in the Weimar Republic." *AHR* 95:331–58.

Clark, Stuart. 1983. "French Historians and Early Modern Popular Culture." *P&P* 100:62–99.

Cockburn, J. S., ed. 1977. *Crime in England, 1550–1800.* London.

Cohen, Stanley, and Andrew Scull, eds. 1983. *Social Control and the State: Historical and Comparative Essays.* Oxford.

Cohn, Bernard S. 1980. "History and Anthropology: The State of Play." *CSSH* 22:198–221.

Cohn, Bernard S. 1981. "History and Anthropology: Towards a Rapprochement?" *JIH* 12:227–52.

Colls, Robert, and Philip Dodd, eds. 1986. *Englishness: Politics and Culture, 1880–1920.* London.

Copley, Antony. 1989. *Sexual Moralities in France, 1780–1980: New Ideas on the Family, Divorce, and Homosexuality: An Essay on Moral Change.* London.

Couvares, Francis G. "Telling a Story in Context; or, What's Wrong with Social History?" *Theory and Society* 9(5):674–76.

Coward, Rosalind. 1984. *Female Desires: How They Are Sought, Bought, and Packaged.* London.

Crossick, Geoffrey, and Gerhard Haupt, eds. 1984. *Shopkeepers and Master Artisans in Nineteenth-Century Europe.* London.

Darnton, Robert. 1980. "Intellectual and Cultural History." In Michael Kammen, ed., *Past before Us,* 332. Ithaca.

Darnton, Robert. 1986. "The Symbolic Element in History." *JMH* 58:218–34.

Davidoff, Leonore, and Catherine Hall. 1987. *Family Fortunes: Men and Women of the English Middle Class, 1780–1850.* London.

Davis, Natalie Zemon. 1975. *Society and Culture in Early Modern France.* Stanford.

Degler, Carl. 1980. "Women and the Family." In Michael Kammen, ed., *Past before Us,* 308–26. Ithaca.

Denning, Michael. 1987. *Mechanic Accents: Dime Novels and Working-Class Culture in America.* London.

Derrida, Jacques. 1988. "Like the Sound of the Sea Deep within a Shell: Paul De Man's War," *Critical Inquiry* 14:590–652.

Donajgrodzki, A. P., ed. 1977. *Social Control in Nineteenth-Century Britain.* London.

Donald, James, ed. 1989. *Fantasy and the Cinema.* London.

Donzelot, Jacques. 1979. *The Policing of Families.* New York.

Eley, Geoff. 1979. "Some Recent Tendencies in Social History." In Georg G. Iggers and Harold T. Parker, eds., *International Handbook of Historical Studies: Contemporary Research and Theory,* 55–70. Westport, CT.

Eley, Geoff. 1984. "Reading Gramsci in English: Observations on the Reception of Antonio Gramsci in the English-Speaking World, 1957–82." *European History Quarterly* 14:441–78.

Eley, Geoff. 1989. "Labor History, Social History, *Alltagsgeschichte:* Experience, Culture, and the Politics of the Everyday—A New Direction for German Social History?" *JMH* 61:297–343.

Eley, Geoff, and Keith Nield. 1980. "Why Does Social History Ignore Politics?" *SH* 5:249–71.

Elliott, Gregory. 1987. *Althusser: The Detour of Theory.* London.

Ellis, Kate. 1989. "Stories without Endings: Deconstructive Theory and Political Practice." *Socialist Review* 19:38.

Elshtain, Jean Bethke. 1981. *Public Man, Private Woman: Women in Social and Political Thought.* Princeton.

Evans, Richard J., ed. 1988. *The German Underworld: Deviants and Outcasts in German History.* London.

Feldman, Gerald D. 1984. "A Collapse in Weimar Scholarship," and "A Response to David Abraham's Reply." *CEH* 17:159–77, 245–67.

Fernandez, James. 1988. "Historians Tell Tales: Of Cartesian Cats and Gallic Cockfights." *JMH* 60:113–27.

Fink, Carole. 1989. *Marc Bloch: A Life in History.* Cambridge.

Forgacs, David. 1989. "Gramsci and Marxism in Britain." *NLR* 176:70–88.

Foucault, Michel. 1965. *Madness and Civilization: A History of Insanity in the Age of Reason.* New York.

Foucault, Michel. 1970. *The Order of Things: An Archaeology of the Human Sciences.* London.

Foucault, Michel. 1972. *The Archaeology of Knowledge.* London.

Foucault, Michel. 1980a. "Body/Power." In Colin Gordon, ed., *Power/Knowledge,* 55–62. Brighton, UK.

Foucault, Michel. 1980b. "The Politics of Health in the Eighteenth Century." In Colin Gordon, ed., *Power/Knowledge,* 166–82. Brighton, UK.

Fox-Genovese, Elizabeth, and Eugene Genovese. 1976. "The Political Crisis of Social History: A Marxian Perspective." *JSH* 10:205–20.

Freifield, Mary. 1986. "Technical Change and the Self-Acting Mule." *SH* 11:319–43.

Frevert, Ute, ed. 1988. *Bürgerinnen und Bürger: Geschlechterverhältnisse im 19. Jahrhundert.* Göttingen, Germany.

Frith, Simon, and Andrew Goodwin, eds. 1990. *On Record: Rock, Pop, and the Written Word.* New York.

Gamman, Lorraine, and Margaret Marshment, eds. 1988. *The Female Gaze. Women as Viewers of Popular Culture.* London.

Gatrell, Peter. 1982. "Historians and Peasants: Studies of Medieval English Society in a Russian Context." *P&P* 96:22–50.

Gattrell, Victor A. C., Geoffrey Parker, and Bruce Lenman, eds. 1980. *Crime and the Law: The Social History of Crime in Western Europe since 1500.* London.

Geertz, Clifford. 1973a. "Ideology as a Cultural System." In *The Interpretation of Cultures,* 193–233. New York.

Geertz, Clifford. 1973b. "Deep Play: Notes on a Balinese Cockfight." In *The Interpretation of Cultures,* 449–53. New York.

Giddens, Anthony. 1981. *A Contemporary Critique of Historical Materialism.* Vol. 1, *Power, Property and the State.* London.

Giddens, Anthony. 1985. *A Contemporary Critique of Historical Materialism.* Vol. 2, *The Nation-State and Violence.* Cambridge.

Gismondi, Michael. 1985. "'The Gift of Theory': A Critique of the *histoire des mentalités.*" *SH* 10:211–30.

Godelier, Maurice. 1980. "Work and Its Representations: A Research Proposal." *HWJ* 10:164–74.

Gordon, Colin, ed. 1980. *Power/Knowledge: Selected Interviews and Other Writings, 1972–1977, by Michel Foucault.* Brighton, UK.

Gray, Robert. 1986. "The Deconstruction of the English Working Class." *SH* 11:363–73.

Gurevitch, Michael, Tony Bennett, James Curran, and Janet Woollacott, eds. 1982. *Culture, Society and the Media.* London.

Hall, Catherine. 1985. "Private Persons versus Public Someones: Class, Gender, and Politics in England, 1780–1850." In Carolyn Steedman, Cathy Urwin, and Valerie Walkerdine, eds. *Language, Gender and Childhood,* 10–33. London.

Hall, John A. 1985. *Powers and Liberties: The Causes and Consequences of the Rise of the West.* Oxford.

Hall, Stuart. 1978. "Some Problems with the Ideology/Subject Couplet." *Ideology and Consciousness* 3:120.

Hall, Stuart, Dorothy Hobson, Andrew Lowe, and Paul Willis, eds. 1980. *Culture, Media, Language.* London.

Harlan, David. 1989. "Intellectual History and the Return of Literature." *AHR* 94:581–609.

Harrison, Rachel, and Frank Mort. 1980. "Patriarchal Aspects of Nineteenth-Century State Formation: Property Relations, Marriage and Divorce, and Sexuality." In Philip Corrigan, ed., *Capitalism, State Formation, and Marxist Theory,* 79–109. London.

Hay, Douglas, Peter Linebaugh, and Edward P. Thompson, eds. 1975. *Albion's Fatal Tree: Crime and Society in Eighteenth-Century England.* London.

Henriques, J., et al., eds. 1985. *Changing the Subject.* London.

Hertz, Deborah. 1983. "Intermarriage in the Berlin Salons." *CEH* 16:303–46.

Hewison, Robert. 1987. *The Heritage Industry: Britain in a Climate of Decline.* London.

Hill, John. 1986. *Sex, Class, and Realism: British Cinema, 1956–1963.* London.

Hirst, Paul Q. 1979. *On Law and Ideology.* London.

Hirst, Paul Q. 1985a. "Anderson's Balance Sheet." In *Marxism and Historical Writing,* 1–28. London.

Hirst, Paul Q. 1985b. "Collingwood, Relativism, and the Purposes of History." In *Marxism and Historical Writing,* 43–56. London.

Hirst, Paul Q. 1985c. "Interview with *Local Consumption.*" In *Marxism and Historical Writing,* 121–48. London.

History Workshop Journal. 1976. Editorial: "Feminist History" (by Sally Alexander and Anna Davin), *HWJ* 1:4–6.

History Workshop Journal. 1976. Editorial: "Sociology and History" (by Raphael Samuel and Gareth Stedman Jones), *HWJ* 1:6–8.

History Workshop Journal. 1977. Editorial: "British Economic History and the Question of Work" (by The Editorial Collective), *HWJ* 3:1–4.

History Workshop Journal. 1980. Editorial: "Language and History," *HWJ* 10:1–5.

History Workshop Journal. 1985. Editorial: "Ten Years After" (by Raphael Samuel and Gareth Stedman Jones), *HWJ* 20:1–4.

Hobsbawm, E. J. 1971. "From Social History to the History of Society." *Daedalus* 100:20–45.

Hochstadt, Steve. 1982. "Social History and Politics: A Materialist View," *SH* 7:75–83.

Houston, Rab, and Richard Smith. 1982. "A New Approach to Family History?" *HWJ* 14:120–31.

Hunt, Lynn, ed. 1989. *The New Cultural History.* Berkeley and Los Angeles.

Hunter, Ian. 1988. *Culture and Government: The Emergence of a Literary Education.* London.

Hutton, Patrick. 1981. "The History of Mentalities: The New Map of Cultural History." *History and Theory* 20:413–23.

Ignatieff, Michael. 1978. *A Just Measure of Pain: The Penitentiary in the Industrial Revolution.* London.

Inglis, Fred. 1990. *Media Theory: An Introduction.* Oxford.

Jackson, Peter. 1989. *Maps of Meaning: An Introduction to Cultural Geography.* London.

John, Angela, ed. 1986. *Unequal Opportunities: Women's Employment in England, 1800–1918.* Oxford.

Johnson, Richard. 1970. "Educational Policy and Social Control in Early-Victorian England." *P&P* 49:96–119.

Johnson, Richard. 1978. "Thompson, Genovese, and Socialist-Humanist History." *HWJ* 6:79–100.

Johnson, Richard. 1979a. "Culture and the Historians." In John Clarke, Chas Critcher, and Richard Johnson, eds., *Working-Class Culture: Studies in History and Theory,* 41–71. London.

Johnson, Richard. 1979b. "Three Problematics: Elements of a Theory of Working-Class Culture." In John Clarke, Chas Critcher, and Richard Johnson, eds., *Working-Class Culture: Studies in History and Theory,* 201–37. London.

Johnson, Richard. 1986–87. "What Is Cultural Studies Anyway?" *Social Text* 16:38–80.

Joyce, Patrick, ed. 1987. *The Historical Meanings of Work.* Cambridge.

Judt, Tony. 1979. "A Clown in Regal Purple: Social History and the Historians." *HWJ* 7:66–94.

Kammen, Michael. 1980. *The Past before Us.* Ithaca.

Kaplan, E. Ann. 1987. "Gender Address and the Gaze in MTV." In *Rocking around the Clock: Music Television, Postmodernism, and Consumer Culture,* 89–142. New York and London.

Kaplan, Steven L., and Cynthia J. Koepp, eds. 1986. *Work in France: Representations, Meaning, Organization, and Practice.* Ithaca.

Katznelson, Ira, and Aristide R. Zolberg, eds. 1986. *Working-Class Formation: Nineteenth-Century Patterns in Western Europe and the United States.* Princeton.

Keane, John, ed. 1988. Introduction to John Keane, ed., *Civil Society and the State: New European Perspectives,* 1–31. London and New York.

Kennedy, Ellen, and Susan Mendus, eds. 1987. *Women in Western Political Philosophy: Kant to Nietzsche.* New York.

Kinser, Samuel. 1981. "Annaliste Paradigm? The Geohistorical Structure of Fernand Braudel." *AHR* 86:63–105.

Kocka, Jürgen, ed. 1988. *Bürgertum im 19. Jahrhundert: Deutschland im europäischen Vergleich.* Munich.

Koshar, Rudy. 1986. *Social Life, Local Politics, and Nazism: Marburg, 1880–1935.* Chapel Hill.

Kramer, Lloyd S. 1989. "Literature, Criticism, and Historical Imagination: The Literary Challenge of Hayden White and Dominick LaCapra." In Lynn Hunt, ed., *New Cultural History,* 97–128. Berkeley and Los Angeles.

Kuhn, Annette. 1990. *Cinema, Censorship, and Sexuality, 1909–1925.* London.

LaCapra, Dominick. 1985. "Is Everyone a *Mentalité* Case? Transference and the 'Culture' Concept." In *History and Criticism,* 71–94. Ithaca.

LaCapra, Dominick. 1988. "Chartier, Darnton, and the Great Symbol Massacre." *JMH* 60:95–112.

Laing, Stuart. 1986. *Representations of Working-Class Life, 1957–1964.* London.

Landes, Joan B. 1988. *Women and the Public Sphere in the Age of the French Revolution.* Ithaca, NY.

Levine, David. 1987. *Reproducing Families. The Political Economy of English History.* Cambridge.

Lovell, Terry, ed. 1990. *British Feminist Thought: A Reader.* Oxford.

Lumley, Robert, ed. 1988. *The Museum Time Machine: Putting Cultures on Display.* London.

Lyotard, Jean-François. 1984. *The Post-Modern Condition.* Minneapolis.

MacCabe, Colin, ed. 1986. *High Theory/Low Culture. Analyzing Popular Television and Film.* Manchester.

Macciocchi, Maria-Antonietta. 1979. "Female Sexuality in Fascist Ideology." *Feminist Review* 1:67–82.

Macintyre, Stuart. 1977. "Interview with Gareth Stedman Jones." *Red Shift* 4:19–23.

Magarey, Susan. 1987. "That Hoary Old Chestnut, Free Will and Determinism: Culture vs. Structure, or History vs. Theory in Britain." *CSSH* 29:626–39.

Mann, Michael. 1986. *The Sources of Social Power, I: A History of Power from the Beginning to A.D. 1760.* Cambridge.

Matthews, Fred. 1990. "The Attack on 'Historicism': Allan Bloom's Indictment of Contemporary American Historical Scholarship." *AHR* 95:429–47.

McDonald, Terrence J. 1985. "The Problem of the Political in Recent American Urban History: Liberal Pluralism and the Rise of Functionalism." *SH* 10:323–45.

McLennan, Gregor. 1981. "Braudel and the Annales Paradigm." In *Marxism and the Methodologies of History,* 129–51. London.

Medick, Hans. 1987. "'Missionaries in the Row Boat'? Ethnological Ways of Knowing as a Challenge to Social History." *CSSH* 29:76–98.

Megill, Allan. 1989. "Recounting the Past: 'Description,' Explanation, and Narrative in Historiography." *AHR* 94:627–53.

Modleski, Tania. 1982. *Loving with a Vengeance: Mass-Produced Fantasies for Women.* New York.

Mort, Frank. 1987. *Dangerous Sexualities: Medico-Moral Politics in England since 1830.* London.

Mouffe, Chantal. 1989. "Rethinking Pluralism." Comparative Studies of Social Transformations (CSST) lecture, 21 Sept. 1989, University of Michigan, Ann Arbor, MI.

Mulvey, Laura. 1989. *Visual and Other Pleasures.* Bloomington and Indianapolis.

Niethammer, Lutz, ed. 1983, 1985, 1986. *Lebensgeschichte und Sozialkultur im Ruhrgebiet, 1930 bis 1960.* 3 vols. Bonn.

Novick, Peter. 1988. *That Noble Dream: The "Objectivity Question" and the American Historical Profession.* Cambridge.

O'Brien, Patricia. 1989. "Michel Foucault's History of Culture." In Lynn Hunt, ed., *The New Cultural History,* 25–46. Berkeley and Los Angeles.

Outram, Dorinda. 1987. "Le langage male de la vertu: Women and the Discourse of the French Revolution." In Peter Burke and Roy Porter, eds., *The Social History of Language,* 120–35. Cambridge.

Outram, Dorinda. 1989. *The Body and the French Revolution: Sex, Class, and Political Culture.* London and New Haven.

Palmer, Bryan D. 1990. *Descent into Discourse: The Reification of Language and the Writing of Social History.* Philadelphia.

Passerini, Luisa. 1987. *Fascism in Popular Memory: The Cultural Experience of the Turin Working Class.* Cambridge.

Pateman, Carole. 1988. *The Sexual Contract.* Cambridge.

Perkin, Harold. 1981. "What Is Social History?" In *The Structured Crowd: Essays in English Social History,* 1–27. Brighton.

Petro, Patrice. 1989. *Joyless Streets: Women and Melodramatic Representation in Weimar Germany.* Princeton.

Pollock, Griselda. 1988. *Vision and Difference: Femininity, Feminism, and the Histories of Art.* London.

Punter, David, ed. 1986. *Introduction to Contemporary Cultural Studies.* London.

Quataert, Jean H. 1983. "A Source Analysis of German Women's History: Factory Inspectors' Reports and the Shaping of Working-Class Lives, 1878–1914." *CEH* 16:99–121.

Quataert, Jean H. 1987. "The Politics of Rural Industrialization: Class, Gender, and Collective Protest in the Saxon Oberlausitz in the Late Nineteenth Century." *CEH* 20:91–124.

Radical History Review. 1978–79. Theme Issue: "Marxism and History: The British Contribution." *RHR* 19.

Radical History Review. 1979. Theme Issue: "Sexuality in History." *RHR* 20.

Radical History Review. 1985. Theme Issue: "The Return of Narrative." *RHR* 31.

Radical History Review. 1986. Theme Issue: "Language, Work, and Ideology." *RHR* 34.

Radstone, Susannah, ed. 1988. *Sweet Dreams: Sexuality, Gender, and Popular Fiction.* London.

Radway, Janice. 1984. *Reading the Romance: Women, Patriarchy, and Popular Culture.* Chapel Hill, NC.

Reddy, William M. 1987. *Money and Liberty in Modern Europe: A Critique of Historical Understanding.* Cambridge.

Rees, A. L., and Frances Borzello, eds. 1988. *The New Art History.* Atlantic Highlands, NJ.

Reid, Donald. 1984. "The Night of the Proletarians: Deconstruction and Social History." *RHR* 28–30:445–63.

Riley, Denise. 1983. *War in the Nursery: Theories of the Child and Mother.* London.

Roper, Michael, ed. 1990. "Recent Books on Masculinity" (reviews by John Tesh, Michael Roper, and Joseph Bristow). *HWJ* 29:184–93.

Rose, Jacqueline. 1984. *The Case of Peter Pan or the Impossibility of Children's Fiction.* London.

Rose, Nikolas. 1985. *The Psychological Complex: Social Regulation and the Psychology of the Individual.* London.

Rose, Nikolas. 1990. *Governing the Soul: The Shaping of the Private Self.* London.

Rose, Sonya O. 1986. "Gender at Work: Sex, Class, and Industrial Capitalism." *HWJ* 21:113–31.

Rose, Sonya O. 1991. *Limited Livelihoods.* Berkeley.

Ryan, Mary P. 1981. *Cradle of the Middle Class: Family and Community in Oneida County, New York, 1780–1865.* Cambridge.

Samuel, Raphael, ed. 1981. *People's History and Socialist Theory.* London.

Samuel, Raphael, ed. 1989. *Patriotism: The Making and Unmaking of British National Identity.* 3 vols. London.

Schöttler, Peter. 1989. "Historians and Discourse Analysis." *HWJ* 27:37–65.

Scott, Joan. 1974. *The Glassworkers of Carmaux: French Craftsmen and Political Action in a Nineteenth-Century City.* Cambridge, MA.

Scott, Joan. 1988. *Gender and the Politics of History.* New York.

Scribner, Robert W. 1981. *For the Sake of Simple Folk: Popular Propaganda for the German Reformation.* Cambridge.

Seccombe, Wally. 1983. "Marxism and Demography." *NLR* 137:22–47.

Sewell, William H., Jr. 1980. *Work and Revolution in France: The Language of Labor from the Old Regime to 1848.* Cambridge.

Sider, Gerald M. 1986. *Culture and Class in Anthropology and History: A Newfoundland Illustration.* Cambridge.

Sinfield, Alan. 1984. *Formations of Nation and People.* London.

Sinfield, Alan. 1989. *Literature, Politics, and Culture in Postwar Britain.* Berkeley and Los Angeles.

Smith, Roger. 1988. "Does the History of Psychology Have a Subject?" *History of the Human Sciences* 1:147–77.

Snyder, Francis, and Douglas Hay, eds. 1987. *Labour, Law, and Crime: An Historical Perspective.* London.

Somers, Margaret R. 1989. "Workers of the World, Compare!" *Contemporary Sociology* 18:325–30.

Somers, Margaret R. 1992. "Narrativity, Narrative Identity, and Social Action: Rethinking English Working-Class Formation." *Social Science History* 16:591–630.

Squire, Corinne. 1989. *Significant Differences: Feminism in Psychology.* London.

Stallybrass, Peter, and Allon White. 1986. *The Politics and Poetics of Transgression.* Ithaca.

Stam, Robert. 1988. "Mikhail Bakhtin and Left Cultural Critique." In E. Ann Kaplan, ed., *Postmodernism and Its Discontents: Theories, Practices,* 116–45. London.

Stead, Peter. 1989. *Film and the Working Class: The Feature Film in British and American Society.* London.

Stedman Jones, Gareth. 1972. "History: The Poverty of Empiricism." In Robin Blackburn, ed., *Ideology in Social Science: Readings in Critical Social Theory,* 96–115. London.

Stedman Jones, Gareth. 1975. "Class Struggle and the Industrial Revolution." *NLR* 90:35–69.

Stedman Jones, Gareth. 1976. "From Historical Sociology to Theoretical History." *British Journal of Sociology* 27:295–305.

Stedman Jones, Gareth. 1977a. "Class Expression versus Social Control? A Critique of Recent Trends in the Social History of 'Leisure'." *HWJ* 4:162–70.

Stedman Jones, Gareth. 1977b. "Society and Politics at the Beginning of the World Economy." *Cambridge Journal of Economics* 1:77–92.

Stedman Jones, Gareth. 1983a. Introduction to *Languages of Class: Studies in English Working-Class History, 1832–1982,* 1–24. Cambridge.

Stedman Jones, Gareth. 1983b. "Rethinking Chartism." In *Languages of Class: Studies in English Working-Class History, 1832–1982,* 90–178. London.

Steedman, Carolyn Kay. 1985. "'The Mother Made Conscious': The Historical Development of a Primary School Pedagogy." *HWJ* 20:149–63.

Steedman, Carolyn Kay. 1986. *Landscape for a Good Woman: A Story of Two Lives.* London.

Stone, Lawrence. 1977. "History and the Social Sciences in the Twentieth Century." In Charles F. Delzell, ed., *The Future of History,* 3–42. Nashville.

Stone, Lawrence. 1979. "The Revival of Narrative." *P&P* 85:3–24.

Swindells, Julia, and Lisa Jardine. 1990. *What's Left? Women in Culture and the Labour Movement.* London.

Tenfelde, Klaus, ed. 1986. *Arbeiter und Arbeiterbewegung im Vergleich: Berichte zur internationalen historischen Forschung.* Historische Zeitschrift-Sonderheft 15 (Munich).

Thane, Pat, and Anthony Sutcliffe, eds. 1986. *Essays in Social History.* Oxford.

Theweleit, Klaus. [1987] 1988. *Male Fantasies.* Minneapolis.

Thompson, Edward P. 1963. *The Making of the English Working Class.* London.

Thompson, Edward P. 1975. *Whigs and Hunters: The Origins of the Black Act.* London.

Thompson, Edward P. 1978. *The Poverty of Theory and Other Essays.* London.

Tilly, Charles. 1980. "Two Callings of Social History." *Theory and Society* 9(5):679–81.

Tilly, Charles. 1990. *Coercion, Capital, and European States, A.D. 990–1990.* Oxford.

Tilly, Louise. 1980. "Social History and Its Critics." *Theory and Society* 9:670.

Tilly, Louise, and Joan Scott. 1978. *Women, Work, and Family.* New York.

Todd, Janet. 1988. "Men in Feminist Criticism." In Mary Eagleton, ed., *Feminist Literary Theory: A Reader,* 118–34. London.

Toews, John E. 1987. "Intellectual History after the Linguistic Turn: The Autonomy of Meaning and the Irreducibility of Experience." *AHR* 92:879–907.

Tomlinson, Alan, ed. 1990. *Consumption, Identity, and Style: Marketing, Meanings, and the Packaging of Pleasure.* London.

Tribe, Keith. 1978. *Land, Labour, and Economic Discourse.* London.

Tribe, Keith. 1989. "The *Geschichtliche Grundbegriffe* Project: From History of Ideas to Conceptual History." *CSSH* 31:180–84.

Vincent, David. 1990. *Literacy and Popular Culture: England, 1750–1914.* Cambridge.

Walden, R., and Valerie Walkerdine. 1985. *Gender and Education: Psychology's Construction of the Feminine.* Milton Keynes.

Wallerstein, Immanuel. 1988. *The Modern World-System.* Vol. 3, *The Second Era of Great Expansion of the Capitalist World-Economy.* New York.

Webster, Duncan. 1988. *Looka Yonder! The Imaginary America of Populist Culture.* London.

Weeks, Jeffrey. 1982. "Foucault for Historians." *HWJ* 14:106–19.

White, Hayden. 1973. *Metahistory: The Historical Imagination in Nineteenth-Century Europe.* Baltimore.

White, Hayden. 1978. *Tropics of Discourse: Essays in Cultural Criticism.* Baltimore.

Widdowson, Peter, ed. 1982. *Re-Reading English.* London.

Williams, Raymond. 1958. *Culture and Society, 1780–1950.* London.

Williams, Raymond. 1961. *The Long Revolution.* London.

Williams, Raymond. 1971. "Literature and Sociology: In Memory of Lucien Goldmann." *NLR* 67:3–18.

Williams, Raymond. 1981. "Marxism, Structuralism, and Literary Analysis." *NLR* 129:51–66.

Williams, Raymond. 1983. *Keywords: A Vocabulary of Culture and Society.* 2d ed. London.

Williams, Raymond. 1986. "The Uses of Cultural Theory." *NLR* 158:19–31.

Williams, Raymond. 1989. "When Was Modernism?" *NLR* 175:48–52.

Williamson, Judith. 1978. *Decoding Advertisements: Ideology and Meaning in Advertising.* London.

Williamson, Judith. 1986. *Consuming Passions: The Dynamics of Popular Culture.* London.

Wood, Ellen Meiksins. 1986. *The Retreat from Class: A New "True" Socialism.* London.

Worpole, Ken. 1983. *Dockers and Detectives: Popular Reading, Popular Writing.* London.

Wright, Patrick. 1985. *On Living in an Old Country: The National Past in Contemporary Britain.* London.

Wrigley, E. A., and Roger S. Schofield. 1981. *The Population History of England, 1541–1871.* Cambridge.

Three Temporalities: Toward an Eventful Sociology

William H. Sewell Jr.

Historical approaches have made remarkable strides in American sociology over the last two decades. Through most of the 1960s, sociology in the United States was utterly dominated by research on contemporary America. But the civil rights and antiwar movements made graduate students trained in the 1960s and early 1970s far more interested than their elders in questions of social change. Rather than seeking timeless laws of the operation of American society—which was implicitly equated with society in general—a new generation began to ask how the world's different societies have been transformed under the impact of capitalism and Western domination. The ideas pioneered by such intrepid historical explorers as Barrington Moore (1966), Charles Tilly (1964), and Immanuel Wallerstein (1974) were consequently taken up by scores of young sociologists in the 1970s and 1980s.[1]

By the early 1980s, historical sociology was recognizable as a major node of growth in the profession. Its prominence has been institutionalized by the formation of two historically inclined official sections of the American Sociological Association (ASA): a Comparative Historical Sociology Section, which a sociologist friend aptly characterizes as "left Weberian," and a Political Economy of the World System Section, which is predominantly Wallersteinian.[2] Although it is doubtful whether historical approaches will ever become dominant in the discipline, their growing prominence already has significantly changed the contours of American sociology.

The leading manifestos and programmatic statements of historical sociologists have generally been concerned with methodological issues and above all with comparative method (e.g., Stinchcombe 1978; Skocpol and Somers, 1980; Skocpol, 1984; Tilly, 1984). The title "Comparative Historical Sociology," adopted by the historical sociologists as the label for their ASA section, is emblematic; it places as much emphasis on comparative method as on historical subject matter. In this respect, historical sociologists reveal themselves to be in the mainstream of American sociology. By stressing comparative method, they participate eagerly in the discipline's obsessive concern to justify itself as a science. Comparative method, after all, is the standard alternative to mainstream statistical methods when the number of cases is insufficiently large. This mode of self-presentation has helped to make historical research acceptable to the rest of the profession. Historical sociology, this rhetoric implies, poses no particular theoretical or epistemological threat; it is simply the sociology of the past, carried on by means as close as feasible to the sociology of the present.

It is not hard to see why historical sociologists have been so self-conscious about method. After all, they have virtually always had to make careers in departments where they were surrounded by skeptical positivists vigilantly on guard against humanistic tendencies. The emphasis on methodology has surely helped historical sociology to establish its secure beachhead in the profession. But it has also served to obscure some of the potentially radical implications of sociology's "historic turn." I believe that historical sociology is now sufficiently secure to risk examining some of these implications in public. In this spirit, I will here attempt to spell out what I see as deep but as yet largely unvoiced challenges that historical sociology poses to the disciplinary mainstream.

Until recently, few historical sociologists have had much to say about what makes their sociology *historical*. If historical sociology is merely the sociology of the past, it is valuable above all because it increases the available number of data points. Many social processes require a significant period of time to work themselves out. If we investigate such processes only in the present, we not only risk studying incomplete sequences but greatly restrict the number of cases. But is history just a matter of more data points? Doesn't making sociology historical imply introducing ideas of temporality that are radically foreign to normal sociological thinking?[3] I maintain that the answer to this question depends on how temporality is conceptualized. The currently dominant modes of conceptualizing temporality in historical sociology—what I will call "teleological" and "experimental" temporality—minimize the challenge to mainstream sociology. But a third, currently subordinate, conceptualization—what I will call "eventful" temporality—is potentially much more subversive.[4] I will argue that the dominant teleological and experimental concepts of temporality are seriously deficient, indeed actually fallacious, and that historical sociology needs to adopt the much more subversive eventful notion of temporality, which sees the course of history as determined by a succession of largely contingent events.

Teleological Temporality

Sociology was born under the sign of teleology. The great nineteenth-century founders, for example, Comte, Marx, Durkheim, and Tonnies, saw history as the temporal working out of an inherent logic of social development—from religious to metaphysical to scientific eras, from feudalism to capitalism to socialism, from mechanical to organic solidarity, or from *Gemeinschaft* to *Gesellschaft*. For these social theorists, history was shaped by transhistorical progressive laws. The direction and meaning of history were a consequence not of the largely contingent events that made up the surface of history but of long-term, anonymous causal forces, of which particular historical events were at best manifestations. The waning of the nineteenth century's virtually universal faith in progress has gradually resulted in an abandonment of explicit teleology in sociological thought. But weaker forms of teleology are still very much with us.

A teleological explanation is the attribution of the cause of a historical happening neither to the actions and reactions that constitute the happening nor to concrete and specifiable conditions that shape or constrain the actions and reactions but rather to abstract transhistorical processes leading to some future historical state. Events in some historical present, in other words, are actually explained by events in the future. Such explanatory strategies, however fallacious, are surprisingly common in recent sociological writing and are far from rare in the works of social historians. They are implied, for example, by the common practice of labeling political or social movements as backward-looking and forward-looking. "Backward-looking" movements, in normal usage, are those that value some aspect of a given period's life and culture that the analyst, with her or his twenty-twenty hindsight, regards as doomed to the dustbin of history, whereas "forward-looking" movements are those valuing aspects of a period's life and culture that turned out to have a bright future. The simple act of labeling movements in this way contains an implicit teleological explanation of their histories.[5] Likewise, the term *modern* often serves as a label for those processes or agents that are deemed by the analyst to be doing the work of the future in some present, while *traditional* labels those equally current forces in the present that the analyst regards as doing the work of the past. The entire modernization school of social science is based on such a teleological conceptualization of temporality. But the teleological fallacy is also widespread in the work of many historical sociologists who regard their work as arising out of an uncompromising critique of modernization theory. I will try to demonstrate this claim by briefly examining the work of two historical sociologists who were particularly influential in overthrowing the theoretical approaches of the modernization school and replacing them with those of contemporary historical sociology: namely, Immanuel Wallerstein and Charles Tilly.

Immanuel Wallerstein as Social Astronomer

Wallerstein is by far the clearer case. In his multivolume history of the modern world-system, Wallerstein proves himself no less anxious than other sociologists to find a secure scientific warrant for his knowledge. But because his object of study is vast and singular—the capitalist "world-system"—the usual quantitative and experimental scientific models are hardly appropriate; there are no other units with which the modern world-system could appropriately be compared. Wallerstein discussed this dilemma in the introduction to his first volume. He worried out loud that there was "only one instance" of his "unit of analysis" and that if this were true he might be reduced to merely writing its history. But he "was not interested in writing its history"; he wanted to discover its *laws:*

> Can there be laws about the unique? In a rigorous sense, there of course cannot be. A statement of causality or probability is made in terms of a series of like phenomena or like instances. . . . There had only been one "modern world." Maybe one day there would be discovered to be comparable phenomena on other planets, or additional modern world-systems on this one. But here and now, the reality was clear—only one. (Wallerstein 1974, 7)

Wallerstein rescued the scientific status of his enterprise by an inspired analogy. If the capitalist world-system is one of a kind, Wallerstein reasoned, its study can be modeled on a fully recognized and powerful natural science that investigates the unique development of a singular system: astronomy, or, more precisely, cosmology, that branch of astronomy that studies the physical universe as a whole. "What," Wallerstein asked himself, "do astronomers do?"

As I understand it, the logic of their arguments involves two separate operations. They use the laws derived from the study of smaller physical

entities, the laws of physics, and argue that (with perhaps certain specified exceptions) these laws hold by analogy for the system as a whole.
Second, they argue *a posteriori*. If the whole system is to have a given
state at time *y*, it most probably had a given state at time *x*. (Wallerstein
1984, 7)

This analogy with cosmology, I would argue, crucially shaped Wallerstein's
intellectual project, although it did so in part by creative misapplication. It
suggested a close relationship between part and whole, where laws found in
investigations of local phenomena are also assumed to operate at the level of
the whole. This key assumption—that local and global processes partake of the
same causalities—was profoundly enabling. It provided Wallerstein with a
powerful unified perspective, one that authorized him to see all sorts of local
events in various times and places as determined not by the accidents of local
conditions but by the dynamics of the world economy of which they were a
part. I believe that it was above all this unique perspective—this ability to see
the dynamic of the whole at work in the dynamics of the parts—that established Wallerstein's reputation as a great historical sociologist and that attracted an entire school of followers.

But in applying the astronomers' assumption about the uniformity of
causalities to the world-system, Wallerstein reversed the direction of the part-
whole relationship. In astronomy, the physical principles discovered in studies
of small-scale earthbound matter—whether these be Galileo's laws of falling
bodies or the findings of contemporary particle physics—are assumed to apply
equally to cosmic matter—to the orbits of planets or to nuclear reactions in
stellar cores. Indeed, such laws are assumed to operate at the level of the
universe as a whole: the great cosmological question of whether the universe
will expand indefinitely or eventually collapse in on itself hinges on calculations of the aggregate gravitational pull of the entire mass of matter in the
cosmos. Astronomy today, as at the time of Newton, remains an example of
reductionist science at its most awesomely successful. In contemporary astronomy, the key to the dynamics of the infinitely large is found in the dynamics of
the infinitely small.

But Wallerstein rejects models, whether derived from behaviorist psychology or microeconomics, that would explain the dynamics of the world-system
by the principles governing its smallest entities—human individuals. Nor does
he argue that the dynamics of local communities provide the key to understanding the development of world society. His point is precisely the opposite: that
the fates of local communities are determined not by local causes but by the

operation of global, system-level causes. The key to understanding the history of Poland or Peru is to recognize their place in the world-systemic division of labor—as peripheral societies dependent on the core. But once we have begun to explain spatially and temporally localized events as a consequence of their place in a totality of world evolution, we are perilously close to teleological explanation.

Wallerstein's misapplied astronomical analogy also encouraged teleology in another, more direct, way. He felt authorized by astronomy to argue a posteriori, to argue back from the recent or current state of the capitalist world-system to its prior state. Most spectacularly, the astronomers project the current velocities of galaxies backward to argue for the existence of a "big bang" at the beginning of time, a primal cosmic event that determined the subsequent character and evolution of the physical universe. Wallerstein the social astronomer devises what in effect is a big bang theory of the origins of capitalism. A European economy already in crisis as a consequence of the disintegration of feudalism was decisively launched on a new and inexorable dynamic by the European geographical expansion known as "the great discoveries." The discoveries, according to Wallerstein, established the key economic, geographical, and political relationships on which the subsequent development of capitalism has been predicated—a spatially differentiated world economy too large to be controlled by any of the competing political units of which it was composed (Wallerstein 1974, 38).

Once again, Wallerstein's misapplication of the analogy with astronomy has served him both well and badly. I am convinced that the particular economic-geographic-political dynamic identified by Wallerstein is indeed crucial in the development of world capitalism and that it was decisively set in motion by the discoveries. But Wallerstein's vision of all the subsequent development of capitalism as somehow inherent in his initial big bang warps his understanding both of the discoveries and of subsequent developments. His work contains some astute eventful analysis of the political and economic history of Europe in his period, although his rhetoric suppresses the narrative's eventful qualities. His discussions of how marginal and tiny Portugal became the initiator of the voyages of discovery (Wallerstein 1974, 50–52), of how the Hapsburgs attempted but failed to gain a political hegemony that would encompass the world economy (165–80), or of how the Dutch Revolt made possible the development of crucial new commercial and financial institutions in the Netherlands (199–214) are actually full of contingency, unanticipated consequences, and fateful choices. But in Wallerstein's analysis, the contingencies, choices, and consequences are foreordained by the necessity built into the world-system from the moment of its creation. Hidden behind Wallerstein's big bang theory is a far more interesting account of how the crucial but open-ended event of the discoveries initiated a long chain of subsequent open-ended events that eventually and far from inevitably led to the emergence of a capitalist world economy.

What makes the astronomers' a posteriori reasoning scientifically acceptable is the plausibility of the assumption that just as the laws of physics hold true across space they also hold true across time. If the laws of motion, gravity, and high-energy physics can be projected backward in time, then it is possible to deduce the timing and characteristics of the big bang that propelled the universe into its current dynamics or the state of the universe ten minutes after the big bang or a hundred billion years from now. But we know that human beings and the societies they create are far more perverse than physical matter. Humans, unlike planets, galaxies, or subatomic particles, are capable of assessing the structures in which they exist and of acting—with imperfectly predictable consequences—in ways that change them. While there certainly are turning points or crucial events in human history, there cannot be big bangs. To construct historical arguments on an analogy with astronomy results in a teleology in which some crucial past event is misconstrued as a pure origin that contains the entire future of the social system *in potentia* and in which the partially contingent events that occur subsequently are robbed of their efficacy and reduced to the status of markers on the road to the inevitable future.

Charles Tilly and the Master Processes of History

Teleology plays a far less obvious role in Tilly's work than in Wallerstein's. Nevertheless, I shall try to demonstrate that two of his most influential contributions—his book on the Vendée rebellion and his work on the history of French collective violence—contain strong doses of teleological temporality (Tilly 1964, 1969, 1972a, 1972b, 1977, 1981, 1986; Tilly, Tilly, and Tilly 1975). This might seem particularly curious in the case of the *The Vendée,* which focuses on a particular event, the great counterrevolutionary revolt that erupted in western France in 1793. But Tilly's book is not a narrative history of the revolt. In fact, his argument is introduced by a very effective polemic against the sociological naivete of the countless existing narrative histories (1964, 6–13). Whereas these narrative histories spoke about the cause of the revolt by rather cavalierly invoking the presumed motives of the rebels, Tilly insisted on asking properly sociological causal questions. He wanted to know what it was about the social organization of the Vendée region that led to a revolt there. Tilly's principal analytical device was to compare two adjacent areas in western France, the Val-Saumurois, which supported the revolution, and the Mauges, which supported the counterrevolution. The principal sociological concept he used to analyze the difference in the social organization of these two areas was "urbanization," which in Tilly's somewhat expanded usage was "a collective term for a set of changes which generally occur with the appearance and expansion of large-scale coordinated activities in a society" (Tilly 1964, 16). Urbanization hence implied not just the growth of cities but an "increased involvement of the members of rural communities in sets of activities, norms, and social relationships that reach beyond the limits of their own localities" (Tilly 1964, 11–12).

Tilly argued that the crucial difference between the Mauges and the Val-Saumurois was the extent and the recentness of their urbanization. The Val-Saumurois was "thoroughly and evenly urbanized" (Tilly 1964, 57); even its rural inhabitants had long lived in sizable, agglomerated villages and sold their produce in regional and national markets. This thorough and even urbanization made the Val-Saumurois well adapted to the more rational and centralized bourgeois regime introduced by the revolution. The Mauges, by contrast, was much less urbanized, but it had experienced very rapid urbanization—especially in the form of rural textile manufacturing—in recent decades. This recent but incomplete urbanization made the social organization of the Mauges far less uniform and led to intense confrontations when the revolution shifted power to the urban bourgeoisie and its agents in the countryside.

Tilly's analysis of how the different forms of social organization of these two regions led to different political and social experiences in the revolution is superb. But his sociological interpretation of these differences is marred by a gratuitous introduction of teleological temporality. For Tilly, the Mauges and the Val-Saumurois represent different points on a single developmental continuum, from less to more urbanized. His procedure, as he puts it, is one "of comparing communities at roughly the same point in time *as if* they were at different stages in a progression from a common origin" (Tilly 1964, 12, emphasis in original). The obvious advantage of this procedure is its generalizability. It means that differences found between two regions are not just a local peculiarity but are comparable to differences in level of urbanization in other places and times. Introducing a single continuum makes it possible to envisage this local study as one contribution to a general scientific sociological account of the effects of urbanization on politics.

The problem is that the difference between the social organization of the Val-Saumurois and that of the Mauges is demonstrably not a matter of different stages in a single master process. The contrasting forms of social organization that Tilly attributes to differences in a progressive development—large nucleated villages surrounded by open fields in the Val-Saumurois as against more isolated small villages and hamlets scattered over hedged fields in the Mauges—were actually constant and virtually unchanging features of the rural environment. The line dividing the Val-Saumurois from the Mauges was an ancient territorial division between what Marc Bloch characterized as distinct "agrarian civilizations" whose characteristics were already in place by the early Middle Ages (Bloch 1970). Tilly, in short, committed the fallacy of transmuting a fixed sociogeographical difference in social organization into putative stages in the linear development of the abstract master process of urbanization.

Tilly's use of urbanization as a linear teleology did not actually spoil his comparative study of the political effects of regional social structures, but it did misrepresent the book's contribution—by casting its subject as a local instance of a universal social process. By doing so, it left unvoiced what I regard as the book's most original accomplishment: its acute analysis of how variations in local social structures made possible a smooth transition from old regime to revolutionary government in the Val-Saumurois but enabled the French Revolution to reconfigure and give new meaning to existing social networks and social cleavages in the Mauges, touching off an escalating and unpredictable chain of confrontational events that culminated in a massive and durable shift in collective identities. It hid a masterwork of eventful sociology behind a veil of misconstrued universalizing science.

One might object that *The Vendée* was Tilly's first book and that his mature work avoids these youthful errors. After all, he subsequently abandoned his overly abstract concept of urbanization, breaking it down into the two more specific notions of state centralization and capitalist development. But in his long and evolving project on French collective violence, which he took up after finishing *The Vendée,* he essentially retained that book's teleological fascination with underlying master processes, while abandoning its superb but insufficiently voiced eventful analysis. Charmed by his own universalizing rhetoric, he pursued the notion that acts of political contestation arise from gradual evolutionary changes in large and anonymous social processes rather than the alternative theme that changes in political regimes reconfigure and give new meaning to existing social networks and cleavages, thereby creating new collective identities.

Tilly argues in his various books and articles on collective violence that the change in forms of violence over the last three centuries—in brief, a change from "reactive," backward-looking, locally oriented violence to "proactive," forward-looking, and nationally oriented violence—was the consequence of the gradual and inexorable rise of state centralization and capitalism.[6] Such an argument is not necessarily teleological. Teleology is not implied, for example, when Tilly argues that changes in the targets and goals of violent protest arise in part from the particular and changing nature of the state presence in localities. But the argument frequently takes on a teleological quality, largely because the asserted causes—capitalist development and state centralization—occur offstage, outside of Tilly's texts, where they are essentially assumed as ever present and ever rising forces, a kind of eternal yeast.[7] The violent incidents that Tilly describes in great number thus figure only as consequences of invisible but ever present causes; they are not *events* in the full sense because they are only effects, never causes, of change. A particularly clear indication that Tilly has abandoned eventful analysis in his more recent work on French collective violence is his denial that even the historians' megaevent, the French Revolution, significantly transformed the nature of collective violence: in his account, it merely caused a certain acceleration of already existing trends (Tilly 1977, 1986). Thus, in spite of the inspired eventful analysis contained in *The Vendée,* the dominant rhetoric of Tilly's work on French collective violence has not broken with a teleological conceptualization of temporality.

Theda Skocpol and Experimental Temporality

If Wallerstein and Tilly exemplify the continuing grip of teleological temporality in historical sociology, Theda Skocpol is the leading prophet and exemplar of experimental temporality. In *States and Social Revolutions,* Skocpol explicitly embraces the standard "scientific" methodology of mainstream American sociology, extending it to historical studies. "Comparative historical analysis," she asserts,

> is distinctively appropriate for developing explanations of macrohistorical phenomena of which there are inherently only a few cases. This is in contrast to more plentiful and manipulable kinds of phenomena suitable for experimental investigations, and in contrast to other phenomena where there are the large numbers of cases required for statistical analyses. Comparative historical analysis is, in fact, the mode of multivariate analysis to which one resorts when there are too many variables and not enough cases. (Skocpol 1979, 36)

Skocpol applies her comparative method to the three great social revolutions of modern times—the French, the Russian, and the Chinese. Her analysis attempts to set up comparative "natural experiments" capable of sorting out the causal factors that explain the occurrence of social revolutions. She explores the histories of the French, Russian, and Chinese revolutions but also of two major political crises that never became revolutions (the Prussian Reform Movement of 1807–14 and the Japanese Meiji Restoration of 1868–73) and of two political revolutions that did not become social revolutions (the English Civil War and Glorious Revolution of 1640–88 and the German Revolution of 1848–50). On the basis of her comparative investigation of these seven cases, Skocpol develops a powerful and sophisticated theory of the causes of social revolutions. She begins by noting that the prerevolutionary French, Russian, and Chinese states had all fallen behind their rivals in military competition. This gave rise to attempts to catch up by instituting far-reaching administrative, economic, and fiscal reforms. But reforms were resisted in all three states by the dominant landlord class, which had a firm enough foothold in the state to block, slow, or subvert the reforms. The consequence was a deep fiscal and political crisis that was broken only by a revolution. These considerations led Skocpol to posit two conditions for social revolution: the existence of a state that fell behind rival states in military competition and a dominant class of landlords who were sufficiently powerful to block state-initiated reforms. She strengthened this specification of causes by examining the Prussian and Japanese cases. In both cases the states were driven into crisis by failure in military competition, but because the Prussian and Japanese dominant classes had little political leverage against the state, reformers from within the state apparatus managed to revitalize the states without the intervention of political revolution.

But Skocpol also finds another necessary condition for the occurrence of social revolutions. Fiscal crises based on military backwardness and exacerbated by the resistance of recalcitrant landlords may have been enough to touch off political revolutions, but for these to become social revolutions—that is, to bring about a transformation of the country's class structure—something more was required: a massive uprising of the peasant class. Social revolutions, therefore, also required the existence of well-organized and autonomous peasant communities capable of taking advantage of the breakdown of state authority in a political revolution. Once again, Skocpol shows how this condition was present in her three cases but absent in the seventeenth-century English and mid-nineteenth century German revolutions, which never advanced from political to social revolutions. In short, Skocpol uses a quasi-experimental, inductive method to discover the three factors necessary for social revolutions: (1)

military backwardness, (2) politically powerful landlord classes, and (3) autonomous peasant communities. As I understand the argument, these factors are conceptualized in this order: factor one induces a political crisis; the addition of factor two turns the political crisis into a political revolution; and the further addition of factor three turns the political revolution into a social revolution.

The explanation Skocpol develops by considering these seven cases is extremely powerful and, quibbling aside, quite convincing. But the power of her explanation cannot derive, as Skocpol claims, from her application of quasi-experimental inductive method. As Michael Burawoy has pointed out in a recent article (1989), a careful examination of Skocpol's logic and evidence indicates that her explanation is by no means proved by the "natural experiments" carried out in her book. In fact, her evidence fails in more than one way. First, as Burawoy remarks, the seventeenth-century English and mid-nineteenth-century German cases actually seem to refute the first stage of her causal theory in that they were genuine political revolutions that were not provoked by military failures: the English Revolution of 1640 certainly arose out of a fiscal crisis but not a fiscal crisis that was provoked by military reverses, and the German Revolution of March 1848 was provoked by neither military reverses nor fiscal crisis. Skocpol's comparisons actually demonstrate that far-reaching political revolutions may arise in the absence of both of her first two factors (Burawoy 1989, 767–68).

Second, the array of cases compared by Skocpol does not demonstrate that the full sequence of three factors is necessary to produce a social revolution. To do so, Skocpol would have had to find a case in which military failure and landlord resistance led to political revolution but in which a social revolution failed to develop due to the absence of autonomous peasant communities. But she has no such case: the Meiji Restoration and the Prussian Reform Movement had only the first factor, the English Revolution only the second, and the German Revolution of 1848 none of the three. On the basis of Skocpol's evidence, it remains logically possible that a combination of military backwardness and a powerful landlord class was by itself sufficient to produce a social revolution.

Indeed, Skocpol's analysis of the Chinese Revolution could actually be read as supporting this proposition. There, a social revolution took place in a country where only the first two of Skocpol's conditions were initially present. Skocpol treats the case as confirming her theory. As she tells the story, the peasantry's lack of autonomy from landlords long prevented the political revolution initiated in 1911 from becoming a social revolution. It was only after

1940 that the Chinese communists organized an autonomous peasantry in the districts they controlled, thereby creating the agrarian striking force necessary to carry through a social revolution (Skocpol 1979, 252–62). But this argument is actually highly ambiguous. One could just as easily say that the long standoff between state and landlords, exacerbated by the Japanese invasion in 1935, created the conditions for a successful social revolution in the areas that the Kuomintang could no longer control. The creation of peasant communities autonomous from landlords was, in this telling, less a precondition for social revolution than a consequence of a locally successful communist-led social revolution touched off by a collapse of the stalemated state in the wake of military failure.

These two flaws in Skocpol's argument invalidate her claim to having confirmed empirically her theory of social revolutions. She has not shown either that political revolutions are explained by a combination of military reverses and effective landlord resistance to reforms or that autonomous peasant communities are necessary for a political revolution to be transformed into a social revolution. It is true that these flaws are not intrinsic to the comparative method per se. Skocpol is working on such a rare phenomenon that she has been unable to amass an array of cases sufficient to test out all the logical possibilities inherent in her theory. It is, perhaps, embarrassing that she jumped to conclusions unwarranted by a strict evaluation of the comparative evidence, but it is hardly fatal for the method she espouses. A historical sociologist working on a somewhat more common phenomenon could surely devise more adequate empirical tests. (See, e.g., Paige [1978], who statistically analyzed a large number of cases of agrarian revolts.) Of course, limiting ourselves to more tractable phenomena would save the comparative method only at a very high cost, inasmuch as it would restrict sociology's ability to say anything valid about rare but world-shaping events like social revolutions. At best, the evidence and arguments presented in *States and Social Revolutions* hardly justifies Skocpol's confidence that comparative historical analysis is a panacea for sociologists working on problems where "there are too many variables and not enough cases" (Skocpol 1979, 36).

Nor do Skocpol's logical difficulties end here. The most troubling flaws of quasi-experimental comparative method come not from the difficulty of amassing enough cases, which affects only some research problems, but from the unhistorical assumptions about temporality that strict adherence to experimental logic requires. The experimental conception of temporality, I shall argue, is inseparable from conventional comparative method, and it can be imposed only by what Burawoy aptly dubs "freezing history"—and, I would extend the metaphor, by fracturing the congealed block of historical time into artificially interchangeable units.

In order for Skocpol's revolutions to be subjected to her comparative method, they must be conceptualized as analogous to separate "trials" of an experiment. This means that the trials must be both equivalent and independent. The principle of equivalence implies that each new trial (in this case, new revolution) be a genuine replication of earlier trials, with all relevant variables held constant. This implies definite assumptions about temporality. The relevant temporality in experimental logic is purely internal to the trial: the posited causal factors must exist prior to their posited consequence. By contrast, the external temporality of historical time—whether one trial precedes or follows another and by how much—must, by definition, be considered irrelevant in order to meet the requirement that experimental trials be strictly equivalent.

This requirement that trials be equivalent poses considerable difficulty for Skocpol's arguments about the causes of social revolutions. In order to use inductive comparison, Skocpol must assume that her three great social revolutions are in fact a uniform class of objects governed by identical causal laws. But this is a highly dubious assumption, in part because new classes and new class relations arise over time. This, in turn, might well alter the conditions necessary and sufficient for social revolution. To take a pertinent example, the Industrial Revolution intervened between the French Revolution and the Russian Revolution, giving rise to a new industrial proletariat. One might consequently assert, with some plausibility, that the revolt of the Petersburg and Moscow proletariat was a necessary condition for social revolution in Russia in 1917, even if it was not a condition in France in 1789. But, as Burawoy points out, Skocpol cannot consider this possibility without breaking the crucial assumption of equivalence between the revolutions. Thus, instead of examining empirical evidence about the role of the industrial proletariat in Russia, she dismisses the possibility out of hand on the grounds that because a proletarian revolt was not necessary in her other two cases it cannot have been necessary in Russia either (Burawoy 1989, 769; Skocpol 1979, 113). The assumption of equivalence, which is a logical foundation of Skocpol's comparative method, does not allow her to pursue questions about how events intervening between revolutions might affect their occurrence and outcome.[8]

The second fundamental assumption of experimental logic, that experimental trials must be independent of one another, also poses serious problems for Skocpol's analysis. For trials to be independent, the outcome of any given trial must have no effect on the outcome of a subsequent trial.[9] But it is absurd to assume that earlier revolutions had no influence on later revolutions. After all, the leadership of the Bolshevik party self-consciously patterned its own revolutionary efforts on what it regarded as the lessons of the French Revolution, and the Chinese communists not only modeled themselves explicitly on the Bolsheviks but received direct aid from them. Once again, this assumption can only be sustained by "freezing" and "fracturing" history, by treating the histories of the three revolutions as if they took place in isolation from one another rather than as a sequence of historically connected events. In short, Skocpol's comparisons are fundamentally deficient logically if viewed from the perspective of experimental method. They fail both the requirement of equivalence and the requirement of independence.

Although it may occasionally be possible to identify a universe of historical objects that simultaneously satisfies the assumptions of equivalence and independence, such occasions are likely to be unusual. With rare exceptions, attempts to assure equivalence in historical cases will actually result in decreasing the independence between cases—and vice versa. The obvious way to assure independence is to compare phenomena that are widely separated in space and time. One can be reasonably sure, for example, that similarities between royal ceremonies in eighteenth-century Japan and ancient Mesopotamia cannot be accounted for by imitation. But the very remoteness that assures independence makes the assumption of equivalence impossible to sustain. In societies with radically different economies, systems of social stratification, religious beliefs, conceptions of gender, and so on, how could we ever be confident that the relevant differences have been controlled for?

It was for precisely this reason that Marc Bloch, in his seminal article on comparative history, cautioned against studying "societies so widely separated in time and space that any analogies observed between them . . . can obviously not be explained either by mutual influence or by a common origin" (Bloch 1967, 46).[10] Bloch believed that such comparisons were too imprecise and therefore opted for a parallel study of societies that are at once neighboring and contemporary, exercising a constant mutual influence, exposed throughout their development to the action of the same broad causes, and owing their existence in part to a common origin. Bloch preferred comparisons of neighboring societies essentially on the grounds that in such societies the assumption of equivalence could reasonably be approximated (Bloch 1967, 47). I suspect that Bloch, as usual, made the wiser choice. But his choice obviously moves comparative history further from the no less logically necessary assumption of independence between the cases. Because the societies Bloch studied exercised a "constant mutual influence" on one another, it is extraordinarily difficult to determine whether a similar outcome in two cases resulted from a posited set of internal causal factors or from the play of influence. With rare exceptions, equivalence between historical cases is bought only at the price of decreasing independence, and vice versa. This paradox, I submit, makes history a singularly unpromising territory for the kind of rigorous experimental induction that Skocpol advocates, but cannot really practice, in *States and Social Revolutions*.

It is remarkable, in view of the logical and empirical failure of Skocpol's program of experimental induction, that her analysis of social revolutions remains so powerful and convincing. This implies that, as was true of both Wallerstein and Tilly as well, something important and valuable is accomplished in the book that remains unvoiced in its explicit theoretical and methodological statements.[11] I would contend that much of this unvoiced work occurs in her handling of events. The bulk of her book is composed not of a rigorous weighing of comparative evidence but of carefully constructed causal narratives specifying how social revolutions are brought about in her three cases. Skocpol's best statement of her narrative strategy is, symptomatically, tucked away in a footnote, where she complains that "social-scientific analyses of revolutions almost *never* . . . give sufficient analytic weight to the conjunctural, unfolding interactions of originally separately determined processes" (Skocpol 1979, 320, emphasis in original).

Specifying the "conjunctural, unfolding interactions of originally separately determined processes" is the distinctive narrative strategy of her book. It is distinct not only from the usual strategy of sociologists but from the usual strategy of historians as well. Sociological analyses of revolutions tend to emphasize the primacy of some single cause of revolutions, systematically subordinating other causes to the chosen explanatory factor. Historical analyses typically attempt to recount the course of a revolution in some semblance of its original complexity, discussing different causal features of the revolutionary process only as they make themselves felt in the unfolding of the story. The problem with the historical strategy is that crucial causal processes tend to get lost in a muddle of narrative detail and are seldom separated out enough to make their autonomous dynamics clear. The trouble with the sociological strategy is that although it successfully specifies the causal dynamics of one factor, it tends either to conflate other causal factors with the chosen cause (as Marxian treatments of revolution have often viewed the state as merely an expression of class power) or to treat them as mere background (as most studies of revolution have done with the international military setting). Skocpol's strategy is an inspired compromise. It appropriates the power of the sociological strategy but applies it to not one but several distinct causal processes. Yet by emphasizing "conjunctural, unfolding interactions" it also appropriates the historical strategy's concern with events, sequence, and contingency. Quite apart from considerations of comparative experimental induction, Skocpol has elaborated in *States and Social Revolutions* an extremely effective strategy for what might be dubbed multiple causal narrative.[12] She has, to put it differently, worked out a kind of incipient theory of revolutionary process, of how events, by straining or rearranging structures, open the door to further transformative events. But this significant rhetorical and theoretical innovation is never signaled in her introduction or conclusion and is only formulated in passing in a footnote in the third chapter. Skocpol's misplaced obsession with quasi-experimental comparative method has virtually obscured her highly original contribution to eventful sociology.

Skocpol's formal comparative method, with its experimental conception of temporality, makes little contribution to her innovations in eventful sociology. Nevertheless, I believe that serious comparative thinking played a crucial role in developing her incipient theory of revolutionary process. The formal logic of comparative method has been developed exclusively as a means of assessing the empirical accuracy of theoretical propositions—to deal with the phase of scientific research that Lakatos has termed the "context of justification." I suspect, however, that the most important role of comparison in *States and Social Revolutions* was actually in the "context of discovery"—that phase of research concerned with generating theoretical ideas. Skocpol's own description of the history of her project suggests as much. She began, she tells us, with the history of the Chinese Revolution, then found that the Chinese developments suggested unsuspected analogies with the French case and finally used an analytic scheme worked out from the Chinese and French cases to interpret Russian history (Skocpol 1979, xii–xiii). One suspects that this mutual reading of each of the cases in terms of the others continued and kept spiraling back, that, for example, Trotsky's emphasis on backward Russia's unsuccessful military competition with the European powers must have suggested parallels in the crisis of the French old regime or that Georges Lefebvre's analyses of the crucial contribution of aristocratic resistance and peasant revolts to the French Revolution must have thrown a sharp light on the roles of landlords and peasants in Russia and China (Trotsky 1960; Lefebvre [1949] 1971, 1973).

I suspect that Skocpol formulated and deepened her interpretations of key revolutionary events by just such a process of critically extending narratives from each of the cases to each of the others. A rough causal logic certainly guided such analogical extensions: if attempts to reform the sprawling agrarian state of Imperial Russia arose in response to the threat of German military prowess, is it not likely that comparable attempts to reform a roughly similar French state might have arisen from repeated defeats at the hands of England? But Skocpol's presentation of comparative method as a means of testing already formulated general propositions gets it the wrong way around. It would be more accurate to say that comparison generated propositions whose potential generality was tested by their ability to illuminate the conjunctural unfolding of analogous causal processes in the three cases. Had the crucial question really been whether Skocpol's posited causes were present or absent in an array of cases, there would have been no need to write a long book; a brief article with a few simple tables would have sufficed. What persuades Skocpol's reader is not the formal logic of a tabular array. It is the fact that all three revolutions can be narrated convincingly in terms of the operation of analogous causal processes, which in practice means above all that narratives based on these analogies make sense of numerous details that otherwise would seem purely accidental. The "proof" is less in the formal logic than in the successful narrative ordering of circumstantial detail. The true payoff of Skocpol's comparative history, then, is not the rigorous testing of abstract generalizations but the discovery of analogies on which new and convincing narratives of eventful sequences can be constructed.[13]

Eventful Temporality

Eventful temporality recognizes the power of events in history. Social life may be conceptualized as being composed of countless happenings or encounters in which persons and groups of persons engage in social action. Their actions are constrained and enabled by the constitutive structures of their societies. Most happenings reproduce social and cultural structures without significant changes (Giddens 1984; Sewell 1992). Events may be defined as that relatively rare subclass of happenings that significantly transform structures. An eventful conception of temporality, therefore, is one that takes into account the transformation of structures by events.

The eventful conception can be clarified by its contrasts with the experimental and teleological conceptions. The experimental conception rests on two fundamental assumptions: a uniformity of causal laws across time and a causal independence of every sequence of occurrences from previous and subsequent occurrences. The eventful conception of temporality denies both of these assumptions. Rather than assuming causal independence through time, it assumes that events are normally "path dependent," that is, that what has happened at an earlier point in time will affect the possible outcomes of a sequence of events occurring at a later point in time. However, path dependence does not necessarily imply that causal structures change over time. In fact, the notion of path dependence was initially formalized by economists, who argued, for example, that different but equally rational choices among alternative technologies at one point in time would imply a divergence in choices at later times even under the standard economists' causal assumption that all actors at all points in time pursue their advantage rationally (Arthur 1988). A fully eventful conception of temporality must also deny the assumption that causal structures are uniform through time. Events must be assumed to be capable of changing not only the balance of causal forces operating but the very logic by which consequences follow from occurrences or circumstances. A fully eventful account of the fate of nobles in the French Revolution, for example, would have to argue that nobles lost power not only because the loss of some of their assets—land, tax privileges, feudal dues, offices—reduced their resources relative to those of other classes but also because the rules of the social and political game were radically redefined, making what had previously been a prime asset—their noble status—into a powerful liability by the time of the Terror. In this case and, I would argue, in general events bring about historical changes in part by transforming the very cultural categories that shape and constrain human action. Because the causalities that operate in social relations depend at least in part on the contents and relations of cultural categories, events have the power to transform social causality.[14]

An eventful concept of temporality, then, assumes a causal dependence of later occurrences on prior occurrences and assumes that social causality is temporally heterogeneous, not temporally uniform. Eventful temporality therefore differs fundamentally from experimental temporality. It also differs from teleological temporality. Teleological and eventful temporality share an assumption of path dependence, but teleological temporality denies temporal heterogeneity or at least general temporal heterogeneity. (Stage theories, one of the subtypes of teleological theories, assume causal homogeneity within stages but may accept radical heterogeneity between stages.) However, teleological and eventful concepts of temporality differ most sharply on the question of contingency. Teleological temporality is compatible with a certain contingency at the surface of social relations, but it is incompatible with the assumption of radical contingency that I regard as fundamental to eventful temporality. For example, a teleological Marxian account might argue that the particular situation in which a conflict between workers and bourgeois occurs may affect the outcome of their struggle and may even result in a local victory for a retrograde form of social organization, say, for handicraft over factory production. But no combination of such local victories can "turn back the clock" definitively. The built-in directionality of underlying causal forces guarantees that local variations are mere surface perturbations with no long-term effect on the course of history.

By contrast, an eventful concept of temporality assumes that contingency is global, that it characterizes not only the surface but the core or the depths of social relations. Contingent, unexpected, and inherently unpredictable events, this view assumes, can undo or alter the most apparently durable trends of history. This does not, of course, imply that human societies are in permanent and universal flux, that social change is easy to accomplish, or that historical changes display no regularities. I am not arguing that capitalism or the global division of labor or sexual inequality would go away if only we wished it or that history is a tale told by an idiot. History displays both stubborn durabilities and sudden breaks, and even the most radical historical ruptures are interlaced with remarkable continuities. To say that events are transformations of structures implies precisely that the structures that emerge from an event are always transformations of preexisting structures, hence that they are both continuous with and different from previous structures. An assumption of global contingency means not that everything is constantly changing but that nothing in social life is ultimately immune to change.

The eventful conception of temporality, then, assumes that social relations are characterized by path dependency, temporally heterogeneous causalities, and global contingency. This is close to the implicit intellectual baggage of most academic historians. Yet most historians take the effectivity of events so much for granted that their accounts of events tend to lack a theoretical edge. Marshall Sahlins, citing Ruth Benedict's aphorism that if deep-sea fish could speak the last thing they would name is water, points out that historians "live in the narrative element" and consequently are remarkably unself-conscious about the event as a theoretical category (Sahlins 1991, 15). My own experience testifies to this dictum. Even as a "social historian" critical of old-fashioned "narrative history," I too swam in the narrative element. It was only sustained encounters with sociological and anthropological discourse, much of it undertaken as a member of an academic sociology department, that made me recognize events as a category in need of theoretical work.

Sociologists, even those whose work contains exemplary analyses of events, are by and large equally unconscious of the event as a theoretical category—as the writings of Wallerstein, Tilly, and Skocpol testify. There are, however, some whose work clearly demonstrates in practice the profound significance of events. In the remainder of this essay I will analyze two such works: *Armies of the Poor* by Mark Traugott (1985) and *Reds or Rackets?* by Howard Kimeldorf (1988). I do not think that either Traugott or Kimeldorf makes much progress toward elaborating the event as a theoretical category. But both of them deploy the highly developed methodological consciousness typical even of nonmainstream sociologists to demonstrate to skeptical readers that events mattered crucially in the cases they are investigating. Although their work does not itself develop a theoretical argument about events, it can be used to develop and illustrate such an argument.

Traugott's Organizational Hypothesis

Traugott's book may be characterized as a study of the differential effect of a great event, the French Revolution of 1848, on two groups of French workers: those enrolled in the government's unemployment relief organization, the National Workshops, who formed the core of the great workers' revolt of June 1848, and those recruited into the paramilitary Mobile Guard, who were instrumental in suppressing it. Traugott's task is to explain why workers associated with these two organizations wound up on opposite sides of the barricades. The leading explanation of their divergent political trajectories has been Marx's. Marx claimed that the Mobile Guard had no scruples about shooting down the proletarian insurrectionaries because it had been recruited exclusively from the rootless *lumpenproletariat,* the scum of the urban poor. Traugott spends much of his book—and doubtless spent even more of his research time—subjecting this argument to a painstaking quantitative test, which shows that the pre-February occupations of the June rebels and the Guardsmen were in fact virtually identical (Traugott 1985, 67–77). The divergent political behavior of Guards and Workshop members cannot be explained by differences in their class backgrounds.

The failure of this standard sociological explanation led Traugott to what he calls the "organizational hypothesis"—that the divergent actions of guardsmen and insurrectionaries were the result not of characteristics of their pre-1848 lives but of their collective experiences between February and June 1848 (Traugott 1985, 83). Traugott tests this hypothesis by means of a "paired comparison" of the organizational histories of the Mobile Guard and the National Workshops. There are many parallels between the two institutions: both were improvised in response to working-class pressures after the February Revolution, and both were intended by the Provisional Government simultaneously to be a means for alleviating unemployment and for co-opting potentially rebellious workers so as to moderate their political sentiments (Traugott 1985, 115). Moreover, both institutions were deeply mistrusted by the conservative bourgeoisie, which feared they would become hotbeds of socialist agitation. By means of his paired comparison, Traugott shows that both were initially highly successful co-optive institutions and that the National Workshops became a nursery of rebellion only when they were organizationally decapitated by a hostile government.

Traugott's organizational analysis borrows from Katherine Chorley's *Armies and the Art of Revolution* (1943). By April of 1848 the initially ragtag Mobile Guard had met Chorley's three crucial conditions for successful military repression of a revolutionary movement: a unified corps of officers, effective isolation from the civilian population, and prompt attention to practical grievances in the ranks. The Mobile Guard's officer corps was supplied by the regular army and supplemented by carefully managed elections from the ranks. By April it became a highly professional and unified body. The guardsmen were isolated from the civilian population because they were housed in barracks, usually not in their own neighborhoods. One practical grievance—a long delay in the provision of uniforms—seriously threatened to undermine the guardsmen's morale, but it was resolved well before June. Hence the potentially unruly Mobile Guard was molded into a disciplined military force that was willing to face down fellow workers in several confrontations in April and May—and to shoot them down when the insurrection broke out in June (Traugott 1985, 86–113).

Although the National Workshops were not a military force, Traugott uses Chorley's model in his analysis of their organizational history as well. The Workshops were actually organized on a military model—with squads, brigades, and companies and a uniformed officer corps. Emile Thomas, the youthful director of the Workshops, assured the unity of his officer corps by recruiting its upper echelons from students at a national engineering school of which he was an alumnus. Lower-level officers were chosen by election from the ranks but subjected to close administrative supervision. The unified officer corps not only enabled Thomas to maintain firm administrative control of the Workshops but contributed to his personal popularity in the ranks. Thomas was less successful in his efforts to overcome practical grievances—mainly because the Workshops were never supplied with enough meaningful work to occupy their full contingent of unemployed laborers (about 120,000 by June). Nor could members of the Workshops be separated fully from the general population—they made up about a third of the working class of Paris and continued to live in their own neighborhoods. But Thomas did his best, insisting that members report to their brigades every day, whether they had work or not, and posting them to peripheral locations when there were demonstrations or political troubles. He also established a National Workshops political club, attempting with considerable success to isolate Workshop members from the political clubs of their neighborhoods (Traugott 1985, 148–65).

This surprisingly effective isolation, together with the unity of the officer corps and Thomas's personal popularity, assured the Workshops' political moderation until nearly the end of May and might have done so indefinitely had the government not decided to sack Thomas and phase out the Workshops. This drove the elected squad and brigade leaders to the left, released them from the political and organizational tutelage of Thomas and his loyal schoolmates, and transformed them from conduits of moderation into a revolutionary cadre (Traugott 1985, 165–68). When the full destruction of the Workshops was announced on June 21, they led their squads and brigades in armed revolt. In short, members of the National Workshops and the Mobile Guard took opposite sides in June not because of divergent class backgrounds but because of the divergent organizational histories of the two institutions in the course of political events.

Traugott justifiably concludes that the "organizational hypothesis" best explains the observed behavior. But the term *organizational hypothesis,* in my opinion, does not capture adequately the nature of Traugott's theoretical argument. The term implies that the organizational hypothesis is just another sociological hypothesis, that he is simply asking his reader to consider another explanatory factor parallel to class background, income, religious preference, or cohort. In fact, he is asking for something much more radical: that sociologists entertain a new and essentially eventful form of explanatory argument. The organizational explanation of why the National Workshops rebelled and the Mobile Guard put down the rebellion is a causal narrative of how these institutions were shaped through time, and it has a characteristically eventful temporality. It incorporates path dependency: the timing of incidents crucially affects their consequences. The fact that the Mobile Guard's deeply felt grievance about lack of uniforms had been rectified well before June assured the Guard's loyalty to the government. Had a revolt broken out before the resolution of this grievance it is uncertain whether the Guard would have followed orders to march against fellow workers. Traugott's temporality is also causally heterogeneous. Consider the role of the Workshops' squad and brigade leaders, who formed the leadership cadre of the insurrection. Their positions of leadership were produced by Emile Thomas's paternalist strategy of cultivating their personal and political loyalties and integrating them tightly into the

Workshops' officer corps. This paternalism had the intended effects of assuring the moderation of the Workshop members as long as Thomas and his schoolmates ran the organization. But when Thomas was sacked, the squad and brigade leaders were also in position to organize the rank and file's resistance to the closing of the Workshops, by armed revolt if necessary. Paradoxically, the organizational structure erected by Thomas to ensure the workers' moderation had the effect of exacerbating the crisis when it came. In brief, the creation of this working-class organizational infrastructure changed the causal dynamics of the situation, greatly amplifying the extent, intensity, and effectiveness of resistance to the government's closing of the Workshops.

It should be clear that the temporality of Traugott's account is interlaced with contingency. Like classical narrative historians, Traugott emphasizes the importance of significant persons. The Workshops were organized as they were largely because of the personal decisions of Emile Thomas, and his removal from the directorship was a decisive cause of their radicalization. A forceful and magnetic person like Thomas, placed in a position of strategic importance, can have a remarkable effect on the course of history. Conscious choice also figures importantly in Traugott's account. Thomas purposely drew his officer corps from his schoolmates so as to enhance its solidarity. The conservative government purposely provoked a crisis by abolishing the Workshops. For all these reasons, the course of the events Traugott analyzes is contingent, not necessary. Had the government maintained the Workshops in existence and kept Thomas as their director, the insurrection might never have happened. Had someone less capable been chosen as director, the revolt would probably have been less effective, but it might well have happened considerably earlier.

Traugott's embrace of eventful temporality does not mean that he has abandoned sociology for narrative history. He is driven to eventful explanation by the austere logic of his sociological method, and he carefully specifies the structural limits within which timing, personality, choice, and contingency operate. Although he comes down in this case for eventful rather than etiological explanations, he does so not to dismiss etiological factors but to specify their mode of effectuation. Class, as he points out, may have an influence, but "any class-based propensities of actors are conditioned by a set of contingent organizational forces" (Traugott 1985, 184). He is arguing not that history is a sequence of pure contingencies but that "an intervening [I would add eventful] level of analysis must demonstrate by what mechanisms macrosociological structures are converted into forms of consciousness and the probability of collective action" (Traugott 1985, 189). Traugott's book, with its careful methodology and its focus on the relationship between structures and events, points the way toward an *eventful* sociology that remains an eventful *sociology*.

Kimeldorf's Multiple Registers of Causation

Kimeldorf's book is a study of the divergent political evolution of longshoremen's unions in New York City and on the West Coast from the 1930s through the 1950s. Kimeldorf, like Traugott, uses a strategy of paired comparison, combines narrative history with structural analysis, and provides powerful arguments for the significance of events in the shaping of workers' politics. Kimeldorf attempts to explain why East Coast and West Coast dockworkers, who did similar work under similar technological and economic conditions, nevertheless formed sharply contrasting labor unions, the durably socialist International Longshoremen's and Warehousemen's Union (ILWU) on the West Coast and the politically conservative and chronically racket-ridden International Longshoremen's Association (ILA) on the East Coast.

Kimeldorf's explanation of the difference between the New York and West Coast unions is complex, multicausal, and irreducibly historical. He shows that the differences cannot be attributed to any single, underlying factor, and that their historical roots go back well before the 1930s. The explanatory factors are of several different types. First, the recruitment and the cultures of the labor forces differed substantially. A high proportion of the West Coast longshoremen were recruited from the lumbering and seafaring industries, which because of their work structures very commonly give rise to high levels of worker solidarity and class conflict, and certainly did so on the American West Coast in the early twentieth century. This labor force, whose prior work experience already inclined it to labor militancy, was widely but only temporarily organized by the radical Industrial Workers of the World (IWW) in the 1910s and 1920s. By the 1930s West Coast dockworkers already had been exposed to a radical work culture that made them ready to heed Harry Bridges's call (Kimeldorf 1988, 20–37). These predisposing factors were entirely absent among the New York dockworkers, where the labor force was recruited from two successive peasant immigrant groups, the Irish and Italians, who, by the 1930s, had established ethnically divided enclaves on the docks. Moreover, the political and work culture was far more conservative, dominated by the Catholic Church in the case of the Irish and by an exploitative (sometimes Mafia-ridden) padrone system in that of the Italians (Kimeldorf 1988, 37–50).

These differences in labor recruitment were reinforced by differences in the ecology of the shipping business and consequently in the class capacities of shipping capitalists. On the West Coast, three American companies dominated the carrying trade and were consequently able to carry on a particularly ferocious and ultimately radicalizing battle against longshore unions. In New York, the carrying trade was divided between a larger number of American and European companies and a large government-owned line. This divided employer class was unable to sustain a unified front against longshore unions, and the companies therefore negotiated separate deals with different union locals (Kimeldorf 1988, 60–75). There were consequently structural factors of a demographic, cultural, and economic nature that made radical unionism more likely on the West Coast than in New York.

But while these structural factors might have been sufficient to rule out radical unionism on the New York docks, they were hardly sufficient to guarantee it on the West Coast. In a chapter entitled "The Strategic Pivot," Kimeldorf moves from relatively stable structural conditions to more contingent conjunctural and volitional causes. The conjuncture, largely shared by the two coasts, was the Depression and the new political climate and nationwide labor militancy it engendered. But the radical potential of this period was seized successfully on the West Coast and missed in New York largely because of the very different strategies of the two areas' Communist Parties. In San Francisco, which became the center of radical longshore unionism, the local Communists ignored the national party's strategy of supporting separate left-wing unions, opting to develop a leftist force within the existing moderate union instead. The consequence was that the Communists and allied left-wingers such as Bridges were in a position to assume leadership in the dramatic and violent strike of 1934 and move the rank and file definitively to the left (Kimeldorf 1988, 81–92). By contrast, the New York party stuck obstinately to an utterly unsuccessful policy of separate left unionism and was thereby deprived of any chance to play a radicalizing role in the New York strike movements of the same year (Kimeldorf 1988, 92–7). Finally, the dramatic radicalization of the West Coast union was rendered enduring by the cultural codification of the "Big Strike" and "Bloody Thursday" (July 5, 1934), which was embodied in a highly self-conscious cohort of " '34 men" who remained a solid block of support for the leftist leadership right through the 1950s and whose prestige among the rank and file created a pervasively leftist and militant work culture on the docks (Kimeldorf 1988, 100–110).

Kimeldorf's book, as I read it, provides a potentially generalizable model of explanation or interpretation in historical sociology, but that model remains largely implicit rather than theoretically voiced. The implicit model not only specifies multiple causes but sorts out what might be characterized as different registers of causation: preexisting structural conditions (cultural, social, demographic, and economic); conjunctural conditions (such as the generalized labor militancy of the 1930s); and contingent strategic or volitional actions. In certain respects, this recapitulates Fernand Braudel's distinction between three different types of histories based on three different scales of duration: structural history, associated with the study of geological, geographic, social, and mental structures that change only glacially; conjunctural history, associated with the study of economic and demographic cycles with durations of decades rather than centuries; and eventful history, associated with what he tended to regard as the ephemera of politics and to disdain as mere froth on the waves of history (Braudel 1958, 1966). Although the time scales of Braudel's and Kimeldorf's histories are very different, both schemes tackle the crucial question of sorting out social processes with very different temporal rhythms. But whereas Braudel's histories remain in their own distinct causal universes, Kimeldorf's registers of causation are brought together in the event, where the action of human subjects can reconfigure preexisting structures and conjunctures—by, for example, forming the solid block of influential '34 men who maintained the leftism of the ILWU. Theorized as I have advocated here, Kimeldorf's account suggests a way of joining structure, conjuncture, and events in a common causal universe, one that centers on acting human subjects.

Kimeldorf's discussion of how the Big Strike and the '34 men attained mythic stature raises another important theoretical issue, but once again the issue is not clearly voiced (Kimeldorf 1988, 109–10). The myth of the Big Strike arose in part from the actions of '34 men, who continually reasserted a moral authority within the union. But the cult of '34 was also fostered by official union policy, which prescribed annual work stoppages on July 5 to commemorate the union's formative battle. The Big Strike, in other words, not only was an objectively important event in the formation of a radical union but was also constructed as a subjectively important event by the radical union in subsequent months and years. This issue, which Kimeldorf discusses almost in passing, actually raises two fundamental theoretical points about events. First, Kimeldorf's account implies that the question of how events are retrospectively appropriated to institute and reproduce structures is just as important for historical sociology as the question of how conjunctures and strategic action make transformative events possible in the first place.[15] Second, the case of the '34 men shows that events transform structures largely by constituting and empowering new groups of actors or by reempowering existing groups in new ways.

An Eventful Sociology?

Traugott and Kimeldorf have written exemplary historical sociologies in the eventful mode. The temporalities sketched out in their books are path dependent, causally heterogeneous, and contingent, and reconfiguration of structures by social action is at the core of their explanatory models. Their books stand as an implicit challenge not only to mainstream sociology but also to mainstream historical sociology. But the challenge remains all too implicit. Although the theoretical modesty of these books is one of their most attractive rhetorical features, it nevertheless has limited their impact by causing them to be classified as little gems of sociological craftsmanship rather than as field-transforming blockbusters. My effort in this essay has been to point out the largely unvoiced theoretical implications of these books and to show why their arguments actually constitute a deeper challenge to the reigning "scientific" orthodoxy of sociology than those of the far more assertive historical sociologists who work in the teleological and experimental modes.

Eventful sociology of the sort produced by Traugott and Kimeldorf challenges the "scientific" orthodoxy on several fundamental questions. It implicitly suggests that sociology's epic quest for social laws is illusory, whether the search is for timeless truths about all societies, ineluctable trends of more limited historical epochs, or inductively derived laws of certain classes of social phenomena. Social processes, it implies, are inherently contingent, discontinuous, and open-ended. Big and ponderous social processes are never entirely immune from being transformed by small alterations in volatile and local social processes. "Structures" are constructed by human action, and "societies" or "social formations" or "social systems" are continually shaped and reshaped by the creativity and stubbornness of their human creators.

All of this implies that adequate eventful accounts of social processes will look more like well-made stories or narratives than like laws of physics. An eventful historical sociology would come to resemble history ever more closely. It is worth noting, in this connection, that both Traugott's and Kimeldorf's books read much like works by social historians. Traditionally, historical sociologists have regarded historians as useful drones more than as genuine intellectual collaborators. Historians would do the tedious work of collecting archival data and producing narratives; historical sociologists would utilize the narratives as raw material for their grander and more theoretically sophisticated analyses. The current generation of historical sociologists has already followed historians into the archives. If they are to construct an eventful sociology, they will increasingly have to look to historians and their narratives for theoretical inspiration as well.

Yet if historical sociology should be involved in more and deeper conversations with history, it will almost certainly continue to be recognizable as sociology. It is important to note that Traugott's and Kimeldorf's narratives and my theorizations of them retain sociology's traditional concern with cause. This is so even if they inflect the usage of cause and causality from the highly abstract and generalizing conceptualizations common in "scientific" sociology toward their more singular and contingent usages in ordinary speech, where giving a causal account of something usually means telling a story about how it came to be. Traugott's and Kimeldorf's work shows that a concern with causal regularities of a recognizably sociological sort is crucial to elaborating a convincing narrative of why things happened as they did. Without Traugott's careful quantitative test of the etiological explanation of differences between the Workshops and the Guards his eventful explanation in terms of organizational histories would have been merely plausible rather than compelling. And Kimeldorf's analysis of the structural differences between the East and West Coast shipping industries and of the different social origins of East and West Coast dockworkers establishes the ground on which the different strategies of organizers operated. The accounts elaborated by both Traugott and Kimeldorf combine diverse causal registers and diverse temporal rhythms. They continue to use conventional structural or etiological strategies of explanation, but these strategies are subsumed in their work within a larger eventful explanatory framework.

This selective appropriation of conventional sociological arguments and methods seems to me to be the proper strategy. I believe that historical sociology—perhaps sociology as a whole—should be remade in an eventful mode, and I believe that such a remaking would constitute a radical departure from current practices. But I also believe that a reconfiguration of sociology could only succeed by appropriating and subsuming existing modes of sociological analysis, just as Traugott and Kimeldorf appropriate and subsume structural and etiological causality. In this spirit, I have tried, in my own critiques of Wallerstein, Tilly, and Skocpol, to show that adopting an eventful approach would not require jettisoning all works that have employed teleological or experimental conceptions of temporality. Instead, I have tried to show how classical teleological and experimental studies might be rethought, seeking out the valuable eventful analyses that have up to now been masked by misconstrued scientific rhetoric. I think we need to rehabilitate such works as

The Modern World System, The Vendée, and *States and Social Revolutions* as rhetorically flawed masterworks of eventful sociology. Likewise, rather than rejecting comparative method, we need to strip it of inappropriate scientific rhetoric and rethink it as a means of theorizing causal narratives through looping contexts of discovery.

The construction of an eventful sociology will require a collective rethinking of the discipline by many scholars. Success in this venture, in my opinion, will hinge on a closer intellectual collaboration of sociologists with historians, anthropologists, political scientists, and others who are themselves engaged in parallel rethinkings.[16] Moreover, we might find assistance in surprising quarters within sociology as well. Charles Tilly has recently published an article in which his central case for historical sociology rests on one of the central claims of the eventful view of temporality, that "social processes are path dependent" (Tilly 1988, 710). In another, he argues that the contingent political struggles of the French Revolution resulted in a fundamental transformation of the French state from indirect to direct means of government and that this innovation was spread to Europe as a whole by French successes in revolutionary and Napoleonic warfare—a classic case of big and general consequences arising from local and particular events (Tilly 1989). And Immanuel Wallerstein has recently written an extremely radical and open-ended call for an "unthinking of the nineteenth century"—in other words, of the deeply held assumptions about social process that we have inherited from the nineteenth century. Although he does not include teleology as one of the assumptions that needs to be unthought, he does include "science itself" and our preference for "elegant sparse laws" over "complex, dense interpretive schema" (Wallerstein 1988, 191). These recent statements suggest that we may ourselves be in the midst of an event in the history of historical sociology, one that could reconfigure previous structures of thought in the field—in the midst, in short, of a historic turn within sociology's historic turn.

NOTES

I am grateful to Nick Dirks, Larry Griffen, and Sherry Ortner for valuable comments on earlier versions of this essay. I would also like to thank my friends and colleagues in the Program on the Comparative Study of Social Transformations (CSST) at the University of Michigan, whose ongoing debates and intellectual companionship made this essay possible. This essay was completed while I was a fellow at the Center for Advanced Study in the Behavioral Sciences. I am grateful for financial support provided by the

National Science Foundation (grant number BNS-870064) and by a fellowship from the John Simon Guggenheim Memorial Foundation. The essay has had an eventful pre-publication history. In 1991, it was awarded a prize as the best recent article in comparative historical sociology by the Comparative Historical Sociology Section of the American Sociological Association. (The following year the section wisely limited the competition to articles already published.) More remarkably, in 1994 the still unpublished essay was subjected to a lengthy and vitriolic attack by Theda Skocpol in the concluding chapter of her collected essays on revolutions (Skocpol, 1994). It is with some relief that I finally present this work to the public.

1. My contention that sociology's historic turn had its origin in a particular moment of domestic and world politics is corroborated by the fact that the work of such liberal historical sociologists as Reinhard Bendix (1956, 1964) and Neil Smelser (1959) has had far less influence on the current generation than that of Moore, Tilly, and Wallerstein. For an interesting autobiographical account of the impact of 1960s politics on a young sociologist, see Theda Skocpol (1988-89).

2. I owe the "left Weberian" tag to Terry Boswell. At the beginning of its existence, the Comparative Historical Sociology section of the ASA was explicitly Weberian in its orientation. Beginning in 1983, a new group of scholars seized control of the section and pointed it in the direction of macropolitical sociology of the nation-state. It should be noted that some of the remaining sections of the ASA, especially those devoted to political sociology and cultural sociology, include many sociologists who do historical work.

3. Recent exceptions to sociologists' silence about this issue include Abbott (1988, 1991), Hall (1984), Aminzade (1992), and Griffin (1992, 1993).

4. The term *eventful* is an anglicization of the French *événementiel*. The term *histoire événementielle* was used widely by French historians of the *Annales* school, but it is particularly associated with Fernand Braudel, who contrasted *histoire événementielle* with *histoire structurelle* and *histoire conjoncturelle* (Braudel 1958, 1966). For Braudel, *histoire événementielle* was largely a term of abuse. My attempt to rehabilitate the term follows Marshall Sahlins (1991). I have, however, anglicized the word differently than has Sahlins, whose *evenemential* seems to me distinctly non-English.

5. Sometimes the judgments embodied in the usage of the backward-forward-looking dichotomy are moral rather than merely anachronistic, with "forward-looking" meaning that which all "progressives" should favor and "backward-looking" meaning that which they should abhor. Least common is the literal and in my opinion quite acceptable usage that would designate as "backward-looking" only those movements that explicitly pattern themselves on what they regard as a past historical condition and as "forward-looking" those that pattern their actions on an imagined future. The dichotomy has, however, been so spoiled by teleological usages that employing it literally for such supposedly "forward-looking" but actually backward-looking movements as the Renaissance or such supposedly "backward-looking" but actually forward-looking movements as early utopian socialism would merely breed confusion.

6. Tilly's terminology shifted more than once over the nearly two decades he devoted to this project, but the underlying categorization of violence has remained essentially constant. For a fuller discussion, see Sewell (1990).

7. Conscience dictates that I attribute this felicitous term to Carl Schorske, who applied it to the ever rising bourgeoisie in a lecture on European intellectual history which I heard as a graduate student at Berkeley in the 1960s.

8. This unwillingness to consider intervening events also gets her into muddy water in her discussion of why the French Revolution consolidated private property when the Russian and Chinese revolutions abolished it (see Sewell 1985, 59).

9. For example, if performing an experiment on the effects of fertilizer on corn yields increases the concentration of helpful soil bacteria on a plot of land, a second trial on that plot will not be independent of the first because the fact that a prior trial has been carried out there will have a positive effect on crop yields.

10. For an exposition of Bloch's comparative method that espouses the sort of experimental logic I have criticized here, see Sewell (1967).

11. Once again, my assessment runs closely parallel to Burawoy's conclusion that Skocpol's work is at its most powerful precisely where it deviates from her announced methodology (Burawoy 1989, 778).

12. Perhaps the best previous model of such a multiple causal narrative is Lefebvre ([1949] 1971), which recounts how four distinct revolutions—an aristocratic revolution, a bourgeois revolution, a municipal revolution, and a peasant revolution—combined to make what we call the French Revolution of 1789. One wonders how much influence this book had on Skocpol's thinking.

13. This critique of conventional comparative method owes much to conversations with Rebecca Scott and Peggy Somers.

14. This has been demonstrated most eloquently, and with greatest theoretical clarity, by the works of Marshall Sahlins (1981, 1985, 1991).

15. For an illuminating study of the political and cultural construction and reconstruction of events, see Coronil and Skurski (1991).

16. I would hesitatingly suggest that enlightening analogies with the eventful sociology I have been advocating in this essay might be found in at least one branch of contemporary natural science: paleontology. I hesitate only because I believe that the development of the social sciences has been bedeviled from the beginning by attempts to adopt the methods and explanatory strategies of supposedly higher or more mature scientific disciplines. But the analogy with paleontology—more specifically, with the version of paleontology set forth by Steven Jay Gould (1989)—seems particularly compelling. The stories of animal evolution that Gould recounts in this book are resolutely narrative and contingent. Indeed, he hails contingency as "the central principle of all history"—including, of course, natural history (Gould 1989, 283). A historical explanation, he goes on, "does not rest on direct deductions from laws of nature, but on an unpredictable sequence of antecedent states, where any major change in any step of the sequence would have altered the final result. This final result is therefore dependent,

or contingent, upon everything that came before—the unerasable and determining signature of history" (1989, 283).

The analogy with natural history as elaborated in *Wonderful Life* is made all the more attractive by Gould's own insistence that scientists need to consider literary and historical narratives as models for their own investigations of evolutionary biology. Remarking that "the theme of contingency, so poorly understood and explored by science, has long been a mainstay of literature" (1989, 285), Gould recommends such novels as *Fatal Inversion* by Barbara Vine [Ruth Rendell] (1987) and *Galapagos* by Kurt Vonnegut (1985) as exemplary texts on the nature of history. Citing paleontology as a scientific warrant for eventful sociology might effectively serve the usual purpose of keeping mainstream colleagues at bay by showing that one's work falls within the sacred precinct of science. After all, the tactic of claiming proper scientific cover for one's procedures may sometimes be unavoidable—especially when the person adopting the rhetorical shield is untenured. But the beauty of invoking the paleontological analogy is that *this* ritual bow toward science also serves the purpose of challenging the conventional assumptions not only of sociology but of science itself. Here is an authentic, exact, and flourishing natural science whose model of explanation resembles that of history and fiction rather than physics. To cite the paleontological model is to argue for the diversity of modes of knowing—as Gould's own plea for a "new taxonomic arrangement of plurality among the sciences" makes clear. Gould argues that "we shall never be able to appreciate the full range and meaning of science until we shatter the stereotype of ordering by status [with physics at the top] and understand the different forms of historical explanation as activities equal in merit to anything done by physics or chemistry" (Gould 1989, 281). Carefully drawn causal narrative, Gould insists, has as much right to claim the laurels of science as mathematical deduction and statistical calculation.

REFERENCES

Abbott, Andrew. 1988. "Transcending General Linear Reality." *Sociological Theory* 6:169–86.

Abbott, Andrew. 1991. "History and Sociology: The Lost Synthesis." *Social Science History* 15:201–38.

Aminzade, Ronald. 1992. "Historical Sociology and Time." *Sociological Methods and Research* 20:456–80.

Arthur, W. Brian. 1988. "Self-Reinforcing Mechanisms in Economics." In *The Economy as an Evolving Complex System.* Edited by Philip W. Anderson, Kenneth J. Arrow, and David Pines, 9–31. Redwood City, CA: Addison-Wesley.

Bendix, Reinhard. 1956. *Work and Authority: Ideologies of Management in the Course of Industrialization.* New York: John Wiley.

Bendix, Reinhard. 1964. *Nation-Building and Citizenship: Studies of Our Changing Social Order.* New York: John Wiley.

Bloch, Marc. 1967. "A Contribution towards a Comparative History of European Societies." In *Land and Work in Medieval Europe.* Translated by J. E. Anderson, 44–81. London: Routledge and Kegan Paul.

Bloch, Marc. 1970. *French Rural History: An Essay on Its Basic Characteristics.* Translated by Janet Sondheimer. Berkeley and Los Angeles: University of California Press.

Braudel, Fernand. 1958. "Histoire et Sciences sociales: La Longue durée." *Annales: Economies. Sociétés Civilisations* 13:725–53.

Braudel, Fernand. 1966. *La Méditerranée et le monde méditerranéen à l'époque de Philippe II.* 2 vols. Paris: Armand Colin.

Burawoy, Michael. 1989. "Two Methods in Search of Science: Skocpol versus Trotsky," *Theory and Society* 18:765–69.

Chorley, Katherine. 1943. *Armies and the Art of Revolution.* London: Faber and Faber.

Coronil, Fernando, and Julie Skurski. 1991. "Dismembering and Remembering the Nation: The Semantics of Political Violence in Venezuela." *Comparative Studies in Society and History* 33:288–337.

Giddens, Anthony. 1984. *The Constitution of Society.* Berkeley and Los Angeles: University of California Press.

Gould, Steven Jay. 1989. *Wonderful Life: The Burgess Shale and the Nature of History.* New York: W. W. Norton.

Griffin, Larry. 1992. "Temporality, Events, and Explanation in Historical Sociology: An Introduction." *Sociological Methods and Research* 20:403–27.

Griffin, Larry. 1993. "Narrative, Event-Structure Analysis, and Causal Interpretation in Historical Sociology." *American Journal of Sociology* 98:1094–133.

Hall, John R. 1984. "Temporality, Social Action, and the Problem of Quantification in Historical Analysis." *Historical Methods* 17:206–18.

Kimeldorf, Howard. 1988. *Reds or Rackets? The Making of Radical and Conservative Unions on the Waterfront.* Berkeley and Los Angeles: University of California Press.

Lakatos, Imre. 1978. *The Methodology of Scientific Research Programmes.* Cambridge: Cambridge University Press.

Lefebvre, Georges. [1949] 1971. *The Coming of the French Revolution.* Translated by R. R. Palmer. Princeton: Princeton University Press.

Lefebvre, Georges. 1973. *The Great Fear: Rural Panic in Revolutionary France.* New York: Pantheon.

Moore, Barrington. 1966. *Social Origins of Dictatorship and Democracy: Lord and Peasant in the Making of the Modern World.* Cambridge: Harvard University Press.

Paige, Jeffrey M. 1978. *Agrarian Revolution: Social Movements and Export Agriculture.* New York: Free Press.

Sahlins, Marshall. 1981. *Historical Metaphors and Mythical Realities: Structure in the Early History of the Sandwich Islands Kingdom.* Ann Arbor: University of Michigan Press.

Sahlins, Marshall. 1985. *Islands of History.* Chicago: University of Chicago Press.

Sahlins, Marshall. 1991. "The Return of the Event, Again: With Reflections on the Beginnings of the Great Fijian War of 1843 to 1855 between the Kingdoms of Bau and Rewa." In *Clio in Oceania: Toward a Historical Anthropology.* Edited by Aletta Biersack, 37–100. Washington, D. C.: Smithsonian Institution Press.

Sewell, William H., Jr. 1967. "Marc Bloch and the Method of Comparative History." *History and Theory* 6:208–18.

Sewell, William H., Jr. 1985. "Ideologies and Social Revolutions: Reflections on the French Case." *Journal of Modern History* 57:57–85.

Sewell, William H., Jr. 1990. "Collective Violence and Collective Loyalties in France: Why the French Revolution Made a Difference." *Politics and Society* 18:527–52.

Sewell, William H., Jr. 1992. "A Theory of Structure: Duality, Agency, and Transformation." *American Journal of Sociology* 98:1–29.

Skocpol, Theda. 1979. *States and Social Revolutions: A Comparative Study of France, Russia, and China.* Cambridge: Cambridge University Press.

Skocpol, Theda. 1988–89. "An 'Uppity Generation' and the Revitalization of Macroscopic Sociology: Reflections at Mid-Career by a Woman from the Sixties." *Theory and Society* 17:627–44.

Skocpol, Theda. 1994. *Social Revolutions in the Modern World.* Cambridge: Cambridge University Press.

Skocpol, Theda, ed. 1984. *Vision and Method in Historical Sociology.* Cambridge: Cambridge University Press.

Skocpol, Theda, and Margaret Somers. 1980. "The Uses of Comparative History in Macrosocial Inquiry." *Comparative Studies in Society and History* 22:174–97.

Smelser, Neil J. 1959. *Social Change in the Industrial Revolution: An Application of Theory to the British Cotton Industry.* Chicago: University of Chicago Press.

Stinchcombe, Arthur, 1978. *Theoretical Methods in Social History.* New York: Academic Press.

Tilly, Charles. 1964. *The Vendée.* Cambridge: Harvard University Press.

Tilly, Charles. 1969. "Collective Violence in European Perspective." In *Violence in America: Historical and Comparative Perspectives.* Edited by Hugh Davis Graham and Ted Robert Gurr, 5–34. Washington, D.C.: U.S. Government Printing Office.

Tilly, Charles. 1972a. "How Protest Modernized in France." In *The Dimensions of Quantitative Research in History.* Edited by William Aydelotte, Allan Bogue, and Robert Fogel, 192–255. Princeton: Princeton University Press.

Tilly, Charles. 1972b. "The Modernization of Political Conflict in France." In *Perspectives on Modernization: Essays in Memory of Ian Weinberg.* Edited by Edward B. Harvey, 50–95. Toronto: University of Toronto Press.

Tilly, Charles. 1977. "Getting It Together in Burgundy." *Theory and Society* 4:479–504.

Tilly, Charles. 1981. "The Web of Contention in Eighteenth-Century Cities." In *Class Conflict and Collective Action*. Edited by Louise Tilly and Charles Tilly, 27–52. Beverly Hills: Sage Publications.

Tilly, Charles. 1984. *Big Structures, Large Processes, Huge Comparisons*. New York: Russell Sage Foundation.

Tilly, Charles. 1986. *The Contentious French*. Cambridge: Harvard University Press.

Tilly, Charles. 1988. "Future History." *Theory and Society* 17:703–12.

Tilly, Charles. 1989. "State and Counterrevolution in France." *Social Research* 56:71–97.

Tilly, Charles, Louise Tilly, and Richard Tilly. 1975. *The Rebellious Century, 1830–1930*. Cambridge: Harvard University Press.

Traugott, Mark. 1985. *Armies of the Poor: Determinants of Working-Class Participation in the Parisian Insurrection of June 1848*. Princeton: Princeton University Press.

Trotsky, Leon. [1932] 1960. *History of the Russian Revolution*. Ann Arbor: University of Michigan Press.

Vine, Barbara [Ruth Rendell]. *A Fatal Inversion*. New York: Bantam Books.

Vonnegut, Kurt. 1985. *Galapagos*. New York: Delacorte Press.

Wallerstein, Immanuel. 1974. *The Modern World-System*. Vol. 1, *Capitalist Agriculture and the Origins of the European World-Economy in the Sixteenth Century*. New York: Academic Press.

Wallerstein, Immanuel. 1988. "Should We Unthink the Nineteenth Century?" In *Rethinking the Nineteenth Century: Contradictions and Movements*. Edited by Francisco O. Ramirez, 185–91. New York: Greenwood.

Resistance and the Problem of Ethnographic Refusal

Sherry B. Ortner

This essay traces the effects of what I call "ethnographic refusal" on a series of studies surrounding the subject of resistance.[1] I argue that many of the most influential studies of resistance are severely limited by the lack of an ethnographic perspective. Resistance studies in turn are meant to stand in for a great deal of interdisciplinary work being done these days within and across the social sciences, history, literature, cultural studies, and so forth.

Ethnography of course means many things. Minimally, however, it has always meant the attempt to understand another life world using the self—as much of it as possible—as the instrument of knowing. As is by now widely known, ethnography has come under a great deal of internal critique within anthropology over the last decade or so, but this minimal definition has not for the most part been challenged.

Classically, this kind of understanding has been closely linked with "fieldwork," in which the whole self physically and in every other way enters the space of the world the researcher seeks to understand. Yet implicit in much of the recent discussions of ethnography is something I wish to make explicit here: that the ethnographic stance (as we may call it) is as much an intellectual (and moral) positionality, a constructive and interpretive mode, as it is a bodily process in space and time. Thus, in a recent useful discussion of "ethnography and the historical imagination," John and Jean Comaroff spend relatively little time on ethnography in the fieldwork sense but a great deal of time on ways of reading historical sources "ethnographically," that is, as if they had been produced through fieldwork (1992).

What then is the ethnographic stance, whether based in fieldwork or not? It is first and foremost a commitment to what Geertz has called "thickness," to producing understanding via richness, texture, and detail rather than parsimony, refinement, and (in the sense used by mathematicians) elegance. The forms that ethnographic thickness have taken have of course changed over time. There was a time when thickness was perhaps synonymous with "exhaustiveness," producing the almost unreadably detailed descriptive ethnography, often followed by the famous "Another Pot from Old Oraibi" kind of journal article. Later, thickness came to be synonymous with "holism," the idea that the object under study was "a" highly integrated "culture" and that it was possible to describe the entire system or at least fully grasp the principles underlying the entire system.

Holism in this sense has also been under attack for some time, and most anthropologists today recognize both the hubris of the "holistic" vision and the irreducible complexity of all societies, including the so-called premodern societies that were imagined to be more integrated and "whole" than us fragmented moderns. Yet I would argue that "thickness" (with traces of both exhaustiveness and holism) remains at the heart of the ethnographic stance. Today issues of thickness focus primarily on issues of (relatively exhaustive) "contextualization." George Marcus, for example, examines the ways in which ethnography in the local and usually bodily sense can be contextualized within the global processes of the world system (1986). And the Comaroffs emphasize the need always to contextualize the data produced through fieldwork and archival research within the forms of practice within which they took shape: "If texts are to be more than literary topoi, scattered shards from which we presume worlds, they have to be anchored in the processes of their production, in the orbits of connection and influence that give them life and force" (1992: 34). Martha Kaplan and John Kelly also insist on a kind of density of contextualization, in their case by articulating the characteristics of the dialogic space within which a political history must be seen as unfolding (1994).

If the ethnographic stance is founded centrally on (among other things, of course) a commitment to "thickness," and if thickness has taken and still takes many forms, what I am calling ethnographic refusal involves a refusal of thickness, a failure of holism or density that itself may take various forms. This essay, then, is about some of the forms of ethnographic refusal, some of its consequences, and some of its reasons, organized around the topic of "resistance." A few words first, then, about "resistance."

Once upon a time, resistance was a relatively unambiguous category, half of the seemingly simple dualism domination/resistance. Domination was a relatively fixed and institutionalized form of power, and resistance was essentially organized resistance to such institutionalized power. This opposition began to be refined (but not abolished) through questionings of both terms. On the one

hand Foucault (e.g., 1978) drew attention to less institutionalized, more pervasive, and more "everyday" forms of power. On the other hand, James Scott
(1985) drew attention to less organized, more pervasive, and more "everyday"
forms of resistance. With Scott's delineation of the notion of "everyday forms
of resistance" (1985), in turn, the question of what is or is not resistance
became much more complicated.[2] When a poor man steals from a rich man is
this "resistance" or simply a survival strategy? The question runs through an
entire collection of essays devoted to everyday forms of resistance (Scott and
Kerkvliet 1986), and different authors attempt to answer it in different ways.
Michael Adas, for example, constructs a typology of forms of everyday resistance, the better to help us place what we are seeing (1986). Brian Fegan
concentrates on the question of intention: if a relatively conscious intention to
resist is not present, the act is not one of resistance (1986). Still others (Stoler
1986; Cooper 1992) suggest that the category itself is not very helpful, and the
important thing is to attend to a variety of transformative processes, in which
things do get changed regardless of the intentions of the actors or in the
presence of very mixed intentions.

In the long run I might agree with Stoler and Cooper, but for the moment I
think resistance, even at its most ambiguous, is a reasonably useful category, if
only because it highlights the presence and play of power in most forms of
relationship and activity. Moreover, we are not required to decide once and for
all whether any given act fits into a fixed box called "resistance." As Marx well
knew, the intentionalities of actors evolve through praxis, and the meanings of
the acts change, both for the actor and for the analyst. In fact, the ambiguity of
"resistance," and the subjective ambivalence of the acts for those who engage
in them, are among the things I wish to emphasize in this essay. In a relationship of power, the dominant often has something to offer, and sometimes a
great deal (though always of course at the price of continuing in power). The
subordinate thus has many grounds for ambivalence about resisting the relationship. Moreover, there is never a single, unitary "subordinate," if only in the
simple sense that subaltern groups are internally divided by age, gender, status,
and other forms of difference, and occupants of differing subject positions will
have different, even opposed—but still legitimate—perspectives on the situation. (I will address the question of whether even a single person is "unitary"
later in the essay.)

Both the psychological ambivalence and the social complexity of resistance
have been noted by several—though not enough—observers.[3] Brian Fegan
talks about being "constantly baffled by the contradictory ways peasants talked
about the tenancy system in general, or about their own relations with particular

landlords" (1986: 92). Moreover, the peasants of Central Luzon who Fegan studied were psychologically uncomfortable with both acts of "resistance" and acts of "collaboration": "Many men talking to me privately about the strategems they use to survive, broke off to say they found theft from the landlord, working for the landlord as guards, arms dealing, etc. distasteful. But what else could a person with children do?" (93)

In a different vein, Christine Pelzer White says "we must add an inventory of 'everyday forms of peasant *collaboration*' to balance our list of 'everyday forms of peasant resistance': both exist, both are important" (1986: 56). She goes on to present examples from postrevolutionary Vietnam of varying alliances between sectors with different interests, including "the state and peasantry against the local elite . . . ; the peasants and the local elite against the state . . . ; the state and individuals [mostly women] against [male] household heads" (60).

Closely related to questions of the psychological and sociopolitical complexity of resistance and nonresistance (and to the need for "thick" ethnography) is the question of "authenticity." Authenticity is another of those highly problematized terms these days insofar as it presumes a naive belief in cultural purity, in "untouched" cultures whose histories are uncontaminated by those of their neighbors or of "the West." I make no such presumptions. Nonetheless, there must be a way to talk about what the Comaroffs call "the endogenous historicity of local worlds" (1992: 27), in which the pieces of reality, however much borrowed from or imposed by others, are woven together through the logic of a group's own locally and historically evolved bricolage. It is this that I will mean by *authenticity* in the discussions that follow, as I turn to a consideration of some of the recent resistance literature.

I should note here that the works to be discussed constitute a very selected and partial set, and I make no claims to covering the entire literature. The works are selected either because they have been very influential or because they illustrate a fairly common problem, or both. In this era of interdisciplinarity, scholarly exhaustiveness is more unattainable than ever. In any event, the point of the discussion is to examine a number of problems in the resistance literature arising from the stance of ethnographic refusal. The discussion will be organized in terms of three forms of such refusal, which I will call sanitizing politics, thinning culture, and dissolving actors.

Sanitizing Politics

It may seem odd to start off by critiquing resistance studies for not containing enough politics. If there is one thing these studies are about, it is politics, front and center. Yet it is always the politics *of* resistance, that is, it is limited to the relationship between the dominant and the subordinate (see also Cooper 1992, 4). If we are to recognize that resistors are doing more than simply opposing domination, more than simply producing a virtually mechanical *re*-action, then we must go the whole way. They have their *own* politics—not just "chiefs and commoners" or "landlords and peasants," categories pulled out because they parallel the macroresistance structure that the study is focused on (say, anticolonialism)—but all the local categories of friction and tension: men and women, parents and children, seniors and juniors; inheritance conflicts among brothers; struggles of succession and wars of conquest between chiefs; struggles for primacy between religious sects; and on and on.

It is the absence of analysis of these forms of internal conflict in many resistance studies that gives them an air of romanticism, of which they are often accused (e.g., Abu-Lughod 1990). Let me take one example from a fine book that I admire on other counts: Inga Clendinnen's *Ambivalent Conquests: Maya and Spaniard in Yucatan, 1517–1570* (1987). Clendinnen recognizes that there were Mayan chiefs who had significant advantages of material resources, political power, and social precedence. She also recognizes that in this sort of polity chiefs had many obligations in turn to their subjects, including the redistribution of (some) wealth through feasts and hospitality and the staging of rituals for the collective well-being. Yet the degree to which she emphasizes the reciprocity over the asymmetry of the relationship systematically excludes from the reader's view a picture of some of the serious exploitation and violence of the Mayan political economy. Chiefs engaged in "extravagant and casual taking" (143), "were allocated the most favoured land for the making of *milpa*" (144), "were given the lords' share of the game taken in a communal hunt [and] levied from the professional hunters" (ibid.). Their land was worked by war captives, and their domestic system was maintained by "female slaves and concubines" (ibid.). Yet Clendinnen balances the mention of each of those instances of systematic exploitation with some mention of how much the chiefs gave in return, culminating in an account of a ritual to protect the villagers from threatened calamity: "In those experiences, when the life of the whole village was absorbed in the ritual process, men learnt that the differences between priest, lord and commoner were less important than their shared dependence on the gods, and the fragility of the human order" (147).

Clendinnen goes on to say (ibid.) that "the cost of all this (although it is far from clear that the Maya regarded it as a cost) was war," waged between chiefs of neighboring groups. In war, "noble captives were killed for the gods; the rest, men, women and children, were enslaved, and the men sold out of the country" (148). What's wrong with this picture? In the first place, one presumes that *some* Maya "regarded it as a cost"—namely, the captives who were to be executed and the men, women, and children who were enslaved, not to mention everyone else in the society who had to live with the permanent possibility of such violence. In the second place, Clendinnen never puts together the pieces of her account to show that the sense of "shared dependence" of chiefs and commoners, insofar as it was successfully established at all, was in large part a product of the displacement of exploitation and violence from the chief's own subjects to those of his neighbors.

There seems to be a virtual taboo on putting these pieces together, as if to give a full account of the Mayan political order, good and bad, would be to give some observers the ammunition to say that the Maya deserved what they got from the Spanish. But this concern is ungrounded. Nothing about Mayan politics, however bloody and exploitative, would condone the looting, killing, and cultural destruction wrought by the Spanish. On the other hand, a more thorough and critical account of precolonial Mayan politics would presumably generate a different picture of the subsequent shape of the colonial history of the region, including the subsequent patterns of resistance and nonresistance. At the very least, it would respect the ambivalent complexity of the Mayan world as it existed both at that time and in the present.[4]

The most glaring arena of internal political complexity glossed over by most of these studies is the arena of gender politics.[5] This is a particularly vexed question. Members of subordinate groups who want to call attention to gender inequities in their own groups are subject to the accusation of undermining their own class or subaltern solidarity, not supporting their men, and playing into the hands of the dominants. "First World" feminist scholars who do the same are subject to sharp attacks from Third World feminist scholars on the same grounds (see C. Mohanty 1988). It seems elitist to call attention to the oppression of women *within* their own class or ethnic group or culture when that class or racial group or culture is being oppressed by another group.

These issues have come into sharp focus in the debates surrounding *sati* or widow-burning in colonial India (Spivak 1988a; Jain, Misra, and Srivastava 1987; Mani 1987). One of the ways in which the British justified their own dominance was to point to "barbaric" practices such as *sati* and to claim that they were engaged in a civilizing mission that would save Indian women from these practices. Gayatri Chakravorty Spivak has ironically characterized this situation as one in which "White men are saving brown women from brown men" (1988a: 296). Thus, feminists who might want to investigate the ways in which *sati* was part of a larger configuration of male dominance in nineteenth-century Indian society cannot do so without seeming to subscribe to the discourse of the colonial administrators. The attempts to deal with this particular set of contradictions have only multiplied the contradictions.

Overall, the lack of an adequate sense of prior and ongoing politics *among* subalterns must inevitably contribute to an inadequate analysis of resistance itself. Many people do not get caught up in resistance movements, and this is not simply an effect of fear (as Scott generally argues [1985, 1990]), naive enthrallment to the priests (as Friedrich argues about many of the nonresisting Mexican peasants [1970]), or narrow self-interest. Nor does it make all nonparticipants collaborators. Moreover, individual acts of resistance, as well as large-scale resistance movements, are often themselves conflicted, internally contradictory, and affectively ambivalent, in large part because of these internal political complexities.

The impulse to sanitize the internal politics of the dominated must be understood as fundamentally romantic. As a partial antidote to this widespread tendency it might be well to reintroduce the work of the so-called structural Marxists in anthropology and their descendants. Structural Marxism (the Bloch [1975] reader is a good place to start; see also Meillassoux 1981; Terray 1972) took shape as a response to this romanticizing tendency within the field of anthropology, and as an attempt to understand non-Western and precapitalist forms of inequality on the analogy of Marx's analysis of class within capitalism. Tackling societies that would have been categorized as "egalitarian" precisely because they lacked class or caste, structural Marxists were able to tease out the ways in which such things as the apparent benevolent authority of "elders" or the apparent altruism and solidarity of kin are often grounded in systematic patterns of exploitation and power.

The structural Marxist project took shape at roughly the same time as did feminist anthropology.[6] The two together made it difficult for many anthropologists, myself included, ever again to look at even the "simplest" society without seeing a politics every bit as complex, and sometimes every bit as oppressive, as those of capitalism and colonialism.[7] Moreover, as anthropologists of this persuasion began taking the historic turn, it seemed impossible to understand the histories of these societies, including (but not limited to) their histories under colonialism and/or capitalist penetration, without understanding how those "external" forces *interacted* with these internal politics. Sahlins's account (1981) of the patterns of accommodation and resistance in play between Hawaiians and Europeans in the eighteenth and nineteenth centuries; some of Wolf's discussions in *Europe and the People without History* (1982); my own (1989) history of Sherpa religious transformations, linking indigenous politics and culture with larger regional (Nepal state and British Raj) dynamics; Richard Fox's (1985) study of the evolution of Sikh identity under colonialism—all of these show that an understanding of political authenticity, of the people's *own* politics, is not only not incompatible with an understanding of resistance but is in fact intrinsic to such an understanding.

Thinning Culture

Just as subalterns must be seen as having an authentic, and not merely reactive, politics, so they must be seen as having an authentic, and not merely reactive, culture. The culture concept in anthropology has (like "ethnography") come under heavy attack in recent years, partly for assumptions of timelessness, homogeneity, uncontested sharedness, and the like that were historically embedded in it and in anthropological practice more generally. Yet those assumptions are not by any means intrinsic to the concept, which can be (re)mobilized in powerful ways without them. Indeed, a radical reconceptualization of culture, including both the historicization and politicization of the concept, has been going on for at least the last decade or so in anthropology, and the attacks upon its traditional form are by now very much in the way of beating a dead horse (see Dirks, Eley, and Ortner 1994). In any event, like James Clifford, one of the major figures in the attack on the culture concept, I do not see how we can do without it (1988: 10). The only alternative to recognizing that subalterns have a certain prior and ongoing cultural authenticity is to view subaltern responses to domination as ad hoc and incoherent, springing not from their own ideas of order, justice, meaning, and the like but only from some set of ideas called into being by the situation of domination itself.

Cultural "thinning" is characteristic of some of the most influential studies of resistance currently on the scene.[8] Some of the problems with this tendency may be brought into focus through a consideration of the way in which "religion" is (or is not) handled in some of these studies. I do not mean to suggest by this that religion is equivalent to all of culture. Nonetheless, religion is always a rich repository of cultural beliefs and values and often has close affinities with resistance movements as well. I will thus consider the treatment of religion in a number of resistance studies before turning to the question of culture more generally.

In one of the founding texts of the subaltern studies "school" of history, for example, Ranajit Guha emphasizes the importance of recognizing and not disparaging the religious bases of tribal and peasant rebellions (1988). Indeed, this is one of the central threads of subaltern studies writings, a major part of its effort to recognize the authentic cultural universe of subalterns, from which their acts of resistance grew. Yet the degree to which the treatment of religion in these studies is actually cultural, that is, is actually an effort to illuminate the conceptual and affective configurations within which the peasants are operating, is generally minimal.[9] Rather, the peasant is endowed with something called "religiosity," a kind of diffuse consciousness that is never further explored as a set of ideas, practices, and feelings built into the religous universe the peasant inhabits. Guha and others in his group are jousting with some Marxist Indian historians who share with bourgeois modernization theorists a view of religion as "backward." The subaltern studies writers in contrast want to respect and validate peasant religiosity as an authentic dimension of subaltern culture, out of which an authentically oppositional politics could be and was constructed. Yet Guha's own notion of peasant religiosity still bears the traces of Marx's hostility toward religion, defining "religious consciousness . . . as a massive demonstration of self-estrangement" (78). Moreover, instead of exploring and interpreting this religiosity of the rebels in any substantive way, he makes a particular textual move to avoid this: he relegates to an appendix (extracts of) the peasants' own accounts of the religious visions that inspired their rebellion.

A similar casualness about religion, while paying it lip service, is evident in James Scott's *Weapons of the Weak* (1985). The point can be seen again not only in what Scott says and does not say but in the very shape of his text. There is no general discussion of the religious landscape of the villagers at all, and the discussion of religious movements in his area, many of which had significant political dimensions, is confined to a few pages toward the end (332–35). During Scott's fieldwork, a number of rumors of religious-political prophecies circulated in his area, as well as a "flying letter" containing similar prophecies. Like the testimonies of Guha's rebels, this letter is reproduced, unanalyzed, in an appendix. The fact that "rarely a month goes by without a newspaper account of the prosecution of a religious teacher accused of propagating false doctrines" is also relegated to a footnote (335).

But cultural thinning, as noted above, need not be confined to marginalizing religious factors, nor is it practiced only by nonanthropologists (like Guha and Scott). In his landmark work *Europe and the People without History* (1982), Eric Wolf devotes a scant five pages at the end of the book to the question of "culture," largely in order to dismiss it. And in his superb study of the Sikh wars against the British (1985), Richard Fox similarly—and much more extensively—argues against the idea that culture informs, shapes, and underpins resistance at least as much as it emerges situationally from it.

There are a number of different things going on here. In part, Wolf and Fox (and perhaps some of the others) are writing from a 1960s-style "materialist" position. Nineteen-sixties-style materialism (in anthropology at least) was opposed to giving culture any sort of active role in the social and historical process, other than mystification of the "real" (i.e., material) causes of formations and events. At the same time, however, Wolf's and Fox's positions converge with later, and not necessarily materialist, critiques of the culture concept (e.g., Clifford and Marcus 1986) as homogenizing, dehistoricizing, and reifying the boundaries of specific groups and/or communities.

Coming from a different direction, however, Raymond Williams (1977) and other Birmingham Cultural Studies scholars (e.g., Hall and Jefferson 1976) were actually revitalizing the culture concept. Williams specifically wanted to overcome the materialism/idealism split and focus on the ways in which structures of exploitation and domination are simultaneously material and cultural. His approach to this was via Gramsci's notion of hegemony, which Williams defined as something very close to the classic anthropological concept of culture, but more politicized, more saturated with the relations of power, domination, and inequality within which it takes shape. This was healthy for the culture concept and for an anthropology that had moved significantly beyond the oppositions of the 1960s. But it raised the old specter of "mystification" and "false consciousness." If domination operates in part culturally, through ideas and—in Williams's phrase—"structures of feeling," then people may accept and buy into their own domination and the possibility of resistance may be undermined. Moreover, as James Scott argued, analysts who emphasize hegemony in this relatively deep, culturally internalized sense, are likely to fail to uncover those "hidden transcripts" of resistance and those nonobvious acts and moments of resistance that do take place (Scott 1985, 1990).

In fact, of course, in any situation of power there is a mixture of cultural dynamics. To some extent, and for a variety of good and bad reasons, people often do buy into the representations that underwrite their own domination. At the same time, they also preserve alternative ("authentic") traditions of belief and value that allow them to see through those representations. Paul Willis's now classic book *Learning to Labour* (1977) is particularly valuable in addressing this mixture of hegemony and authenticity (though not in those terms) involved in relationships of power. Willis's discussion of the ways in which the subculture of the working-class lads embodies both "penetrations" of the dominant culture and limitations on those penetrations—limitations deriving from the lads' own subcultural perspectives on gender—is highly illuminating. Some recent work by Martha Kaplan and John D. Kelly (1994) similarly underscores the cultural complexity of power and resistance. Drawing on Mikhail Bakhtin and, less explicitly, Marshall Sahlins, they frame their study of colonial Fiji as an analysis of contending discourses within a dialogic space. Setting aside for the most part the category of "resistance," they insist on the thickness of the cultural process in play in colonial "zones of transcourse" where "multiple grammars operate through contingently categorized people" (129, 127). The result is a complex but illuminating picture of shifting loyalties, shifting alliances, and above all shifting categories as British, native Fijians, and Fiji Indians contended for power, resources, and legitimacy (see also Kaplan 1990; Orlove 1991; and Turner 1991 and n.d.).

Indeed, there is a large alternative tradition of resistance studies that shows clearly that cultural richness does not undermine the possibility of seeing and understanding resistance. Quite the contrary, it allows us to understand better both resistance *and its limits.* Many of the great classics of social history—for example, E. P. Thompson's *The Making of the English Working Class* (1966) and Eugene Genovese's *Roll, Jordan, Roll* (1976)—are great precisely because they are culturally rich, providing deep insight not only into the fact of resistance but into its forms, moments, and absences. Other outstanding examples of the genre include Clendinnen's *Ambivalent Conquests* (1987) (despite its weakness on Mayan politics, discussed above), William H. Sewell Jr.'s *Work and Revolution in France* (1980), and Jean Comaroff's *Body of Power, Spirit of Resistance* (1985).

Dissolving Subjects

The question of the relationship of the individual/person/subject to domination carries the resistance problematic to the level of consciousness, subjectivity, intentionality, and identity. This question has taken a particular form in debates surrounding—once again—the subaltern studies school of historians, with literary critics in particular taking the other side. I should say here that I do not launch so much criticism against the subaltern studies historians because they are (in Guha's term) "terrible." On the contrary, I find myself returning to their work not only because much of it is insightful and provocative but also because it is situated at that intersection of anthropology, history, and literary studies that so many of us find ourselves occupying—often awkwardly—in contemporary scholarly work.[10]

In any event, Gayatri Chakravorty Spivak has taken the subaltern studies school to task for creating a monolithic category of "subaltern" who is presumed to have a unitary identity and consciousness (1988a, 1988b). Given the arguments I made above about the internal complexity of subaltern politics and culture, I would certainly agree with this point. Yet Spivak and others who deploy a certain brand of poststructuralist (primarily Derridean) analysis go to the opposite extreme, dissolving the subject entirely into a set of "subject effects" that have virtually no coherence. Because these writers are still concerned with subalternity in some sense, they themselves wind up in incoherent positions with respect to "resistance."

Let me say again that in some ways I am sympathetic with what they are trying to do, which is to introduce complexity, ambiguity, and contradiction into our view of the subject, in ways that I have argued above must be done with "politics" and "culture" (and "resistance"). Yet the particular poststructuralist move they make toward accomplishing this goal paradoxically destroys the object (the subject) who should be enriched rather than impoverished by the act of complexification.

This final form of ethnographic refusal may be illustrated by examining an article entitled " 'Shahbano' " (Pathak and Rajan 1989). The authors, who acknowledge their debt to Spivak's work, address the case of a Muslim Indian woman called Shahbano, who went to civil court to sue for support from her husband after a divorce. The court awarded her the support she sought, but this set off a national controversy of major proportions because the court's award (and indeed Shahbano's decision to bring the case to a civil court in the first place) controverted local Islamic divorce law. In the wake of the controversy, Shahbano wrote an open letter to the court rejecting its award and expressing solidarity with her co-Muslims.

The authors' argument about the case runs as follows. The court's award, and the larger legal framework within which it was made, operated through a discourse of "protection" for persons who are seen to be weak. But "to be framed by a certain kind of discourse is to be objectified as the 'other,' represented without the characteristic features of the 'subject,' sensibility and/or volition" (563). Within the context of such discursive subjectification, the appropriate notion of resistance is simply the "refusal of subjectification" (571), the refusal to occupy the category being foist upon one. Shahbano's shifting position on her own case—first seeking, then rejecting, the award— represented such a refusal of subjectification, the only one open to her given her situation. "To live with what she cannot control, the female subaltern subject here responds with a discontinuous and apparently contradictory subjectivity" (572). But "her apparent inconstancy or changeability must be interpreted as her refusal to occupy the subject position [of protectee] offered to her" (ibid.).

Basically, I agree with the authors' argument that every moment in the developing situation foregrounded a different aspect of Shahbano's multiplex identity—as a woman, as a poor person, as a Muslim. Indeed, it does not require sophisticated theorizing to recognize that every social being lives such multiplicity, and every social context creates such shifting of foreground and background. I also agree (although the authors never quite put it this way) that, for certain kinds of compounded powerlessness (female *and* poor *and* of minority status), the "refusal of subjectification" may be the only strategy available to the subject. Yet there are several problems with the interpretation that need to be teased out.

First, returning to an earlier discussion in this essay, there is an inadequate analysis of the internal politics of the subaltern group, in this case of the gender/ethnic politics of the Muslim community surrounding Shahbano. The authors make it clear that this is disallowed, for it would align one with the general discourse of protection and with the specific politics of the Hindu court vis-à-vis the minority Muslims: transforming Spivak's previously cited aphorism, the situation is one in which "Hindu men are saving Muslim women from Muslim men" (566), and any author who addresses Muslim gender politics moves into the same position. Yet one cannot help but feel a nagging suspicion about the on-the-ground politics surrounding Shahbano's open letter rejecting the court's award in the name of Muslim solidarity. Is "refusal to occupy the subject position offered to her" (572) an adequate account of what happened here, or might we imagine some rather more immediately lived experience of intense personal pressures from significant social others—kin, friends, neighbors, male and female—who put pressure on Shahbano in the name of their own agendas to renounce a monetary award that she desperately needed and had been seeking for ten years? Might one not say that "her refusal to occupy the subject position offered to her"—the only kind of agency accorded her by the authors—is the real "effect" in view here, that is, the (analytic) by-product of her agency rather than the form of it? In my reading, Shahbano was trying to be an agent, to pursue a coherent agenda, and rather creatively at that. The shifting quality of her case is not to be found in her shifting identity (whether essentialized as subaltern consciousness or seen as "strategic") but in the fact that she is at the low end of every form of power in the system and is being quite actively pushed around by other, more powerful agents.

This brings us to the second problem with the discussion, and here again we must turn textual analysis against the authors' own text. The whole point of the poststructuralist move is to de-essentialize the subject, to get away from the ideological construct of "that unified and freely choosing individual who is the normative male subject of Western bourgeois liberalism" (572). And indeed the freely choosing individual *is* an ideological construct, in multiple senses: because the person is culturally (and socially, historically, politically, etc.) constructed, because few people have the power to freely choose very much, and so forth. The question here, however, is how to get around this ideological construct and yet retain some sense of human agency, the capacity of social beings to interpret and morally evaluate their situation, and to formulate projects and try to enact them.

The authors of "'Shahbano'" realize that this is a problem: "Where, in all these discursive displacements, is Shahbano the woman?" (565). But they specifically refuse to attend to her as an intentionalized being with her own hopes, fears, desires, projects. They have only two models for such attending—either psychological perspectives that attempt to tap her "'inner' being," or a perspective that assumes "individualized and individualistic" heroic resistors—and they reject both (570). Instead, their strategy is to focus on the mechanical interaction of a variety of disembodied forces: "multiple intersections of power, discursive displacements, discontinuous identities refusing subjectification, the split legal subject" (577). Thus, despite certain disclaimers at the end of the article, Shahbano as subject (or agent? or person?) quite literally disappears. The irrelevance of her understandings and intentions (not to mention her social universe, her history, and so forth) to this analytic project is starkly brought home by the authors' own textual strategy of refusing to reproduce and interpret two press interviews Shahbano gave, one to a newspaper and one on national television. The authors say "We have not privileged these as sources of her subjectivity" (570). In fact, they have not even presented them.

The de(con)struction of the subject in this way cannot be the only answer to the reified and romanticized subject of many resistance studies. On the contrary, the answer to the reified and romanticized subject must be an actor understood as *more fully* constructed socially and culturally. The breaks and splits and incoherencies of consciousness, no less than the integrations and coherencies, are equally products of cultural and historical formation. Indeed, one could question whether the splits and so forth should be viewed as incoherencies or simply as alternative forms of coherence; not to do so implies that they are a form of "damage." Of course, oppression *is* damaging, yet the ability of social beings to weave alternative, and sometimes brilliantly creative, forms of coherence across the damages is one of the heartening aspects of human subjectivity (see also Cooper's [1992] critique of Fanon). A similar point may be made with respect to "agency." Agency is not something that exists apart from cultural construction (nor is it something one has only when one is whole or when one is "an individual"). Every culture, every subculture, every historical moment constructs its own forms of agency, its own modes of enacting the process of reflecting on the self and the world and acting simultaneously within and upon what one finds there. To understand where Shahbano or any other figure in a resistance drama is coming from, one must explore the particularities of all these constructions, as both cultural and historical products, and as personal creations building on those precipitates of culture and history.

A brilliant example of this alternative perspective may be seen in Ashis Nandy's *The Intimate Enemy: Loss and Recovery of the Self under Colonialism* (1983). Nandy begins by exploring the homology between sexual and political dominance as this took shape in the context of British colonialism in India. He then goes on to consider Indian literary efforts to react against colonialism that were in fact highly hegemonized, works that were "grounded in reinterpreted sacred texts but in reality dependent on core values [particularly of hypermasculinity] borrowed from the colonial world view and then legitimized according to existing concepts of sacredness" (22). But the main effort of the book is to examine individual literary, religious, and political figures who sought "to create a new political awareness which would combine a critical awareness of Hinduism and colonialism with cultural and individual authenticity" (27). He is particularly interested in the ways in which Gandhi and other major voices of anticolonialism mobilized (and partly reordered) Indian categories of masculinity, femininity, and androgyny in formulating both resistance to colonialism and an alternative vision of society. Again and again, he views these oppositional figures, even when severely victimized in their personal lives (see especially the discussion of Sri Aurobindo), as drawing upon cultural resources to transform their own victimhood and articulate a model of self and society that is neither the hyperrational and hypermasculine self of the West (itself, of course, an ideology) nor the various "Indias" (of the warrior or the mystic) that the West invented or called into being.[11]

But finally Nandy comes back to the ordinary person, who does not write novels, launch new religious systems, or lead movements of national resistance. In this context, he seems to come close to the position of the authors of "'Shahbano'", for he argues (in a more psychological language) that cultural and psychological survival may require the kind of fragmented and shifting self that Shahbano seemed to display (107). Yet Nandy's discussion has a different tone. Partly this comes from his exploration of broad cultural patterns, showing that the boundaries between such things as self and other, masculine and feminine, and myth and history, are both differently configured and differently valued in various strands of Indian thought. The shifting subject in turn is both drawing on and protecting these alternative cultural frames, as opposed to making a seemingly ad hoc response to an immediate situation of domination. In addition, Nandy's subjects paradoxically retain a kind of coherent agency in their very inconstancy: "these 'personality failures' of the Indian could be another form of developed vigilance, or sharpened instinct or faster reaction to man-made suffering. They come . . . from a certain talent for and faith in life" (110). Thus, Nandy's subjects, whether prominent public figures or common men and women, retain powerful voices throughout his book, while Shahbano representationally disappears.

Finally, however, it must be emphasized that the question of adequate representation of subjects in the attempt to understand resistance is not purely a matter of providing better portraits of subjects in and of themselves. The importance of subjects (whether individual actors or social entities) lies not so much in who they are and how they are put together as in the projects that they construct and enact. For it is in the formulation and enactment of those projects that they both become and transform who they are, and sustain or transform their social and cultural universe.

Textual Resistance

Running through all these works, despite in some cases deep theoretical differences between them, is a kind of bizarre refusal to know and speak and write of the lived worlds inhabited by those who resist (or do not, as the case may be). Of the works discussed at length in this essay, Clendinnen goes to greater lengths than the others to portray the precolonial Mayan world in some depth and complexity, yet in the end she chooses to pull her punches and smooth over what the material has told her. Scott, Guha, and Pathak and Rajan, on the other hand, quite literally refuse to deal with the material that would allow entry into the political and cultural worlds of those they discuss. The "flying letters" of Scott's peasants, the peasants' testimonies of their visions in Guha, Shahbano's press interviews—these are texts that could be read in the richest sense to yield an understanding of both the meanings and the mystifications upon which people are operating. What might emerge is something like what we see in Carlo Ginzburg's *The Night Battles* (1985), an extraordinarily rich and complicated world of beliefs, practices, and petty politics whose relationship to the encroachment of Christianity and the Inquisition in the Middle Ages is confused and unheroic yet also poignantly stubborn and "authentic"—a very Nandyesque story.

There are no doubt many reasons for this interpretive refusal. One is surely to be found in the so-called crisis of representation in the human sciences. When Edward Said says in effect that the discourse of Orientalism renders it virtually impossible to know anything real about the Orient (1979); when Gayatry Spivak tells us that "the subaltern cannot speak" (1988a); when James Clifford informs us that all ethnographies are "fictions" (1986, 7); and when of course *in some sense* all of these things are true, then the effect is a powerful inhibition on the practice of ethnography broadly defined—the effortful practice, *despite all that,* of seeking to understand other peoples in other times and places, and especially people not in dominant positions.

The ethnographic stance holds that ethnography is never impossible. For people not only resist political domination; they resist, or anyway evade, textual domination as well. The notion that colonial or academic texts are able completely to distort or exclude the voices and perspectives of those being written about seems to me to endow these texts with far greater power than they have. Many things shape these texts, including, dare one say it, the point of view of those being written about. Nor does one need to resort to various forms of textual experimentation to allow this to happen; it is happening all the time. Of course, there is variation in the degree to which different authors and different forms of writing allow this process to show, and it is certainly worthwhile to reflect—as Clifford and others have done—on the ways in which this process can be enhanced. But it seems to me grotesque to insist on the notion that the text is shaped by everything but the lived reality of the people the text claims to represent.

Take the case of a modern female suicide discussed in Spivak's famous paper, a paper that concludes with the statement that "the subaltern cannot speak" (308). It is perhaps more difficult for any voice to break through Spivak's theorizing than through the most typifying ethnography, yet even this dead young woman, who spoke to no one about her intentions and left no note before her death, forces Spivak to at least try to articulate, in quite "realist" and "objectivist" fashion, the truth of the suicide from the woman's point of view:

The suicide was a puzzle since, as Bhuvaneswari was menstruating at the time, it was clearly not a case of illicit pregnancy. Nearly a decade later, it was discovered that she was a member of one of the many groups involved in the armed struggle for Indian independence. She had finally been entrusted with a political assassination. Unable to confront the task and yet aware of the practical need for trust, she killed herself.

Bhuvaneswari had known that her death would be diagnosed as the outcome of illegitimate passion. She had therefore waited for the onset of menstruation. . . . Bhuvaneswari Bhaduri's suicide is an unemphatic, ad hoc, subaltern rewriting of the social text of *sati*-suicide. (307–8)

With this discussion, it seems to me, Spivak undermines her own position (see also Coronil 1992). Combining a bit of homely intepretation of the "text" of the woman's body (the fact that she was menstruating) with a bit of objective history (the woman's participation in a radical political group), Spivak arrives at what any good ethnography provides: an understanding of both the meaning and the politics of the meaning of an event.

Another angle on the problem of ethnographic refusal may be gained from considering the implications of the "fiction" metaphor. Reverberating with ordinary language, the fiction metaphor implies (though this is not exactly what Clifford meant) that ethnographies are "false," "made up," and more generally that they are products of a literary imagination that has no obligation to engage with "reality." Yet the obligation to engage with reality seems to me precisely the difference between the novelist's task and that of the ethnographer (or the historian). The anthropologist and the historian are charged with representing the lives of living or once-living people, and as we attempt to push these people into the molds of our texts *they push back*. The final text is a product of our pushing and their back-pushing, and no text, however "dominant," lacks the traces of this counterforce.

Indeed, if the line between fiction and ethnography is being blurred, the blurring has had at least as much impact on fiction as on ethnography. The novelist's standard disclaimer—"any resemblance to persons living or dead is coincidental"—is less and less invoked,[12] or less and less accepted. The response to Salman Rushdie's *The Satanic Verses* (1989) shows in particularly dramatic form that the novelist can no longer pretend that, in contrast to "ethnography" or "history," there is nobody on the other side of his or her text and that fiction can escape resistance.[13]

Finally, absolute fictionality and absolute silencing are impossible not only because those being written about force themselves into the author's account, but because there is always a multiplicity of accounts. The point is simple, yet it seems to get lost in the discussions just considered. It is strange in this era of the "death of the author" to find theorists like Spivak and Clifford acting as if texts were wholly self-contained, as if every text we wrote had to embody (or could conceivably embody) in itself all the "voices" out there, or as if every text we read had boundaries beyond which we were not allowed to look. On the contrary, in both writing and reading we enter a corpus of texts in which, in reality, a single representation or misrepresentation or omission never goes wholly unchallenged. Our job, in both reading and writing, is precisely to refuse to be limited by a single text, or by any existing definition of what should count as the corpus, and to play the texts (which may include, but never be limited to, our own field notes) off against one another in an endless process of coaxing up images of the real.

Conclusions

The point of this essay can be stated very simply: resistance studies are thin because they are ethnographically thin—thin on the internal politics of dominated groups, thin on the cultural richness of those groups, and thin on the subjectivity—the intentions, desires, fears, projects—of the actors engaged in these dramas. Ethnographic thinness in turn derives from several sources (other than sheer bad ethnography, of course—always a possibility). The first is the failure of nerve surrounding questions of the internal politics of dominated groups and the cultural "authenticity" of those groups. The second is the set of issues surrounding the "crisis of representation"—that is, the possibility of truthful portrayals of others (or Others), and the capacity of the subaltern to be heard. Taken together, and for different reasons, the two sets of issues converge to produce a kind of ethnographic black hole.

Filling in the black hole would certainly deepen and enrich resistance studies, but there is more to it than that. It would, or should, reveal the ambivalences and ambiguities of resistance itself. These ambivalences and ambiguities, in turn, emerge from the intricate webs of articulations and disarticulations that always exist between dominant and dominated. For the politics of external domination and the politics within a subordinated group may link up with, as well as repel, one another; the cultures of dominant groups and of subalterns may speak to, even while speaking against, one another;[14] and—as Nandy so eloquently argues—subordinated selves may retain oppositional authenticity and agency by drawing on aspects of the dominant culture to criticize their *own* world as well as the situation of domination. In short, one can only appreciate the ways in which resistance can be more than opposition, can be truly creative and transformative, if one appreciates the multiplicity of projects in which social beings are always engaged and the multiplicity of ways in which those projects feed on as well as collide with one another.

NOTES

1. An earlier and very different version of this chapter was written for "The Historic Turn" conference organized by Terrence McDonald for the Program in the Comparative Study of Social Transformations (CSST) at the University of Michigan. The extraordinarily high level of insightfulness and helpfulness of critical comments from my colleagues in CSST has by now become almost routine, and I wish to thank them collectively here. In addition, for particularly close and detailed readings of the text, I wish to thank Frederick Cooper, Fernando Coronil, Nicholas Dirks, Val Daniel, Geoff Eley, Ray Grew, Roger Rouse, William Sewell Jr., Julie Skurski, and Ann Stoler. I have incorporated many of their suggestions and know that I have ignored some at my peril. Finally, for valuable comments as well as for the heroic job of organizing the conference, I wish especially to thank Terrence McDonald.

2. Scott was of course drawing on a wealth of earlier scholarship.

3. The notion of ambivalence has become central to colonial and postcolonial studies more generally and is worth an essay in itself. See, for example, Hanks (1986) and Bhabha (1985).

4. A parallel to the monolithic portrayal of resistors is the monolithic portrayal of the dominants. This is beginning to be broken down, as for example in Stoler (1989).

5. The absence of gender considerations in generic resistance studies, and some implications of this absence, have been addressed particularly by O'Hanlon (1989). See also White (1986). For valuable ethnographic studies of gender resistance per se see Abu-Lughod (1986) and Ong (1987).

6. The beginnings of (Franco-British) structural Marxism in anthropology were also contemporary with the beginnings of British (Marxist) cultural studies. The impact of structural Marxism on anthropology, as well as the fact that the field was still mired in the materialism/idealism split in that era, probably accounts in good part for the delay of the impact of cultural studies. See Ortner (1984) for a review of anthropological theory from the 1960s to the 1980s.

7. Some important early feminist anthropology drew directly on structural Marxism. See especially Collier and Rosaldo (1981).

8. The work of the British cultural studies scholars is seemingly a major exception to this point. I would argue if I had space, however, that for much of the work in this field the treatment of both culture and ethnography is also "thin" (Willis [1977] is a major exception). In any event, my focus in this section is on influential work that is much more obviously problematic with respect to culture.

9. Of course the subaltern studies school is complex, and a variety of tendencies appear within it. Shahid Amin's "Gandhi as Mahatma" (1988) is more fully cultural than many of the other writings, as is Gyanendra Pandey's "Peasant Revolt and Indian Nationalism" (1988).

10. The same is true of other postcolonial historiographies (African studies, for

example), but I am less familiar with their literatures. Indian anthropology and history touch upon my own long-term research in Nepal.

11. For another strong work on Gandhi's cultural genius, see Fox (1989).

12. See, for example, the quite different disclaimer in Don deLillo's fictionalization of the Kennedy assassination, *Libra* (1989).

13. I am indebted to Nick Dirks for pushing me on this point.

14. Nandy (1983) and Comaroff (1985) make a point of discussing the ways in which subalterns may effectively, and for their own benefit, draw on some of the latent oppositional categories and ideologies of Western culture.

REFERENCES

Abu-Lughod, Lila. 1986. *Veiled Sentiments: Honor and Poetry in a Bedouin Society.* Berkeley and Los Angeles: University of California Press.

Abu-Lughod, Lila. 1990. "The Romance of Resistance: Tracing Transformations of Power through Bedouin Women." *American Ethnologist* 17(1): 41–55.

Adas, Michael. 1986. "From Footdragging to Flight: The Evasive History of Peasant Avoidance Protest in South and Southeast Asia." *Journal of Peasant Studies* 13 (2): 64–86.

Amin, Shahid. 1988. "Gandhi as Mahatma." In *Selected Subaltern Studies.* Edited by R. Guha and G. C. Spivak, 288–350. New York and Oxford: Oxford University Press.

Bhabha, Homi K. 1985. "Signs Taken for Wonders: Questions of Ambivalence and Authority under a Tree outside Delhi." *Critical Inquiry* 12(1): 144–65.

Bloch, Maurice. 1975. *Marxist Analyses and Social Anthropology.* New York: John Wiley.

Bourdieu, Pierre. 1977. *Outline of a Theory of Practice.* Translated by R. Nice. Cambridge: Cambridge University Press.

Clendinnen, Inga. 1987. *Ambivalent Conquests: Maya and Spaniard in Yucatan, 1517–1570.* Cambridge: Cambridge University Press.

Clifford, James. 1986. "Introduction: Partial Truths." In *Writing Culture: The Poetics and Politics of Ethnography.* Edited by James Clifford and George Marcus, 1–26. Berkeley and Los Angeles: University of California Press.

Clifford, James. 1988. *The Predicament of Culture: Twentieth-Century Ethnography, Literature, and Art.* Cambridge: Harvard University Press.

Clifford, James, and George E. Marcus. 1986. *Writing Culture: The Poetics and Politics of Ethnography.* Berkeley and Los Angeles: University of California Press.

Collier, Jane, and Michelle Z. Rosaldo. 1981. "Politics and Gender in 'Simple' Societies." In *Sexual Meanings: The Cultural Construction of Gender and Sexuality.* Edited by S. Ortner and H. Whitehead, 275–329. New York: Cambridge University Press.

Comaroff, Jean. 1985. *Body of Power, Spirit of Resistance: The Culture and History of a South African People.* Chicago: University of Chicago Press.

Comaroff, John, and Jean Comaroff. 1992. *Ethnography and the Historical Imagination.* Boulder, CO: Westview Press.

Cooper, Frederick. 1992. "The Dialectics of Decolonization: Nationalism and Labor Movements in Post-War Africa." Paper presented at the "Power" conference, Program in the Comparative Study of Social Transformations, University of Michigan, January, Ann Arbor.

Coronil, Fernando. 1994. "Listening to the Subaltern: The Poetics of Subaltern States." *Poetics Today* 15(4): 643–58.

DeLillo, Don. 1989. *Libra.* New York: Penguin Books.

Dirks, Nicholas B., Geoff Eley, and Sherry B. Ortner. 1994. "Introduction" to *Culture/ Power/History: A Reader in Contemporary Social Theory,* 3–46. Princeton: Princeton University Press.

Fanon, Frantz. [1952] 1967. *Black Skin, White Masks.* Translated by C. L. Markmann. New York: Grove Press.

Fegan, Brian. 1986. "Tenants' Non-Violent Resistance to Landowner Claims in a Central Luzon Village." *Journal of Peasant Studies* 13(2): 87–106.

Foucault, Michel. 1978. *The History of Sexuality.* Translated by R. Hurley. New York: Pantheon.

Fox, Richard G. 1985. *Lions of the Punjab: Culture in the Making.* Berkeley and Los Angeles: University of California Press.

Fox, Richard G. 1989. *Gandhian Utopia: Experiments with Culture.* Boston: Beacon Press.

Friedrich, Paul. 1970. *Agrarian Revolt in a Mexican Village.* Englewood Cliffs, NJ: Prentice-Hall.

Genovese, Eugene D. 1976. *Roll, Jordan, Roll: The World the Slaves Made.* New York: Vintage Books.

Ginzburg, Carlo. 1985. *The Night Battles: Witchcraft and Agrarian Cults in the Sixteenth and Seventeenth Centuries.* Translated by J. Tedeschi and A. Tedeschi. New York: Penguin Books.

Guha, Ranajit. 1988. "The Prose of Counter-Insurgency." In *Selected Subaltern Studies.* Edited by R. Guha and G. C. Spivak, 45–88. New York: Oxford University Press.

Hall, Stuart, and Tony Jefferson, eds. 1976. *Resistance through Rituals: Youth Subcultures in Post-War Britain.* London: Hutchinson.

Hanks, William F. 1986. "Authenticity and Ambivalence in the Text: A Colonial Maya Case." *American Ethnologist* 13(4): 721–44.

Jain, Sharada, Nirja Misra, and Kavita Srivastava. 1987. "Deorala Episode: Women's Protest in Rajasthan." *Economic and Political Weekly* 22, no. 45 (November 7): 1891–94.

Kaplan, Martha. 1990. "Meaning, Agency, and Colonial History: Navosavakadua and the *Tuka* Movement in Fiji." *American Ethnologist* 17(1): 3–22.

Kaplan, Martha, and John Kelly. 1994. "Rethinking Resistance: Dialogics of 'Disaffection' in Colonial Fiji." *American Ethnologist* 21(1): 123–51.

Mani, Lata. 1987. "Contentious Traditions: The Debate on Sati in Colonial India." *Cultural Critique* 7 (fall): 119–56.

Marcus, George. 1986. "Contemporary Problems of Ethnography in the Modern World System." In *Writing Culture: The Poetics and Politics of Ethnography.* Edited by J. Clifford and G. Marcus, 165–93. Berkeley and Los Angeles: University of California Press.

Meillassoux, Claude. 1981. *Maidens, Meal, and Money: Capitalism and the Domestic Community.* New York: Cambridge University Press.

Mohanty, Chandra. 1988. "Under Western Eyes: Feminist Scholarship and Colonial Discourse." *Feminist Review* 30:61–88.

Nandy, Ashis. 1983. *The Intimate Enemy: Loss and Recovery of the Self under Colonialism.* Delhi: Oxford University Press.

O'Hanlon, Rosalind. 1989. "Cultures of Rule, Communities of Resistance: Gender, Discourse, and Tradition in Recent South Asian Historiographies." *Social Analysis* 25 (September): 94–114.

Ong, Aihwa. 1987. *Spirits of Resistance and Capitalist Discipline: Factory Women in Malaysia.* Albany: State University of New York Press.

Orlove, Benjamin S. 1991. "Mapping Reeds and Reading Maps: The Politics of Representation in Lake Titicaca." *American Ethnologist* 18(1): 3–38.

Ortner, Sherry B. 1984. "Theory in Anthropology since the Sixties." *Comparative Studies in Society and History* 26(1): 126–66.

Ortner, Sherry B. 1989. *High Religion: A Cultural and Political History of Sherpa Buddhism.* Princeton: Princeton University Press.

Pandey, Gyanendra. 1988. "Peasant Revolt and Indian Nationalism." In *Selected Subaltern Studies.* Edited by R. Guha and G. C. Spivak, 233–87. New York: Oxford University Press.

Pathak, Zakia, and Rajeswari Sunder Rajan. 1989. "'Shahbano.'" *Signs* 14(3): 558–82.

Rushdie, Salman. 1989. *The Satanic Verses.* New York: Viking Press.

Sahlins, Marshall D. 1981. *Historical Metaphors and Mythical Realities: Structure in the Early History of the Sandwich Islands Kingdoms.* Ann Arbor: University of Michigan Press.

Said, Edward. 1979. *Orientalism.* New York: Vintage Books.

Scott, James C. 1985. *Weapons of the Weak: Everyday Forms of Peasant Resistance.* New Haven: Yale University Press.

Scott, James C. 1990. *Domination and the Arts of Resistance.* New Haven: Yale University Press.

Scott, James C., and Benedict J. Tria Kerkvliet. 1986. "Everyday Forms of Peasant Resistance in South-East Asia" (special issue). *Journal of Peasant Studies* 13, no. 2 (January).

Sewell, William H., Jr. 1980. *Work and Revolution in France: The Language of Labor from the Old Regime to 1848.* Cambridge: Cambridge University Press.

Spivak, Gayatri Chakravorty. 1988a. "Can the Subaltern Speak?" In *Marxism and the Interpretation of Cultures.* Edited by C. Nelson and L. Grossberg, 271–316. Urbana: University of Illinois Press.

Spivak, Gayatri Chakravorty. 1988b. "Subaltern Studies: Deconstructing Historiography." In *Selected Subaltern Studies.* Edited by R. Guha and G. C. Spivak, 3–34. New York: Oxford University Press.

Stoler, Ann. 1986. "Plantation Politics and Protest on Sumatra's East Coast." *Journal of Peasant Studies* 13(2): 124–43.

Stoler, Ann. 1989. "Rethinking Colonial Categories: European Communities and the Boundaries of Rule." *Comparative Studies in Society and History* 31(1): 134–61.

Terray, Emmanuel. 1972. *Marxism and "Primitive" Societies.* Translated by M. Klopper. New York: Monthly Review Press.

Thompson, E. P. 1966. *The Making of the English Working Class.* New York: Vintage Books.

Turner, Terence. 1991. "Representing, Resisting, Rethinking: Historical Transformations of Kayapo Culture and Anthropological Consciousness." In *Post-Colonial Situations: The History of Anthropology,* Vol. 7. Edited by G. Stocking, 285–313. Madison: University of Wisconsin Press.

Turner, Terence. n.d. "The Mebengokre Kayapo: History, Social Consciousness and Social Change from Autonomous Communities to Inter-Ethnic System." Unpublished manuscript.

White, Christine Pelzer. 1986. "Everyday Resistance, Socialist Revolution, and Rural Development: The Vietnamese Case." *Journal of Peasant Studies* 13(2): 49–63.

Williams, Raymond. 1977. *Marxism and Literature.* Oxford: Oxford University Press.

Willis, Paul. 1977. *Learning to Labour: How Working-Class Kids Get Working Class Jobs.* New York: Columbia University Press.

Wolf, Eric R. 1982. *Europe and the People without History.* Berkeley and Los Angeles: University of California Press.

The Rise and Domestication of Historical Sociology

Craig Calhoun

Historical sociology is not really new, though it has enjoyed a certain vogue in the last twenty years. In fact, historical research and scholarship (including comparative history) was central to the work of many of the founders and forerunners of sociology—most notably Max Weber but also in varying degrees Karl Marx, Emile Durkheim, and Alexis de Tocqueville among others. It was practiced with distinction more recently by sociologists as disparate as George Homans, Robert Merton, Robert Bellah, Seymour Martin Lipset, Charles Tilly, J. A. Banks, Shmuel Eisenstadt, Reinhard Bendix, Barrington Moore, and Neil Smelser. Why then, should historical sociology have seemed both new and controversial in the 1970s and early 1980s?

The answer lies less in the work of historical sociologists themselves than in the orthodoxies of mainstream, especially American, sociology of the time. Historical sociologists picked one battle for themselves: they mounted an attack on modernization theory, challenging its unilinear developmental tendencies, its problematic historical generalizations and the dominance (at least in much of sociology) of culture and psychology over political economy. In this attack, the new generation of historical sociologists challenged the most influential of their immediate forebears (and sometimes helped to create the illusion that historical sociology was the novel invention of the younger generation). The other major battle was thrust upon historical sociologists when many leaders of the dominant quantitative, scientistic branch of the discipline dismissed their work as dangerously "idiographic," excessively political, and in any case somehow not quite 'real' sociology.

Historical sociology has borne the marks of both battles, and in some sense, like an army always getting ready to fight the last war, it remains unnecessarily preoccupied with them. Paying too much attention to culture or to historically specific action thus seemed to invite being labeled unscientific. Focusing on culture also raised the specter of association with Parsonsian functionalism and modernization theory. Historical sociologists remain disproportionately tied to political economy, even though most have abandoned the Marxism that gave that a political point. At the same time that old defense mechanisms remain in place, many of the old aspirations to transform sociology have dimmed. Above all, historical sociology has not succeeded enough in historicizing social theory and is itself becoming too often atheoretical.

In this essay, I will first examine the process by which historical sociology achieved a certain legitimation within sociology but in doing so became domesticated as a subfield, losing much of its critical edge and challenge to mainstream sociology. I will argue that the genuine importance of historical sociology is obscured by attempts to grasp it as a form of research method rather than as part of a substantive reorientation of inquiry. Second, I will say a little about the current importance for historical sociology of confronting problems of culture and action if it is to live up to more of its promise within sociology and also participate more effectively in interdisciplinary historical discourse. Finally, I shall point to the importance of developing approaches to historical sociology that do not just address past times but clarify the nature and theoretical significance of basic, categorical transformations in social life.

The Rise and Domestication of Historical Sociology

The 1960s upset the confident development of mainstream sociology, which was based on the balanced split between grand theory and abstracted empiricism of which C. Wright Mills (1958) wrote so critically. A variety of mostly antifunctionalist schools of theory contended with each other, in some ways undermining the very centrality of theory. Despite antiempiricist diatribes, however, the hegemony of largely quantitative, predominately scientistic empirical sociology only grew more complete. Its dominance failed to impart a sense of security to its adherents, however, as critiques from many quarters—phenomenology and ethnomethodology, Marxism and Weberian hermeneutics—challenged sociologists' very idea of what made their discipline a science. This disciplinary unease gained added force from the broader political turmoil of the 1960s and early 1970s.

In this context, historical sociology grew not just as scholarly innovation or renewal but as a sort of social movement. Recruitment to historical sociology drew on several important sources beyond simply the intrinsic merits of the perspective: for example, political dissatisfaction with current American and more broadly Western power regimes encouraged research into their origins and trajectories, and both the success and the collapse of the civil rights, student protest, and antiwar movements prompted inquiry into their antecedents and attempts to develop stronger theoretical foundations and longer historical perspectives for the future development of such movements. In more specifically disciplinary terms, many young sociologists reacted against the narrowness and abstractness of much existing sociology. And finally, the excitement generated by several interdisciplinary discourses with substantial historical and political components drew the involvement of many sociologists despite mainstream claims to disciplinary autonomy. Marxism was probably the most important, but the "new social history," labor studies, and (a bit later for the most part) feminism were also prominent.

Against this backdrop, an increasing turn to historical sociology provoked controversy where none had existed before (and, overdetermined by political ideologies and a tight job market, sometimes led to negative or difficult tenure and promotion decisions). The work of Bellah (1957), Smelser (1958), Eisenstadt (1963), and Tilly (1964) never provoked a similar controversy. Certainly, earlier historical sociologists had sometimes felt some isolation within the profession, and a few once tried to create a subsidiary association, but this never involved the conflicts of the later resurgence of historical sociology. This was partly because such earlier works were generally not tied to new and/or politically loaded theoretical perspectives. It was also because in the earlier period historical sociologists did not offer so substantial a claim to reorienting sociology in general and because the hegemony of ahistorical quantitative studies was much less complete.

In the 1970s and early 1980s, sociologists oriented to increasingly sophisticated quantitative methods, and largely disconnected from theoretical discourse, enjoyed hegemony in most of sociology's research centers. Many nonetheless manifested a certain siege mentality. Internal challenges were coupled with a sense that sociology lacked prestige in a broader scientific field. Elite or would-be elite sociologists turned away from the long tradition of work oriented to "social problems" and increasingly borrowed approaches from economics while treating economists as a crucial reference group.[1] In this context, hegemonic sociologists were apt to see historical research as dangerously unscientific because apparently idiographic, as not only unacceptably interdisciplinary but as linking sociology to the wrong other disciplines, and as attempting to reshape sociology in accord with left political concerns.

The period of this early fighting, though full of painful moments, was also the "golden age" of historical sociology—or comparative historical sociology—as a movement. Historical sociologists enjoyed glory days waging war on an old sort of functionalism, especially modernization theory, and its counterpart, a spuriously universalistic but in fact ethnocentric positivism. Classical modernization theory had given widespread credence to a universalistic, unilinear account of social and cultural change, one that led harmoniously to modern Western liberalism. Researchers who looked less at such global narratives were still likely to lose touch with historical specificity by seeking to discover universal features of those processes of social change itself. Even many of the most distinguished historical sociologists of the preceding period could be faulted on this issue.

The new historical sociologists spoke out for greater variability in processes of social change, for the impact of earlier developmental patterns on later development efforts, and for basic tensions and contradictions in the processes of historical change that made it a matter of active struggle rather than automatic unfolding. They also placed a needed emphasis on political economy, trying especially to show the centrality of power regimes, exploitation, and class division. Where many modernization theorists emphasized transformations of cultural values and "becoming individually modern," the new historical sociologists often bent over backward to avoid cultural interpretation and sociopsychological accounts. With the bathwater of untenable assumptions, however, historical sociologists were too often ready to throw out the babies of meaningful human action and concern for only what amounts to a basic historical change, especially an epochal transformation of cultural categories and forms of social relationship.[2]

Part of the reorientation was a shift in substantive concerns. Historical sociologists worked first to establish the importance of political economy and then in some cases the importance and relative autonomy of state processes against narrowly economic or cultural explanation (Evans, Rueschemeyer, and Skocpol 1986; Poulantzas's [1974] more theoretical effort within the Marxist tradition was also extremely influential). Ironically, this focus on the state, initially inspired in part by the concerns of politically committed sociologists, often deflected attention away from the study of popular political action and toward the study of formal structures, state elites, and state-centered policy formation. Politics became more a matter of structure and function than action.[3]

The reorientation was also linked to the way historical sociologists sought to win respect for their work in a discipline dominated by quantitative research and scientistic self-understanding. In Britain, calls for historical sociology were often linked to criticism of precisely these dominant orientations (often under the rubric of "positivism"). But the most rapid growth of historical sociology came not in response to these arguments but out of the empirical debates over social change that galvanized much of American sociology in the 1960s and 1970s. The leading American historical sociologists—for example, Charles Tilly and Theda Skocpol—elected to play on the turf of their mainstream colleagues, not just in placing an emphasis on empirical research ahead of theory and epistemological critique but in putting forward a methodological argument for the nature and conduct of historical sociology. This was a crucial step in domesticating the once radical and challenging movement for historical sociology and rendering it merely a disciplinary subfield distinguished by methodology.

Claiming Legitimacy from Methods

Rather than emphasizing sociology's substantive need for history—the need for social theory to be intrinsically historical—Skocpol, Tilly, and others argued that historical sociology should be accepted because it was or could be comparably rigorous to other forms of sociology.[4] Where Tilly emphasized the operationalization of quantitative sociological research and analytic methods for historical use, Skocpol placed a distinctive stress on comparison.[5] This was all the more influential because it provided an account of the analytic rigor that qualitative researchers might use. Together with Margaret Somers, Skocpol (1980; see also Skocpol 1984) mobilized John Stuart Mill to distinguish between parallel demonstration of theory, contrast of contexts, and their favored combination of the two: macrocausal analysis. There is much good sense in Skocpol and Somers' analysis, and reflection on our methods is important. But in this and other similar arguments there is also a curious tendency to try to describe historical sociology in terms of method or approach rather than substance.[6] Skocpol and Somers, for example, ask at the outset of their article "What purposes are pursued—and how—through the specific modalities of *comparative* history?" Though they use a variety of substantive studies as examples, however, by "purposes pursued" they mean generic categories of methodological purposes. Does one pursue parallel demonstration of a theory, for example, or does one seek to contrast contexts? They do not mean "What substantive theoretical or empirical problems does one aim to solve?"

For Skocpol and Somers, this methodological emphasis is part of a strategy of disciplinary legitimation.[7] They are the best representatives of an effort, implicit or explicit, to convince mainstream sociologists of the utility of historical research by playing into the penchant of mainstream sociologists for formal analytic techniques. They seek, in other words, to give largely qualitative historical sociology a status analogous to statistical research methods. There is some ambiguity as to whether this portrayal of historical analysis as a method is meant to call attention to the data gathering process— that is, historical sociology is like survey methods—or to the data analysis process—that is, historical sociology is like Lisrel. Either way, the substantive importance of historical work is underemphasized. Too often, this version of historical sociology can also be surprisingly ahistorical. It problematizes neither temporal processes nor the specificities of time and place but rather amounts to doing conventional sociology with data drawn from the past.[8] Finally, this account of historical work as a method obscures its true methodological diversity. Historians and historical sociologists may use an enormously wide variety of techniques to gather and analyze data.

Goldthorpe's (1991) critique of historical sociology is instructive and may serve as a focus for discussion, as he is a more than usually sophisticated exponent of a widespread view rooted in a conventional understanding of science. Goldthorpe seeks to dissuade sociologists from doing historical research except when absolutely necessary. The purposes of sociology are to be nomothetic, to seek the most generalizable explanations of social processes and structures, while those of history are correspondingly specific to time and place. "History may serve as, so to speak, a 'residual category' for sociology, marking the point at which sociologists, in invoking 'history,' thereby curb their impulse to generalize or, in other words, to explain sociologically, and accept the role of the specific and of the contingent as framing—that is, as providing both the setting and the limits—of their own analyses" (1991, 14). While history's positive role for sociologists is thus reduced, Goldthorpe emphasizes the negative: the price sociologists will have to pay in quality and comprehensiveness of data when they turn from contemporary to historical research.

Though he focuses his critical attention partly on Skocpol, Goldthorpe's real target is those who would deny a basic difference between history and sociology. This is a substantial and diverse crew—more so than Goldthorpe seems to realize. Not just Giddens and Abrams, but Pierre Bourdieu (Bourdieu and Wacquant 1989), Gareth Stedman Jones (1976), Fernand Braudel (1980) and Eric Hobsbawm (1971) have all argued that history and sociology are, as Braudel puts it, "one single intellectual adventure" (1980, 69; see review of this discussion in Calhoun [1987] and [1992a]). As should be evident, this is not just a list of armchair sociologists anxious to have historians serve as their "under-laborers," digging up facts for them to theorize. Their claims are simply that a strong understanding of social life must be both historical and sociological at the same time. Goldthorpe grants in passing that sociologists ought to know about the historical contexts and limits of their findings, but his main argument is that sociology and history need to be kept distinct on methodological grounds. Historians can only interpret the "relics" of the past, while sociologists can create new and better data through contemporary research. Sociologists who turn to history take on (often poorly recognized) challenges posed by the paucity of available data. This much is undoubtedly true. What is more in doubt is whether this proposition offers any principle for distinguishing history from sociology. Goldthorpe inadvertently reveals how confusing the definition of boundaries can be when he takes the work of a prominent historian, Michael Anderson, as an example of the limits of historical sociology and categorizes Charles Tilly as a historian. Beyond such gaffes—and Goldthorpe's attempt to demonstrate his case by critique of Barrington Moore and Kai Erickson rather than any of the major newer works—there are more fundamental problems with his argument.

The distinction between historical facts as inferences from relics and the facts of social science as the results of new, more perspicuous, and more complete and repeatable observations has more limited purchase than Goldthorpe imagines. It reflects both the ideology of many historians, which overstates the extent to which they rely solely on the relics they have inspected in archives (the dustier the better), and the ideology of sociologists, that it is possible rigorously to study such objects as class, industrial organization, or social integration entirely from controlled, contemporary observations without massive (and usually unexamined) historical inductions. No doubt it is correct that contemporary data gathered specifically to address an analytical problem are better suited for many sociological purposes. Specifically, to the extent that we seek generalizable, lawlike statements about specific aspects of social life, contemporary data will usually be better (though just as we would want this data to reflect a wide range of contemporary settings and subjects in order to avoid spurious claims to generality, so we would presumably want to test its historical scope as well). This tells us nothing, however, about how adequate a knowledge of social life we can in fact construct from such more or less generalizable statements about various of its specific aspects. It tells us nothing about where the categories of our sociological inquiries come from and how they remain shaped by their empirical and practical origins.

All this also tells us too little about how to differentiate sociological from historical data. How old, we might ask, does demographic data have to be before it counts as a historical relic rather than purpose-built sociological information? The data a field worker can generate from observation and interview are indeed enormously richer than those normally available to historians on some aspects of social life but not on all. If the field worker is studying a protest movement, will she refrain from consulting such "relics" as handbills passed out by the protesters, television footage, or police records (if they are promptly rather than only "historically" available)? More basically, we need to grasp how extraordinarily limited the practice of historians would be if they could rely only on first-order inferences from relics. History would be reduced to the narrowest of primary-source investigations with no broader attempts at understanding historical phenomena based on the intersection of many projects. And, perhaps more surprisingly, sociology would also be radically narrowed. Sociologists would no longer seek to answer such time-and-place-specific questions as: Is racial violence increasing in France? How have fertility patterns changed in postwar America? Have recent British educational reforms increased social mobility? They would seek, on Goldthorpe's account, only to understand racial violence, fertility, and social mobility as more or less generalizable phenomena.

Goldthorpe's methodological arguments against historical sociology could largely be rephrased as useful advice: pay attention to the availability, biases, and limits of primary sources, for example, or be careful to consider how historical facts are not "modular" and easily lifted from a book but often deeply implicated in complex interpretations. This amounts to saying that historical sociologists ought to take the same sort of care over evidence that historians do, which is quite right but hardly a convincing basis for declaring the two disciplines to be necessarily separate. Indeed, on this dimension of his argument, Goldthorpe seems mainly to be saying either that history is too hard for sociologists or that one who pays careful attention to historical evidence cannot reasonably address questions of any breadth beyond the immediate case (not even, for example, asking rigorously what it is a case of).

Goldthorpe's more basic argument for a separation of disciplines lies in his call for nomothetically generalizable observations.[9] Interestingly, he is in agreement with Theda Skocpol here (though unaware of it). She has never argued that sociology and history are indistinguishable and indeed has suggested that the disciplinary turf of historical sociology needs to be kept distinct from that of history. Her call for macroanalytic comparative strategies is, in fact, designed precisely to encourage the very pursuit of generalizable explanations (rather than accounts of specific cases) that Goldthorpe also advocates. Thus, Skocpol (1979) tries to use her case studies not to advance analysis of the French, Russian, or Chinese revolutions as such but to develop a better sociological account of states and social revolutions in general. This is why comparison is methodologically so important to her.[10] Along with Somers, she also perceives a need to answer—with something more than just substantive argument—arguments such as Goldthorpe's about either (*a*) what aspects of social life sociologists would be forced to ignore if they did not rely on historical research or (*b*) the ways in which sociological theory depends intrinsically on historical understanding (and therefore had best develop it seriously rather than relying on happenstance, casual reading, and secondary school education.[11]

At a minimum, the first of these two sorts of arguments involves recognizing four sorts of social phenomena that cannot be dealt with adequately through purely contemporaneous data sources:

1. Some important sociological phenomena, like revolutions (Skocpol 1979; Goldstone 1991) or settler societies (McMichael 1984) occur only in a small number of cases. This makes it impossible to study them by most statistical techniques and often difficult or impossible to use interviews, experiments, or other contemporary research methods to good effect because the rarity of the events means that a researcher might have to wait decades for the chance and/or it might be difficult to be on the scene at the right time.

2. Some particular events or cases of a broader phenomenon are theoretically important or have an intrinsic interest. For example, the case of Japan is crucial to all arguments about whether the origins of capitalist economic development depended on some specific cultural features of Western civilization (i.e., Europe and societies settled by Europeans). Could capitalism have developed elsewhere had Europeans not gotten to it first (Anderson 1975)?[12]

3. Some phenomena simply happen over an extended period of time. Many sociological research topics focus on fairly brief events, like marriages and divorces, adolescence, or the creation of new businesses. Other phenomena of great importance, however, happen on longer time scales. For example, industrialization, state formation, the creation of the modern form of family, and the spread of popular democracy all took centuries. Simply to look at present-day cases would be to examine only specific points in a long trajectory or course of development. This could lead not only to faulty generalizations but to a failure to grasp the essential historical pattern of the phenomenon in question.

4. For some phenomena, changing historical context is a major set of explanatory variables. For example, changes in the structure of interna-

tional trade opportunities, political pressures, technologies, and the like all shape the conditions for economic development. The world context is an important determinant of what strategies work, which ones fail, and how far development will get (Wallerstein 1974–88). When Britain became the world's first industrial capitalist country in the late eighteenth and early nineteenth centuries, it did not have to compete with any other such powerful economic producer. When Japan became an industrial capitalist power, there were already many such, and there are even more to compete with new capitalist producers today.

Even an emphasis on the empirical holes that must be left in a sociology that neglects history does not, however, fully bring out the importance of historical sociology. The rest of that importance lies in the challenge that historical sociology poses, ideally, to (a) the canonical histories (and anthropologies) that have been incorporated into classical social theory and its successors, (b) the attempt to apply concepts and develop generalizations without attention to their cultural and historical specificity, and (c) the neglect of the historicity of all of social life. It is for these reasons that *all* sociologists need to be historical, at least in some part. A strategy of disciplinary legitimation that results in a historical sociology compartmentalized as a subfield, especially one defined vaguely by methodological approach, greatly impoverishes its potential contributions.[13]

A Lost Theoretical Agenda

In the 1960s and 1970s, when modernization research was still a formidable antagonist, historical sociologists often took up a Marxist standard in their theoretical polemics.[14] Sociologists as different as Wallerstein, Tilly, and Skocpol all paid obeisances of various sorts to Marxist theory, though this seems to have mattered deeply only in Wallerstein's case. Perhaps more basically, Marxist and Marxist-influenced historiography exerted a wide influence through the work of Thompson, Hobsbawm, Braudel, and many others. Even for non-Marxist scholars, Marxism framed many of the key research questions. As time went on, however, the specific influence of Marxism waned in most versions of historical sociology. Weber's influence grew somewhat, but more basically historical sociology ceased to be characterized by any particular theoretical or political agenda (though historical sociologists made use of various theories and continued vaguely to think of themselves as Young Turks).

Most historical sociology remained within the classical sociological traditions insofar as it took its basic topics and questions from the attempt to understand the change processes, major events, and international impacts of Western modernity. Relatively few historical sociologists studied earlier epochs or parts of the histories of non-Western societies that had little to do with the impact of the West or the modern world system (Mann 1986 and Abu-Lughod 1989 are exceptions). Though the new wave of historical sociologists emphasized variation and comparison more, they actually did less work in Third World settings than did their predecessors among modernization researchers. Historical sociology of the last twenty years has spared itself important challenges by focusing overwhelmingly on the modern West, especially on the more industrial countries (and for that matter especially on the larger Western European countries and North America). Like its predominantly empiricist character, this helped to keep it in or near the sociological mainstream.

Much the same story of domestication could be told of social history, of course, despite Hobsbawm's anticipation twenty years ago that "social history can never be another specialization like economic or other hyphenated histories because its subject matter cannot be isolated" (1971, 5). Social history has indeed been compartmentalized. It too has lost its insurgent, cutting-edge character. To many historians, cultural history appears to have taken that place (Hunt 1989). Feminist scholarship is another, overlapping, candidate, and recently feminist historians have in fact debated whether or not they ought to throw in their lot with social history or maintain a broader engagement with the discipline as a whole (Scott 1988; Tilly 1989; Bennett 1989). Both social history and historical sociology have ceased to be intellectual movements and have instead become mere subfields. They have senior gatekeepers and junior aspirants, contending schools of thought, and prominent professors promoting the careers of their students. Their protagonists fight not for their academic lives or for radical social or political movements but for the next departmental appointment. In both cases, this is unfortunate in several ways, although good for graduate students seeking jobs.

None of this is to say that the old enemies should become heroes. Modernization theory deserved the attack it received. And in this age of collapsing communism, it is still important to challenge theories of unilinear progress. Nor have the old virtues lost all their luster. Finding a middle path between overly abstract grand theory and the overly grand pretensions of abstracted empiricism is still one of the important accomplishments of historical sociology. But the old fights between Marxists and functionalists, *dependistas* and modernization theorists, have gone the way of decks of punched computer cards and the double-knit leisure suits once all too common at ASA meetings. Key debates are now more apt to concern modernity and postmodernity, cultural interpretation and rational action models. Historical sociology (whether practiced by sociologists or historians or others) has important, indeed crucial, contributions to make to these discourses. The methodological focus of much reflection on the project of historical sociology, however, tends (*a*) to neglect the way in which it can shape such basic discourses and help to make them more than idle academic competitions and (*b*) to emphasize rather a view of the field that reflects its struggle for acceptance fifteen years ago.

Culture, Action, and Historical Sociology

The battle against modernization theory in the 1970s was not the first time sociologists found themselves constructing an exaggerated dichotomy between culture and society. This time, as before, many complemented it with a further split between action and structure. Previous historical writing, especially "old-fashioned" narrative, was accused of suggesting that individuals and groups were able somehow to translate their ideologies directly into historical outcomes, that we could understand what happened in the Russian Revolution, for example, by understanding what was in Lenin's head. It was not that analysts saw no role for action. The social structures that made action possible and the strategies that made it rational were both accepted as important concerns. It was attempts to interpret what made action *meaningful* that were portrayed as lapses into naive voluntarism or impressionistic fuzziness. And, of course, there was enough naive voluntarism about to make this plausible, just as there were enough culturalists who were prepared to present culture as an autonomous and free-floating system, independent of any social organization or creative action. It was this, for example, that diminished the effectiveness of calls like Geertz's (1958) to take culture more seriously and avoid the pitfalls of sociologism and psychologism.[15] In sociology, professional biases and powers were stacked against any interpretative account of culture or action. Phenomenology was as much the victim of this as cultural studies.

The anti-interpretative biases have remained as the sociology of culture has grown. It is an odd mix, born, like the methodological account of historical sociology, of a need for disciplinary legitimation. Indeed, the methodological arguments about comparative historical sociology seem to have influenced at least some of the recent efforts to take culture more seriously. Robert Wuthnow, one of America's foremost sociologists of culture, has recently branched into historical work with a monumental study of the Protestant Reformation, the Enlightenment, and European socialism (Wuthnow 1989). A guiding principle of Wuthnow's work is that it is important for sociologists to approach culture as object and correspondingly to avoid the interpretation of meaning. His historical study attempts to examine its three sociocultural movements solely through attention to the social factors affecting the production, selection, and institutionalization of dominant or enduring ideologies. Wuthnow offers some useful arguments, largely centered on the importance of the state as distinct from the economy. But note what factors Wuthnow feels constrained *not* to consider by virtue of his calling as sociologist: the intentions of individual actors, the force of ideas themselves, the fit between innovative ideas and existing cultural traditions, and the practical problems that made people open to shifting from one way of thinking to another. Wuthnow's approach to culture without action or meaning keeps it well within the sociological mainstream. The fact that the study is of historical movements (or that they form a chronological series) becomes coincidental. These are just cases for exploring the more general phenomenon of how movements of ideas reach critical takeoff points (reason no. 1 above for historical sociology). It is not even clear, pace Goldthorpe, that there are compelling reasons for turning to historical cases to explore this phenomenon, unless one can say something about what makes these specific cases distinctive.[16] In fact, of course, the three cases are all fascinating and much of the interest of the book inheres in the historical importance of the Reformation, the Enlightenment, and socialism. But Wuthnow cannot admit this for to do so would be to place the stress on the interpretation of the substance of the cases rather than on his methodological principles for systematic analysis.

In the last twenty years, a good deal has been done to join action and structure in a less dualistic account of structuration.[17] Culture and society are still widely opposed, however, and for every sociologist stressing the primacy of social relations, there is a historian, literary critic, or symbolic anthropologist prepared to grant culture an utter autonomy. Yet this failure to join cultural and social analysis together makes it much harder to grapple with "structuration" and throws enormous impediments in the way of grasping basic qualitative transformations in human life. Think, for example, of how social as well as cultural factors are needed to understand and substantiate George Steiner's comment on qualitative change in 1789: "In ways which no preceding historical phenomenon had accomplished, the French Revolution mobilized historicity itself, seeing itself as historical, as transformative of the basic conditions of human possibility, as invasive of the individual person." (1988, 150) The French Revolution both reflected and furthered a fundamental categorical transformation in human self-understanding, a remaking of the person, and an expansion of the capacities of social action. Yet this was not an event in culture alone or a cultural outcome imaginable separately from the social struggles and material conditions that made it possible. To begin to speak not just of "cultural systems" but of communications media, literary markets and patronage, and shifting relations between public and private spaces and identities is to enter a discourse where the cultural cannot be separated from the social. It is within this discourse that we can see the constitution and transformation of basic categories of human life.

The search for a sociology that can take human action seriously without lapsing into a naive voluntarism or a naturalistic rationalism depends upon a complex, historical understanding of culture. It requires, for example, an understanding of how what it means to be a human actor can vary, an understanding that can only be gained as part of a culturally and historically specific inquiry into the constitution of the person.[18] At the same time, an actorless account of culture, such as that characteristic of most anthropology and more recently of poststructuralism, cannot provide the necessary dynamism or normative purchase for either good history or critical theory. Finally, an account of the most basic transformations in history must appeal to action of some sort if it is to offer an endogenous account of crucial changes and one that avoids either mechanistic determinism or the imputation that change is just an unfolding of potentials structurally inherent in a cultural or social-relational starting point. And it must work in terms of the transformation of cultural categories, not only to avoid a simple voluntarism but to be able to identify what should count as qualitatively new rather than merely quantitatively different. Thus, capitalism is not merely different from feudalism on a range of variables, such as tendency to expand productivity or reliance on money-mediated markets, it is incommensurable with feudalism because basic categories and practices—like labor, as it is transformed by abstraction and sale into a commodity—either exist only in one or have sharply distinct meanings in each and cannot be carried on in both senses at once.

Getting some purchase on culture—as meaningful activity, not mere objective products—must be among the next tasks of a historical sociology that has avoided this dimension of human life as part of its reaction against modernization theory and its strategy for disciplinary legitimation. Unfortunately, three "professional deformations" distort historical sociologists' efforts in this arena. The first is the idea that one can or should avoid culture. The second is the notion that culture is simply a topical area referring to certain objective products of human activity.[19] The third is the idea that culture should be addressed only in subjectless, actorless, "structuralist" guise.[20] Each of these last two falls afoul of Leroi Jones's admonition that "hunting is not those heads on the wall" by failing to address the ubiquitous role of meaningful action in the creation of all social arrangements.

The Historical Constitution of Sociological Categories

Poststructuralism (which is really a more direct outgrowth of structuralism than the name implies) has enormously revitalized contemporary cultural discourse. Poststructuralist ideas are at the heart of the explanation for why the emphases of historians have shifted from the once "new" social history in which sociology was influential to a currently fashionable "new cultural history" (Hunt 1989). Nonetheless, we need to see three closely linked weaknesses that keep poststructuralism from meeting all the needs of historical sociology. The first is that it works within and perpetuates the separation of culture and society. The second is that it grants little if any role to action. These both stem from an internal approach to culture, one that stresses its unity and closure as a system, even if that is only for the purpose of deconstructing it. As Weber (1987) has argued, the very claim to deconstruct a text is a move that holds that text within an interpretive framework or community, which fixes it within a context. Poststructuralism, in its reliance on texts and textual metaphors and in its general antisubjectivist analytic strategies, constructs culture as a system of objects. It is in this sense sharply opposed to a view of both culture and society as matters of practice. Bourdieu's work (especially 1976, 1990), for example (though arguably in many ways an instance of "poststructuralism," insofar as that creation of English language analysts has any purchase on actual French currents of thought), shows not only how actors participate in the reproduction as well as creation or change of structure but also how the categories of social and cultural analysis merge in an account of the forms of practice. The forms are that part—usually the vast majority—of action that can be theorized and properly analyzed. Beyond them lies the particularity or singularity of action that can only be described.

Even Bourdieu, however, does not offer all the strength we need to counter the third weakness of poststructuralism. This is its universalizing of difference. When difference is universalized it is, ironically, trivialized. When any grouping of commonalities is simply the normalizing discourse of power, we lose our capacity to distinguish greater or lesser differences. This is linked to the notorious incapacity of poststructuralist work to ground its own (or any other) normative orientations. Shifting to a theory of practice helps. It reveals, first of all, that as activity culture has a temporal direction, a history. Shifts from one position to another are not made from among the choices in an abstract field of possibilities (as both logical positivists and poststructuralists often imply). Rather, they are practical moves from weaker to stronger positions; they are made to solve practical problems. In the realm of knowledge, Charles Taylor (1989) has called this "epistemic gain." But outside epistemology a similar process is also at work, obligating us to understand the meaning of ideas, political actions, or institutions at least partly in terms of their creation. We need to grasp them not just as they are, in a static sense, but as they could have been arrived at in a historical process. "It is essential to an adequate understanding of certain problems, questions, issues, that one understand them genetically" (Taylor 1984, 17). In other words, we understand a position by knowing why and from where or what one might have moved to it.[21]

In addition, working in a theory of practice points up that not all differences necessitate clashes or resolutions. We can and do allow many to coexist happily. But for at least a few this is impossible. These differences involve incommensurable practices, courses of action that cannot be pursued simultaneously any more than one can play rugby and basketball by making the same moves (see Bernstein 1983; Calhoun 1991a; Taylor 1985). An analysis of practices, and more particularly of the various habituses and implicit strategies that they reveal, is basic to establishing where the truly important lines of social conflict lie. But such an analysis of practices and strategies is not enough. It is still internal to a sociocultural formation. It does not give us purchase, any more than typical poststructuralist approaches do, on the source and nature of categorical transformations in history. Bourdieu's account of the various forms of capital, for example, generalizes the idea of capital for the analysis of any and all strategizing in any historical or cultural setting (see Calhoun 1993b). In this way, it undercuts even Bourdieu's own earlier analyses of the tensions between Kabyle society and the incursions of French society and economic practices in Algeria (Bourdieu 1962, 1976). Bourdieu's scheme does not elucidate what, if anything, might be distinctive to modern capitalism, for example, or how the various individual and collective strategic pursuits that are the source of constant quantitative changes in social arrangements ever are reorganized by more basic qualitative changes (though aspects of this are part of his current work on the development of the modern French state). Bourdieu's work is similar, in this connection, to Foucault's. Both begin with analyses that make a good deal of contrasts between modernity and pre- or nonmodern social forms. Yet each is led to universalize his critical analytic tools, the bodily inscription and discourse of power, and the convertible forms of capital.

This is not just a question of where particular concepts or generalizations apply, a matter of scope statements (Walker and Cohen 1985). The notion of historical constitution of categories is more basic. Durkheim, in *The Elementary Forms of Religious Life* (1968), took on the challenge of giving a sociological account of the origins of the basic categories of thought. This sociologization of the Kantian categories is fascinating and a neglected feature of Durkheim's thought. But it is crucial to note that Durkheim operates primarily in static terms. His idea of "elementary forms" is not simply an idea of origins but rather of universals that are more visible in their earlier and simpler appearances. His account of the categories—time and space, for example—makes the experience of living in society their basis. It does not focus on how variations in social organization or processes of historical transformation might reconstitute such basic categories. If this is an issue (within the neo-Kantian framework) for categories like space and time, it is at least as much so for "rationality," "individual," "nation," or "society." These and a host of other basic terms of analysis derive their specific meanings from processes of historical change (within specific cultural traditions and often refracted through highly developed intellectual frameworks), not from abstract definition.

Social theory has been heavily shaped by the construction of its "canon" of classical works. Parsons played the most substantial role (though the real canonizers were those who taught theory and wrote texts). The major innovation since Parsons's death has been the addition of Marx to the ranks of founders. Simmel continues to appear only on the fringes, and other than Marx, the history of social theory before the late nineteenth century remains widely ignored. This not only reduces the range of theoretical ideas most sociologists use, it inhibits interdisciplinary discourse (e.g., with political theory that remains in active dialogue with earlier theories). Perhaps even more basically, the construction of the canon shaped the standard historical views of most sociologists—these have come not so much from the study of history as from the study of what Weber, Durkheim, and other classical theorists have had to say about history. Such study has tended, moreover, to discount the study of historical change as such in favor of typologies: traditional/modern, mechanical/organic, and so on. Though Durkheim's account of the division of labor does offer some causal arguments (e.g., about the role of "dynamic density"), it is not mainly a historical account of change so much as an elaboration of the functioning of two different forms of social solidarity. Weber, far more a historian than Durkheim, is nonetheless taught to sociologists largely through his abstract definitions and typologies in the opening pages of *Economy and Society,* together with *The Protestant Ethic and the Spirit of*

Capitalism. His writings about the complexity of historical variation and change are generally ignored or relegated to secondary status.

From the works of classical theorists, sociologists were apt to draw schematic accounts of how modern societies came into being, which they would then treat as both settled and sufficient. Sociologists—like most political scientists and economists—were primarily concerned with the operation of the existing institutions of modern societies. They did not focus on the historical transformations that brought those societies into being or on the idea that they might be fundamentally transformed.[22] One of the most important impacts of Marxism, when it was revitalized in the 1960s, was that it introduced such a notion of basic transformations into social science discourse. The important role of Marxism in the resurgence of historical sociology did not put culture or the interpretation of meaningful human action in the foreground, but it did help to maintain a central place for the problematic of basic historical change. Marxism is one of the theories most attuned to the need to specify clear breaks between epochs and to develop historically specific conceptual tools for understanding each.[23] A category like labor, for instance, gains its full theoretical meaning only in terms of the whole categorical structure of capitalism. Its meaning is fundamentally altered if it is reduced to "work," in the sense in which productive activity is characteristic of all historical periods. See Postone (1993) for a sophisticated reading of Marx's mature theory as being historically specific to capitalism.

This is part, for example, of what Hobsbawm (1971) meant by distinguishing the history of society from social history in general. Social historians may study innumerable ways in which people are social; they may identify a host of commonalties or divergences in the routines of daily life. Simply looking at these specifics, however, does not give us a grip on basic transformations in fundamental forms of social arrangements. Consider, for example, the notion of "everyday forms of resistance," made popular recently by the subaltern studies group. There are indeed innumerable ways in which subalterns may resist the will of those who dominate them or at least may resist submerging their identities in the hegemonic culture imposed on them. By means of dialect and the outright refusal of discourse, they insulate their worlds from the scrutiny of those from dominant groups. They move slowly, instill distrust in their children, and develop a range of other "weapons of the weak" (Scott 1984). This is an important fact of social life. But noting it, or distinguishing tactics of maneuver from position, does not take away from the observation that organized, sustained, and cumulative political action by such subalterns has been historically exceptional, restricted primarily to the modern era, and effective in securing changes in ways that everyday resistance could never rival. Hobsbawm overstates this, particularly by implying that formalization and conscious control are essential to influence and subjectivity, but he is not altogether off the mark:

> "The poor," or indeed any subaltern group, become a subject rather than an object of history only through formalized collectivities, however structured. Everybody always has families, social relations, attitudes toward sexuality, childhood and death, and all other things that keep social historians usefully employed. But, until the past two centuries, as traditional historiography shows, "the poor" could be neglected most of the time by their "betters," and therefore remained largely invisible to them, precisely because of their active impact on events was occasional, scattered and impermanent. (1978, 48)

This capacity to organize, to create institutionalized forces for change, of course depended on other social changes, including the growth of the state and capitalist industry. Changes like these help to define categorical breaks in history, as distinct from mere differences and fluctuations.

Marxism is not unique in stressing such breaks. Foucault (1966, 1969), unquestionably influenced by Marx (and Hegel) though equally without question no Marxist in his mature work, laid great stress on the discovery of historical "ruptures." Modernization theory itself proposed at least one set of changes so basic as to amount to a fundamental transformation, the defining "before" and "after" of tradition and modernity (though after this one historical break all further change was seen in terms of an evolutionary continuum). For the most part, however, historians and sociologists have rejected, or at least abandoned, consideration of such breaks. Even the fate of Foucault's emphasis on ruptures is instructive. Foucault has become enormously influential, in part precisely because historians are prepared to take a search of the power/knowledge link and other fundamental categories of Foucauldian analysis into virtually any and every conceivable historical context. Indeed, Foucault himself did this in the later volumes of his *History of Sexuality* (1978–88), abandoning the argument about the distinctiveness of modernity that was so central to his earlier work. So used, Foucault's categories become, ironically, as universalist as rational choice theory or any other product of the Enlightenment discourses he began by criticizing.

This use of Foucault is particularly American and fits with a more general tendency to turn French structuralist discourse into a normalized academic doctrine. Where the French structuralists and poststructuralists argued in a strong polemical relationship to Marxism, phenomenology, and other analytic strategies, their American disciples have tended, ironically, to reproduce deconstructionism and postmodernism as monological discourses of truth, losing sight of the agonistic dimension of their origins (see Weber [1987], for a perceptive discussion focused on literary criticism). Of course, the poststructuralists (to take a single name for this tendency) argue about the importance of difference and conflict; they do not ignore them. But too often they universalize these features of discourse and culture, making it impossible to grasp differences in the production and character of difference, for example, and obscuring attention to other dimensions of culture and social life.

At its best, one of the points that Foucault's work (especially 1965, 1966, 1969, 1977) makes is that we need an understanding of the historical constitution of basic categories of understanding, and we need to see the costs entailed in their construction. Foucault's work is not very widely read by historical sociologists, though, and at least partly for an instructive reason. Foucault appears in the guise of a student of culture, and historical sociology is still locked in a reaction formation against cultural analysis that dates from its battles with modernization theory. Yet, this failure to take culture seriously not only impedes addressing basic categorical breaks in history, it hinders historical sociology's shift of attention to the emerging central issue of the constitution of actors. Even though many historical sociologists study collective action, they commonly adopt a kind of objectivism and fail to give adequate attention to culture (i.e., to actors' constructions of their own identities, to the categories through which they understand the world, etc.). This objectivism is equally manifest in rational choice theory and structuralism, which are two sides of the same coin in mainstream sociology. In the work of Tilly, for example, collective action is the product of interests (in an analysis not far from rational choice theory) and structure but seldom of culture. More precisely, Tilly does not pursue a cultural analysis of the constitution of interests or structures.

One of the key differences of critical theory from traditional social theory is that the former demands a reflexive and historical grounding of its own categories, while the latter typically adopts transhistorical, putatively neutral, and universally available categories. In other words, the critical theorist takes on the obligation to ask in strong senses "why do I use these categories, and what are their implications?" while the traditional theorist asks simply "have I defined my categories clearly?" The division is evident even within the Marxist tradition. Many Marxists thus treat labor as a transhistorical, universal category rather than one specific to capitalism. Reducing labor to work, however, deculturalizes and dehistoricizes Marx's analysis of capitalism. It negates the effort of *Capital* to show how a categorical break distinguishes earlier accumulation of wealth from capitalism and demands the new analytic categories and changed relationships among terms established in the opening chapter.[24] Similarly, other theorists, recognizing cultural and historical diversity, have attempted to overcome its more serious implications by subsuming it into a common, often teleological, evolutionary framework. Unlike biological evolutionary theories, which stress the enormous qualitative diversity within the common processes of speciation, inheritance, mutation, selection, and so forth, sociological theories have generally relied on claimed universal features of all societies—like technology, held by Lenski, Lenski, and Nolan (1990) to be the prime mover of evolutionary change—to act as basic, transhistorical variables. Such theories do indeed pay attention to the problem of establishing qualitative changes in patterns of social organization, but rather than showing the historical constitution and particularity of their own categories and analytical approach, they position themselves outside of history as neutral observers of the whole.

As the foremost contemporary critical theorist, Habermas has been ambivalent on the issue of historical grounding of categories. His early work, especially *The Structural Transformation of the Public Sphere,* works in exemplary historical fashion. It develops its concept as specific to a stage of capitalist development and state formation, as varying among national histories, and as transformed by transitions within capitalism and state organization. In Habermas's later work, however, especially in his magnum opus, *The Theory of Communicative Action,* he sheds this historical constitution of categories for an evolutionary construct. Although he wants to stress the special importance of the opposition between instrumental and communicative reason in the contemporary era, for example, he locates the distinction in a primordial split, a sort of communicative expulsion from the Garden of Eden. His theory becomes more Rousseauian (and Kantian) and less Marxian. It also becomes much less historically specific, with the result that he is no longer able within its terms to locate basic qualitative transformations within history (such as the rise of capitalism). This has the effect of laying his theory open to the common poststructuralist (or postmodernist) charge of unjust universalization—more so indeed than even his widely criticized normative claims.

Poststructuralist and postmodern thought has emphasized difference in a radical but generally salutary way and with the idea of postmodernity itself such thought has suggested a historical shift that required a commensurate shift in categories and modes of analysis. Unfortunately, this shift has been asserted rather more than demonstrated—particularly where social rather than cultural factors are at issue (Calhoun 1993a). It is also difficult—and often rejected as a goal—to ground the poststructuralist account of difference in an analysis of its own historical and theoretical conditions. It is impossible within its strong claims as to the incommensurability of language games to construct a conclusive argument as to why we should in fact be tolerant or encouraging of other language games, or why other than by chance we should participate in any one. This then has the ironic result of granting "the other" legitimacy comparable to ourselves but of denying the possibility of meaningful discourse across the cultural gulf that separates us. What is needed to resolve this dilemma is the recognition that processes of communication and cross-cultural relations are themselves historical and part of materially consequential social practices. Translation is an inapt metaphor for what most important cross-cultural communication must mean. Any account of the confrontation of, say, aboriginal Australians with Europeans must go beyond an attempt to translate cultural contents to a recognition that all communication was a part of relations that transformed each party, though asymmetrically; that were conducted by means of material power as well as cultural signification; and that focused on social practices not abstract discourse. To say such communication—or less extreme and less violent communication across basic cultural divides—is historical is to say that arriving at mutual understanding is not primarily a process of translation but rather of transformation. Both parties must change into the sort of people who can understand each other (and a good deal else is likely to change in the same process).[25]

If it is to be able to deal effectively with either basic cross-cultural comparisons or fundamental historical transformations, social theory needs the capacity to ground its categories historically. This is something that historical sociology (and history) should provide. The category of the person is a good example. Inquiries of the kind begun by Marcel Mauss (cf. n. 18) need to be continued. Perhaps the most important contemporary exemplar of such work is Charles Taylor's recent *The Sources of the Self*. We could read this work as, among other things, an almost diametric opposition to Foucault on a crucial point. Foucault used historical studies to uncover the construction of selves (and "the self") and then took this as the basis for an account of the unreality of such constructed selves. He remained, ironically, caught within a "jargon of authenticity" (Adorno 1973). Historicity was taken as a rebuttal of claimed authenticity that would have had to be "original" to be accepted (see discussion in Berman 1989). Taylor, by contrast, shows a whole series of subtle stations through which the modern notion of the self passes as it is constituted and reconstituted. Each of these, he suggests, must be treated as authentic (see Calhoun 1991b).

Taylor's inquiry, however, remains within the realm of (a rather philosophical) intellectual history. Taylor focuses conceptual attention on practices, but does not try to concretize and substantiate his account of the transformations of the self through a broader sociocultural history. This is a problem with intellectual history more generally, though current trends are in a positive direction. Recent intellectual history has branched out beyond semibiographical attention to "great thinkers," placing their work not just in the context of "their times" or their intellectual influences and adversaries but in that of a more theoretically serious analysis of systems of signification and discourse (see, e.g., White 1978, 1987; LaCapra 1983). But signification and discourse are still typically treated as though they existed independently of broader social and material processes.[26]

Conclusion

Historical scholarship and research rose to the forefront of sociology as an alternative to modernization research and related approaches to social change. It rose also in response to an unfortunate narrowing of much mainstream sociological research and inattention to major questions, including some posed by classical social theorists. The political orientations of early practitioners and their challenge to the prevailing orthodoxies of mainstream sociology aroused controversy and hostility. When it was not simply ad hominem attack, this often focused on the closely related claims that historical research was "idiographic" and/or always a matter of interpretation and therefore unable to make contributions to the project of a cumulative social science. Some of the historical sociologists most influential in winning disciplinary legitimacy for the field did so partly by claiming for historical sociology a distinctive (usually comparative) methodology. Framing the project of historical sociology in methodological rather than substantive terms, however, has had the unfortunate effects of weakening ties to social theory and reducing much historical sociology to conventional mainstream sociological research using data from the past. The thematic importance of historicity as such is too often lost.

The legitimation of historical sociology first and foremost as rigorous method rather than substantive challenge, the predominance of political-economic foci, and the continued emphasis on rejecting the culturally oriented modernization approach combine to inhibit development of work oriented more to matters of culture and meaningful social action. Even where culture is addressed, there is a strong tendency to try to do so in objectivistic terms rather than through interpretation of meaning.

In order to realize its potential both within sociology and in relation to an interdisciplinary historical and theoretical discourse, however, historical sociology needs to address problems of the changing constitution of social actors, the shifting meanings of cultural categories, and the struggle over identities and ideologies. These need to be conceived as part and parcel of social relations, not separate topics of inquiry, and still less as the turf of other disciplines. It is important thus to regain for historical sociology the agenda of changing social theory rather than accepting domestication as a "safe" subdiscipline. It is also important to resist arguments for the sharp separation of sociology from interdisciplinary discourse in history and social theory.

In its early years, historical sociology played a major role in reopening serious theoretical discourse about large-scale social transformations. This remains a vital agenda. This is not to say that studies with other foci are illegitimate or unimportant. But to reduce historical sociology to conventional sociology applied to past times is both to deprive it of its main significance and to open the door to challenges of methodologically minded conventional sociologists. Historical sociologists thus should continue to push forward with theoretical discourse on basic social transformations rather than being altogether domesticated within the positivity of contemporary sociological research. In order to do so, however, it is crucial to focus much more centrally and richly on problems of culture and meaningful action. Blind spots or weaknesses in these areas are problematic legacies of historical sociology's initial conflict with modernization theory and its struggle for legitimation. Social theory, however, needs not just a historical approach to culture and action as objects of analysis but an approach that opens up inquiry into the historical constitution of basic theoretical categories. This is especially important for any theorist who aspires to be reflexively aware of the conditions of her or his own thought. A reflexivity limited to the here and now or to a positive recognition of one's own interpretative tradition cannot suffice as the grounding for a truly critical theory.

NOTES

1. I have shown elsewhere a striking increase in the rate of citations to economics journals by articles in the leading American sociology journals during this period (Calhoun 1992a).

2. This was certainly not true for all, though few approaches combined both attention to epochal transformation and to culture. An account of what makes the modern world categorically distinctive is central to Wallerstein's world-systems theory (though culture as a substantive domain is less so). In this sense, his work is among the most historical of historical sociologies (even though Wallerstein sharply distinguishes his focus on social change from an interest in the idiosyncratic past for its own sake). That is, he works by studying a process of change in all its phases rather than by abstracting several events—for example, revolutions—from their historical contexts in order to look for general features of revolutions. Similarly, historical transformations in cultural and sociopsychological processes have been addressed importantly by Sennett (1976) and others. More typical, however, are accounts that reduce culture to ideology and social psychology to rational interests. Various other babies have also been thrown out with the bathwater of modernization theory—for example, attention to the effect of built environment or physical infrastructure (e.g., transportation and communications facilities) on social life has been abandoned (Calhoun 1992b).

3. In this the new political sociologists moved close to much American political science, itself often distanced from politics by the objectification of its objects of study.

4. They certainly agreed that sociology needed historical work but less on theoretical grounds than in order to fill in neglected empirical territory. In this sense, it is wrong to lump, as Goldthorpe (1991) does, Skocpol's position together with the theoretical argument for a unity of sociology and history advanced by Giddens (1985), Abrams (1982), and others. Of course, these two sorts of claims were not contradictory, though the difference in rationales is significant. Skocpol's methodological emphasis was distinctively important in the context of American sociology. It was linked to a much more rapid growth of empirical historical research by sociologists than that developed in Britain (see Calhoun 1987), but much of this research lost touch with the agenda of making social theory itself more historical.

5. Tilly was and is also an advocate of comparison, and some of his earlier collaborative work was very influential in promoting specifically comparative historical sociology (Tilly, Tilly, and Tilly 1975; Tilly 1975). The difference from Skocpol in this regard is one of emphasis and formalization.

6. Charles Tilly (1988), for example, has proposed a hierarchy moving from the epochal "world-historical" level down through world-system analysis and macrohistory to microhistory, with his own preferences lying in the latter two categories. This is perfectly plausible, but it reveals the same tendency to categorize mainly on nonsubstantive features of analytic strategy. Charles Ragin and David Zaret (1983) have offered a different methodological program, drawing on Weber and developed by Ragin (1988) through Boolean algebra and other techniques.

7. Concern for legitimation was not unreasonable, whatever the merits of the specific strategy. Mainstream sociology was for a time strongly biased against historical work and influenced heavily by its scientism and the categories of the *methodenstreit,* the contrast of putatively nomothetic and idiographic disciplines. Too much of this

nonsense lives on. At the same time, enough historians are hostile to theory and to systematic reflection on the production of their knowledge to give credence to the disciplinary split from their side of the fence. But the emotions of the dispute are now fairly remote, and it is a little strange to read through the numerous debates over whether and how history and sociology should link up (see reviews in Abrams 1982 and Calhoun 1987). For all their frequent good sense, these told us little about what was to happen when the disciplines did join forces, and they underestimated the needs that would remain unmet even when historians and sociologists spoke freely. Gareth Stedman Jones was (along with Hobsbawm) one of the few clearly to articulate the central issue: "there is no distinction in principle between history and any of the other 'social sciences.' The distinction is that between theory brought to bear" (1976, 305). Similarly, we might add, it was naive for optimists to assume that there would be no serious or enduring clash of analytic perspectives and that the differences between sociologists and historians were purely complementary—different sorts of data, say, or mere data versus analytic techniques.

8. Similarly, sociologists doing longitudinal analyses with data plucked out of historical context now often jump on the bandwagon of historical sociology—at least when there appear to be benefits.

9. In drawing on this terminological heritage of the *methodenstreit,* sociologists in recent decades have implied that theory must be exclusively a matter of the so-called nomothetic. This reflects a very distinct and problematic view of theory, however, and accordingly neglects both the extent of genuine theory developed in historically and culturally specific—putatively idiographic—analyses and conversely the extent to which even apparently very general theory is intrinsically specific itself, its conceptualizations rooted in their empirical referents (Calhoun 1991a).

10. Goldthorpe really has a further claim about the level of analysis in works like Skocpol's and Moore's. He leaves this rather undeveloped, however, because he confounds it with the easier task of showing that Moore's (1966) use of historical sources is sloppy (something that has been argued at length before). He doesn't really develop the underlying argument, which, I think, would need to go something like this: Moore and Skocpol work by putting together accounts of individual cases at the national level from published historical works. Such cases are apt to reflect both inadequate grasp of the historical specifics of the individual cases and a poor ability to discriminate among the conflicting arguments of historians. Even where this were not true, such works would still be too "grand" in their aims. By attempting to explain very big questions directly with variables that they can only measure based on extremely complex inferences from inferences from inferences (and which in any case are composites of other more specific variables), they render their analyses dubious at best. Crucially, they are not able (because of the limits of historical data) to get at the really basic variables that constitute the more complex phenomena and that would need to be examined to produce a really satisfying explanation. They are like biologists reasoning from phenotypes in the absence of genetic information (or even a good classification based on reproductive

organization and descent rather than appearance). This improved form of Goldthorpe's argument has some merit but (*a*) has little purchase on the distinguishing of history from sociology except insofar as sociologists imagine that historical relics are adequate sources of data for developing knowledge of such quasiuniversal building blocks of social life and (*b*) implies an assumption on Goldthorpe's part that microsociology is intrinsically simpler than macro (because it is about building blocks rather than complex structures built of them) and (*c*) implies the further assumption that it is potentially possible to aggregate an adequate understanding of the whole social world (including its largest scale structures and dynamics) from such building blocks.

11. I refer to Somers only as coauthor of the influential 1980 article with Skocpol. As her paper in the present volume reveals, she has since changed her position (if it was ever fully represented by that article).

12. In general, case studies are important supplements to statistical research because they allow detailed knowledge of specific instances of a more general phenomenon, as well as statements about the average or the overall pattern. Case studies are often misunderstood by those who ask whether cases are "typical" or "representative." Case studies are often especially illuminating when focused on nontypical examples where they point up the limits to theoretical generalizations.

13. It would be hard in any case to find the methodological principle that unifies the major "classics" of the resurgence of historical sociology in the 1970s. Is it a method (or set of methods) that joins *The Modern World-System* (Wallerstein 1974–88), *The Rebellious Century* (Tilly, Tilly, and Tilly 1975), *Lineages of the Absolutist State* (Anderson 1974), and *States and Social Revolutions* (Skocpol 1979) in a common discourse or makes them exemplars to generations of graduate students? One might at least as well point to their common bias in favor of broadly "structural" accounts and against either voluntaristic approaches to action or cultural interpretation. Surely, however, the importance of the works just mentioned derives primarily from their contributions to addressing important substantive theoretical or empirical problems or questions.

14. The "new social history" was also often Marxist or political-economic, but not so biased toward the "macro." Indeed, family history was important to social history in a way it never was to historical sociology (despite several good historical works by sociologists). Much family history, too, it should be noted, was carried out within the broad framework of political economy, concerns for class and attentions to the struggles people faced both within and about families during the course of industrialization. But links to cultural analysis were more readily made in history, partly because the Young Turks challenged an older generation of "conventional" macropolitical historians rather than culturally oriented modernization theorists. Feminist scholarship (e.g., Rose 1992) has recently helped to link family history, cultural analysis, and historical sociology.

15. In "Ideology as a Cultural System" (1958), Geertz was writing with the basic Parsonsian conception of three subsystems of action—social, personality, and cultural—and calling for a renewed appreciation of the relative autonomy of the last.

16. This analysis of Wuthnow is developed further in Calhoun (1992c).

17. This term arises earlier in Pierre Bourdieu's work (e.g., 1971) but has become more widely associated in English with Anthony Giddens.

18. This is a problem charted early on for sociology in Marcel Mauss's classic—and all but forgotten—essay on the category of the person (reprinted with commentary in Carrithers, Collins, and Lukes 1985). The major contemporary exploration of this problem is Charles Taylor's *The Sources of the Self* (1989); see also Calhoun (1991b).

19. "Hunting is not those heads on the wall" is the title of a brilliant essay on writing by Leroi Jones (Amiru Baraka) *City Lights Review,* 1968, 56–71.

20. This is raised in an interesting exchange between Theda Skocpol and William Sewell Jr. Sewell opened the exchange with a critique of Skocpol's (1979) argument against ideological explanation of revolution. He advocated a more sophisticated and complex analytic approach that would allow for a better grasp of culturally and historically concrete phenomena. Recognizing that culture has been dismissed by historical sociologists (and most other sociologists) as too closely linked to a voluntarist account of agency, he argued that attention to culture need not involve theories that take the conscious intentions of agents to be historically or sociologically decisive. This was how Skocpol ruled out the autonomous power of ideology: she showed that "any line of reasoning that treats revolutionary ideologies as blueprints for revolutionary outcomes cannot sustain scrutiny" (1979, 170). Sewell claims authority from Althusser, Foucault, Geertz, and Williams for an alternative view of ideology as the anonymous and impersonal operation of ideological state apparatuses, epistemes, cultural systems, or structures of feeling. This view of ideology is structural, he suggests, just as are the forces of class, state, and international relations that form the basis of Skocpol's analysis. Skocpol, therefore, dealt with only a "naive voluntarist conception of ideology" (Sewell 1985, 61). In reply, Skocpol accepts Sewell's criticism of her earlier treatment of ideology but challenges his argument that the concept of ideology should be used in an entirely impersonal, anonymous, and structuralist sense. Ironically, given her reputation as an extreme proponent of structural analysis and the frequent criticism of her neglect of both culture and intentional action, Skocpol argues for these notions against Sewell's ideological structuralism. The central difficulty with Sewell's argument, Skocpol contends, is his failure to distinguish between a notion of culture which is "transpersonal" and anonymous, and ideology and cultural idioms as these are brought into use by specific actors in revolutionary transformation.

21. This emphasis on a fundamentally historical form of understanding is shared in varying degrees by a variety of intellectual traditions, from postfundamentalist and post-Kuhnian philosophy of science through parts of poststructuralism and above all Gadamer's hermeneutics, in which practice and historicity is basic to the critique of earlier hermeneutic claims to find truth by radically overcoming historical distance (Gadamer 1975; Bernstein 1983 argues the case for a convergence among different scholarly traditions). The Gadamer-Taylor argument shows the insufficiency of the familiar division posed by speech act theory (and appropriated by Habermas) between constative and performative utterances. Poststructuralists are often keen to show how

putative constatives (e.g., neutral truth claims) are really performatives (grabs for power). On Taylor's account we see that demonstrating performativity need not be the end of analysis, and that performativity is not antithetical to a discourse of at least proximate truth or rightness.

22. Modernization theorists looked outside the modern West but for the most part dropped the idea of basic historical transformations for a notion of evolutionary continuum. They did not study the transformations of modernity but rather the "becoming modern" of those who missed the first opportunity.

23. It should not be thought that all Marxists are equally attentive to this need. It has been common for many to turn Marxism into a more or less evolutionary theory, and/or to treat the basic concepts of Marx's account of capitalism as transhistorical.

24. See Postone (1993) for a discussion of this.

25. I have discussed this at much greater length in Calhoun (1991a).

26. Intellectual history, in fact, has been a particularly active and productive field of late, fruitfully transcending its boundaries as part of the new cultural history (see discussion in Kramer 1989). Poststructuralist thought has played an important role in this.

REFERENCES

Abrams, Philip. 1982. *Historical Sociology.* Ithaca, NY: Cornell University Press.

Abu-Lughod, Janet. 1989. *Before European Hegemony: The World System, A.D. 1250–1350.* New York: Oxford University Press.

Adorno, T. W. 1973. *The Jargon of Authenticity.* Evanston, IL: Northwestern University Press.

Anderson, Perry. 1974. *Lineages of the Absolutist State.* London: New Left Books.

Bellah, Robert. 1957. *Tokugawa Religion: The Values of Pre-Industrial Japan.* Glencoe, IL: Free Press.

Bennett, Judith. 1989. "Comment on Tilly: Who Asks the Questions for Women's History?" *Social Science History* 13 (4): 471–78.

Berman, Marshall. 1989. *Modern Culture and Critical Theory.* Madison: University of Wisconsin Press.

Bernstein, Richard. 1983. *Beyond Objectivism and Relativism.* Philadelphia: University of Pennsylvania Press.

Bourdieu, Pierre. 1962. *The Algerians.* Boston: Beacon Press.

Bourdieu, Pierre. 1971. "Genese et Structure du Champ Religieux." *Revue francais de Sociologie* 12:295–334. Translation, "Genesis and structure of the Religious Field." *Comparative Social Research* 13(1991): 1–44.

Bourdieu, Pierre. 1976. *Outline of a Theory of Practice.* Cambridge: Cambridge University Press.

Bourdieu, Pierre. 1990. *The Logic of Practice.* Stanford: Stanford University Press.

Bourdieu, Pierre, and L. Wacquant. 1989. "Toward a Reflexive Sociology: A Workshop with Pierre Bourdieu," *Sociological Theory* 7:26–63.

Braudel, Fernand. 1980. *On History.* London: Weidenfeld and Nicolson.

Calhoun, Craig. 1987. "History and Sociology in Britain: A Review Article." *Comparative Studies in Society and History* 29 (3): 615–25.

Calhoun, Craig. 1991a. "Culture, History, and the Problem of Specificity in Social Theory." In S. Seidman and D. Wagner, eds., *Embattled Reason: Postmodernism and Its Critics,* 244–88. New York and Oxford: Basil Blackwell.

Calhoun, Craig. 1991b. "Morality, Identity, and Historical Explanation: Charles Taylor on the Sources of the Self." *Sociological Theory* 9 (2): 232–63.

Calhoun, Craig. 1992a. "Sociology, Other Disciplines, and the Project of a General Understanding of Social Life." In *Sociology and its Publics,* 137–95. Edited by T. Halliday and M. Janowitz. Chicago: University of Chicago Press.

Calhoun, Craig. 1992b. "The Infrastructure of Modernity: Indirect Relationships, Information Technology, and Social Integration." In *Social Change and Modernity,* 205–36. Edited by Neil Smelser and Hans Haferkamp. Berkeley and Los Angeles: University of California Press.

Calhoun, Craig. 1992c. "Beyond the Problem of Meaning: Robert Wuthnow's Historical Sociology of Culture." *Theory and Society,* 21: 419–44.

Calhoun, Craig. 1993a. "Postmodernism as Pseudohistory." *Theory, Culture and Society.* 10 (1): 75–96.

Calhoun, Craig. 1993b. "Rationality, Habitus, and Field of Power: The Question of Historical Specificity." In *Bourdieu. Critical Perspectives,* 61–88. Edited by C. Calhoun, E. LiPuma, and M. Postone. Cambridge, MA: Polity Press.

Carrithers, Michael, Steven Collins, and Steven Lukes, eds. 1985. *The Category of the Person: Anthropology, Philosophy, History.* Cambridge: Cambridge University Press.

Durkheim, Emile. [1915] 1968. *The Elementary Forms of Religious Life.* New York: Free Press, 1968.

Durkheim, Emile. 1950. *Leçons de Sociologie.* Paris: Presses Universitaires de France.

Durkheim, Emile. 1980. *Textes.* 3 vols. Edited by V. Karady. Paris: Editions de Minuit.

Eisenstadt, Shmuel. 1963. *The Political Systems of Empires.* Glencoe, IL: Free Press.

Evans, Peter, Dietrich Rueschemeyer, and Theda Skocpol. 1985. *Bringing the State Back In.* Cambridge: Cambridge University Press.

Foucault, Michel. 1965. *Madness and Civilization.* New York: Random House.

Foucault, Michel. 1966. *The Order of Things: An Archaeology of the Human Sciences.* New York: Random House.

Foucault, Michel. 1969. *The Archaeology of Knowledge.* New York: Pantheon.

Foucault, Michel. 1977. *Discipline and Punish: The Birth of the Prison.* New York: Pantheon.

Foucault, Michel. 1978–88. 4 vols. *The History of Sexuality.* New York: Pantheon.

Gadamer, Hans-Georg. 1975. *Truth and Method.* New York: Seabury.

Geertz, Clifford. [1958] 1973. "Ideology as a Cultural System." In *The Interpretation of Cultures,* 193–233. New York: Basic Books.

Giddens, Anthony. 1985. *The Constitution of Society.* Berkeley and Los Angeles: University of California Press.

Goldstone, Jack. 1991. *Revolution and Rebellion in the Early Modern World.* Berkeley and Los Angeles: University of California Press.

Goldthorpe, John. 1991. "The Uses of History in Sociology: Reflections on Some Recent Tendencies (T. H. Marshall Lecture, 1989)." *British Journal of Sociology* 42(2): 211–30.

Habermas, Jürgen. [1962] 1989. *The Structural Transformation of the Public Sphere.* Cambridge: MIT Press.

Habermas, Jürgen. [1984] 1988. *The Theory of Communicative Action.* Boston: Beacon Press.

Hobsbawm, Eric. 1971. "From Social History to the History of Society." In *Essays in Social History,* 1–22. Edited by M. W. Flinn and T. C. Smout. Oxford: Oxford University Press.

Hobsbawm, Eric. 1978. "Should the Poor Organize?" *New York Review of Books,* March 23, 44–49.

Hunt, Lynn, ed. 1989. *The New Cultural History.* Berkeley and Los Angeles: University of California Press.

Jones, Gareth Stedman. 1976. "From Historical Sociology to Theoretical History." *British Journal of Sociology* 27:295–305.

Kramer, Lloyd S. 1989. "Literature, Criticism, and Historical Imagination: The Literary Challenge of Hayden White and Dominick LaCapra." In *The New Cultural History,* 97–130. Edited by L. Hunt. Berkeley: University of California Press.

LaCapra, Dominick. 1983. *Rethinking Intellectual History: Texts, Contexts, Language.* Ithaca, NY: Cornell University Press.

Lenski, Gerhard, Jean Lenski, and Patrick Nolan. 1990. *Human Societies.* 6th ed. New York: McGraw-Hill.

Mann, Michael. 1986. *The Sources of Social Power.* Cambridge: Cambridge University Press.

McMichael, Philip. 1984. *Settlers and the Agrarian Question.* Cambridge: Cambridge University Press.

Mills, C. Wright. 1958. *The Sociological Imagination.* Harmondsworth, UK: Penguin.

Moore, Barrington. 1966. *The Social Origins of Dictatorship and Democracy.* Boston: Beacon Press.

Postone, Moishe. 1993. *Marx's Critique of Labor and Time.* Cambridge: Cambridge University Press.

Poulantzas, Nicos. 1974. *Political Power and Social Classes.* London: New Left Books.

Ragin, Charles. 1988. *Beyond Quality and Quantity.* Berkeley and Los Angeles: University of California Press.

Ragin, Charles, and David Zaret. 1983. "Theory and Method in Comparative Research: Two Strategies." *Social Forces* 61 (3): 731–54.

Rose, Sonya O. 1992. *Limited Livelihoods: Gender and Class in Nineteenth-Century England.* Berkeley and Los Angeles: University of California Press.

Scott, James. 1984. *Weapons of the Weak.* New Haven: Yale University Press.

Scott, Joan Wallach. 1988. *Gender and the Politics of History.* New York: Columbia University Press.

Sennett, Richard. 1976. *The Fall of Public Man.* New York: Alfred Knopf.

Sewell, William H., Jr. 1985. "Ideologies and Social Revolutions: Reflections on the French Case." *Journal of Modern History* 57 (1): 57–85.

Skocpol, Theda. 1979. *States and Social Revolutions.* Cambridge: Cambridge University Press.

Skocpol, Theda. 1985. "Cultural Idioms and Political Ideologies in the Revolutionary Reconstruction of State Power: A Rejoinder to Sewell." *Journal of Modern History* 57 (1): 86–96.

Skocpol, Theda, ed. 1984. *Vision and Method in Historical Sociology.* New York: Cambridge University Press.

Skocpol, Theda, and Margaret Somers. 1980. "The Uses of Comparative History in Macrosocial Inquiry." *Comparative Studies in Society and History* 22 (2): 174–97.

Smelser, Neil. 1958. *Social Change in the Industrial Revolution.* London: Routledge and Kegan Paul.

Steiner, George. 1988. "Aspects of Counter-Revolution." In *The Permanent Revolution: The French Revolution and Its Legacy,* 129–54. Edited by G. Best. Chicago: University of Chicago Press.

Taylor, Charles. 1984. "Philosophy and Its History." In *Philosophy in History,* 17–30. Edited by R. Rorty, J. B. Schneewind, and Q. Skinner. Cambridge: Cambridge University Press.

Taylor, Charles. 1985. *Philosophy and the Human Sciences: Philosophical Papers.* Vol. 2. Cambridge: Cambridge University Press.

Taylor, Charles. 1989. *The Sources of the Self: The Making of the Modern Identity.* Cambridge: Harvard University Press.

Tilly, Charles. 1964. *The Vendée.* Cambridge: Harvard University Press.

Tilly, Charles. 1988. *Coercion, Capital, and European States, A.D. 990–1990.* Cambridge, MA: Blackwell Publishers.

Tilly, Charles, ed. 1975. *The Formation of Nation-States in Western Europe.* Princeton: Princeton University Press.

Tilly, Charles, Louise A. Tilly, and Richard Tilly. 1975. *The Rebellious Century, 1830–1930.* Cambridge: Harvard University Press.

Tilly, Louise. 1989. "Gender, Women's History, and Social History." *Social Science History* 13 (4): 439–63.

Walker, Henry, and Bernard P. Cohen. 1985. "Scope Statements: Imperatives for Evaluating Theory." *American Sociological Review* 50 (3): 288–301.

Wallerstein, Immanuel. 1974–88. *The Modern World-System.* 3 vols. New York: Academic Press.

Weber, Max. [1902] 1985. *The Protestant Ethic and the Spirit of Capitalism.* New York: Free Press.

Weber, Max. [1922] 1968. *Economy and Society.* Berkeley and Los Angeles: University of California Press.

Weber, Samuel. 1987. "Capitalizing History: The Political Unconscious." In *Institution and Interpretation,* 40–58. Minneapolis: University of Minnesota Press.

White, Hayden. 1978. *Tropics of Discourse: Essays in Cultural Criticism.* Baltimore: Johns Hopkins University Press.

White, Hayden. 1987. *The Content of the Form: Narrative Discourse and Historical Representation.* Baltimore: Johns Hopkins University Press.

Wuthnow, Robert. 1989. *Communities of Discourse: Ideology and Social Structure in the Reformation, the Enlightenment, and European Socialism.* Cambridge: Harvard University Press.

Zald, Mayer N., and John D. McCarthy, eds. 1979. *The Dynamics of Social Movements.* Cambridge, MA: Winthrop.

The Past as Authority and as Social Critic: Stabilizing and Destabilizing Functions of History in Legal Argument

Robert W. Gordon

In the last twenty years there has been a remarkable revival of interest world-wide in history among lawyers and legal scholars and dramatically so in the United States, the country that Europeans like to accuse of lacking any consciousness of its past. Here, legal and constitutional history are unquestionably living subjects, the indispensable resources of the characteristically legalized forms of our political argumentation.

There is nothing at all new, of course, in the fact of lawyers resorting to history for their argumentative materials. Lawyers and historians have always cohabited in a relationship of intimate antagonism. Lawyers have always needed history, appealed to it for authority, and made significant contributions to writing it. They have also persistently been accused—especially since the emergence among professional historians of the historicist viewpoint that the past is a "foreign country" (Lowenthal 1985) different from the present and to be understood "on its own terms"—of abusing history, distorting the past, and making demands upon it to carry burdens of current relevance that it cannot possibly sustain. The revival that is now taking place relies mostly on ways of making history relevant to legal argument that have been around for some time, some of them from early modern Europe, others of more recent eighteenth- and nineteenth-century invention (see generally Kelley 1970; Kelley 1990; Franklin 1963; Pocock 1957; Walker 1981; Wieacker 1967; Grossi 1981; Burrow 1981; Stein 1980; Dawson 1968; Whitman 1990; Lieberman 1990; Siegel 1990). Much of this essay will be given over to sketching some of these recurrent modes by which lawyers have resorted to history, along with some modern examples. But I will also want eventually to suggest, though very tentatively, that there may be something new in the current revival after all, some ways of using history that do not quite repeat familiar patterns.

Lawyers' History—Some Standard Modes

First to explain the apparent paradox, namely, why lawyers keep going back to history and keep—as the historians see it—abusing it. The need to resort to history is obvious: law derives its authority from things that happened in the past, sometimes the quite distant past, from ancient documents or enactments, precedents, customs, or traditions. Yet however ancient, these texts must usually be given present effect, forcibly ripped from their originating contexts and put to work for purposes, and under circumstances, that their framers could quite literally not have imagined. Past practices are also looked to as sources of tradition as well as direct authority, especially in the Anglo-American legal culture with its preference for reasoning from precedent rather than from conceptual system. The common law method of adjudication—often extended to statutory and constitutional interpretation as well, so that in construing an old text the judges will look as often to their own past constructions as to the text itself—is inescapably to some extent backward-looking. But the invocation of tradition in law is usually for conservative rather than reactionary purposes. The legal enterprise is usually committed to stabilizing present advantages and expectations—or at most to encouraging incremental reforms—rather than to rolling back to the past in a way that would require radical undoings of the present dispensation. Law is often called upon to legitimate entitlements that have vested only after considerable social dislocations.[1] The past is therefore chiefly serviceable to lawyers only insofar as it can be seen as being of a homogeneous—or at least continuous—piece with the present.

A closer look at some of the conventional modes of lawyers' history will quickly reveal why it is—indeed, usually must be—tortured history by the standards of historians.

1. The most basic and unavoidable lawyers' resort to historical materials is to texts that are themselves the operative law, that is, whose authoritative reading will actually resolve (or anyway bear on) a legal dispute—a constitution, statute, charter, grant, contract, or testamentary instrument, and the like. The lawyer-historian's contribution may be actually to discover the text, or simply to help interpret it, possibly with the aid of whatever contemporaneous records that may be helpful to the task. Sometimes the question posed to the text is authentically antiquarian ("What distinction was understood by the Constitution's drafters and their contemporaries to exist between the powers to

'make' and to 'declare' war?"). But much more often it is aggressively anachronistic ("Did the Framers of the Constitution confer upon the federal government the power to construct an interstate highway system?" "Would they have approved the legislative veto as a device to maintain congressional oversight over bureaucratic rule-making?" "Would the framers or ratifiers of the Fourteenth Amendment have wanted racial integration of the public schools?"), a question that a conscientious historian cannot really help to answer—or, to put this more cautiously, can help to answer only very indirectly—given that the present dispute is likely to be one that the text's authors could hardly have been able to approach with anything like a modern's experience, tacit knowledge, or pictures of the probable consequences of putting their views into practice.

The lawyer's easiest as well as most orthodox course, naturally, is to textualism—to reading the document as if it had been uttered in her own time, wrenching it out of history altogether and relocating it in a modern context. The main alternative usually proposed, reconstruction in detail of the contemporaneous understandings of its original authors or audience, is attended by terrific practical difficulties (see Brest 1978; Powell 1987; Tushnet 1988): for example, their intentions may be undiscoverable, they may have disagreed fundamentally, they may have left intentions deliberately or unintentionally vague or ambiguous in order to accommodate conflicting opinions or the possibility of changing circumstances, or they may have drastically revised their views after a very short experience observing how they worked out in practice. If the lawyer bypasses these difficulties and partially succeeds in reconstructing intentions with some particularity, she is likely to find herself in an alien and unrecapturable social and conceptual world, one in which the most elementary terms such as *liberty* and *property* have connotations that have long since vanished and whose political concerns seem at least in some respects parochially preoccupied with transient problems and are in any case quite remote from those they have been resurrected to address. (No wonder that when such detailed reconstructions actually are accomplished by historians, they are often ignored in the profession and the courts.)

2. One middle way between anachronism and antiquarianism is to reconstruct the consciousness of the text's historical authors at a level of generality that will comfortably straddle both past and present so as to be able to claim with apparent truth that legal principles do not change, though their applications must vary with changing circumstances. The level of generality may sometimes rise very high to make the straddle ("The founders were suspicious of concentrated power"), so high indeed as to soar above the specific intentions of historical legislators to the general mode of thinking of their age or even to

the "spirit" or "genius" of "our Constitution and institutions" (e.g., "Teutonic democracy," "Anglo-Saxon norms of fair procedure").

Within this middle way there have been two major variations, one stressing the timelessness of the basic principles, the other their adaptation over time to changing circumstances. The choice of one path or the other can lead—as Pocock has shown in his contrast of seventeenth-century English conceptions of "immemorial" common law custom, one (Sir Edward Coke's) insisting on its foundation in the ancient Gothic constitution, the other (Sir Matthew Hale's) emphasizing its ceaseless adaptability—to radically divergent views of legal change (Pocock 1957).

(a) The first method usually privileges a particular historical moment or age—Rome in the period of classical legal science, pre-Conquest Anglo-Saxon England, the founding American generation of 1787—as having exemplified the principles in an exceptionally pure form. Everything since must, if not decline, at least struggle to recover that idyllic purity. Again, this sort of lapsarian history is not necessarily or even usually a reactionary method in the hands of a jurist willing to believe, let's say, that the ur-principles of common law or Roman law legal science or the American Constitution are devoted to the promotion of individual free will through protection of the owner's security and powers to dispose of private property. Thus interpreted, the principles have proved as recruitable to the same service as any ahistorical and a priori positivism or natural law theory or even for that matter any aggressively modernist project to shuck off the deadweight of the past. But it is obviously an antihistorical method for all its privileging of past authority (and despite the fact that much valuable historical research has been done, as it were, on the side by those who believed in it). As a method, it casually links together records from completely different periods and contexts as evidence of the same timeless principles. Its only notion of historical change is of lapses from and restorations of the true constitution.

(b) The second method of dynamic rather than static tradition, given somewhat variant forms in Matthew Hale, Edmund Burke, and Friedrich Karl von Savigny's Historical School, seems at first much friendlier to the historical sensibility. And of course Hale, Savigny, and Savigny's disciples did distinguished historical work. But the story of legal change as one in which law (mostly) unconsciously records the spontaneous underground modifications of thousands of particular customs to adapt to changing circumstances can be extremely resistant to historical analysis. Hale's view in fact seemed to be that the history of the common law was unknowable in that it has been fed by so many springs and sources over so long a time. One can never say therefore whether a given application is of fresh or ancient origin and what contextual influences or causes may have shaped it. Moreover, on this view the authority of law lies in its unbroken continuity, which repels any type of historical account of discontinuous change. The German school had no doubt that legal history was accessible to science. But ultimately for many members of that school the aim of studying multiple manifestations of legal forms over time was once again to distill their essential core of principle, to weed out the inessential (the arbitrary, anomalous, purely contingent debris of history) from the essential and, once this was done, to abandon historical inquiry altogether for the more urgent task of weaving the historically derived principles together into a system (see Reimann 1990).

(*c*) Much conventional legal argument of the last two centuries has relied on a lazy synthesis of these two competing views, seeing law as both unchanging in root principles but adaptive in particulars. It has combined the two views with a Whiggish notion of law as progress, so that, by means of gradual adaptation, the ancient and essential principles of legal order may be seen as ever more efficiently and purely realized (with some allowances for lapses and setbacks) in practice. In this synthesis, legal history is often written as the story of the genetic ancestors or "origins" of the legal forms of the present and of the gradual developing of these embryos into their mature modern condition.

3. There did, nonetheless, develop a mode of legal-historical writing that for some considerable time bridged the gulf between the dogmatic, authoritarian, stabilizing purposes of the lawyers and the integrity of a dominant historical method. This was the historiography of the "comparative method" of study, by means of comparative legal history as well as anthropology and linguistics, of societies from the relatively "primitive" to the most "advanced," with the purpose of discovering the laws governing the evolution of "progressive" societies (see Burrow 1966; Stein 1980). In fact, some of the great contributors to comparative evolutionary theory were lawyers like Adam Smith and Henry Sumner Maine. This symbiosis held enormous advantages for both historiography and law. Lawyers could write respectable historical scholarship of the most advanced kind without falling into anachronism yet also put it to use without threatening the conservatizing functions of their vocation. By the mid-nineteenth century, it was no longer necessary to insist that private property had been the basis of ancient societies in order to legitimate it as the basis of modern societies. Communal property simply belonged to an earlier "stage" and was functional to society in that stage as absolute individual property is functional to civilization in its present and more advanced condition.[2]

Such studies, if their subtleties were pruned away, were also congenial to

Whiggish views of legal evolution as being a central component of the simultaneous progress of commerce, liberty, and science. So useful in fact has been this mode of history—in which progressive societies evolve in stages and in each stage develop legal forms that are functional to their social needs—to lawyers that it has remained the dominant mode in legal argument and scholarship in this country ever since, even after many of the universalistic and deterministic premises on which it is based have been blasted into bits by scholars in other fields. But the lawyers often adopted the mode of thinking behind evolutionary functionalism without making any commitment to continuing the type of research on which that thinking was based. Thus, for the most part the promise of Adam Smith's and Henry Maine's efforts, that lawyers might develop a tradition of comparative historical sociology, was never fulfilled. The work of scholars like Theodor Mommsen, Max Weber, and Paul Vinogradoff, for example, was almost completely ignored by legal scholars in their own time, and no attempt was made to integrate it into conventional legal argument.[3] So instead of continuing to investigate the relations between changes in legal and in social forms, most legal writers were content simply to assume that such relations existed and that they were (save for some instances in which legal change "lagged" behind social and economic change) functional. A common reason for ignoring context—social history—in the writing of legal history was simply to posit that courts or jurists have been the authoritative recorders of customary practices, the best and truest representatives of the *Volk,* so there was no need to go behind their writings. One could even take this view if one believed—as Oliver Wendell Holmes, Jr. did, for example—that legal change was conflictual and Darwinian rather than harmonious and consensual, that the courts and jurists simply registered the outcome of the struggle, the practices of the winners. The social change that supposedly drives legal change through its functional requirements thus tends to appear in legal writing only as vaguely specified background processes or "forces"— "the decline of feudalism," "modernization," "the rise of industrial capitalism," "the growth of the regulatory welfare state," and so forth—rather than as richly described environmental influences.

Stabilizing and Critical Functions of Lawyers' History

As I said earlier, and as the preceding examples mostly demonstrate, lawyers' uses of history have generally been apologetic, designed to endow currently dominant claims to entitlements and distributions of legal advantage and modes of legitimating property and power with the authority of the past. Yet, that is only part of the story. In actual deployment, many legal-historical modes, including some of the modes just discussed, have (though not always intentionally) served critical and destabilizing functions, operating to challenge ruling authorities and assumptions about how the world works. In promoting a customary common law, Lord Coke and his fellows were opposing to centralized royal power what could be taken as, and later was often turned into, an ideology of popular pre-Norman liberties against central royal power. Adam Smith was of course challenging the entire system of mercantilist regulation and what he believed to be dysfunctional "feudal" survivals such as entails. Even Savigny, though an aristocratic conservative politically, was, as my colleague James Whitman has shown (Whitman 1990) concerned to develop a view of Roman property principles as gradually ripening possession into ownership in order to emancipate the German peasantry from serfdom without the need for either legislation or revolution. Modern "conservatives" like Robert Bork appeal to the authority of the "original understanding" in the hope of undoing a generation of settled constitutional precedent.

Some of the standard modes of historically based argument in law have always assumed an inherently critical rather than complacent stance toward the past. This is the commonplace argument that an old text should not be applied to present circumstances because its originating context is too alien from our own. At the end of the nineteenth century, lawyers such as F. W. Maitland and O. W. Holmes tried to generalize this critical-historicist mode of argument into the main purpose of legal history: that is, the modernist project of liberating the present from the past by revealing how much current law was merely "survivals" of ancient forms that had lost their functions or else by showing up authority as having been rooted in a context of ugly or barbaric or obsolete social practices. They also shook up the hardening complacency of evolutionary views of history by using their research into the history of legal forms to *invert* the conventional patterns of "progressive" social development. Maitland, for example, concluded that English law had evolved away from the "individualism" of medieval village societies toward more cooperative and communal forms in modern associational life, while Holmes concluded that the common law in the same period had abandoned its concern for individual moral culpability to treat persons as standardized units in the service of collective social welfare. The fact that lawyers may be recruited to serve different power centers and opposing economic and social interests has meant that these critical uses of history have also found their outlets in legal argument.

Even when lawyers adopted historical models for primarily apologetic principles the resulting engagement with history could not help but bring with it destabilizing consequences. For example, when nineteenth-century histo-riography began to identify the Germanic collectivistic *Mark* rather than the Roman *dominium* as the "basic" or "original" form of European landholding, it removed one of the primary authoritative props to the order of absolute individ-ual ownership—even though the same historians, like Maine, had the ready response that modern needs required new forms of ownership. As Paolo Grossi has pointed out in his great study of nineteenth-century debates over the history of property law (Grossi 1981), collectively held property through these re-searches acquired an entirely different status from any it had held before. It was no longer just a utopian fantasy or dangerous socialist projection but repre-sented the actual lived experience of ancestors—and, as it turned out, of quite a lot of forgotten or marginalized though still existing European communes as well. The same could be said, to cite more recent examples, of the lawyers and historians who revived the extensive history of pre-Civil War state planning to demonstrate that the New Deal violated no sanctified American tradition of laissez-faire or for that matter, of legal scholars who have been raiding the historical revival of the "republican" tradition of civic virtue in the hope of finding counterweights to the politically regnant modes of unbridled "liberal," self-serving individualism. Just as conservative lawyers' appeals to tradition invite critical lawyers to discover countertraditions, so the conservatives' pic-ture of the law of their own time as the result of a gradual evolutionary process encourages critics to argue that many existing areas of law are backward or lagging sectors that have failed to keep pace with the general tendencies of evolutionary change.

In other words, whenever the lawyers embraced historical methods and evidence, they could never get rid of them, even when their company became uncomfortable. The historicizing of the legal-dogmatic categories of property relations and the acceptance of nonlegal evidence regarding them moved them into the domain of historical, sociological, and political-economic debate, where they became vulnerable to intellectual revisionists who sometimes shared none of the lawyers' stabilizing agenda.

Examples from Recent American Histories of Law

My discussion so far has been somewhat abstract. In this section I will try to give it more body and immediacy by matching up some of the recent work in American legal history to the main modes of lawyers' history just described. I will also try to indicate where this work falls on the divides between histor-ically based argument that reinforces and stabilizes current dominant authorities and advantages and argument that seeks to challenge and destabilize. I should warn that the recent literature is vast; the examples that follow are illustrative rather than exhaustive and are confined to a few selected fields and omit mention of many works of high quality; and finally (and most earnestly) that sorting by crude labels such as those employed here does not begin to capture the complexity or variety of most of this work.

The Core Narrative of Liberal Progress: a Theme with Variations

Americans, of course, venerate their federal Constitution and sacralize the moment of its making. Its text is their polity's supreme law. Nonetheless, the dominant mode of history among American lawyers has been dynamic rather than static—not surprising in a culture that prefers more to extol than to deplore progress, to see the present as, at least potentially, a fulfillment rather than a betrayal of the past. This needs some qualification: the founding period has the status of a golden age, and below the major themes of progress in American legal writing there has always been a strong minor subtheme of the jeremiad, lamenting declension from our origins. But the basic story told in American legal writing—until, as we shall see, quite recently—is the story of Western liberalism, the story told by the Scottish Enlightenment political thinkers of the hand-in-hand progress of commerce and liberty, the gradual emancipation of individual freedom and reason from the shackles of feudal and mercantilist restraints on land, labor, and capital and from the tyranny and superstition of the rule of despots, nobles, and established churches. This story in turn has effortlessly modulated in legal narratives into the generally accepted paradigm of Western history as a movement "from status to contract" or simply of "modernization" and of legal history as the gradual evolution of forms functional to that modernizing process. The middle classes rise, and after long struggle with the ancien régime, finally triumph. (In America, of course, the ancien régime was pretty weak and vestigial to start with.) The remnants of the regime—primogeniture, established churches, seditious libel, imprisonment for debt and hostility to bankruptcy, customary monopolies, labor-conspiracy prosecutions, married women's disabilities, indentured servitude, eventually even slavery itself, and after slavery Jim Crow—gradually disappear under the modernizing pressures of commercial development. The basic theme is the emancipation of the freely choosing self: the release of individual energy, the opening of opportunity, the removal of restrictions on choice, gradual progress to the point where virtually all social relations in which people may find themselves may be seen as instituted by their voluntary consent. More and more groups shed special incidents of status and become eligible to participate as legal equals in the polity and economy. In these histories the merit badges for lawyers go to those who help transform economic and political institutions in the direction of liberal development. Even lawyers who in their time may have been perceived as fairly conservative, such as Alexander Hamilton, John Marshall, Joseph Story, Lemuel Shaw, or James Kent, are cast as liberal pioneers, statesmanlike architects of the frameworks for a liberal-pluralist market society (see, for example, Hurst 1978; Newmyer 1985; and Levy 1957).

Needless to say, there are deep political splits even within the liberal tradition. The biggest divide is between parties one might call Classics and Progressives. Classical legal liberalism flourished around the end of the nineteenth century and is now experiencing a major revival. For its major nineteenth-century exponents, lawyers like Thomas M. Cooley, John Norton Pomeroy, and James Coolidge Carter, the gradual evolution of judicially recognized custom, assisted by a legal science devoted to eliciting its core of principle, had produced a system of common law and constitutional principles that came close to perfecting the framework for a libertarian polity (see Siegel 1990; Horwitz 1992 for good accounts of the Classical mindset). For its modern admirers, it remains the high point of liberal development: most legal change since then has been a slide into the "serfdom" and inefficiency of the regulatory welfare state.[4]

But it was the Progressives who began to criticize the Classical generation in the 1890s and whose ideas came gradually to be institutionalized in state social legislation and administrative commissions and ultimately in the New Deal, whose view of history achieved something close to total domination after World War Two. Progressivism dominated not only the work of professional legal historians but much of the ordinary rhetoric of legal argument and judicial opinions. Its hegemony has been subjected to serious challenge only in the last twenty-five years. For the Progressives, the Classics' late-nineteenth-century high point—symbolized by *Lochner v New York*,[5] the case that in modern liberal-legal mythology is equivalent to the worst excesses of Stuart despotism—is our legal system's all-time historical low, a terrible deviation from the general pattern of advance. Some versions have it that there was a massive failure of policy and imagination during a "lag" period in which law failed to come to grips with the realities of large-scale capitalism and its effects of urban squalor, unassimilated immigrant populations, destruction of the natural resource base, industrial accidents, labor strife, monopoly power, periodic depression and mass unemployment, and skewed wealth-and-income distribution. Other versions believed that well-organized corporate interests captured the legal system and made it do their bidding until underdog groups could counterorganize. The course of liberalization could only resume once the managers of the legal system accepted that state and federal governments would have to supply specialized regulatory mechanisms coordinating economic activity and controlling its worst side effects. After the New Deal, the Progressive legal historians returned to the antebellum period to find a rich variety of state interventions into economic life, so that the New Deal could be seen not as drastic innovation on a landscape of laissez-faire tradition but as one more stage in a long tradition of pragmatic state policies toward the economy (see, for example, Handlin and Handlin 1947; and Hartz 1948; and see Scheiber 1972 for an excellent critical synthesis of this body of work).

The masters of modern American legal history have been on the whole Progressives,[6] but rather somber and disenchanted ones. Their dour outlook befits a generation that has lived through the cold war, Vietnam, and many failures or shortfalls of Progressive-minded policies. These have included the failed war on poverty; the collapsed collective-bargaining regime (now shrunk to cover only 15 percent of the workforce); disappointed aspirations to racial integration, affordable housing, a universal social wage, redistribution through progressive taxation, effective public education, and taming the political power of big business through antitrust policy; and waning confidence in regulatory bureaucracy as the instrument of such policies. It is not surprising that from the 1950s onward some Progressive historians would be stressing maturation as an important element of progress, meaning coming to terms with the tragic limits of human capacities and rational planning and the imperfections of legal and administrative institutions as instruments of policy (see, for example, Hurst 1979).

Soon after the Progressives began to sense the limitations of their political vision, the vision itself came under bruising assaults from both right- and left-wing critics, who offered remarkably convergent reasons to question the beneficence of Progressive state policies in "the public interest." The state, critics on both sides contended, had simply been captured by special interests for their own ends: economic regulation was thinly disguised cartel enforcement; spending programs were mostly subsidies for corporate or middle-class beneficiaries; and taxing policies riddled with special deals neither promoted economic growth nor genuinely redistributed income.[7] The critiques paved the way for both radical and conservative challenges to the long-standing Progressive story.

The Radical Challenge: Progress Thwarted, Promises Betrayed

Perhaps the earliest of the recent pressures to revise the Progressive narrative came from left-liberal and radical legal activists and scholars, inspired by the civil rights and antiwar movements and the general ferment of the 1960s.[8] In the last ten years it has been these radical reinterpretations that have been among the most consequential for legal-historical scholarship. They have had relatively little influence, compared to the older Progressive-liberal and the newly influential conservative paradigms, on the work of the practicing bar outside small enclaves of activists such as the National Lawyers Guild. But in the legal academy they have transformed the field. Many of the generation who came of intellectual age in the late 1960s or 1970s trained as historians under the stars of Christopher Hill, E. P. Thompson, Eric Hobsbawm, Eugene Genovese, Herbert Gutman, and David Montgomery. Seeing there were no jobs in history, they went to law school and ended up as legal scholars. These were scholars who explicitly sympathized with the subordinated groups of history and sought to recreate not only their distinctive patterns of life but their struggles with their overlords and their political, economic, and moral ideals.

Most conservative and some liberal historians tend somewhat to identify with the lawyers and judges and jurists they write about, or at least with their situation.[9] For such historians, clearly, legal and constitutional history is in part professional training in statecraft:[10] we look to past masters to see what to emulate, what mistakes they made, and what to avoid and to learn maxims of prudential wisdom. Lawmaking has often been misguided, but well-made law, sound doctrine, and sensible policy is basically benign.

Radical-populist history, by contrast, sees law from the bottom up, from the perspectives of oppressed or disempowered groups.[11] It thus sees it as ruling-class measures to repress or co-opt such groups, qualified only by whatever concessions such groups have managed to extract by struggle. Legal history in this mode is a dialectical story of progressively self-conscious but repeatedly thwarted, subordinated-group insurgency. The early workingmen's associations, for example, meet with indictments for criminal conspiracy. They overcome these only to enter a fearful new regime of regulation by injunction. They mobilize to win state legislative protections for labor picketing and organization and then see these statutes nullified by hostile courts. Finally, they achieve national defeat of injunctions and the legal rights to organization and recognition in the New Deal. But the New Deal protections are rolled back by the Taft-Hartley Act of 1947, by a series of adverse court rulings, and, since 1970, by renewed employer militance and a Labor Board ranging from ineffective to positively hostile (see, for example, Tomlins 1985; Holt 1984; Avery 1988; Forbath 1989; Klare 1978; Stone 1981; and Rogers 1990). Victims of industrial accidents run up against fellow-servant and assumption-of-risk defenses to tort suits in the mid-nineteenth century, only just begin to erode the defenses when the system is sidetracked onto low-payout workers' compensation, and ultimately win a generic right to safe workplaces in the Occupational Safety and Health Act of 1970, only to find it unenforced (see, for example, Weinstein 1968; Abel 1985; and Noble 1986). Organizers for black rights see the ambitious hopes of Radical Reconstruction go down the drain with the Supreme Court's encouragement, the Southern legal system rebuilt around Jim Crow segregation maintained by corrupt officials and juries and the toleration of unofficial violence; and the Southern economy organized around the legal forms of sharecropping and tenant farming that trap blacks at the bottom of the occupational ladder. The *Brown* decision integrating the schools, painfully extracted from the courts after thirty years of patient NAACP litigation, runs into "massive resistance" from Southern political leadership, is left unenforced until a black civil rights movement organizes to challenge segregation, and remains unenforced to this day to the extent that integration and affirmative action may substantially threaten interests of middle-class whites (see, for example, R. Kennedy 1989a; Tushnet 1987; Bell 1980; Burns 1981; Crenshaw 1988; Freeman 1990). These are just a few examples. Obviously one could add similar stories for women, paupers and welfare recipients, immigrant groups, or radical dissenters.

In the radical legal histories law appears in (at least) two somewhat different and conflicting guises, an ambivalence nicely captured in a well-known passage from E. P. Thompson's *Whigs and Hunters* (Thompson 1975, 258–69) that characterizes the law as *both* a medium of ruling-class oppression *and* as a practically effective expression of the ideal of limits on such oppression. (*a*) In one of its aspects, law appears as broken promises. Law embodies universally good norms of equal rights and of fair procedures, protection against arbitrary and tyrannical rule, and protection of the conditions of self-realization—such as individual autonomy, solidarity in association with others, and participation in self-government. The problem is that these norms have been twisted and manipulated by dominant groups to their own advantage. Lawyers, who ought to have been the standard-bearers of the norms embodied in law, have instead repeatedly perverted them on behalf of powerful clients. (The theme of lawyers as betrayers of legal ideals is prominent in Horwitz 1977, chap. 5; Konefsky 1983; and especially Auerbach 1976.) Nonetheless, subordinated groups can make use of the utopian and unfulfilled norms of justice as resources. They can refashion, out of the same norms they nominally share with their oppressors, constitutions and rights that effectively articulate their grievances and ideals— property rights in employment or in squatters' tenure or as traditional use-rights in grazing or fishing grounds; or freedom of contract defined as legal equalization of bargaining advantages. (*b*) Law also appears less advantageously as a bunch of snares and delusions, albeit with some exploitable loopholes. In this view, the utopian promises of the legal system are just ideological window dressing, masks for power. Yet the needs of the powerful to make them *seem* benign, to frame them in formal terms of general rights and obligations, delivers some resources to employ the norms and procedures of the system against itself. The danger of such tactics, however, is that they may only serve to reinforce the ideological legitimacy of the system as a whole.

This ambivalent attitude toward the legal system, like the history it generated of legal change as periodically resurgent and repeatedly thwarted subordinated-group mobilization, perfectly expressed the professional and political situation of legal activists for social movements. These activists had witnessed a remarkable blossoming of opportunities for law-driven (indeed court-driven) social change in the 1950s and 1960s, only to see them wither away or come to disaster in the 1970s and 1980s.

That same experience of disillusionment also delivered some real benefits to the radicals' legal-historical writing. It freed them from one of the besetting diseases of legal history, its filiopietism toward tradition and the heroic lawyers and judges of the past. It also markedly changed the portrayal of background "social forces." Appropriating the work of left social historians, the radicals emphasized the suffering and violence underlying what had often been told as a story of gradual and impersonal social changes—"evolution," "modernization," and "development."[12] "The re-organization of industry around mass-production techniques," to take one example of a phrase describing a disembodied process, was in reality a prolonged and bloody business: ragged armies of strikers, often by the tens of thousands, confronting troops and armed guards for months at a time in violent standoffs (see, for example, Montgomery 1987; Edwards 1979; and Forbath 1989). Legal elites, who in the most complacent orthodox accounts figure as the statesmanlike vanguard of progressive policies ceaselessly adapting law to the evolving needs of society, in fact often actively participated in and apologized for the worst injustices, or tried not to see them. Progress toward equal and decent treatment of minorities and a more inclusive democracy usually came, when it came at all, from disruptive movements from below, aided in their early phases by few lawyers and those few as often as not considered outcasts and pariahs.[13] Moreover, there is never any assurance that ground thus gained will not be lost again and the gainers again dispossessed of power. There is no reliable trend toward ever increasing pluralism, incorporation of new groups into the economy and polity as equal players. Rather there are periods of struggle for incorporation, often followed by periods of intense reaction, sometimes xenophobic and hysterical, sometimes quite nicely calculated by established powers.[14]

The picture of law as a historical instrument of class, race, and gender subordination and even more of its history as a story of thwarted progress and broken promises, remains of course very important to the projects of lawyers, judges, and politicians trying to extend the reach of equal protection and due process norms to subordinated groups. There is no claim with more practical effect than one that generally accepted legal norms have been regularly perverted so as to systematically benefit privileged insiders at the expense of despised or helpless outsiders. Simple justice, say the claimants, requires ending the unequal treatment, restructuring the offending institutions, and redistributing wealth and social advantage to ensure equality. But on the whole the *scholarly* enterprise of left-of-center legal history has moved somewhat beyond this set of concerns—to historical accounts of law as a set of ideological representations of social reality and to accounts of the indigenous notions of legality fashioned by subordinated groups themselves. I will return to this later scholarship in a moment.

Neotraditionalism

In mainstream legal writing and argument, as distinct from academic legal history, the most pronounced tendency of the last two decades has been to move away from dynamic views of history-as-progress to look for authority and inspiration in a rediscovered past. This neotraditionalist revival has taken many different forms.

There are still some modern representatives of the adaptationist school of customary law. Some conservative legal historians stress the Burkean qualities of the legal system. They celebrate the common law as encoding the gradually evolving "spontaneous order" of society (in F. A. Hayek's phrase, frequently echoed in Bridwell and Whitten 1977). They echo the early Federalist (and Tocqueville's) *thèse nobiliaire:* that in America, lawyers and judges are an aristocracy with a social-stabilizing function; they restrain popular enthusiasms and leveling legislatures; they maintain, by means of transmitted professional habits and adherence to precedent, traditional principles and continuity with the past against radical revisions, sharp discontinuities, and excessively "abstract" principles; they are agents of social integration, promoting cultural and national unity and customary morality through the shared values of legalism and the constitutional norms of liberty, property, and due process. (For neo-Burkeanism, see, for example, Bickel 1975; McClellan 1971; Bridwell and Whitten 1977; and Presser and Hurley 1984; see Horwitz 1973 for a critique). The Burkean temper also briefly surfaced in a milieu where one would least expect to find it, namely, among Chicago lawyer-economists, who for a season formalized adaptationism as the "efficiency of the common law hypothesis." The hypothesis was that common law decision making had an inherent tendency to reach increasingly efficient—wealth-maximizing or transaction-cost-reducing—results over time. And considerable ingenuity went into describing the mechanisms that might explain how the common law could have relentlessly pursued economic efficiency even though its judges obviously hadn't a clue that that's what they were doing (see, for example, Priest 1977; Rubin 1977). The difficulty with all the "conservative" schools of adaptationism was that the last thing most of them wanted to do was to sanctify the most recent phase of evolution, the Progressive transformations of law and government over the last seventy-five years. Generally they defend nineteenth-century corrective justice against twentieth-century redistributive justice, nineteenth-century common law rules against social-welfare legislation, and morals legislation against novel constitutional rights to sexual self-expression. The closest thing to a truly Burkean state of mind, in fact, belongs to the Progressive defenders of the legacy of the New Deal and Warren Court and the reformist, "evolving" Constitution.

The most prominent as well as most remarkable neotraditionalist movement—remarkable because one would have thought it had been so long and so thoroughly discredited among historically sophisticated lawyers—has been the revival of "originalism": the view that the *exclusive* guide to the current legal meanings of legal texts (especially the federal Constitution) should be the specific intentions of their historical framers or ratifiers. Obviously there is nothing new or surprising in the appeal to original intentions, especially of the founders of 1787. In American (unlike British) legal practice, legislators' statements of their views are one among several acceptable supplemental sources—along with evidence of the broad historical context of enactment that reveals the "mischiefs" that the law was designed to remedy and of subsequent constructions of the law that show how judges and other officials have applied it in practice over time—in which judges may hunt for guidance for the meaning of ambiguous or vague textual provisions. In the case of federal constitutional interpretation, the prestige of the drafters and the sacralization of the drafting moment naturally lend the exegesis of intentions unusual rhetorical force. The oddity of the new originalism lies in its insistence that historical reconstruction of drafters' or ratifiers' intentions must be the sole guide to judicial interpretation—even if the effect would be to undo generations of precedent—and in its vigorous assertions that the historical method will in fact usually yield a single determinate meaning.

This robust version of originalism seems to have come into being in response to the race relations decisions of the Supreme Court under Chief Justice Earl Warren. The Warren Court undertook an expansive rereading of the Reconstruction amendments and civil rights acts as not only mandating an end to official segregation but as authorizing civil and criminal remedies against even "private" discrimination in areas like restaurants and housing. Some of these decisions relied in part on detailed if somewhat tortured analyses of the historical intentions of the Reconstruction congresses (see, for example, *Bell v Maryland* [1964], and *Jones v Alfred H. Mayer* [1968]). To critics of these decisions it seemed not only that the court had got its history wrong but was dangerously out of control. The reaction grew sharper as federal judges in the 1960s and 1970s pioneered the "rights revolution"—the fashioning of novel legal rights and remedies on behalf of blacks, women, aliens, welfare recipients, inmates of prisons and mental asylums, schoolchildren, and other excluded or dependent groups; and the invention of new constitutional rights to contraception and abortion. History—meaning here, not history as historians understand it, but the narrow project of the search for intentions—was proposed as the corrective to judicial discretion run riot. If the meanings of the great open-ended "due process" and "equal protection" clauses could be tied down to the specific views of the enacting generation, the whole rights revolution could be branded an illegitimate outbreak of "government by judiciary" (Berger 1977) and could be repudiated by later, more conservative executive action and judicial rulings.

The "originalist" position achieved the rare distinction for a hermeneutic theory (at least, in a secular polity) of becoming official government policy in the Justice Department under Attorney General Edwin Meese (see Meese 1985). It was Judge Robert Bork's rallying cry in his unsuccessful campaign for confirmation to the Supreme Court (Bork 1990).[15] Originalism in the Reagan era attracted many supporters: the young Federalist Society lawyers in the Justice Department (some of whom went on to form a new cadre of conservative law teachers and think tank scholars), the older Straussian scholars favored for constitutional-bicentennial grants by the National Endowment for the Humanities, fundamentalist Christians with their own attachments to textual literalism, and—not least—the new chief justice of the United States William Rehnquist (elevated in 1986) and a new associate justice, Antonin Scalia (appointed in 1986).[16]

Inevitably, as soon as the conservatives had designated the past, particularly the eighteenth-century founding, as the terrain on which modern constitutional quarrels would be settled, their ground was immediately invaded by contending armies with entirely different political and intellectual aims.[17] Suddenly, every school of constitutional theory, not just conservatives, felt the need to be regrounded in historical tradition. Valuable, fresh work was done by all parties on the venerable issues of framers' intentions—especially on the background of the religion clauses (see, for example, McConnell 1990; Laycock 1986, 1991), the Reconstruction amendments (see, for example, Kaczorowski 1986; Maltz 1985; and Nelson 1988), and the framers' views of property (Nedelsky 1990). Many of the most interesting disputes between parties searching for versions of the past to put to immediate use shift to a higher level of abstraction, over how best to characterize the general principles or "spirit" of the ancient constitution and founding age, either to shore up selected aspects of the present dispensation or to redeem the present from decadence through the founders' wisdom. Thus, the more sophisticated conservatives reconstruct eighteenth-century systems less so that we can slavishly imitate the details than that we may appreciate the principles and attitudes of mind informing them. Some examples of this include the conception of liberty as customary law restraining governmental power (Reid 1988a); the separation of law from politics in John Marshall's jurisprudence (Haskins and Johnson 1981); the Federalists' marvelous balance of temperament that could combine realism about self-interest with faith in civic virtue, respect for theory with distrust of overabstract systems, suspicion of political power with confidence that complex institutional mechanisms could both contain ambition and channel it productively, and disdain for the masses with optimistic projects for educating them to responsible citizenship (Lerner 1979); and even the High Federalist vision of an organic-hierarchical political community founded on deference to patrician men of virtue (Presser 1991). Perhaps the most ambitious (as well as the most resolutely antihistorical although purportedly based on history) conservative attempt to synthesize an unchanging ancient constitution for modern use has been Richard Epstein's assertion of a absolute libertarian right to property secure from all private and public encroachments, which he claims took the same basic form in Roman law, the liberal philosophies of Hobbes and Locke, the thought of the constitutional framers, and the (mostly late-nineteenth-century) "common law" (Epstein 1985)! Epstein's vision, though often cited as ideological authority by powerful people—libertarian policy makers and lawyers—is of course in most respects in the modern world a radical one in that its literal realization would entail the demolition of all the taxing, spending, and regulatory activities of the modern state.

Meanwhile, responding in kind to the Reaganite intellectuals' excavation of eighteenth-century tradition to buttress cultural-conservative and libertarian-economic views, center-left liberals have come up with their own ancient constitution. The key components have been lifted from the revival of interest in "republican" or "civic-humanist" thought in the pioneering work of J. G. A. Pocock (Pocock 1975). Republicanism seems to solve a lot of problems (while raising some new ones) for modern heirs to Progressive liberalism. It infuses the Constitution-making moment with a communitarian, public-welfare-regarding ideology not handicapped by associations with European socialism. The legal scholar Cass Sunstein, for example, extrudes from the republican tradition as represented by Madison the norm of "deliberative democracy" in order to argue—against reductionist liberal conceptions such as those of public-choice theory—for a conception of politics as an arena in which prefer-ences are shaped and transformed as well as simply given effect. Republicans, like liberals, favor legal rights such as rights to property but prefer that rights be allocated to facilitate the participation in self-government of independent and relatively equal citizens (Sunstein 1985, 1988; for other influential pieces in the "republican revival," see Michelman 1986; Sherry 1986).[18] Other scholars, most notably Bruce Ackerman, have found even more ingenious devices for adjusting their commitments to the regulatory-welfare state legacy of the New Deal to the exigencies of the new traditionalism. Ackerman ad-vances a theory of "dualist democracy," distinguishing normal politics, the ordinary tug-and-haul of self-interested groups, from transformative political moments in which the people refashion the basic constitutional framework. He suggests that the Constitution has been "amended" by such transformations twice since the founding—once after the Civil War and again in the New Deal. He takes the task for constitutional theory to be one of creative synthesis of the core principles of each transformation (Ackerman 1991). By such devices the authority of original foundations is preserved as the basis of our legal system without entailing the undoing of the modern state.

Even populist legal scholarship has been pulled into the search for the authority of original intentions and traditions. As I said earlier, the governing convention of radical work has been to tell legal history as a tale of thwarted progress and betrayed promises—that is, to construct a radical-egalitarian version of legal origins (for example, out of the Declaration of Independence's assertion that "all men are created equal") against which present uses of law may be judged and seen to fall woefully short. First-rate work in this vein continues to appear. One thinks of Lea Vandervelde's recovery of the "free labor" ideology that informed the drafting of the Thirteenth Amendment, making that amendment capable of being read as a standing constitutional argument against all kinds of intensely subordinate or dependent labor relations as remnants or "badges" of slavery (Vandervelde 1989); or Karl Klare's story of how the original radical potential of the National Labor Relations (Wagner) Act was leeched away by later conservative Supreme Court interpretations (Klare 1978); or Akhil Amar's populist-libertarian theory of the original Bill of Rights (Amar 1991). Such work has lately been supplemented by legal history taking a rather different approach—reconstructing what Hendrik Hartog has called "the Constitution of aspiration" (Hartog 1988), an underground tradition of radical social-legal ideas that rarely had a chance of authoritative enactment when first uttered. These are accounts that show how subordinated groups appropriate the symbols and norms and procedures of legality from the dominant culture and use them to manufacture materials for their own emancipation out of the very systems meant to subdue them—as the slaves in Eugene Genovese's classic account (Genovese 1974) were said to have appropriated the Christianity of the slaveholders to fashion images of benevolent protective masters and their own release from bondage to the Promised Land (for legal histories with such themes, see, for example, Crenshaw 1988; Forbath 1989; Hartog 1985, 1988a,b; R. Kennedy 1989b; Luban 1989; Minow 1985; Siegel 1992; Simon 1991; Weisbrod 1986; and Wiecek 1977. For similar work by nonlawyer historians see, for example, Litwack 1979; Kerber 1980; Lebsock 1984; Sewell 1980; Hahn 1983; Pollack 1987; and Wilentz 1984.) Some of those counter-constitutions eventually achieve some recognition in the dominant legal culture; most are crushed or co-opted and lost to history. This is history that incorporates the legal realists' and legal sociologists' insights that the law of any period is not a fixed constellation of rules, articulated from the top, but is rather a plastic medium whose actual content is fought over and practically shaped by thousands of interpreters at all levels of society.

Law as Plural, Contested, Constructed

As the last set of examples shows, history in the legal academy is, broadly speaking, taking two different roads.

One road leads to direct engagement with the conservative revival of origins and traditions. Following long-standing custom in critical legal thought, scholars on this path advance rival and, they claim, superior interpretations of the same traditional sources. Or they seek to establish different and additional sources as competing fonts of tradition. Or, finally, they use the time-honored techniques of historicist criticism to discredit particular fonts of traditional authority as obsolete and unworthy of present preservation.

But another set of critics is using both conventional methods of social, cultural, and intellectual history and the more modish methods of the "new historicism" to undermine the very idea of authoritative traditions. The project of the historicizers is to show legal ideas, rules, institutions, and procedures as contingent products of time and circumstances: contested in their content, multiple in their forms, variable across time, place, and social group in the ways they are put to practical use. Some of these scholars have no conspicuous agenda save the historicist one of rescuing the past from the distortions of the present-minded and of emphasizing the embeddedness of legal forms in the particularities of context. These have produced groundbreaking studies of the legal culture of the American Revolution and early republic (see especially Reid 1988a, 1988b, and 1989 on the Revolution; Conrad 1984, 1988, and 1989 on the legal thought of James Wilson; and White 1988 on the cultural matrix of John Marshall's Supreme Court.)

For many legal historians critical of the revival of tradition, however, the demonstration of contingency has a political as well as intellectual purpose: to try to convince living lawyers and other civic actors that the jumble of forms of legal-social life and thought that we have become used to are not the ones that we are stuck with. The premise is that if we can show how past forms were made and unmade, and how present forms in their turn came to be put together, we can make the present seem more plastic, more amenable to present re-imagination and change. That premise clearly drives much of the work already described on the counter-constitutions of the oppressed. The aim of such work is to displace altogether ruling modes of legal thought, past and present, from their privileged position on center stage, to supplement or even displace the customary hieratic sources such as the appellate courts or elite treatise writers with popular sources of legal tradition ("Everyman's Constitution"), and to replace their master narratives with alternative stories whose heroes and hero-ines endure and resist dominant ideas of legality and struggle to forge their own normative orders.

The same premise may be seen at work in studies of dominant legal ide-ologies themselves. Until quite recently, most critical legal history approached dominant legal ideas and institutions in a debunking spirit. The aim was to show ruling systems as biased and hypocritical, dressed up in the costumes of neutral legality, but actually devoted to reinforcing the ability of the powerful to protect their privileges and subordinate the weak. Clearly, law and the state have frequently been recruited to exactly this service, and legal historians have continued to do valuable work uncovering the grimy details (see, for example, Harring 1983; Holt 1984, 1986; Tomlins 1988 on labor law; Siegel 1992 on laws restricting abortion and contraception; and Williams 1990 on European legal ideas about native American peoples). But some of the most exciting critical legal history of the last few years adopts a quite different approach: namely, taking dominant legal ideologies at their own estimation and trying to see how their components are assembled (see, for example, Olsen 1983; Steinfeld 1991). One of the large dividends of this approach has been a dramatic revision of the received (Progressive) view of the core ideas of the law of the Classical period of 1870–1920[19] (see Friedman 1985, 358–63; Paul 1960; D. Kennedy 1980; Benedict 1985; Keller 1977, 362–70; Jones 1967; McCurdy 1975; Siegel 1984; Urofsky 1985; Casebeer 1985; May 1989; Hovenkamp 1988a, 1988b; and Soifer 1987). The revisionists found that the Classical lawyers and judges had been unduly demonized by their Progressive critics as partisan ideologues of big capital. Classical common and constitutional law, they argued, was the stepchild of Jacksonian, Free Soil, and abolitionist "equal rights" ideology, not of the "trusts." It distrusted all forms of legal privilege and legal disability; it aimed at classless formal-general neutrality, such as perfectly symmetrical treatment of capital and labor combinations. Some of the Classical lawyers and judges were hostile toward or at least troubled by the rise of large business enterprises, believing that they threatened individual autonomy and political independence. Corporations as parties often lost in the courts while most Progressive social legislation survived judicial review under the quite expansive scope that Classical judges gave to the state police power to regulate health, safety, and morals. The effect of this rehabilitation, if one may call it that, of the Classical system, establishes it not as some sort of massive conspiracy or period of collective myopia but as a formidably plausible system for organizing perceptions of reality—sorting experience into categories that highlighted some types of economic pressure (such as labor boycotts) as intolerably coercive and others (such as employers' power to hire and fire) as simply natural facts about the world. It was only after a sustained assault by generations of Progressive critics that a new common sense could emerge— namely, that the Classical system's apparent neutrality was illusory, that it inevitably papered over a mass of unacknowledged biases and implicit policy judgments, that it privileged as somehow natural a particular and very controversial distribution of social power—and every key premise of the Classical world could be challenged and transformed (see Peller 1985; Horwitz 1992). The lesson, whether or not it was made explicit in the historian's work, is clear: what happened to the Classics can and will happen to us; our commonsense legal views of fault and necessity, accident and causation, consent and coercion, property and trespass, the public sphere and the private, the domains of the market and the family, are what they are under the sun of governing paradigms that structures perception and constrains imagination in certain systematic ways. The lesson is doubtless all the more sharply pointed because the reigning conservative lawyers and judges have been urging the reinstatement of so many features of the old Classical scheme—without however recognizing the wide scope even the Classics allowed for regulation or the cogency of the most acute Progressive critiques of the scheme's basic premises.

Perhaps the most original as well as controversial of these efforts to reveal the backstage devices employed in the construction of dominant legal forms is the work of one school of the critical legal studies movement (for a fuller account see Gordon 1984), which argues that legal systems from Blackstone's time to the present day may be seen as a series of successive attempts to mediate between objectives that liberal thought holds to be in fundamental tension—for example, fusing with others in cooperative association versus preserving a sphere of autonomy against others' invasion; doing justice as rule-following versus justice as equitable particularism; promoting freedom of action in contracting versus protecting security; and so on. Each generation of lawyers holds out the hope that the objectives can be harmoniously reconciled or balanced through appropriate rule-systems. But each attempt at mediation proves to be unstable as it breaks down along the fault line of the contradiction. The school was founded by a brilliant (albeit so gnomic as to have remained almost unread) essay by Duncan Kennedy on Blackstone's *Commentaries* (D. Kennedy 1979). That essay helped spawn several monographs on very diverse topics (colonial property, preferences in bankruptcy, conditional gifts to heirs, tortious interference with contracts, among others), but which all shared an organization of the history of subfields of legal doctrine around attempts to mediate, minimize, or make disappear a basic structural contradiction, (see, for example, Frug 1980; Nockleby 1983; Olsen 1983; Mensch 1982; Alexander 1985; Bone 1986; Singer 1982; Kainen 1982; and Weisberg 1986).

The potentially constructive as well as critical bite to this work derives from the insight that if the legal rules and processes that in part constitute the workings of a liberal-capitalist society are contradictory at the core, there must always be alternative arrangements—already built in, as it were—to those that a society at any given time happens to privilege. To make this more concrete: the law defines what "private property" is and which "harms" to property may be compensated and enjoined and which must be suffered in silence. It sets the ground rules of economic conflict, marking the limits on how competitors and employers and workers may combine to do each other damage, and it supplies processes for resolving such issues (juries, administrative boards, adversary litigation, etc.) that also distribute advantages to those best able to manipulate them. The critical historians' main point about these legal arrangements is that the basic principles behind them are so indeterminate, and their historical interpretations so variable and multiform, that one cannot plausibly speak of a single "capitalist" order at all. A commitment to "private property rights" in the abstract can tell you nothing about whether homeowners can stop a coal company from polluting their groundwater; downstream riparian owners can sue upstreamers for diversion; or workers, creditors, suppliers, or customers have a right to participate in corporate decisions affecting their interests. The legal system has to decide how to define the property rights in question and to whom it will assign them. It has to decide whether the rights will be lumped together in one "owner" or spread among many, whether they will be protectible by injunction or only by damages, or not at all. In its actual history—as several excellent recent histories of property rights have confirmed (see, for example, Horwitz 1977; Scheiber 1984; Selvin 1980; and Rose 1986)—our legal system has resolved these questions and thousands more like them in strikingly different ways, reaching contradictory answers at different times and even in the same periods. It has moved property rights around to different categories of owners and continually abolished old rights and invented new ones. Thus, in the United States as elsewhere in the capitalist world, there have been many actual historical capitalisms—and one might add, many forms of patriarchy, many variations on the theme of white racial supremacy—and there might have been many more. Such legal histories usefully supplement work in comparative policial economy that sharply challenges determinist accounts of the emergence of such institutional forms as eventually achieved predominance in the American economy[20] like "Fordist" methods of workplace organization or the giant multidivisional enterprise. Such work argues instead that there was nothing in the least inevitable about the appearance of these particular forms, that there have been plenty of variations on them within "capitalist" societies, and that the emergence of particular forms has been tied to quite contingent variations in politics, ideology, culture, and—not least— legal ideas and institutions (see, for example, Piore and Sabel 1984; Sabel and Zeitlin 1985; Berk 1994; Kuisel 1981; Reddy 1984; Wright 1986; Maier 1987;

Goldthorpe 1984; and Rogers 1990). The point is that our current economic and legal institutions got to be the way they are not through some logic of linear development but through a process rather more nearly resembling that of biological evolution. Multiple forms are continually being produced. Some disappear, killed off by predators or random external shocks; some survive for contingent reasons, and some are selected for certain functional purposes then sidetracked and co-opted for other purposes entirely. The political lesson of such demonstrations, clearly, is to illustrate what might be called the radical potential of conservative arrangements: to show that there exist, already immanent in such familiar ideals and institutions as private property and free contract, possibilities for transforming the society and economy in more democratic and egalitarian—as well as to be sure more autocratic and unequal—directions.[21]

Conclusion

The reader will have noticed that most of the the examples of recent American uses of history by lawyers and legal scholars follow the familiar patterns I sketched in the first section of this essay. For most of this century, the dominant resort to history was the Progressives' appeal to the notion of law as the product of a gradual and incremental evolutionary progress. This mode of history was readily adapted to critical purposes by legal activists claiming that progress had not moved far or fast enough or that the Progressive telos had been fundamentally sidetracked or sabotaged. The modest payoffs from this very activism in the "rights revolution" of the 1960s and 1970s prompted a backlash in the form of a rejection of modernism and the teleology of progress and the renewed interest in history as a source of traditional legal authority. But the conservatives' turn to history in search of authority, as has usually been the case, has been disappointing and ultimately somewhat subversive of its own ends. The project of recovering the past invites the participation of more critical lawyers with a historicist agenda that is often intensely antimythological. For example, the Magna Carta, once professionally reconstructed, is presented as a baffling technical quarrel over feudal privileges and the founding fathers as a diverse collection of politicians enmeshed in complex factional, regional, and ideological squabbles carried on in almost archaic political language. The search for tradition serves as an incitement to restore radical traditions as well as conservative ones, to appeal to the authority of the polity's past antiauthoritarianism and its eagerness to break radically with the encumbering past of the wicked Old World.

So far, as I say, these uses of history repeat familiar themes. Every time conservatives invoke the past for the purpose of shutting down further change, reform-minded lawyers dredge the same sources to brand the present as a corrupt deviation from its true principles, to recover buried countertraditions or counter-constitutions to oppose to present orthodoxy, to suggest that evolutionary long-term trend lines point toward the triumph of reformist society, or finally just to suggest that the future is not determined by the past at all but is within the control of present generations. The main differences that I perceive about much modern work, particularly the radical or critical work, is a much sharper awareness, in the form of a kind of postmodern skepticism, about the contingency, fragility, and revisability of all models of the past, their own as well as the established ones they are trying to displace. This skepticism is by no means universal. There is still plenty of legal history that uses critical-historicist methods to destroy claims that some dominant conservative position is rooted in tradition or original intentions. But such history then goes on to assert that its own countertraditions are more authoritative because more authentically rooted in lived experience or in normative longings that would be generally shared if no longer repressed by the powerful, or simply in the virtue and clarity of perception that results from injustice and suffering. On the whole, however, one less often has the sense now of dogma being swept aside so that a new dogmatics may take its place and counterauthority set on the throne of authority. The point seems to be rather simply (1) to soften up existing structures by becoming aware of the conflicts and ambiguities in the very foundations of the way they were constructed, (2) to recover suppressed alternatives less to establish them as a new orthodoxy than to suggest the perpetual malleability of structures and the possible experimental directions for their revision, (3) to stress the multiplicity of legal traditions and the perpetually contested and contradictory nature of basic legal ideals, (4) to reveal the backstage mechanics of how ideals are constructed in order to dissipate myths that they are natural or determined by the course of history, and (5) to spin out alternative narratives to break the spell of dominant master narratives. But with this loss of dogmatism, this newly playful awareness of contingency, has also come some sense of loss of direction. The erosion of faith in the Progressive paradigm of progress has weakened the moral force of the older critique's claim that the cause of progress had been unacceptably delayed or betrayed. The notion that every form of legality is a constructed artifact rather than a natural or determined fact is useful for understanding the genealogy of current conditions but at the same time tends, understandably, to deprive people of any strong basis for confidence in transcendent standpoints for critique of the present order. Thus, at this writing, the potential contributions of historical learning to rebuilding society—as contrasted simply to combating the fatalistic sense that no change is possible—are still not so clear.

NOTES

Grateful thanks to Stephen Diamond, Terrence McDonald, and Gunther Teubner for comments on earlier drafts, and to Laura Dickinson for help in preparing the manuscript.

1. Legal elites of the industrializing societies of the nineteenth century, for example, used their roles as guardians of the "traditional rights of property" to help rationalize the process of wholesale destruction of existing property rights and their transfer and consolidation into the hands of entrepreneurial users (see, e.g., Horwitz [1977]).

2. This is not to say that at the time these historical conclusions were not violently controversial. On the nineteenth-century debates among historians and lawyers on the history of property and its legal forms, see especially Grossi (1981) and Burrow (1974).

3. Otto von Gierke's work on medieval associations as "group-persons" (Gierke [1913]) is a remarkable exception to this tale of neglect; it supplied the materials for reconceptualizing corporate personality in the era of giant concerns.

4. The most influential Classical liberal in modern times is, of course, F. A. Hayek (see, e.g., Hayek [1960]). More recently the mission of bolstering a libertarian legal theory with historical models has fallen to Richard Epstein (see, e.g., Epstein [1983, 1984, 1985]). Yet with the significant exception of work by Chicago School economists on the history of regulation, surprisingly little legal history has as yet been written from a Classical-liberal perspective. As the ranks of right-libertarian academics increase, we may expect this to be one of the growth areas of legal historiography in the near future.

5. 198 U.S. 45 (1905). In this famous case, the U.S. Supreme Court struck down a New York state law limiting work in bakeries to ten hours a day on the ground that the law violated the "liberty of contract" protected by the Fourteenth Amendment to the federal Constitution.

6. I am thinking here primarily of Willard Hurst, Lawrence Friedman, Oscar and Mary Handlin, Louis Hartz, Harry Scheiber, Morton Keller, and even for some purposes (though his Progressive-liberal persona alternates with a radical one) Morton Horwitz.

7. Disillusioned liberal historians themselves played a leading part in this revision: for a classic treatment of law as the product of interest group politics, see Friedman and Ladinsky (1967). But the pendulum of historical revision always swings back (and some of the critiques were rather overbroad anyway). In recent years, historians have begun to rehabilitate the Progressive vision. Some have reemphasized the idealistic aims of Progressive reforms, as opposed to their self-interest-promoting and social control aims, and presented them as, though flawed, still basically admirable (see, e.g., Crunden [1982]; Kloppenberg [1986]). Others, notably including some legal writers, have reex-

amined specific policies and programs of the Progressive and New Deal eras, finding in them both evidence of motives to pursue the public interest (see, e.g., Hovenkamp [1988c] on Progressive railroad regulation) and continuing relevance for the remedy of current policy failures (see, e.g., Simon [1985] on the New Deal social workers).

8. The 1960s generation did not, of course, invent radical or populist critiques of the law and its history: these have been generated, especially by labor movements and their lawyers, since the beginning of the republic. And indeed the rediscovery of these critiques has been one of the accomplishments of the new critical legal histories. But with rare exceptions, such critical views did not reach the ordinary arguments of practicing lawyers or the profession's major journals until the late 1960s.

9. There is a clear generational difference here. Hurst clearly sees legal history as the handmaiden to current policymakers. In his *History of American Law* (2d ed. [1987]) Friedman is considerably less engaged, more ironic and detached.

10. For Hurst, to be sure, it is *democratic* statecraft, decision making at the humdrum administrative and state-legislative levels, not just the commanding heights.

11. I say "populist" rather than "Marxist" because very little work by American legal historians is strongly or distinctively Marxist in approach, if one means by that history that seeks to explain most legal forms and outcomes as epiphenomena of the class struggle incident to the "relations of production," which are in turn determined by material-technological "forces of production." These days, ironically, it is likely to be right-wing Chicago economists who suggest that law is best explained as instrumentally fashioned by groups pursuing their material interests or as functional adaptations to master processes of economic change. The radical historians, by contrast, usually treat law as expressing ideologies and ideals that are partly "autonomous" from economic interests and "forces." I bring this up because the term *Marxist* is carelessly applied, often as a smear label, to almost any writer who shows sympathy with the underdogs of history or indignation at the ways in which political and economic elites used the legal system against them.

12. This exaggerates, as the critical generation of the 1960s was prone to do, the complacency of the previous accounts. In legal as in general historiography, the principal charge was that the historians of the 1950s had emphasized ideological "consensus" at the expense of "conflict" in the American past and had uncritically celebrated that consensus. The charge might have been valid enough against certain works of the period—let's say, for instance, Daniel Boorstin's *The Genius of American Politics* (Boorstin [1953])—but vastly overdrawn with respect to its best work. Willard Hurst, for example—like Richard Hofstadter and Louis Hartz—was acutely aware of the defects of the liberal consensus. Hurst characterized the dominant nineteenth-century consensus as "bastard pragmatism," fixated on market calculation, incapable of any but the most short-term assessment of the consequences of action, and basically irresponsible in ways that imposed heavy social costs (see Hurst [1964]). Later histories in tune with the liberal-progressive sensibility, like Lawrence Friedman's *A History of Ameri-*

can Law (2d ed. [1985]), fully incorporate the "bottom-up" perspectives of the New Social History.

13. The Boston legal establishment of the antebellum years, with a few notable exceptions, supported the segregation of the city's school system, setting a precedent that was to be fatally drawn upon in the construction of postbellum Jim Crow institutions (see Kousser [1988]). After the Civil War, most of the leaders of the Northeastern city bar cheered on the judicial evisceration of the Reconstruction amendments (see van Ee [1986]). In the post-*Brown* South, despite the stirring example of courage and firmness set by the Eisenhower-appointed judges of the Fifth Circuit in dismantling racial segregation, it was almost impossible to find white lawyers willing to take on a civil rights case (see Bass [1981]).

14. One obvious example is the turn, after rapid progress had been made in the courts toward a libertarian view of the First Amendment in the 1930s and 1940s, to prosecutions of and legislative and administrative sanctions against dissidents and supposed "subversives" in the loyalty-security investigations and purges of the 1950s—many of which, though fortunately not all, survived judicial review (see Belknap [1977]; Kutler [1982]; and Caute [1978]).

15. Judge Bork was a fairly recent convert to originalism, a method that earlier in his career he had often derided as an unsatisfactory guide to interpretation. See Boyle (1991) for a comprehensive guide to Bork's intellectual migrations.

16. It should be mentioned that the most intellectually sophisticated of the Reagan appointees, such as Judge Richard Posner (of the Court of Appeals for the Seventh Circuit and formerly of the University of Chicago Law School) and Professor Charles Fried (of Harvard University Law School and Solicitor General of the United States under Reagan), never adopted the originalist position.

17. The politicians not surprisingly failed to maintain much interest in originalism except as a vague rhetorical aspiration. Nobody really wants to revive the political culture of the eighteenth century in any detail, to turn Washington, D.C., into some sort of Colonial Williamsburg. Some conservatives may want to repeal the New Deal, but few if any would seriously maintain what the framers clearly believed, that the issuance of paper money violates the Constitution. The Reagan Administration's legal scholars and ideologues were doubtless sincere in their faith in original intent. But for their political masters, presumably, originalism was only useful so long as it was expedient and was forgotten the moment it began to yield the wrong answers. Conservatives are very fond of original-intent analysis when it suggests that the framers approved of the death penalty, sodomy laws, and state efforts to promote religion or that they would have been baffled by the idea of procreative liberty or abortion as a fundamental right. The originalist approach is a lot less friendly to conservatives' claims of a broad presidential prerogative in foreign and national security affairs in that it is fairly clear that the original Constitution supposed that the Congress would share with the President primary authority over the design of foreign and war-making policy. More generally, the

key originalist claim that original-intent research will fetter judges because it yields clear, single answers to legal questions cannot plausibly survive any serious scholarly enterprise in a field where there are no agreed-upon criteria even on what evidence should count as legally authoritative (e.g., should arguments in the Philadelphia Convention be given determinative weight? Weight only as evidence of contemporary views of meaning? No weight at all because the convention's proceedings were secret and uncommunicated to ratifiers?) and where every issue of historical fact is so hotly contested. It is thus hardly surprising that Judge Bork's recent book, even while affirming originalism as the only sure guide to constitutional interpretation, should fail to cite a single historian's work (Bork [1990]).

18. There has even been a revival—in one of those interesting legal historians' invocations of a lost cause as a competing source of tradition—of the thought of the opponents of the federal Constitution, the Anti-Federalists (Symposium [1989]).

19. Contrary to what one might expect, most of this work has not been done by free market conservatives trying to revive the pre-Progressive status quo ante as a model for present imitation but by scholars who seem mostly left-liberal in their general sympathies.

20. Such accounts may take many forms, from liberal efficiency-based accounts (e.g., Chandler [1977]) to Marxist accounts of the logic of monopoly capitalism (e.g., Braverman [1974]).

21. See, for example, D. Kennedy (1982) (revealing tradition of paternalist and redistributive motives in ordinary contract and tort doctrine); Lynd (1988); and Singer (1980) (showing how traditional contract and property doctrine justify giving workers and communities affected by plant closings a property interest in the plant). The legal scholar most insistent on the plasticity of economic institutions and the most conscientiously detailed in proposals for reconstruction is Roberto Mangabeira Unger (see especially Unger [1987]).

REFERENCES

Abel, Richard. 1985. "Risk as an Arena of Struggle." *Michigan Law Review* 83:772–94.

Ackerman, Bruce. 1991. *We the People. Vol. 1: Foundations.* Cambridge: Harvard University Press.

Alexander, Gregory. 1985. "The Dead Hand and the Law of Trusts in the Nineteenth Century." *Stanford Law Review* 37:1189–266.

Amar, Akhil. 1991. "The Bill of Rights as a Constitution." *Yale Law Journal* 100:1131–210.

Auerbach, Jerold. 1976. *Unequal Justice: Lawyers and Social Change in Modern America.* New York: Oxford University Press.

Avery, Dianne. 1988. "Images of Violence in Labor Jurisprudence: The Regulation of Labor and Boycotts, 1894–1921." *Buffalo Law Review* 37:1–117.

Bass, Jack. 1981. *Unlikely Heroes: The Dramatic Story of the Southern Judges of the Fifth Circuit Who Translated the Supreme Court's* Brown *Decision into a Revolution for Equality.* New York: Simon and Schuster.

Belknap, Michael. 1977. *Cold War Political Justice: The Smith Act, the Communist Party, and American Civil Liberties.* Westport, CT: Greenwood Press.

Bell, Derrick. 1980. *Race, Racism, and American Law.* 2d ed. Boston: Little, Brown.

Bell v Maryland 378 US 226 (1964).

Benedict, Michael Les. 1985. "Laissez-Faire and Liberty: A Re-Evaluation of the Meaning and Origins of Laissez-Faire Constitutionalism." *Law and History Review* 3:293–331.

Berger, Raoul. 1977. *Government by Judiciary: The Transformation of the Fourteenth Amendment.* Cambridge: Harvard University Press.

Berk, Gerald. 1994. *Alternative Tracks: The Corporation and the Constitution of American Industrial Order, 1865–1917.* Baltimore: Johns Hopkins University Press.

Bickel, Alexander. 1975. *The Morality of Consent.* New Haven: Yale University Press.

Bone, Robert. 1986. "Normative Theory and Legal Doctrine in American Nuisance Law: 1850–1920." *Southern California Law Review* 59:1101–226.

Boorstin, Daniel. 1953. *The Genius of American Politics.* Chicago: University of Chicago Press.

Bork, Robert. 1990. *The Tempting of America.* New York: Free Press.

Boyle, James. 1991. "A Process of Denial: Bork and Post-Modern Conservatism." *Yale Journal of Law and the Humanities* 3:263–314.

Braverman, Harry. 1974. *Labor and Monopoly Capital: The Degradation of Work in the Twentieth Century.* New York: Monthly Review Press.

Brest, Paul. 1978. "The Misconceived Quest for the Original Understanding." *Boston University Law Review* 25:75–110.

Bridwell, Randall, and Ralph U. Whitten. 1977. *The Constitution and the Common Law.* Lexington, MA: Lexington Books.

Burns, Haywood. 1981. "From Brown to Bakke and Back: Race, Law, and Social Change in America." *Daedalus* 110 (spring): 219–31.

Burrow, J. W. 1966. *Evolution and Society: A Study in Victorian Social Theory.* Cambridge: Cambridge University Press.

Burrow, J. W. 1974. "The 'Village Community' and the Uses of History in Late Nineteenth Century England." In Neil McKendrick, ed., *Historical Perspectives: Studies in English Thought and Society in Honor of J. H. Plumb,* 260–75. London: Europa.

Burrow, J. W. 1981. *A Liberal Descent: Victorian Historians and Their Past.* Cambridge: Cambridge University Press.

Casebeer, Kenneth. 1985. "Teaching an Old Dog New Tricks: *Coppage* v. *Kansas* and At-Will Employment Revisited." *Cardozo Law Review* 6:765–97.

Caute, David. 1978. *The Great Fear: The Anti-Communist Purge under Truman and Eisenhower.* New York: Simon and Schuster.

Chandler, Alfred. 1977. *The Visible Hand: The Managerial Revolution in American Business.* Cambridge: Harvard University, Belknap Press.

Conrad, Stephen A. 1984. "Polite Foundation: Citizenship and Common Sense in James Wilson's Republican Theory." *Supreme Court Review* 1984: 359–88.

Conrad, Stephen A. 1988. "Metaphor and Imagination in James Wilson's Theory of Federal Union." *Law and Social Inquiry* 13:1–70.

Conrad, Stephen A. 1989. "James Wilson's Assimilation of the Common-Law Mind." *Northwestern University Law Review* 89:186–219.

Crenshaw, Kimberle Williams. 1988. "Race, Reform, and Retrenchment: Transformation and Legitimation in Anti-Discrimination Law." *Harvard Law Review* 101:1331–87.

Crunden, Robert. 1982. *Ministers of Reform: The Progressives' Achievement in American Civilization, 1889–1920.* New York: Basic Books.

Dawson, John P. 1968. *Oracles of the Law.* Ann Arbor: University of Michigan Law School.

Edwards, Richard. 1979. *Contested Terrain: The Transformation of the Workplace in the Twentieth Century.* New York: Basic Books.

Epstein, Richard. 1983. "A Common Law for Labor Relations: A Critique of the New Deal Labor Legislation." *Yale Law Journal* 92:1357–408.

Epstein, Richard. 1984. "In Defense of the Contract at Will." *University of Chicago Law Review* 51:947–82.

Epstein, Richard. 1985. *Takings: Private Property and the Power of Eminent Domain.* Cambridge: Harvard University Press.

Foner, Eric. 1988. *Reconstruction: America's Unfinished Revolution, 1863–1877.* New York: Harper and Row.

Forbath, William. 1989. "The Shaping of the American Labor Movement." *Harvard Law Review* 102:1111–256.

Franklin, Julian. 1963. *Jean Bodin and the Sixteenth Century Revolution in the Methodology of Law and History.* New York: Columbia University Press.

Freeman, Alan. 1990. "Antidiscrimination Law: The View from 1989." In David Kairys, ed., *The Politics of Law: A Progressive Critique,* 121–150. New York: Pantheon Books.

Friedman, Lawrence. 1985. *A History of American Law.* 2d ed. New York: Simon and Schuster.

Friedman, Lawrence, and Jack Ladinsky. 1967. "Social Change and the Law of Industrial Accidents." *Columbia Law Review* 67:50–82.

Frug, Gerald. 1980. "The City as a Legal Concept." *Harvard Law Review* 93:1059–154.

Garrow, David. 1986. *Bearing the Cross: Martin Luther King Jr. and the Southern Christian Leadership Conference.* New York: W. Morrow.

Genovese, Eugene. 1974. *Roll, Jordan, Roll.* New York: Pantheon.

Gierke, Otto Friedrich von. 1913. *Political Theories of the Middle Age,* F. W. Maitland, trans. and intro. Cambridge: Cambridge University Press.

Goldthorpe, John. 1984. *Order and Conflict in Contemporary Capitalism.* Oxford: Clarendon Press.

Gordon, Robert W. 1984. "Critical Legal Histories." *Stanford Law Review* 36:57–125.

Grossi, Paolo. 1981. *An Alternative to Private Property: Collective Property in the Juridical Consciousness of the Nineteenth Century,* Lydia C. Cochrane, trans. Chicago: University of Chicago Press.

Hahn, Stephen. 1983. *The Roots of Southern Populism: Yeoman Farmers and the Transformation of the Georgia Upcountry, 1850–1890.* New York: Oxford University Press.

Handlin, Oscar, and Mary Handlin. 1947. *Commonwealth: A Study of the Role of Government in the American Economy: Massachusetts, 1774–1861.* Cambridge: Harvard University Press.

Harring, Sidney. 1983. *Policing a Class Society.* New Brunswick, NJ: Rutgers University Press.

Hartog, Hendrik. 1985. "Pigs and Positivism." *Wisconsin Law Review* 1985:899–935.

Hartog, Hendrik. 1988a. "Mrs. Packard on Dependency." *Yale Journal of Law and the Humanities* 1:79–103.

Hartog, Hendrik. 1988b. "The Constitution of Aspiration and the 'Rights that Belong to Us All.'" In David Thelen, ed., *The Constitution and American Life.* Ithaca: Cornell University Press.

Hartz, Louis. 1948. *Economic Policy and Democratic Thought: Pennsylvania, 1776–1860.* Cambridge: Harvard University Press.

Haskins, George Lee, and Herbert A. Johnson. 1981. *Foundations of Power: John Marshall 1801–1815, Part One.* New York: Macmillan.

Hayek, Friederich A. von. 1960. *The Constitution of Liberty.* Chicago: University of Chicago Press.

Holt, Wythe. 1984. "Labour Conspiracy Cases in the United States: Bias and Legitimation in Common Law Adjudication, 1805–1842." *Osgoode Hall Law Journal* 22:591–663.

Holt, Wythe. 1986. "Recovery by the Worker Who Quits: A Comparison of the Mainstream, Legal Realist, and Critical Legal Studies Approaches to a Problem of Nineteenth Century Contract Law." *Wisconsin Law Review* 1986:677–732.

Horwitz, Morton. 1973. "The Conservative Tradition in the Writing of American Legal History." *American Journal of Legal History* 17:275–94.

Horwitz, Morton. 1977. *The Transformation of American Law, 1780–1860.* Cambridge: Harvard University Press.

Horwitz, Morton. 1992. *The Transformation of American Law, 1870–1960: The Crisis of Legal Orthodoxy.* New York: Oxford University Press.

Hovenkamp, Herbert. 1988a. "Labor Conspiracies in American Law, 1880–1930." *Texas Law Review* 66:919–65.

Hovenkamp, Herbert. 1988b. "The Political Economy of Substantive Due Process." *Stanford Law Review* 40:379–447.

Hovenkamp, Herbert. 1988c. "Regulatory Conflict in the Gilded Age: Federalism and the Railroad Problem." *Yale Law Journal* 97:1017–72.

Howe, Daniel Walker. 1979. *The Political Culture of the American Whigs*. Chicago: University of Chicago Press.

Hurst, James Willard. 1964. *Law and Economic Growth: The Legal History of the Lumber Industry in Wisconsin, 1836–1915*. Cambridge: Harvard University Press.

Hurst, James Willard. 1978. "Alexander Hamilton, Law Maker." *Columbia Law Review* 78:483–547.

Hurst, James Willard. 1979. "Old and New Dimensions of Research in United States Legal History." *American Journal of Legal History* 23:1–20.

Hyman, Harold, and William M. Wiecek. 1982. *Equal Justice under Law: Constitutional Development, 1835–1875*. New York: Harper and Row.

Jones, Alan. 1967. "Thomas M. Cooley and Laissez-Faire Constitutionalism." *Journal of American History* 53:751–71.

Jones v Alfred H. Mayer, 392 US 409 (1968).

Kaczorowski, Robert J. 1985. *The Politics of Judicial Interpretation*. Dobbs Ferry, NY: Oceana Publications.

Kaczorowski, Robert J. 1986. "Revolutionary Constitutionalism in the Era of the Civil War and Reconstruction." *New York University Law Review* 61:863–940.

Kainen, James. 1982. "Nineteenth Century Interpretation of the Federal Contract Clause: The Transformation from Vested to Substantive Rights against the State." *Buffalo Law Review* 31:381–480.

Kairys, David. 1982. *The Politics of Law: A Progressive Critique*. New York: Pantheon Books.

Keller, Morton. 1977. *Affairs of State: Public Life in Late Nineteenth Century America*. Cambridge: Harvard University, Belknap Press.

Kelley, Donald. 1970. *Foundations of Modern Historical Scholarship*. New York: Columbia University Press.

Kelley, Donald. 1990. *The Human Measure: Social Thought in the Western Legal Tradition*. Cambridge: Harvard University Press.

Kennedy, Duncan. 1979. "The Structure of Blackstone's Commentaries." *Buffalo Law Review* 28:209–382.

Kennedy, Duncan. 1980. "Toward an Historical Understanding of Legal Consciousness: The Case of Classical Legal Thought in America, 1850–1940." *Research on Law and Society* 3:3–24.

Kennedy, Duncan. 1982. "Distributive and Paternalist Motives in Contract and Tort Law, with Special Reference to Compulsory Terms and Unequal Bargaining Power." *Maryland Law Review* 41:563–658.

Kennedy, Randall. 1989a. "Reconstruction and the Politics of Scholarship." *Yale Law Journal* 98:521–39.

Kennedy, Randall. 1989b. "Martin Luther King's Constitution: A Legal History of the Montgomery Bus Boycott." *Yale Law Journal* 98:999–1067.

Kerber, Linda. 1980. *Women of the Republic.* Chapel Hill: University of North Carolina Press.

Klare, Karl. 1978. "Judicial Deradicalization of the Wagner Act." *Minnesota Law Review* 62:265–339.

Kloppenberg, James. 1986. *Uncertain Victory: Social Democracy and Progressivism in European and American Thought, 1870–1920.* New York: Oxford University Press.

Kluger, Richard. 1976. *Simple Justice: The History of* Brown v. Board of Education *and Black America's Struggle for Equality.* New York: Alfred Knopf.

Konefsky, Alfred S. 1983. Preface to Alfred S. Konefsky and Andrew King, eds., *The Papers of Daniel Webster: Legal Papers,* Vol. 1. Hanover, NH: University Press of New England.

Kousser, J. Morgan. 1988. "The Supremacy of Equal Rights: The Struggle against Racial Discrimination in Ante-Bellum Massachusetts and the Foundations of the Fourteenth Amendment." *Northwestern Law Review* 82:941–1010.

Kuisel, Richard. 1981. *Capitalism and the State in France: Renovation and Economic Management in the Twentieth Century.* New York: Cambridge University Press.

Kutler, Stanley I. 1982. *The American Inquisition: Justice and Injustice in the Cold War.* New York: Hill and Wang.

Laycock, Douglas. 1986. "'Non-Preferential' Aid to Religion: A False Claim about Original Intent." *William and Mary Law Review* 27:875–923.

Laycock, Douglas. 1991. "'Noncoercive' Support for Religion: Another False Claim about the Establishment Clause." *Valparaiso University Law Review* 26:37–67.

Lebsock, Suzanne. 1984. *The Free Women of Petersburg: Status and Culture in a Southern Town, 1784–1860.* New York: W. W. Norton.

Lerner, Ralph. 1979. "Recovering the Revolution." Prologue to Ralph Lerner, *The Thinking Revolutionary: Principle and Practice in the New Republic,* 1–38. Ithaca, NY: Cornell University Press.

Levy, Leonard Williams. 1957. *The Law of the Commonwealth and Chief Justice Shaw.* Cambridge: Harvard University Press.

Lieberman, David. 1990. *The Province of Legislation Determined.* Cambridge: Cambridge University Press.

Litwack, Leon. 1979. *Been in the Storm So Long: The Aftermath of Slavery.* New York: Alfred Knopf.

Lofgren, Charles. 1987. *The Plessy Case: A Legal-Historical Interpretation.* New York: Oxford University Press.

Lowenthal, David. 1985. *The Past Is a Foreign Country.* Cambridge: Cambridge University Press.

Luban, David. 1989. "Difference Made Legal: The Court and Dr. King." *Michigan Law Review* 87:2152–224.

Lynd, Staughton. 1988. "The Genesis of the Idea of a Community Right to Industrial Property in Youngstown and Pittsburgh, 1977–1987." In David Thelen, ed., *The Constitution in American Life,* 266–98. Ithaca: Cornell University Press.

Maier, Charles. 1987. *In Search of Stability: Explorations in Historical Political Economy.* New York: Cambridge University Press.

Maltz, Earl M. 1985. "The Concept of Equal Protection of the Laws: A Historical Inquiry." *San Diego Law Review* 22:499–540.

May, James. 1989. "Antitrust in the Formative Era: Political and Economic Theory in Constitutional and Anti-Trust Analysis: 1880–1918." *Ohio State Law Journal* 50:257–395.

McClellan, James. 1971. *Joseph Story and the American Constitution.* Norman: University of Oklahoma Press.

McConnell, Michael. 1990. "The Origins and Historical Understanding of Free Exercise of Religion." *Harvard Law Review* 103:1409–517.

McCurdy, Charles. 1975. "Justice Field and the Jurisprudence of Government-Business Relations." *Journal of American History* 61:970–1005.

Meese, Edwin. [1985] 1990. "Interpreting the Constitution." In Jack N. Rakove, ed., *Interpreting the Constitution: The Debate Over Original Intent,* 13–22. Boston: Northeastern University Press.

Mensch, Elizabeth. 1982. "The Colonial Origins of Liberal Property Rights." *Buffalo Law Review* 31:635–735.

Michelman, Frank I. 1986. "Foreword: Traces of Self-Government." *Harvard Law Review* 100:4–77.

Minow, Martha. 1985. "Forming Underneath Everything That Grows: Toward a History of Family Law." *Wisconsin Law Review* 1985:819–98.

Montgomery, David. 1987. *Fall of the House of Labor: The Workplace, the State, and American Labor Activism, 1865–1925.* New York: Cambridge University Press.

Moore, Barrington. 1966. *Social Origins of Dictatorship and Democracy: Lord and Peasant in the Making of the Modern World.* Boston: Beacon Press.

Nedelsky, Jennifer. 1990. *Private Property and the Limits of American Constitutionalism.* Chicago: University of Chicago Press.

Nelson, William. 1988. *The Fourteenth Amendment: From Political Principle to Judicial Doctrine.* Cambridge: Harvard University Press.

Newmyer, Kent. 1985. *Supreme Court Justice Joseph Story: Statesman of the Old Republic.* Chapel Hill: University of North Carolina Press.

Noble, Charles. 1986. *Liberalism at Work: The Rise and Fall of OSHA.* Philadelphia: Temple University Press.

Nockleby, John. 1983. "Tortious Interference with Contractual Relations in the Nineteenth Century." *Harvard Law Review* 93:1510–39.

Olsen, Frances. 1983. "The Family and the Market: A Study of Ideology and Legal Reform." *Harvard Law Review* 96:1497–578.

Paul, Arnold. 1960. *Conservative Crisis and the Rule of Law: Attitudes of Bar and Bench, 1887–1895.* Ithaca, NY: Cornell University Press.

Peller, Gary. 1985. "The Metaphysics of American Law." *California Law Review* 73:1152–290.

Piore, Michael, and Charles Sabel. 1984. *The Second Industrial Divide: Possibilities for Prosperity.* New York: Basic Books.

Pocock, J. G. A. 1957. *The Ancient Constitution and the Feudal Law.* Cambridge: Cambridge University Press.

Pocock, J. G. A. 1975. *The Machiavellian Moment: Florentine Political Thought and the Atlantic Republican Tradition.* Princeton: Princeton University Press.

Pollack, Norman. 1987. *The Just Polity: Populism, Law, and Human Welfare.* Urbana: University of Illinois Press.

Powell, T. Jefferson. 1987. "Rules for Originalists." *Virginia Law Review* 73:659–99.

Presser, Stephen. 1991. *The Original Misunderstanding: The English, the Americans, and the Dialectic of Federalist Jurisprudence.* Durham, NC: Carolina Academic Press.

Presser, Stephen, and Becky Bair Hurley. 1984. "Saving God's Republic: The Jurisprudence of Samuel Chase." *University of Illinois Law Review* 1984:771–822.

Priest, George L. 1977. "The Common Law and the Efficient Selection of Legal Rules." *Journal of Legal Studies* 6:65–82.

Reddy, William. 1984. *The Rise of Market Culture: The Textile Trade and the Rise of French Society, 1750–1900.* New York: Cambridge University Press.

Reid, John Phillip. 1986–91. *Constitutional History of the American Revolution.* Vol. 1-3. Madison: University of Wisconsin Press.

Reid, John Phillip. 1988a. "Liberty and the Original Understanding," In *Essays in the History of Liberty: Seaver Institute Lectures at the Huntington Library.* Vol. 1. Pasadena, CA: Huntington Library.

Reid, John Phillip. 1988b. *The Concept of Liberty in the Age of the American Revolution.* Chicago: University of Chicago Press.

Reid, John Phillip. 1989. *The Concept of Representation in the Age of the American Revolution.* Chicago: University of Chicago Press.

Reimann, Mathias. 1990. "Nineteenth Century German Legal Science." *Boston College Law Review* 31:837–97.

Rogers, Joel. 1990. "Divide and Conquer: Further Reflections on the Distinctive Character of American Labor Laws." *Wisconsin Law Review* 1990:1–147.

Rose, Carol. 1986. "The Comedy of the Commons: Custom, Commerce, and Inherently Public Property." *University of Chicago Law Review* 53:711–81.

Rubin, Paul H. 1977. "Why Is the Common Law Efficient?" *Journal of Legal Studies* 6:51–64.

Sabel, Charles F., and Jonathan Zeitlin. 1985. "Historical Alternatives to Mass Production." *Past and Present* 108 (August): 133–76.

Scheiber, Harry. 1972. "Government and the Economy: Studies of the Commonwealth Policy in Nineteenth Century America." *Journal of Interdisciplinary History* 3:135–51.

Scheiber, Harry. 1984. "Public Rights and the Rule of Law in American Legal History." *California Law Review* 75:415–44.

Selvin, Molly. 1980. "The Public Trust Doctrine in American Law and Economic Policy, 1789–1920." *Wisconsin Law Review* (1980):1403–42.

Sewell, William H., Jr. 1980. *Work and Revolution in France: The Language of Labor from the Old Regime to 1848.* New York: Cambridge University Press.

Sherry, Suzanna. 1986. "Civic Virtue and the Feminine Voice in Constitutional Adjudication." *Virginia Law Review* 72:543–616.

Siegel, Reva. 1992. "Reasoning from the Body: A Historical Perspective on Abortion Regulation and Questions of Equal Protection." *Stanford Law Review* 44: 261–381.

Siegel, Stephen. 1984. "Understanding the Lochner Era: Lessons from the Controversy over Railroad and Utility Rate Regulation." *Virginia Law Review* 70:187–263.

Siegel, Stephen. 1990. "Historism in Late Nineteenth-Century Constitutional Thought." *Wisconsin Law Review* (1990):1431–47.

Simon, William. 1985. "The Invention and Reinvention of Welfare Rights," *Maryland Law Review* 44:1–37.

Simon, William. 1991. "Social-Republican Property." *UCLA Law Review* 38:1335–413.

Singer, Joseph. 1980. "The Reliance Interest in Property." *Stanford Law Review* 40:611–751.

Singer, Joseph. 1982. "The Legal Rights Debate in Analytical Jurisprudence from Bentham to Hohfeld." *Wisconsin Law Review* 1982:975–1059.

Soifer, Aviam. 1987. "The Paradoxes of Paternalism and Laissez-Faire Constitutionalism: United States Supreme Court, 1888–1921." *Law and History Review* 5:249–79.

Stein, Peter. 1980. *Legal Evolution: The Story of an Idea.* Cambridge: Cambridge University Press.

Steinfeld, Robert. 1991. *The Invention of Free Labor: The Employment Relation in English and American Law and Culture, 1350–1870.* Chapel Hill: University of North Carolina Press.

Stone, Katherine van Wezel. 1981. "The Post-War Paradigm in American Labor Law." *Yale Law Journal* 90:1509–80.

Story, Joseph. 1835. Inaugural discourse, "The Value and Importance of Legal Studies." In William W. Story, ed., *The Miscellaneous Writings,* 503–48. Boston: J. Munroe and Company.

Sunstein, Cass. 1985. "Interest Groups in American Public Law." *Stanford Law Review* 38:29–87.

Sunstein, Cass. 1988. "Beyond the Republican Revival." *Yale Law Journal* 97:1539–90.

Symposium. 1989. "Roads Not Taken: Undercurrents of Republican Thinking in Modern Constitutional Theory." *Northwestern University Law Review* 84:1–249.

Thompson, E. P. 1975. *Whigs and Hunters: The Origin of the Black Act.* New York: Pantheon Books.

Tomlins, Christopher. 1985. *The State and the Unions: Labor Relations, Law, and the Organized Labor Movement in America, 1880–1960.* Cambridge: Cambridge University Press.

Tomlins, Christopher. 1988. "A Mysterious Power: Industrial Accidents and the Legal Construction of Employment Relations in Massachusetts, 1800–1850." *Law and History Review* 6:375–438.

Tushnet, Mark. 1987. *The NAACP Campaign against Segregated Education, 1925–1950.* Chapel Hill: University of North Carolina Press.

Tushnet, Mark. 1988. *Red, White, and Blue: A Critical Analysis of Constitutional Law.* Cambridge: Harvard University Press.

Unger, Roberto Mangabeira. 1987. *Politics: Part I, False Necessity—Anti-Necessitarian Social Theory in the Service of Radical Democracy.* Cambridge: Cambridge University Press.

Urofsky, Melvin. 1985. "State Courts and Protective Legislation during the Progressive Era." *Journal of American History* 72:63–91.

Vandervelde, Lea. 1989. "The Labor Vision of the Thirteenth Amendment." *University of Pennsylvania Law Review* 138:437–504.

van Ee, Daun. 1986. *David Dudley Field and the Reconstruction of the Law.* New York: Garland.

Walker, Mack. 1981. *Johann Jakob Moser and the Holy Roman Empire of the German Nation.* Chapel Hill: University of North Carolina Press.

Weinstein, James. 1968. *The Corporate Ideal in the Liberal State: 1900–1918.* Boston: Beacon Press.

Weisberg, Robert. 1986. "Commercial Morality, the Merchant Character, and the History of the Voidable Preference." *Stanford Law Review* 39:3–138.

Weisbrod, Carol. 1986. "Images of the Woman Juror." *Harvard Women's Law Journal* 9:59–82.

White, G. Edward. 1988. *The Marshall Court and Cultural Change: 1815–1835.* New York: Macmillan.

Whitman, James. 1990. *The Legacy of Roman Law in the German Romantic Era.* Princeton: Princeton University Press.

Wieacker, Franz. 1967. *Privatrechtsgeschichte der Neuzeit.* 2d ed. Goettingen: Vandenhoek & Reprecht.

Wiecek, William. 1977. *The Sources of Antislavery Constitutionalism in America, 1760–1848.* Ithaca, NY: Cornell University Press.

Wilentz, Sean. 1984. *Chants Democratic: New York City and the Rise of the American Working Class.* New York: Oxford University Press.

Williams, Robert A. 1990. *The American Indian in Western Legal Thought: The Discourse of Conquest.* New York: Oxford University Press.

Wright, Gavin. 1986. *Old South, New South: Revolutions in the Southern Economy since the Civil War.* New York: Basic Books.

The Evidence of Experience

Joan Wallach Scott

Becoming Visible

A section of Samuel Delany's magnificent autobiographical meditation, *The Motion of Light in Water,* dramatically raises the problem of writing the history of difference, the history, that is, of the designation of "other," of the attribution of characteristics that distinguish categories of people from some presumed (and usually unstated) norm (Minow 1987). Delany (a gay man, a black man, a writer of science fiction) recounts his reaction to his first visit to the St. Marks bathhouse in 1963. He describes standing on the threshhold of a "gym-sized room" dimly lit by blue bulbs. The room was full of people, some standing, the rest

> an undulating mass of naked, male bodies, spread wall to wall.
>
> My first response was a kind of heart-thudding astonishment, very close to fear.
>
> I have written of a space at certain libidinal saturation before. That was not what frightened me. It was rather that the saturation was not only kinesthetic but visible. (Delany 1988, 173)

Watching the scene establishes for Delany a "fact that flew in the face" of the prevailing representation of homosexuals in the 1950s as "isolated perverts," as "subjects gone awry." The "apprehension of massed bodies" gave him (as it does, he argues, anyone "male, female, working or middle class") a "sense of political power":

> what *this* experience said was that there was a population—not of individual homosexuals . . . not of hundreds, not of thousands, but rather of millions of gay men, and that history had actively and already created for

379

us whole galleries of institutions, good and bad, to accommodate our sex. (Delany 1988, 174)

The sense of political possibility is frightening and exhilarating for Delany. He emphasizes not the discovery of an identity but a sense of participation in a movement. Indeed, it is the extent (as well as the existence) of these sexual practices that matters most in his account. Numbers—massed bodies—constitute a movement, and this, even if subterranean, belies enforced silences about the range and diversity of human sexual practices. Making the movement visible breaks the silence about it, challenges prevailing notions, and opens new possibilities for everyone. Delany imagines, even from the vantage point of 1988, a future utopian moment of genuine sexual revolution "once the AIDS crisis is brought under control":

> That revolution will come precisely because of the infiltration of clear and articulate language into the marginal areas of human sexual exploration, such as this book from time to time describes. . . . Now that a significant range of people have begun to get a clearer idea of what has been possible among the varieties of human pleasure in the recent past, heterosexuals and homosexuals, females and males will insist on exploring them even further. (Delany 1988, 175)

By writing about the bathhouse Delany seeks not, he says, to "romanticize that time into some cornucopia of sexual plenty" but rather to break an "absolutely sanctioned public silence" on questions of sexual practice, to reveal something that existed but that had been suppressed.

> Only the coyest and the most indirect articulations could occasionally indicate the boundaries of a phenomenon whose centers could not be spoken or written of, even figuratively; and that coyness was medical and legal as well as literary; and, as Foucault has told us, it was, in its coyness, a huge and pervasive discourse. But what that coyness means is that there is no way to gain from it a clear, accurate, and extensive picture of extant public sexual institutions. That discourse only touched on highly select margins when they transgressed the legal and/or medical standards of a populace that firmly wished to maintain that no such institutions existed. (Delany 1988, 175–76)

The point of Delany's description, indeed of his entire book, is to document the existence of those institutions in all their variety and multiplicity, to write about and thus to render historical what has hitherto been hidden from history.

As I read it, a metaphor of visibility as literal transparency is crucial to his project. The blue lights illuminate a scene he has participated in before (in darkened trucks parked along the docks under the West Side Highway, in men's rooms in subway stations) but understood only in a fragmented way. "No one ever got *to see* its whole" (Delany 1988, 174). He attributes the impact of the bathhouse scene to its visibility: "You could *see* what was going on throughout the dorm" (Delany 1988, 173). Seeing enables him to comprehend the relationship between his personal activities and politics: "the first direct sense of political power comes from the apprehension of massed bodies" (173). Recounting that moment also allows him to explain the aim of his book: to provide a "clear, accurate, and extensive *picture* of extant public sexual institutions" so that others may learn about and explore them (Delany 1988, 174, 176). Knowledge is gained through vision; vision is a direct apprehension of a world of transparent objects. In this conceptualization the visible is privileged; writing is then put at its service (Bhabha 1987). Seeing is the origin of knowing. Writing is reproduction, transmission—the communication of knowledge gained through (visual, visceral) experience.

This kind of communication has long been the mission of historians documenting the lives of those omitted or overlooked in accounts of the past. It has produced a wealth of new evidence previously ignored about these others and has drawn attention to dimensions of human life and activity usually deemed unworthy of mention in conventional histories. It has also occasioned a crisis for orthodox history, by multiplying not only stories but subjects and by insisting that histories are written from fundamentally different—indeed irreconcilable—perspectives or standpoints, none of which is complete or completely "true." Like Delany's memoir, these histories have provided evidence for a world of alternative values and practices whose existence gives the lie to hegemonic constructions of social worlds, whether these constructions vaunt the political superiority of white men, the coherence and unity of selves, the naturalness of heterosexual monogamy, or the inevitablity of scientific progress and economic development. The challenge to normative history has been described, in terms of conventional historical understandings of evidence, as an enlargement of the picture, a corrective to oversights resulting from inaccurate or incomplete vision, and it has rested its claim to legitimacy on the authority of experience and the direct experience of others as well as of the historian who learns to see and illuminate the lives of those others in his or her texts.

Documenting the experience of others in this way has been at once a highly successful and a limiting strategy for historians of difference. It has been successful because it remains so comfortably within the disciplinary frame-work of history, working according to rules that permit calling old narratives into question when new evidence is discovered. The status of evidence is, of course, ambiguous for historians. On the one hand, they acknowledge that "evidence only counts as evidence and is only recognized as such in relation to a potential narrative, so that the narrative can be said to determine the evidence as much as the evidence determines the narrative" (Gossman 1989, 26). On the other hand, historians' rhetorical treatment of evidence and their use of it to falsify prevailing interpretations depends on a referential notion of evidence that denies that it is anything but a reflection of the real (LaCapra 1985, 15–44). Michel de Certeau's description is apt. "Historical discourse," he writes,

> gives itself credibility in the name of the reality which it is supposed to represent, but this authorized appearance of the "real" serves precisely to camouflage the practice which in fact determines it. Representation thus disguises the praxis that organizes it. (de Certeau 1986, 203)

When the evidence offered is the evidence of "experience," the claim for referentiality is further buttressed—what could be truer, after all, than a sub-ject's own account of what he or she has lived through? It is precisely this kind of appeal to experience as uncontestable evidence and as an originary point of explanation—as a foundation upon which analysis is based—that weakens the critical thrust of histories of difference. By remaining within the epistemologi-cal frame of orthodox history, these studies lose the possibility of examining those assumptions and practices that excluded considerations of difference in the first place. They take as self-evident the identities of those whose experi-ence is being documented and thus naturalize their difference. They locate resistance outside its discursive construction and reify agency as an inherent attribute of individuals, thus decontextualizing it. When experience is taken as the origin of knowledge, the vision of the individual subject (the person who had the experience or the historian who recounts it) becomes the bedrock of evidence upon which explanation is built. Questions about the constructed nature of experience, about how subjects are constituted as different in the first place, about how one's vision is structured—about language (or discourse) and history—are left aside. The evidence of experience then becomes evidence for the fact of difference rather than a way of exploring how difference is estab-lished, how it operates, and how and in what ways it constitutes subjects who see and act in the world.[1]

To put it another way, the evidence of experience, whether conceived through a metaphor of visibility or in any other way that takes meaning as transparent, reproduces rather than contests given ideological systems—those that assume that the facts of history speak for themselves and those that rest on notions of a natural or established opposition between, say, sexual practices and social conventions and between homosexuality and heterosexuality. Histories that document the "hidden" world of homosexuality, for example, show the impact of silence and repression on the lives of those affected by it and bring to light the history of their suppression and exploitation. But the project of making experience visible precludes critical examination of the workings of the ideological system itself: its categories of representation (homosexual/ heterosexual, man/woman, black/white as fixed immutable identities), its premises about what these categories mean and how they operate, and its notions of subjects, origin, and cause. Homosexual practices are seen as the result of desire, which is conceived as a natural force operating outside of or in opposition to social regulation. In these stories, homosexuality is presented as a repressed desire (experience denied) and made to seem invisible, abnormal, and silenced by a "society" that legislates heterosexuality as the only normal practice (Bersani 1976). Because this kind of (homosexual) desire cannot ultimately be repressed—because experience is there—it invents institutions to accommodate itself. These institutions are unacknowledged but not invisible. Indeed, it is the possibility that they can be seen that threatens order and ultimately overcomes repression. Resistance and agency are presented as driven by uncontainable desire; emancipation is a teleological story in which desire ultimately overcomes social control and becomes visible. History is a chronology that makes experience visible but in which categories appear as nonetheless ahistorical: desire, homosexuality, heterosexuality, femininity, masculinity, sex, and even sexual practices become so many fixed entities being played out over time but not themselves historicized. Presenting the story in this way excludes, or at least understates, the historically variable interrelationship between the meanings "homosexual" and "heterosexual," the constitutive force each has for the other, and the contested and changing nature of the terrain that they simultaneously occupy. "The importance—an importance—of the category 'homosexual,'" writes Eve Sedgwick,

comes not necessarily from its regulatory relation to a nascent or already-constituted minority of homosexual people or desires, but from its potential for giving whoever wields it a structuring definitional leverage over the whole range of male bonds that shape the social constitution. (Sedgwick 1985, 86)

Not only does homosexuality define heterosexuality by specifying its negative limits, not only is the boundary between the two a shifting one, but both operate within the structures of the same "phallic economy"—an economy whose workings are not taken into account by studies that seek simply to make homosexual experience visible. One way to describe this economy is to say that desire is defined through the pursuit of the phallus—that veiled and evasive signifier that is at once fully present but unattainable and that gains its power through the promise it holds out but never entirely fulfills (Gallop 1982; de Lauretis 1984; Sedgwick 1985; Lacan 1977). Theorized this way, homosexuality and heterosexuality work according to the same economy, their social institutions mirroring one another. The social institutions through which gay sex is practiced may invert those associated with dominant heterosexual behavior (promiscuous versus restrained, public versus private, anonymous versus known, and so on), but they both operate within a system structured according to presence and lack.[2] To the extent that this system constructs desiring subjects (those who are legitimate as well as those who are not), it simultaneously establishes them and itself as given and outside of time, as the way things work, the way they inevitably *are*.

The project of making experience visible precludes analysis of the workings of this system and of its historicity. Instead, it reproduces its terms. We come to appreciate the consequences of the closeting of homosexuals, and we understand repression as an interested act of power or domination. Alternative behaviors and institutions also become available to us. What we do not have is a way of placing those alternatives within the framework of (historically contingent) dominant patterns of sexuality and the ideology that supports them. We know they exist but not how they have been constructed. We know their existence offers a critique of normative practices but not the extent of the critique. Making visible the experience of a different group exposes the existence of repressive mechanisms but not their inner workings or logics. We know that difference exists, but we do not understand it as relationally constituted. For that, we need to attend to the historical processes that, through discourse, position subjects and produce their experiences. It is not individuals who have experience but subjects who are constituted through experience. Experience in this definition then becomes not the origin of our explanation, not the authoritative (because seen or felt) evidence that grounds what is known but rather that which we seek to explain, that about which knowledge is produced. To think about experience in this way is to historicize it as well as to historicize the identities it produces. This kind of historicizing represents a reply to the many contemporary historians who have argued that an unproblematized "experience" is the foundation of their practice. It is a historicizing that implies critical scrutiny of all explanatory categories usually taken for granted, including the category of "experience."

The Authority of Experience

History has been largely a foundationalist discourse. By this I mean that its explanations seem to be unthinkable if they do not take for granted some primary premises, categories, or presumptions. These foundations (however varied, whatever they are at a particular moment) are unquestioned and unquestionable. They are considered permanent and transcendent. As such, they create a common ground for historians and their objects of study in the past and so authorize and legitimize analysis. Indeed, analysis seems not to be able to proceed without them.[3] In the minds of some foundationalists, in fact, nihilism, anarchy, and moral confusion are the sure alternatives to these givens, which have the status (if not the philosophical definition) of eternal truths.

Historians have had recourse to many kinds of foundations, some more obviously empiricist than others. What is most striking these days is the determined embrace, the strident defense, of some reified, transcendent category of explanation by historians who have used insights drawn from the sociology of knowledge, structural linguistics, feminist theory, or cultural anthropology to develop sharp critiques of empiricism. This turn to foundations even by antifoundationalists appears, in Fredric Jameson's characterization, as "some extreme form of the return of the repressed" (Jameson 1991, 199).

"Experience" is one of the foundations that has been reintroduced into historical writing in the wake of the critique of empiricism. Unlike "brute fact" or "simple reality," its connotations are more varied and elusive. It has recently emerged as a critical term in debates among historians about the limits of interpretation and especially about the uses and limits of poststructuralist theory for history. In these debates, those most open to interpretive innovation— those who have insisted on the study of collective mentalities; of economic, social, or cultural determinations of individual behavior; and even of the influences of unconscious motives on thought and action—are among the most ardent defenders of the need to attend to "experience." Feminist historians critical of biases in "male-stream" histories and seeking to install women as viable subjects, social historians insisting upon the materialist basis of the discipline on the one hand and on the "agency" of individuals or groups on the other, and cultural historians who have brought symbolic analysis to the study of behavior have joined both political historians whose stories privilege the purposive actions of rational actors and intellectual historians who maintain that thought originates in the minds of individuals. All seem to have converged on the argument that experience is an "irreducible" ground for history.

The evocation of "experience" appears to solve a problem of explanation for professed antiempiricists even as it reinstates a foundational ground. For this reason, it is interesting to examine the uses of "experience" by historians. Such an examination allows us to ask whether history can exist without foundations and what it might look like if it did.

In *Keywords,* Raymond Williams sketches the alternative senses in which the term *experience* has been employed in the Anglo-American tradition. These he summarizes as "(i) knowledge gathered from past events, whether by conscious observation or by consideration and reflection; and (ii) a particular kind of consciousness, which can in some contexts be distinguished from 'reason' or 'knowledge'" (Williams 1985, 126). Until the early eighteenth century, he says, experience and experiment were closely connected terms, designating how knowledge was arrived at through testing and observation (the visual metaphor here is important). In the eighteenth century, experience still contained this notion of consideration or reflection on observed events, of lessons gained from the past, but it also referred to a particular kind of consciousness. This consciousness, in the twentieth century, has come to mean "a full and active 'awareness'" including feeling as well as thought (Williams 1985, 127). The notion of experience as subjective witness, writes Williams, "is offered not only as truth, but as the most authentic kind of truth," as "the ground for all (subsequent) reasoning and analysis" (Williams 1985, 128). According to Williams, experience has acquired another connotation in the twentieth century different from these notions of subjective testimony as immediate, true, and authentic. In this usage, it refers to influences external to individuals—social conditions, institutions, forms of belief or perception—"real" things outside them that they react to and does not include their thought or consideration (Rorty 1979).

In the various usages described by Williams, "experience," whether conceived as internal or external, subjective or objective, establishes the prior existence of individuals. When it is defined as internal, it is an expression of an individual's being or consciousness; when external, it is the material on which consciousness then acts. Talking about experience in these ways leads us to take the existence of individuals for granted (experience is something people have) rather than to ask how conceptions of selves (of subjects and their identities) are produced.[4] It operates within an ideological construction that not only makes individuals the starting point of knowledge but that also naturalizes categories such as man, woman, black, white, heterosexual, and homosexual by treating them as given characteristics of individuals.

Teresa de Lauretis's redefinition of experience exposes the workings of this ideology. "Experience," she writes, is the

> process by which, for all social beings, subjectivity is constructed. Through that process one places oneself or is placed in social reality and so perceives and comprehends as subjective (referring to, originating in oneself) those relations—material, economic, and interpersonal—which are in fact social, and, in a larger perspective, historical. (de Lauretis 1984, 159)

The process that de Lauretis describes operates crucially through differentiation. Its effect is to constitute subjects as fixed and autonomous and as reliable sources of a knowledge that comes from access to the real by means of their experience.[5] When talking about historians and other students of the human sciences it is important to note that this subject is both the object of inquiry—the person one studies in the present or the past—and the investigator him- or herself—the historian who produces knowledge of the past based on "experience" in the archives or the anthropologist who produces knowledge of other cultures based on "experience" as a participant-observer.

The concepts of experience described by Williams preclude inquiry into processes of subject construction. They avoid examining the relationships between discourse, cognition, and reality; the relevance of the position or situatedness of subjects to the knowledge they produce; and the effects of difference on knowledge. Questions are not raised about, for example, whether it matters for the history they write that historians are men, women, white, black, straight, or gay. Instead, as de Certeau writes, "the authority of the 'subject of knowledge' [is measured] by the elimination of everything concerning the speaker" (de Certeau 1986, 218). His knowledge, reflecting as it does something apart from him, is legitimated and presented as universal, accessible to all. There is no power or politics in these notions of knowledge and experience.

An example of the way "experience" establishes the authority of a historian can be found in R. G. Collingwood's *The Idea of History,* the 1946 classic that has been required reading in historiography courses for several generations. For Collingwood, the ability of the historian to reenact past experience is tied to his autonomy, "where by autonomy I mean the condition of being one's own authority, making statements or taking action on one's own initiative and not because those statements or actions are authorized or prescribed by anyone else" (Collingwood 1956, 274–75). The question of where the historian is situated—who he is, how he is defined in relation to others, what the political effects of his history may be—never enters the discussion. Indeed, being free of these matters seems to be tied to Collingwood's definition of autonomy, an issue so critical for him that he launches into an uncharacteristic tirade about it. In his quest for certainty, the historian must not let others make up his mind for him, Collingwood insists, because to do that means

> giving up his autonomy as an historian and allowing someone else to do for him what, if he is a scientific thinker, he can only do for himself. There is no need for me to offer the reader any proof of this statement. If he knows anything of historical work, he already knows of his own experience that it is true. If he does not already know that it is true, he does not know enough about history to read this essay with any profit, and the best thing he can do is to stop here and now. (Collingwood 1956, 256)

For Collingwood, it is axiomatic that experience is a reliable source of knowledge because it rests on direct contact between the historian's perception and reality (even if the passage of time makes it necessary for the historian to imaginatively reenact events of the past). Thinking on his own means owning his own thoughts, and this proprietary relationship guarantees an individual's independence, his ability to read the past correctly, and the authority of the knowledge he produces. The claim is not only for the historian's autonomy but also for his originality. Here "experience" grounds the identity of the researcher as a historian.

Another very different use of "experience" can be found in E. P. Thompson's *The Making of the English Working Class,* the book that revolutionized social and labor history. Thompson specifically set out to free the concept of "class" from the ossified categories of Marxist structuralism. For this project "experience" was a key concept. "We explored," Thompson writes of himself and his fellow New Left historians, "both in theory and in practice, those junction-concepts (such as 'need,' 'class,' and 'determine') by which, through the missing term, 'experience,' structure is transmuted into process, and the subject re-enters into history" (Thompson 1978, 170).

Thompson's notion of experience joined ideas of external influence and subjective feeling, the structural and the psychological. This gave him a mediating influence between social structure and social consciousness. For him, experience meant "social being"—the lived realities of social life, especially the affective domains of family and religion and the symbolic dimensions of expression. This definition separated the affective and the symbolic from the economic and the rational. "People do not only experience their own experience as ideas, within thought and its procedures," he maintained, "they also experience their own experience as *feeling*" (Thompson 1978, 171). This statement grants importance to the psychological dimension of experience, and it allows Thompson to account for agency. Feeling, Thompson insists, is "handled" culturally as "norms, familial and kinship obligations and reciprocities, as values or (through more elaborated forms) within art and religious beliefs" (171). At the same time, it somehow precedes these forms of expression and so provides an escape from a strong structural determination: "For any living generation, in any 'now,'" Thompson asserts, "the ways in which they 'handle' experience defies prediction and escapes from any narrow definition of determination" (171).

And yet in his use of it, experience, because it is ultimately shaped by relations of production, is a unifying phenomenon, overriding other kinds of diversity. Because these relations of production are common to workers of different ethnicities, religions, regions, and trades they necessarily provide a common denominator and emerge as a more salient determinant of "experience" than anything else. In Thompson's use of the term, experience is the start of a process that culminates in the realization and articulation of social consciousness, in this case, a common identity of class. It serves an integrating function, joining the individual and the structural and bringing together diverse people into that coherent (totalizing) whole that is a distinctive sense of class (Butler 1990, 22–25). "'Experience' (we have found) has, in the last instance, been generated in 'material life,' has been structured in class ways, and hence 'social being' has determined 'social consciousness'" (Thompson 1978, 171). In this way, unequivocal and uniform identity is produced through objective circumstances, and there is no reason to ask how this identity achieved predominance—it had to.

The unifying aspect of experience excludes whole realms of human activity by simply not counting them as experience, at least with any consequences for social organization or politics. When class becomes an overriding identity, other subject-positions are subsumed by it, those of gender, for example (or, in other instances of this kind, of history, race, ethnicity, and sexuality). The positions of men and women and their different relationships to politics are taken as reflections of material and social arrangements rather than as products of class politics itself. They are part of the "experience" of capitalism. Instead of asking how some experiences become more salient than others, how what matters to Thompson is defined as experience, and how differences are dissolved, experience becomes itself cumulative and homogenizing, providing the common denominator on which class consciousness is built.

Thompson's own role in determining the salience of certain things and not others is never addressed. Although his author's voice intervenes powerfully with moral and ethical judgments about the situations he is recounting, the presentation of the experiences themselves is meant to secure their objective status. We forget that Thompson's history, like the accounts offered by political organizers in the nineteenth century of what mattered in workers' lives, is an interpretation, a selective ordering of information that through its use of originary categories and teleological accounts legitimizes a particular kind of politics (it becomes the only possible politics) and a particular way of doing history (as a reflection of what happened, the description of which is little influenced by the historian if, in this case, he only has the requisite moral vision that permits identification with the experiences of workers in the past).

In Thompson's account, class is finally an identity rooted in structural relations that preexist politics. What this obscures is the contradictory and contested process by which class itself was conceptualized and by which diverse kinds of subject-positions were assigned, felt, contested, or embraced. As a result, Thompson's brilliant history of the English working class, which set out to historicize the category of class, ends up essentializing it. The ground may seem to be displaced from structure to agency by insisting on the subjectively felt nature of experience, but the problem Thompson sought to address is not really solved. Working-class "experience" is now the ontological foundation of working-class identity, politics, and history.[6]

This kind of use of experience has the same foundational status if we substitute "women's" or "black" or "lesbian" or "homosexual" for "working-class" in the previous sentence. Among feminist historians, for example, "experience" has helped to legitimize a critique of the false claims to objectivity of traditional historical accounts. Part of the project of some feminist history has been to unmask all claims to objectivity as being an ideological cover for masculine bias by pointing out the shortcomings, incompleteness, and exclusiveness of mainstream history. This has been achieved by providing documentation about women in the past that calls into question existing interpretations made without consideration of gender. But how do we authorize the new knowledge if the possibility of all historical objectivity has been questioned? The answer is by appealing to experience, which in this usage connotes both reality and its subjective apprehension—the experience of women in the past and of women historians who can recognize something of themselves in their foremothers.

Judith Newton, a literary historian writing about the neglect of feminism by contemporary critical theorists, argues that women, too, arrived at the critique of objectivity usually associated with deconstruction or the new historicism. This feminist critique came "straight out of reflection on our own, that is, women's experience, out of the contradictions we felt between the different ways we were represented even to ourselves, out of the inequities we had long experienced in our situations" (Newton 1988, 93). Newton's appeal to experience seems to bypass the issue of objectivity (by not raising the question of whether feminist work can be objective), but it rests firmly on a foundational ground (experience). In her work, the relationship between thought and experience is represented as transparent (the visual metaphor combines with the visceral) and so directly accessible, as it is in historian Christine Stansell's insistence that "social practices" in all their "immediacy and entirety" constitute a domain of "sensuous experience" (a prediscursive reality directly felt, seen, and known) that cannot be subsumed by "language" (Stansell 1987, 28).[7] The effect of these kinds of statements, which attribute an indisputable authenticity to women's experience, is to establish incontrovertibly women's identity as people with agency. It is also to universalize the identity of women and thus to ground claims for the legitimacy of women's history in the shared experience of historians of women and those women whose stories they tell. In addition, it literally equates the personal with the political, for the lived experience of women is seen as leading directly to resistance to oppression, to feminism.[8] Indeed, the possibility of politics is said to rest on, to follow from, a preexisting women's experience.

"Because of its drive toward a political massing together of women," writes Denise Riley, "feminism can never wholeheartedly dismantle 'women's experience,' however much this category conflates the attributed, the imposed, and the lived, and then sanctifies the resulting mélange." The kind of argument for a women's history (and for a feminist politics) that Riley criticizes closes down inquiry into the ways in which female subjectivity is produced, the ways in which agency is made possible, the ways in which race and sexuality intersect with gender, and the ways in which politics organize and interpret experience—in sum, the ways in which identity is a contested terrain and the site of multiple and conflicting claims. In Riley's words, "it masks the likelihood that . . . [experiences] have accrued to women not by virtue of their womanhood alone, but as traces of domination, whether natural or political"

(Riley 1988, 99, 100). I would add that it masks the necessarily discursive character of these experiences as well.

But it is precisely the discursive character of experience that is at issue for some historians because attributing experience to discourse seems somehow to deny its status as an unquestionable ground of explanation. This seems to be the case for John Toews, who wrote a long article in the *American Historical Review* in 1987 called "Intellectual History after the Linguistic Turn: The Autonomy of Meaning and the Irreducibility of Experience." The term *linguistic turn* is a comprehensive one used by Toews to refer to approaches to the study of meaning that draw on a number of disciplines but especially on theories of language, "since the primary medium of meaning was obviously language" (Toews 1987, 881). The question for Toews is how far linguistic analysis has gone and should go, especially in view of the poststructuralist challenge to foundationalism. Reviewing a number of books that take on questions of meaning and its analysis, Toews concludes that

> the predominant tendency [among intellectual historians] is to adapt traditional historical concerns for extralinguistic origins and reference to the semiological challenge, to reaffirm in new ways that, in spite of the relative autonomy of cultural meanings, human subjects still make and remake the worlds of meaning in which they are suspended, and to insist that these worlds are not reactions *ex nihilo* but responses to, and shapings of, changing worlds of experience ultimately irreducible to the linguistic forms in which they appear. (Toews 1987, 882)

By definition, he argues, history is concerned with explanation. It is not a radical hermenutics but an attempt to account for the origin, persistence, and disappearance of certain meanings at "particular times and in specific sociocultural situations." For him, explanation requires a separation of experience and meaning, and experience is that reality that demands meaningful response. "Experience" as Toews uses it is taken to be so self-evident that he never defines the term. This is telling in an article that insists on establishing the importance and independence—the irreducibility—of "experience." The absence of definition allows experience to resonate in many ways, but it also allows it to function as a univerally understood category—the undefined word creates a sense of consensus by attributing to it an assumed, stable, and shared meaning.

Experience, for Toews is a foundational concept. While recognizing that meanings differ and that the historian's task is to analyze the different meanings produced in societies and over time, Toews protects "experience" from this kind of relativism. In so doing he establishes the possibility for objective knowledge and so for communication among historians, however diverse their positions and views. This has an effect (among others) of removing historians from critical scrutiny as active producers of knowledge.

The insistence on the separation of meaning and experience is crucial for Toews, not only because it seems the only way to account for change but also because it protects the world from "the hubris of wordmakers who claim to be makers of reality" (Toews 1987, 906). Even if Toews here uses "wordmakers" metaphorically to refer to those who produce texts, those who engage in signification, his opposition between "words" and "reality" echoes the distinction he makes earlier in the article between language (or meaning) and experience. This opposition guarantees both an independent status for human agents and the common ground on which they can communicate and act. It produces a possibility for "intersubjective communication" among individuals despite differences between them and also reaffirms their existence as thinking beings outside the discursive practices they devise and employ.

Toews is critical of John Pocock's vision of "intersubjective communication" based on rational consensus in a community of free individuals, all of whom are equally masters of their own wills. "Pocock's theories," he writes, "often seem like theoretical reflections of familiar practices because the world they assume is also the world in which many contemporary Anglo-American historians live or think they live" (Toews 1987, 893). Yet the separation of meaning and experience that Toews offers does not really provide an alternative. A more diverse community can be posited, of course, with different meanings given to experience. Because the phenomenon of experience itself can be analyzed outside the meanings given to it, the subjective position of historians then can seem to have nothing to do with the knowledge they produce.[9] In this way, experience authorizes historians and it enables them to counter the radical historicist stance that, Toews says, "undermines the traditional historians' quest for unity, continuity and purpose by robbing them of any standpoint from which a relationship between past, present and future could be objectively reconstructed" (Toews 1987, 902). Here he establishes as self-evident (and unproblematic) the reflective nature of historical representation and he assumes that it will override whatever diversity there is in the background, culture, and outlook of historians. Attention to experience, he concludes, "is essential for our self-understanding, and thus also for fulfilling the historian's task of connecting memory with hope" (Toews 1987, 907).[10]

Toews's "experience" thus provides an object for historians that can be known apart from their own role as meaning makers, and it then guarantees not only the objectivity of their knowledge but their ability to persuade others of its importance. Whatever diversity and conflict may exist among them, Toews's community of historians is rendered homogeneous by its shared object (experience). But as Ellen Rooney has so effectively pointed out, using the field of literary theory as her example, this kind of homogeneity can exist only because of the exclusion of the possibility that "historically irreducible interests divide and define reading communities" (Rooney 1989, 6). Inclusiveness is achieved by denying that exclusion is inevitable, that difference is established through exclusion, and that the fundamental differences that accompany inequalities of power and position cannot be overcome by persuasion. In Toews's article, no disagreement about the meaning of the term *experience* can be entertained because experience itself lies somehow outside its signification. For that reason, perhaps, Toews never defined it.

Even among those historians who do not share all of Toews's ideas about the objectivity or continuous quality of history writing, the defense of "experience" works in much the same way: it establishes a realm of reality outside of discourse, and it authorizes the historian who has access to it. The evidence of experience works as a foundation that provides both a starting point and a conclusive kind of explanation, beyond which few questions can or need to be asked. And yet it is precisely the questions precluded—questions about discourse, difference, and subjectivity as well as about what counts as experience and who gets to make that determination—that would enable us to historicize experience and to reflect critically on the history we write about it rather than to premise our history on it.

Historicizing "Experience"

Gayatri Chakravorty Spivak begins an essay addressed to the subaltern studies collective with a contrast between the work of historians and literary scholars:

> A historian confronts a text of counterinsurgency or gendering where the subaltern has been represented. He unravels the text to assign a new subject-position to the subaltern, gendered or otherwise. A teacher of literature confronts a sympathetic text where the gendered subaltern has been represented. She unravels the text to make visible the assignment of subject-positions. . . . The performance of these tasks, of the historian and the teacher of literature, must critically "interrupt" each other, bring each other to crisis, in order to serve their constituencies; especially when each seems to claim all for its own. (Spivak 1987, 241)

Spivak's argument here seems to be that there is a difference between history and literature that is both methodological and political. History provides categories that enable us to understand the social and structural positions of people (as workers, subalterns, and so on) in new terms, and these terms define a collective identity with potential political (maybe even revolutionary, but certainly subversive) effects. Literature relativizes the categories history assigns and exposes the processes that construct and position subjects. In Spivak's discussion, both are critical operations, although she clearly favors the deconstructive task of literature.[11] Although her essay has to be read in the context of a specific debate within Indian historiography, its general points must also be considered. In effect, her statements raise the question of whether historians can do other than construct subjects by describing their experience in terms of an essentialized identity.

Spivak's characterization of the subaltern studies historians' reliance on a notion of consciousness as a "strategic use of positivist essentialism" does not really solve the problem of writing history either because, whether it is strategic or not, essentialism appeals to the idea that there are fixed identities, visible to us as social or natural facts (Spivak 1987 and 1989; Fuss 1989). A refusal of essentialism seems particularly important once again these days within the field of history, as disciplinary pressure builds to defend the unitary subject in the name of his or her "experience." Neither does Spivak's invocation of the special political status of the subaltern justify a history aimed at producing subjects without interrogating and relativizing the means of their production. In the case of colonial and postcolonial peoples, but also of various others in the West, it has been precisely the imposition of a categorical (and universal) subject-status (*the* worker, *the* peasant, *the* woman, *the* black) that has masked the operations of difference in the organization of social life. Each category taken as fixed works to solidify the ideological process of subject-construction, making the process less rather than more apparent and naturalizing rather than analyzing it.

It ought to be possible for historians (as for the teachers of literature Spivak so dazzlingly exemplifies) to "make visible the assignment of subject-positions," not in the sense of capturing the reality of the objects seen but of trying to understand the operations of the complex and changing discursive processes by which identities are ascribed, resisted, or embraced. These processes themselves are unremarked; indeed they achieve their effect because they are *not* noticed. To do this a change of object seems to be required, one that takes the emergence of concepts and identities as historical events in need of explanation. This does not mean that one dismisses the *effects* of such concepts and identities, that one does not explain behavior in terms of their operations. It does mean assuming that the appearance of a new identity is not inevitable or determined, not something that was always there simply waiting to be expressed, and not something that will always exist in the form it was given in a particular political movement or at a particular historical moment. Stuart Hall writes:

> The fact is "black" has never been just there either. It has always been an unstable identity, psychically, culturally and politically. It, too, is a narrative, a story, a history. Something constructed, told, spoken, not simply found. People now speak of the society I come from in totally unrecognizable ways. Of course Jamaica is a black society, they say. In reality it is a society of black and brown people who lived for three or four hundred years without ever being able to speak of themselves as "black." Black is an identity which had to be learned and could only be learned in a certain moment. In Jamaica that moment is the 1970s. (Hall 1987, 45)

To take the history of Jamaican black identity as an object of inquiry in these terms is necessarily to analyze subject-positioning, in part at least, as the effect of discourses that placed Jamaica in a late-twentieth-century international racist political economy. It is to historicize the "experience" of blackness (Carby 1987; Fields 1982).[12]

Treating the emergence of a new identity as a discursive event is not to introduce a new form of linguistic determinism nor to deprive subjects of agency. It is to refuse a separation between "experience" and language and to insist instead on the productive quality of discourse. Subjects are constituted discursively, but there are conflicts among discursive systems, contradictions within any one of them, multiple meanings possible for the concepts they deploy (Bono 1990; Poovey 1988). And subjects do have agency. They are not unified, autonomous individuals exercising free will but rather subjects whose agency is created through situations and statuses conferred on them. Being a subject means being "subject to definite conditions of existence, conditions of endowment of agents and conditions of exercise" (Adams and Minson 1978, 52; Nussbaum 1989; de Bolla 1989). These conditions enable choices, although they are not unlimited. Subjects are constituted discursively and experience is a linguistic event (it does not happen outside established meanings), but neither is it confined to a fixed order of meaning. Because discourse is by definition shared, experience is collective as well as individual. Experience can both confirm what is already known (we see what we have learned to see) and upset what has been taken for granted (when different meanings are in conflict we readjust our vision to take account of the conflict or to resolve it—that is what is meant by "learning from experience," though not everyone learns the same lesson or learns it at the same time or in the same way). Experience is a subject's history. Language is the site of history's enactment. Historical explanation cannot, therefore, separate the two.

The question then becomes how to analyze language, and here historians often (though not always and not necessarily) confront the limits of a discipline that has typically constructed itself in opposition to literature. (These are not the same limits Spivak points to. Her contrast concerns the different kinds of knowledge produced by history and literature; mine is about different ways of reading and the different understandings of the relationship between words and things implicit in those readings. In neither case are the limits obligatory for historians; indeed recognition of them makes it possible for us to get beyond them.) The kind of reading I have in mind would not assume a direct correspondence between words and things, confine itself to single meanings, or aim for the resolution of contradiction. It would neither render process as linear nor rest explanation on simple correlations or single variables. Rather, it would grant to "the literary" an integral, even irreducible, status of its own. To grant such status is not to make "the literary" foundational but to open new possibilities for analyzing discursive productions of social and political reality as complex, contradictory processes.

The reading I offered of Delany at the beginning of this essay is an example of the kind of reading I want to avoid. I would like now to present another reading—one suggested to me by literary critic Karen Swann—as a way of indicating what might be involved in historicizing the notion of experience. It is also a way of agreeing with and appreciating Swann's argument about "the importance of 'the literary' to the historical project."[13]

For Delany, witnessing the scene at the bathhouse (an "undulating mass of naked male bodies" seen under a dim blue light) was an event. It marked what in one kind of reading we would call a coming to consciousness of himself, a recognition of his authentic identity, one he had always shared, would always share with others like himself. Another kind of reading, closer to Delany's preoccupation with memory and the self in this autobiography, sees this event not as the discovery of truth (conceived as the reflection of a prediscursive reality) but as the substitution of one interpretation for another. Delany presents this substitution as a conversion experience, a clarifying moment, after which he sees (that is, understands) differently. But there is all the difference between subjective perceptual clarity and transparent vision; one does not necessarily follow from the other even if the subjective state is metaphorically presented as a visual experience. Moreover, as Swann has pointed out, "the properties of the medium through which the visible appears—here, the dim blue light, whose distorting, refracting qualities produce a wavering of the visible" make any claim to unmediated transparency impossible. Instead, the wavering light permits a vision beyond the visible, a vision that contains the fantastic projections ("millions of gay men" for whom "history had, actively and already, created . . . whole galleries of institutions") that are the basis for political identification. "In this version of the story," Swann notes, "political consciousness and power originate, not in a presumedly unmediated experience of presumedly real gay identities, but out of an apprehension of the moving, differencing properties of the representational medium—the motion of light in water."

The question of representation is central to Delany's memoir. It is a question of social categories, personal understanding, and language, all of which are connected and none of which are or can be a direct reflection of the others. What does it mean to be black, gay, a writer, he asks, and is there a realm of personal identity possible apart from social constraint? The answer is that the social and the personal are imbricated in one another and that both are historically variable. The meanings of the categories of identity change and with them the possibilities for thinking the self:

> at that time, the words "black" and "gay"—for openers—didn't exist with their current meanings, usage, history. 1961 had still been, really, part of the fifties. The political consciousness that was to form by the end of the sixties had not been part of my world. There were only Negroes and homosexuals, both of whom—along with artists—were hugely devalued in the social hierarchy. It's even hard to speak of that world. (Delany 1988, 242)

But the available social categories are not sufficient for Delany's story. It is difficult, if not impossible, to use a single narrative to account for his experience. Instead, he makes entries in a notebook: at the front about material things, at the back about sexual desire. These are "parallel narratives, in parallel columns" (Delany 1988, 29). Although one seems to be about society, the public, and the political, and the other about the individual, the private, and the psychological, in fact both narratives are inescapably historical. They are discursive productions of knowledge of the self, not reflections either of external or internal truth. "That the two columns must be the Marxist and the Freudian—the material column and the column of desire—is only a modernist prejudice. The autonomy of each is subverted by the same excesses, just as severely" (Delany 1988, 212). The two columns are constitutive of one another, yet the relationship between them is difficult to specify. Does the social and economic determine the subjective? Is the private entirely separate from or completely integral to the public? Delany voices the desire to resolve the problem: "Certainly one must be the lie that is illuminated by the other's truth" (Delany 1988, 212). And then he denies that resolution is possible because answers to these questions do not exist apart from the discourses that produce them:

> If it *is* the split—the space between the two columns (one resplendent and lucid with the writings of legitimacy, the other dark and hollow with the voices of the illegitimate)—that constitutes the subject, it is only after the Romantic inflation of the private into the subjective that such a split can even be located. That locus, that margin, that split itself first allows, then demands the appropriation of language—now spoken, now written—in both directions, over the gap. (Delany 1988, 29–30)

It is finally by tracking "the appropriation of language . . . in both directions, over the gap," and by situating and contextualizing that language that one historicizes the terms by which experience is represented and so historicizes "experience" itself.

Conclusion

Reading for "the literary" does not seem at all inappropriate for those whose discipline is devoted to the study of change. It is not the only kind of reading I am advocating, although more documents than those written by literary figures are susceptible to such readings. Rather it is a way of changing the focus and the philosophy of our history, from one bent on naturalizing "experience" through a belief in the unmediated relationship between words and things, to one that takes all categories of analysis as contextual, contested, and contingent. How have categories of representation and analysis—such as class, race, gender, relations of production, biology, identity, subjectivity, agency, experience, even culture—achieved their foundational status? What have been the effects of their articulations? What does it mean for historians to study the past in terms of these categories and for individuals to think of themselves in these terms? What is the relationship between the salience of such categories in our own time and their existence in the past? Questions such as these open consideration of what Dominick LaCapra has referred to as the "transferential" relationship between the historian and the past, that is, of the relationship between the power of the historian's analytic frame and the events that are the object of his or her study (LaCapra 1985, 71–94). And they historicize both sides of that relationship by denying the fixity and transcendence of anything that appears to operate as a foundation, turning attention instead to the history of foundationalist concepts themselves. The history of these concepts (understood to be contested and contradictory) then becomes the evidence by which "experience" can be grasped and by which the historian's relationship to the past she writes about can be articulated. This is what Foucault meant by genealogy:

> If interpretation were the slow exposure of the meaning hidden in an origin, then only metaphysics could interpret the development of humanity. But if interpretation is the violent or surreptitious appropriation of a system of rules, which in itself has no essential meaning, in order to impose a direction, to bend it to a new will, to force its participation in a different game, and to subject it to secondary rules, then the development of humanity is a series of interpretations. The role of genealogy is to record its history: the history of morals, ideals, and metaphysical concepts, the history of the concept of liberty or of the ascetic life; as they stand for the emergence of different interpretations, they must be made to appear as events on the stage of historical process. (Foucault 1977, 151–52)

Experience is not a word we can do without, although, given its usage to essentialize identity and reify the subject, it is tempting to abandon it altogether. But *experience* is so much a part of everyday language, so implicated in our narratives that it seems futile to argue for its expulsion. It serves as a way of talking about what happened, of establishing difference and similarity, of claiming knowledge that is "unassailable" (Pierson n.d.). Given the ubiquity of the term, it seems to me more useful to work with it, to analyze its operations, and to redefine its meaning. This entails focusing on processes of identity production and insisting on the discursive nature of "experience" and on the politics of its construction. Experience is at once always already an interpretation *and* something that needs to be interpreted. What counts as experience is neither self-evident nor straightforward; it is always contested, always therefore political. The study of experience, therefore, must call into question its originary status in historical explanation. This will happen when historians take as their project *not* the reproduction and transmission of knowledge said to be arrived at through experience but the analysis of the production of that knowledge itself. Such an analysis would constitute a genuinely nonfoundational history, one that retains its explanatory power and its interest in change but does not stand on or reproduce naturalized categories.[14] It also cannot guarantee the historian's neutrality, for the choice of which categories to historicize is inevitably political, necessarily tied to the historian's recognition of his or her stake in the production of knowledge. Experience is, in this approach, not the origin of our explanation but that which we want to explain. This kind of approach does not undercut politics by denying the existence of subjects; it instead interrogates the processes of their creation and, in so doing, refigures history and the role of the historian, opening new ways for thinking about change (de Bolla 1986).

NOTES

I am grateful to Tom Keenan for inviting me to the conference ("History Today—and Tonight," Rutgers and Princeton Universities, March 1990) where I tried out some of these ideas and to the many people there whose questions and comments led to a first round of revisions and reformulations. The students in my graduate seminar at Rutgers in the spring of 1990 helped immeasurably in the clarification of my ideas about "experience" and about what it means to historicize. Criticisms from members of the "History" seminar during 1990–91 in the School of Social Science at the Institute for Advanced Study helped give this essay its final—and, I think, much improved—form. As usual, Elizabeth Weed provided the crucial suggestions for the conceptualization of this essay. I also appreciate the important contributions of Judith Butler, Christina Crosby, Nicholas Dirks, Christopher Fynsk, Clifford Geertz, Donna Haraway, Susan Harding, Gyan Prakash, Donald Scott, and William Sewell Jr. Karen Swann's astute comments led me to rethink and rewrite the final section of this essay. I learned a great deal from her and from that exercise. In a letter he wrote in July 1987, Reginald Zelnick challenged me to articulate a definition of "experience" that might work for historians. Although I'm not sure he will find this essay the answer he was looking for, I am indebted to him for that early provocation.

1. Vision, as Donna Haraway points out, is not passive reflection. "All eyes, including our own organic ones, are active perceptual systems, building in translations and specific *ways* of seeing—that is, ways of life." In another essay she pushes the optical metaphor further: "The rays from my optical device diffract rather than reflect. These diffracting rays compose *interference* patterns, not reflecting images. . . . A diffraction pattern does not map where differences appear, but rather where the *effects* of differences appear" (Haraway, "The Promises of Monsters: Reproductive Politics for

Inappropriate/d Others," unpublished manuscript). In this connection, see also Minnie Bruce Pratt's discussion of her eye that "has only let in what I have been taught to see" in Pratt (1984), and the analysis of Pratt's autobiographical essay by Biddy Martin and Chandra Talpade Mohanty (1986).

2. Discussions with Elizabeth Weed on this point were helpful.

3. I am grateful to Judith Butler for discussions on this point.

4. Bhabha puts it this way: "*To see* a missing person, or *to look* at Invisibleness, is to emphasize the subject's *transitive* demand for a *direct* object of self-reflection; a point of presence which would maintain its privileged enunciatory position *qua subject*" (Bhabha 1987, 5).

5. Gayatri Spivak describes this as "positing a metalepsis":

A subject-effect can be briefly plotted as follows: that which seems to operate as a subject may be part of an immense discountinuous network . . . of strands that may be termed politics, ideology, economics, history, sexuality, language, and so on. . . . Different knottings and configurations of these strands, determined by heterogeneous determinations which are themselves dependent upon myriad circumstances, produce the effect of an operating subject. Yet the continuist and homogenist deliberative consciousness symptomatically requires a continuous and homogeneous cause of this effect and thus posits a sovereign and determining subject. This latter is, then, the effect of an effect, and its positing a metalepsis, or the substitution of an effect for a cause. (Spivak 1987, 204)

6. For a different reading of Thompson on experience, see Sewell (1990). I have also benefited from Sylvia Schafer's "Writing about 'Experience': Workers and Historians Tormented by Industrialization" (unpublished manuscript).

7. Often this kind of invocation of experience leads back to the biological or physical "experience" of the body. See, for example, the arguments about rape and violence offered by Hawkesworth (1989).

8. This is one of the meanings of the slogan "the personal is the political." Personal knowledge, that is, the experience of oppression is the source of resistance to it. This is what Mohanty calls "the feminist osmosis thesis: females are feminists by association and identification with the experiences which constitute us as female" (Mohanty 1987. See also King [1986]).

9. De Certeau puts it this way:

That the particularity of the place where discourse is produced is relevant will be naturally more apparent where historiographical discourse treats matters that put the subject-producer of knowledge into question: the history of women, of blacks, of Jews, of cultural minorities, etc. In these fields one can, of course, either maintain that the personal status of the author is a matter of indifference (in relation to the objectivity of his or her work) or that he or she alone authorizes or invalidates the discourse (according to whether he or she is "of it" or not). But this debate requires what has been concealed by an epistemology, namely, the impact of subject-to-subject relationships (men and women, blacks and whites, etc.) on the use of apparently "neutral" techniques and in the organization of discourses that are, perhaps, equally scientific. For example, from the fact of the differentiation of the sexes, must one conclude that a woman produces a different historiography from that of a man? Of course, I do not answer this question, but I do assert that this interrogation puts the place of the subject in question and requires a treatment of it unlike the epistemology that constructed the "truth" of the work on the foundation of the speaker's irrelevance. (de Certeau 1986, 217–18)

10. Here we have an example of what Foucault characterized as "continuous history": "the indispensable correlative of the founding function of the subject: the guarantee that everything that has eluded him may be restored to him; the certainty that time will disperse nothing without restoring it in reconstituted unity" (Foucault 1972).

11. Her argument is based on a set of oppositions between history and literature, male and female, identity and difference, practical politics and theory, and she repeatedly privileges the second set of terms. These polarities speak to the specifics of the debate she is engaged in with the (largely male) subaltern studies collective, historians working within a Marxist, and especially Gramscian, frame.

12. Fields's article (1982) is notable for its contradictions: the way, for example, that it historicizes race, naturalizes class, and refuses to talk at all about gender.

13. Karen Swann's comments on this paper were presented at the Little Three Faculty Colloquium on "The Social and Political Construction of Reality" at Wesleyan University in January 1991. The comments exist only in typescript.

14. Conversations with Christopher Fynsk helped clarify these points for me.

REFERENCES

Adams, Parveen, and Jeff Minson. 1978. "The 'Subject' of Feminism." *m/f* 2:43–61.
Bersani, Leo. 1976. *A Future for Astyanax: Character and Desire in Literature.* Boston: Little, Brown.
Bhabha, Homi K. 1987. "Interrogating Identity." In *Identity: The Real Me,* 5–11. Edited by Lisa Appignanesi. London: ICA Publications.
Bono, James J. 1990. "Science, Discourse, and Literature: The Role/Rule of Metaphor in Science." In *Literature and Science: Theory and Practice,* 59–89. Edited by Stuart Peterfreund. Boston: Northeastern University Press.
Butler, Judith. 1990. *Gender Trouble: Feminism and the Subversion of Identity.* New York: Routledge.
Carby, Hazel. 1987. *Reconstructing Womanhood: The Emergence of the Afro-American Woman Novelist.* New York: Oxford University Press.

Certeau, Michel de. 1986. "History: Science and Fiction." In *Heterologies: Discourse on the Other*, 199–224. Translated by Brian Massumi. Minneapolis: University of Minnesota Press.

Collingwood, R. G. [1946] 1956. *The Idea of History*. Oxford: Oxford University Press.

de Bolla, Peter. 1986. "Disfiguring History." *Diacritics* 16:49–58.

de Bolla, Peter. 1989. *The Discourse of the Sublime: Readings in History, Aesthetics, and the Subject*. Oxford: Basil Blackwell.

Delany, Samuel R. 1988. *The Motion of Light in Water: Sex and Science Fiction Writing in the East Village, 1957–1965*. New York: Plume.

de Lauretis, Teresa. 1984. *Alice Doesn't: Feminism, Semiotics, Cinema*. Bloomington: Indiana University Press.

Fields, Barbara J. 1982. "Ideology and Race, in American History." In *Region, Race, and Reconstruction: Essays in Honor of C. Vann Woodward*, 143–77. Edited by J. Morgan Kousser and James M. McPherson. New York: Oxford University Press.

Foucault, Michel. 1972. *The Archaeology of Knowledge*. Translated by A. M. Sheridan Smith. New York: Harper.

Foucault, Michel. 1977. "Nietzsche, Genealogy, History." In *Language, Counter-Memory, Practice: Selected Essays and Interviews*, 139–64. Translated by Donald F. Bouchard and Sherry Simon. Edited by Bouchard. Ithaca, NY: Cornell University Press.

Fuss, Diana. 1989. *Essentially Speaking: Feminism, Nature, and Difference*. New York: Routledge.

Gallop, Jane. 1982. *The Daughter's Seduction: Feminism and Psychoanalysis*. Ithaca, NY: Cornell University Press.

Gossman, Lionel. 1989. "Towards a Rational Historiography." *Transactions of the American Philosophical Society* n.s. 79, pt. 3.

Hall, Stuart. 1987. "Minimal Selves." In *Identity: The Real Me*, 44–46. Edited by Lisa Appignanesi. London: ICA Publications.

Haraway, Donna. 1988. "Situated Knowledges: The Science Question in Feminism and the Privilege of Partial Perspective." *Feminist Studies* 14 (fall): 575–600.

Haraway, Donna. n.d. "The Promises of Monsters: Reproductive Politics for Inappropriate/d Others." Unpublished manuscript.

Hawkesworth, Mary E. 1989. "Knowers, Knowing, Known: Feminist Theory and Claims of Truth." *Signs* 14:533–57.

Jameson, Fredric. 1991. "Immanence and Nominalism in Postmodern Theory." In *Postmodernism, or, the Cultural Logic of Late Capitalism*. Durham, NC: Duke University Press.

King, Katie. 1986. "The Situation of Lesbianism as Feminism's Magical Sign: Contests for Meaning and the U.S. Women's Movement, 1968–1972." *Communication* 9:65–91.

Lacan, Jacques. 1977. "The Signification of the Phallus." In *Écrits: A Selection*, 281–91. Translated by Alan Sheridan. New York: W. W. Norton.

LaCapra, Dominick. 1985. "Rhetoric and History." In *History and Criticism.* Ithaca, NY: Cornell University Press.

Martin, Biddy, and Chandra Talpade Mohanty. 1986. "Feminist Politics: What's Home Got to Do With It?" In *Feminist Studies/Critical Studies,* 191–212. Edited by Teresa de Lauretis. Bloomington: Indiana University Press.

Minow, Martha. 1987. "Justice Engendered." Foreword to "The Supreme Court, 1986 Term." *Harvard Law Review* 101:10–95.

Mohanty, Chandra Talpade. 1987. "Feminist Encounters: Locating the Politics of Experience." *Copyright* 1 (Fall 1987).

Newton, Judith. 1988. "History as Usual? Feminism and the 'New Historicism.'" *Cultural Critique* 9 (spring): 87–121.

Nussbaum, Felicity A. 1989. *The Autobiographical Subject: Gender and Ideology in Eighteenth-Century England.* Baltimore: Johns Hopkins University Press.

Pierson, Ruth Roach. 1991. "Experience, Difference, and Dominance in the Writings of Canadian Women's History." In *Writing Women's History: International Perspectives,* 79–106. Edited by Karen Offen, Ruth Roach Pierson, and Jane Rendall. Bloomington: Indiana University Press.

Poovey, Mary. 1988. *Uneven Developments: The Ideological Work of Gender in Mid-Victorian England.* Chicago: University of Chicago Press.

Pratt, Minnie Bruce. 1984. "Identity: Skin Blood Heart." In *Yours in Struggle: Three Feminist Perspectives on Anti-Semitism and Racism.* Edited by Elly Bulkin, Minnie Bruce Pratt, and Barbara Smith. Brooklyn, NY: Long Haul.

Riley, Denise. 1988. *"Am I That Name?": Feminism and the Category of Women in History.* Minneapolis: University of Minnesota Press.

Rooney, Ellen. 1989. *Seductive Reasoning: Pluralism as the Problematic of Contemporary Theory.* Ithaca, NY: Cornell University Press.

Rorty, Richard. 1979. *Philosophy and the Mirror of Nature.* Princeton, NJ: Princeton University Press.

Schafer, Sylvia. n.d. "Writing about 'Experience': Workers and Historians Tormented by Industrialization." Unpublished manuscript.

Sedgwick, Eve Kosofsky. 1985. *Between Men: English Literature and Male Homosocial Desire.* New York: Columbia University Press.

Sewell, William H., Jr. 1990. "How Classes Are Made: Critical Reflections on E. P. Thompson's Theory of Working-Class Formation." In *E. P. Thompson: Critical Perspectives,* 50–77. Edited by Harvey J. Kaye and Keith McClelland. Philadelphia: Temple University Press.

Spivak, Gayatri Chakravorty. 1987. "Subaltern Studies: Deconstructing Historiography." In *In Other Worlds: Essays in Cultural Politics,* 197–205. New York: Routledge.

Spivak, Gayatri Chakravorty. 1988. *In Other Worlds: Essays in Cultural Politics.* New York: Routledge.

Spivak, Gayatri Chakravorty, and Ellen Rooney. 1989. "In a Word: Interview." *differences* 1:124–54.

Stansell, Christine. 1987. "A Response to Joan Scott." *International Labor and Working-Class History* 31 (spring): 21–29.

Thompson, E. P. 1966. *The Making of the English Working Class.* New York: Vintage Books.

Thompson, E. P. 1978. "The Poverty of Theory or an Orrery of Errors." In *The Poverty of Theory and Other Essays,* 1–210. New York: Monthly Review Press.

Toews, John E. 1987. "Intellectual History after the Linguistic Turn: The Autonomy of Meaning and the Irreducibility of Experience." *American Historical Review* 92 (4): 879–907.

Williams, Raymond. 1961. *The Long Revolution.* London: Chatto & Windus.

Williams, Raymond. 1979. *Politics and Letters: Interviews with New Left Review.* London: Verso.

Williams, Raymond. 1985. *Keywords: A Vocabulary of Culture and Society.* Rev. ed. New York: Oxford University Press.

Contributors

Craig Calhoun is Professor of Sociology and History and Director of the University Center for International Studies at the University of North Carolina, Chapel Hill. His most recent books include *Neither Gods Nor Emperors: Students and the Struggle for Democracy in China* (University of California Press, 1994), and *Critical Social Theory: Culture, History, and the Challenge of Difference* (Blackwell, 1995). He is the editor of the American Sociological Association's journal, *Sociological Theory*, and is currently engaged in comparative historical research on nationalism, democracy, and public life.

Nicholas B. Dirks is Professor of Anthropology and History and Director of the Advanced Study Center of the International Institute at the University of Michigan. He is the author of *The Hollow Crown: Ethnohistory of an Indian Kingdom* (Cambridge University Press, 1987; 2nd edition, University of Michigan Press, 1993), and editor of *Colonialism and Culture* (University of Michigan Press, 1992) and—with Geoff Eley and Sherry Ortner—*Culture/Power/History: A Reader in Contemporary Social Theory* (Princeton University Press, 1994). He is currently completing a book on caste in India.

Geoff Eley is Professor of History at the University of Michigan. He is the author of *Reshaping the German Right: Radical Nationalism and Political Change after Bismarck* (Yale University Press, 1980; new edition University of Michigan Press, 1991); *The Peculiarities of German History. Bourgeois Society and Politics in Nineteenth-Century Germany* (Oxford University Press, 1984), with David Blackbourn; and *From Unification to Nazism: Reinterpreting the German Past* (Routledge, 1986). He is the editor of *Culture/Power/History: A Reader in Contemporary Social Theory* (Princeton University Press, 1994), with Nicholas B. Dirks and Sherry B. Ortner; and *Becoming National: A Reader* (Oxford University Press, 1996), with Ronald Grigor Suny. He is completing a general study of the European Left from the mid-nineteenth century to the present, and a book with Keith Nield on current debates in social and cultural history.

Robert W. Gordon is Professor of Law at Yale University.

Terrence J. McDonald is Professor of History at the University of Michigan. He has written extensively on the relationship between history and the social sciences, including, most recently, "Institutions and Institutionalism in the Stream of History," *Polity* 28, no. 1 (1995): 129–35; and "Theory and Practice in the 'New' History: Re-reading Arthur Meier Schlesinger's *The Rise of the City, 1878–1898*," 257–71, in Stanley I. Kutler, ed., *American Retrospectives: Historians on Historians* (Johns Hopkins University Press, 1995).

Steven Mullaney is Associate Professor of English and Director of the Program in British Studies at the University of Michigan. He has published extensively on Renaissance literature and culture and on the European encounter with the Americas, and is the author of *The Place of the Stage: License, Play, and Power in Renaissance England,* which has recently been reprinted by the University of Michigan Press. Currently he is completing a study of the historical and cultural construction of affect, titled *Before Emotions: Structures of Feeling in Early Modern England.*

Sherry B. Ortner is Professor of Anthropology at the University of California, Berkeley. She is the author of several monographs on Sherpa ethnography, and has published extensively on feminist theory and social theory. Her most recent book is a volume, co-edited with Nicholas B. Dirks and Geoff Eley, entitled *Culture/Power/History: A Reader in Contemporary Social Theory* (1994). A collection of her essays in feminist theory, entitled *Making Gender: The Politics and Erotics of Culture,* is coming out in the fall of 1996.

Joan Wallach Scott is Professor of Social Science at the Institute for Advanced Study. She is the author, most recently, of *Only Paradoxes to Offer: French Feminists and the Rights of Man* (Harvard University Press, 1996).

William H. Sewell, Jr. is Professor of Political Science and History at the University of Chicago, but he is also a card-carrying sociologist. He is the author of *Work and Revolution in France: The Language of Labor from the Old Regime to 1848; Structure and Mobility: The Men and Women of Marseille, 1820–1870;* and *A Rhetoric of Bourgeois Revolution: The Abbé Sieyes and What Is the Third Estate?* He is currently writing a book on historical change and social theory.

Rogers M. Smith is Professor of Political Science at Yale University. He has written extensively on American constitutional law and liberalism as well as the "new institutionalism" in political science. His most recent book is *Civic*

Ideals: Conflicting Visions of Citizenship in American Public Law (Yale University Press, 1996).

Margaret R. Somers is Associate Professor of Sociology at the University of Michigan, and a European Forum Fellow at the European University Institute, Florence, Italy (1995–96). Her recent publications include "Narrating and Naturalizing Civil Society and Citizenship Theory," *Sociological Theory:* 13 (3) 1995; "What's Political or Cultural about Political Culture and the Public Sphere?" *Sociological Theory:* 13 (2) 1995; "The Narrative Constitution of Identity," *Theory and Society* 23 (5) 1994; and "Citizenship and the Place of the Public Sphere," *American Sociological Review* 58 (5) 1993.

Index